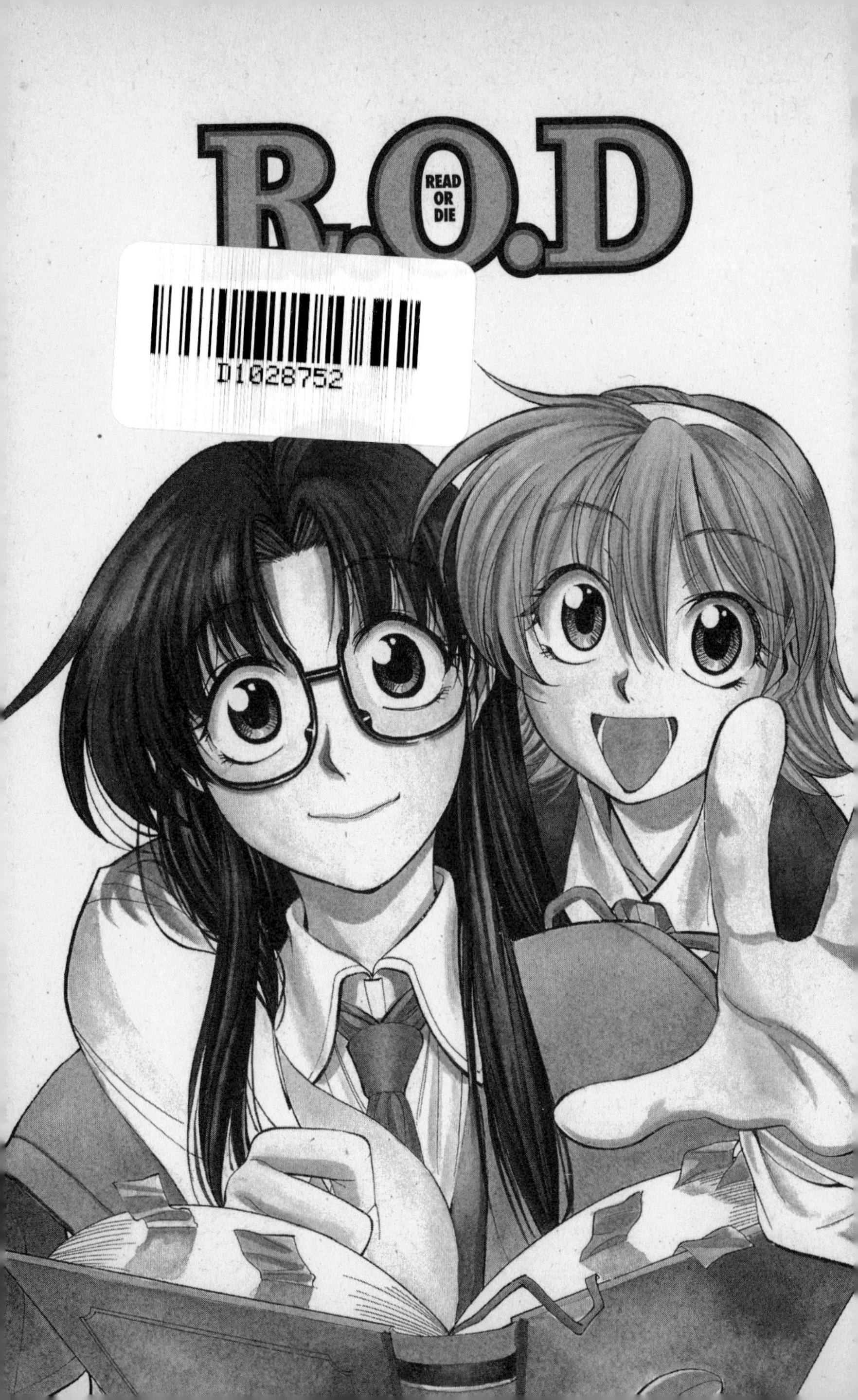
R.O.D
READ OR DIE

CONTENTS

THE LAST LITERATURE D-LINE OF U.K. AGENT YOMIKO READMAN "THE PAPER"

EPISODE ONE

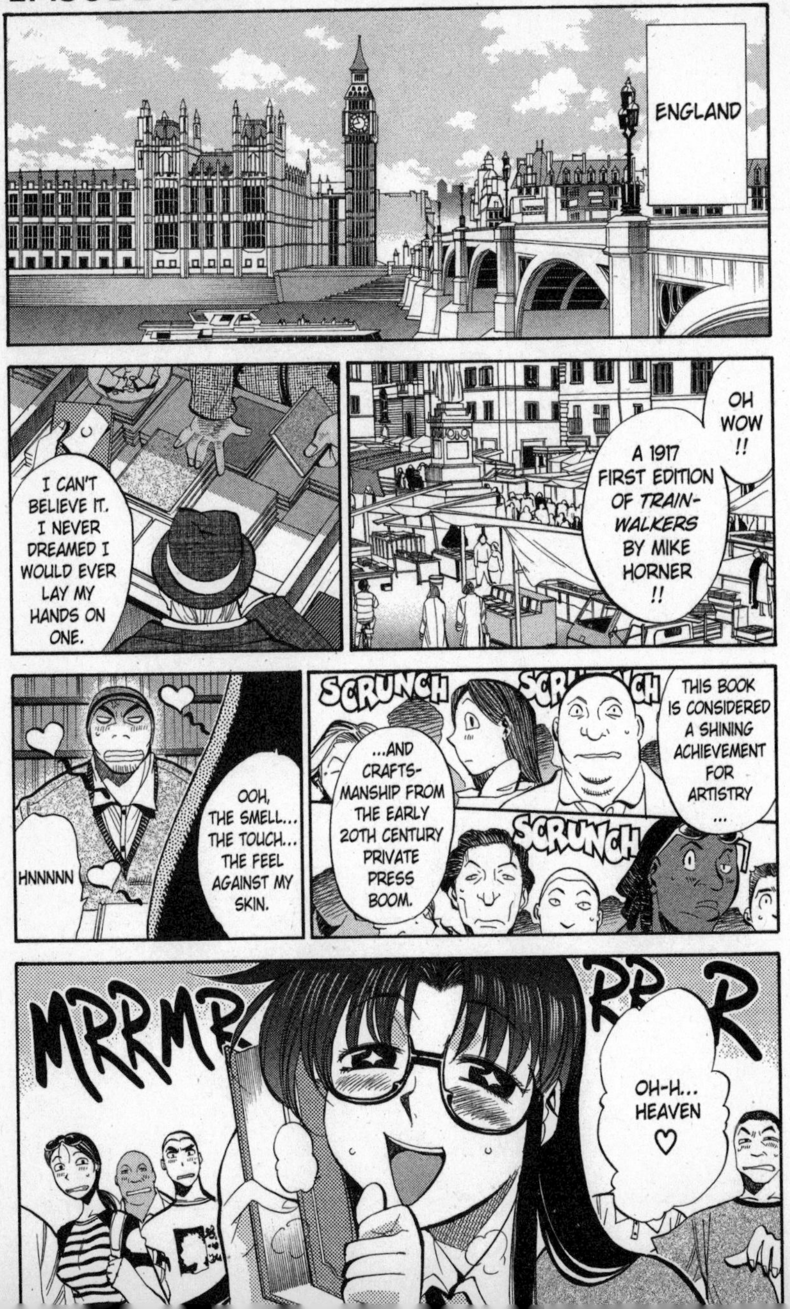
ENGLAND
OH WOW !!
A 1917 FIRST EDITION OF *TRAIN-WALKERS* BY MIKE HORNER !!
I CAN'T BELIEVE IT. I NEVER DREAMED I WOULD EVER LAY MY HANDS ON ONE.
SCRUNCH
SCRUNCH
THIS BOOK IS CONSIDERED A SHINING ACHIEVEMENT FOR ARTISTRY ...
...AND CRAFTSMANSHIP FROM THE EARLY 20TH CENTURY PRIVATE PRESS BOOM.
SCRUNCH
OOH, THE SMELL... THE TOUCH... THE FEEL AGAINST MY SKIN.
HNNNNN
MRRMR
R
OH-H... HEAVEN ♡

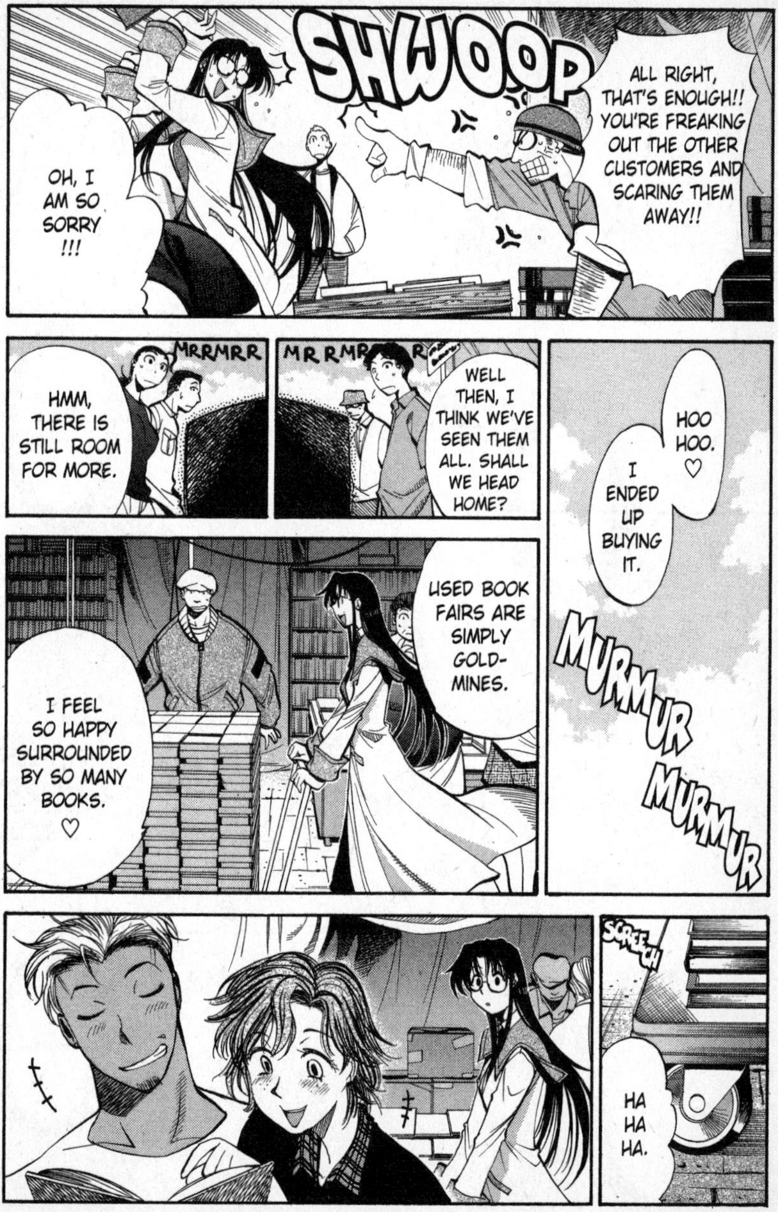
SHWOOP
ALL RIGHT, THAT'S ENOUGH!! YOU'RE FREAKING OUT THE OTHER CUSTOMERS AND SCARING THEM AWAY!!
OH, I AM SO SORRY !!!
HOO HOO. ♡
I ENDED UP BUYING IT.
MURMUR MURMUR
MRRMRR
WELL THEN, I THINK WE'VE SEEN THEM ALL. SHALL WE HEAD HOME?
MRRMRR
HMM, THERE IS STILL ROOM FOR MORE.
USED BOOK FAIRS ARE SIMPLY GOLD-MINES.
I FEEL SO HAPPY SURROUNDED BY SO MANY BOOKS. ♡
SCREECH
HA HA HA.

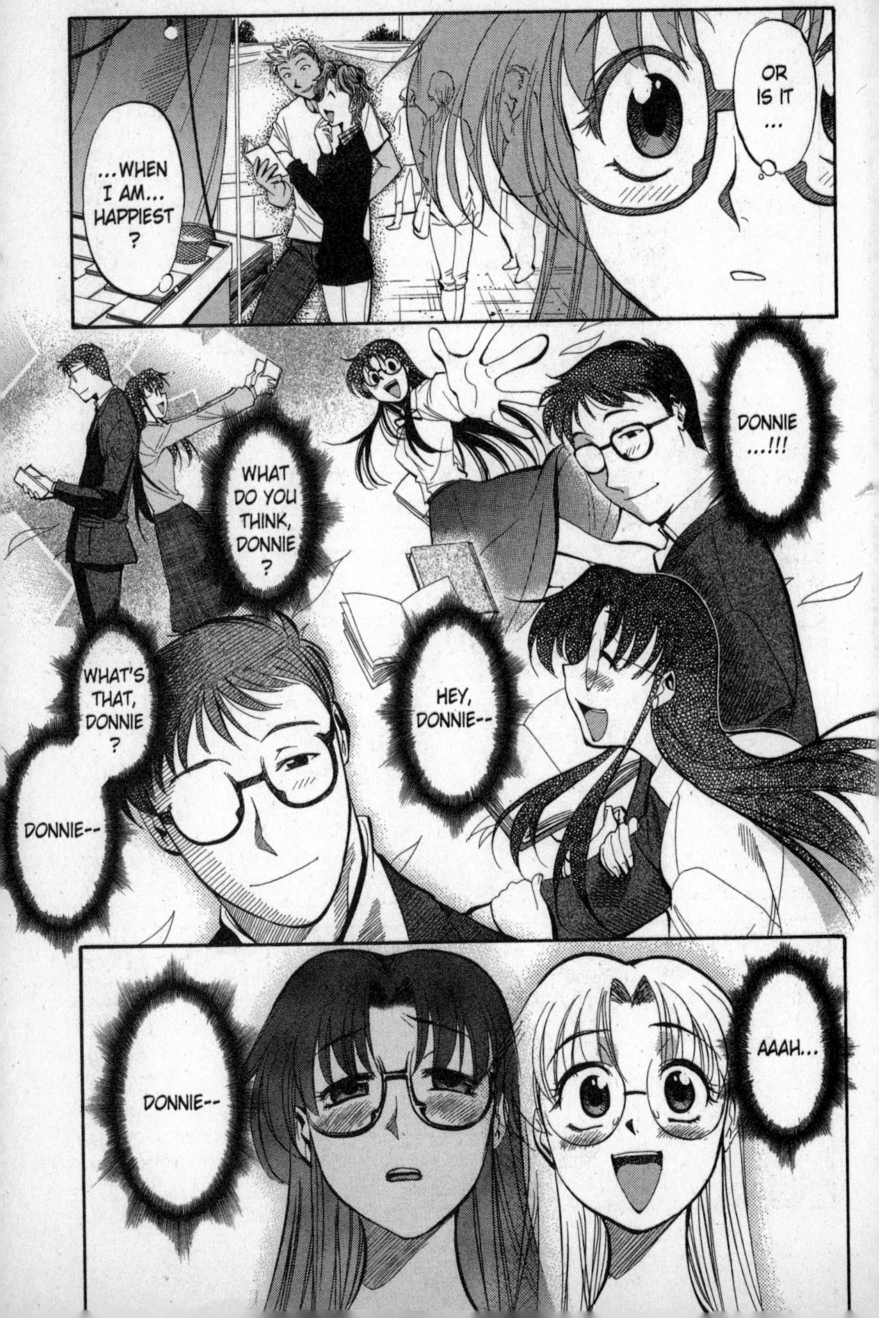
OR IS IT ...
...WHEN I AM... HAPPIEST ?
DONNIE ...!!!
WHAT DO YOU THINK, DONNIE ?
HEY, DONNIE--
WHAT'S THAT, DONNIE ?
DONNIE--
AAAH...
DONNIE--

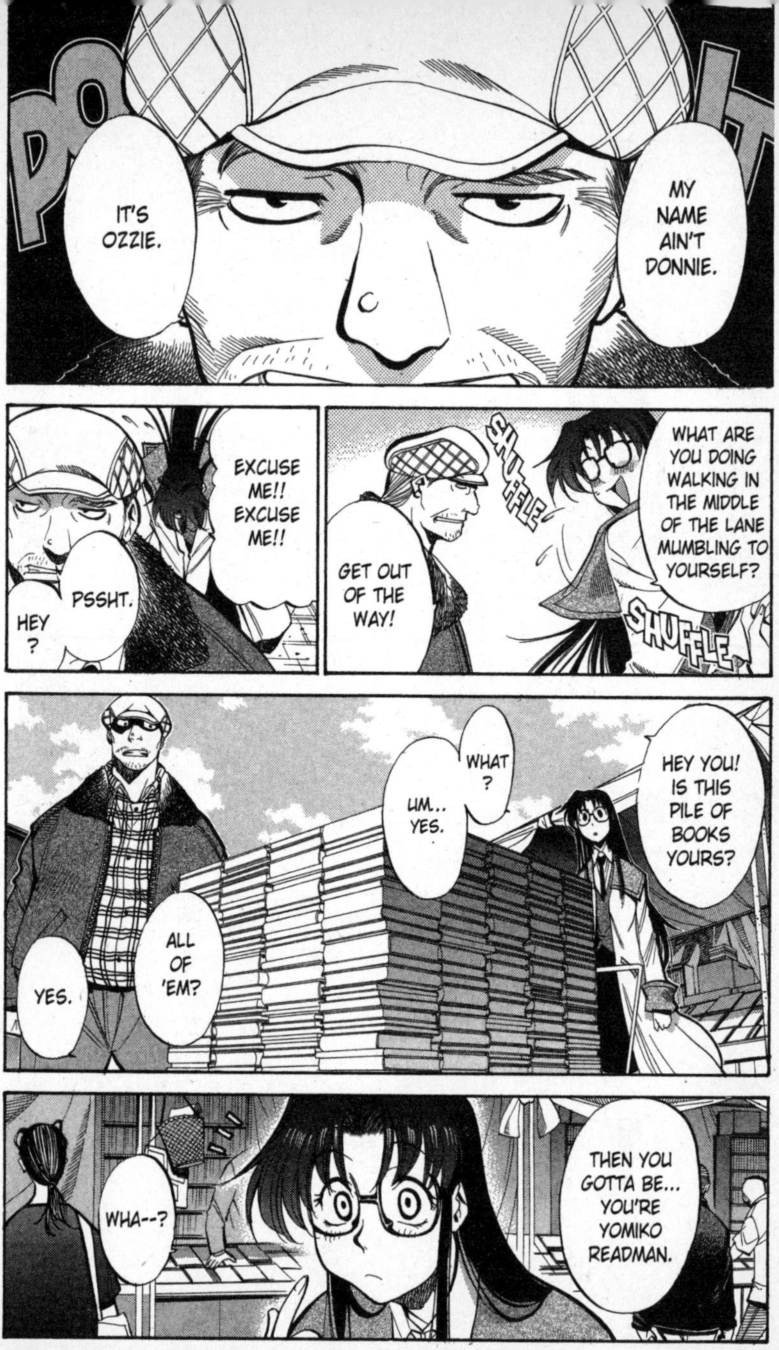
MY NAME AIN'T DONNIE.
IT'S OZZIE.
WHAT ARE YOU DOING WALKING IN THE MIDDLE OF THE LANE MUMBLING TO YOURSELF?
SHUFFLE
SHUFFLE
GET OUT OF THE WAY!
EXCUSE ME!! EXCUSE ME!!
PSSHT.
HEY ?
HEY YOU! IS THIS PILE OF BOOKS YOURS?
WHAT ?
UM... YES.
ALL OF 'EM?
YES.
THEN YOU GOTTA BE... YOU'RE YOMIKO READMAN.
WHA--?

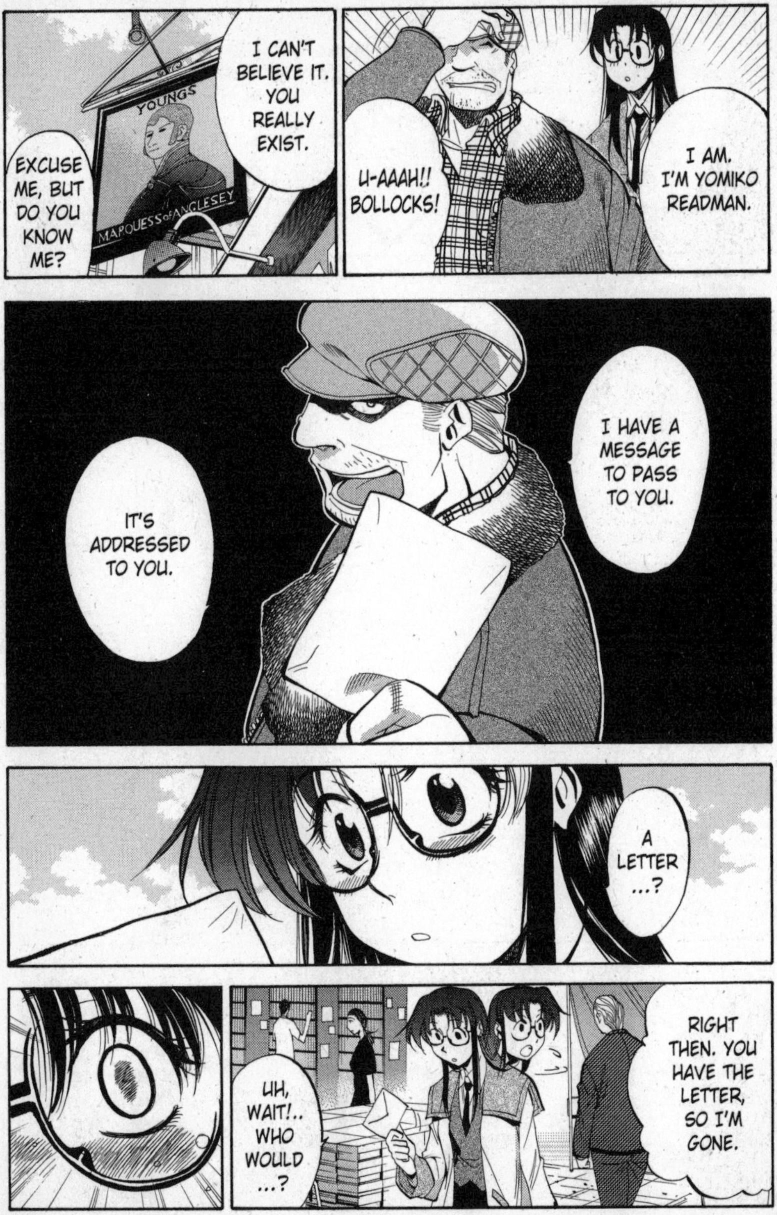
I AM. I'M YOMIKO READMAN.
U-AAAH!! BOLLOCKS!
I CAN'T BELIEVE IT. YOU REALLY EXIST.
YOUNGS
MARQUESS of ANGLESEY
EXCUSE ME, BUT DO YOU KNOW ME?
I HAVE A MESSAGE TO PASS TO YOU.
IT'S ADDRESSED TO YOU.
A LETTER ...?
RIGHT THEN. YOU HAVE THE LETTER, SO I'M GONE.
UH, WAIT!.. WHO WOULD ...?

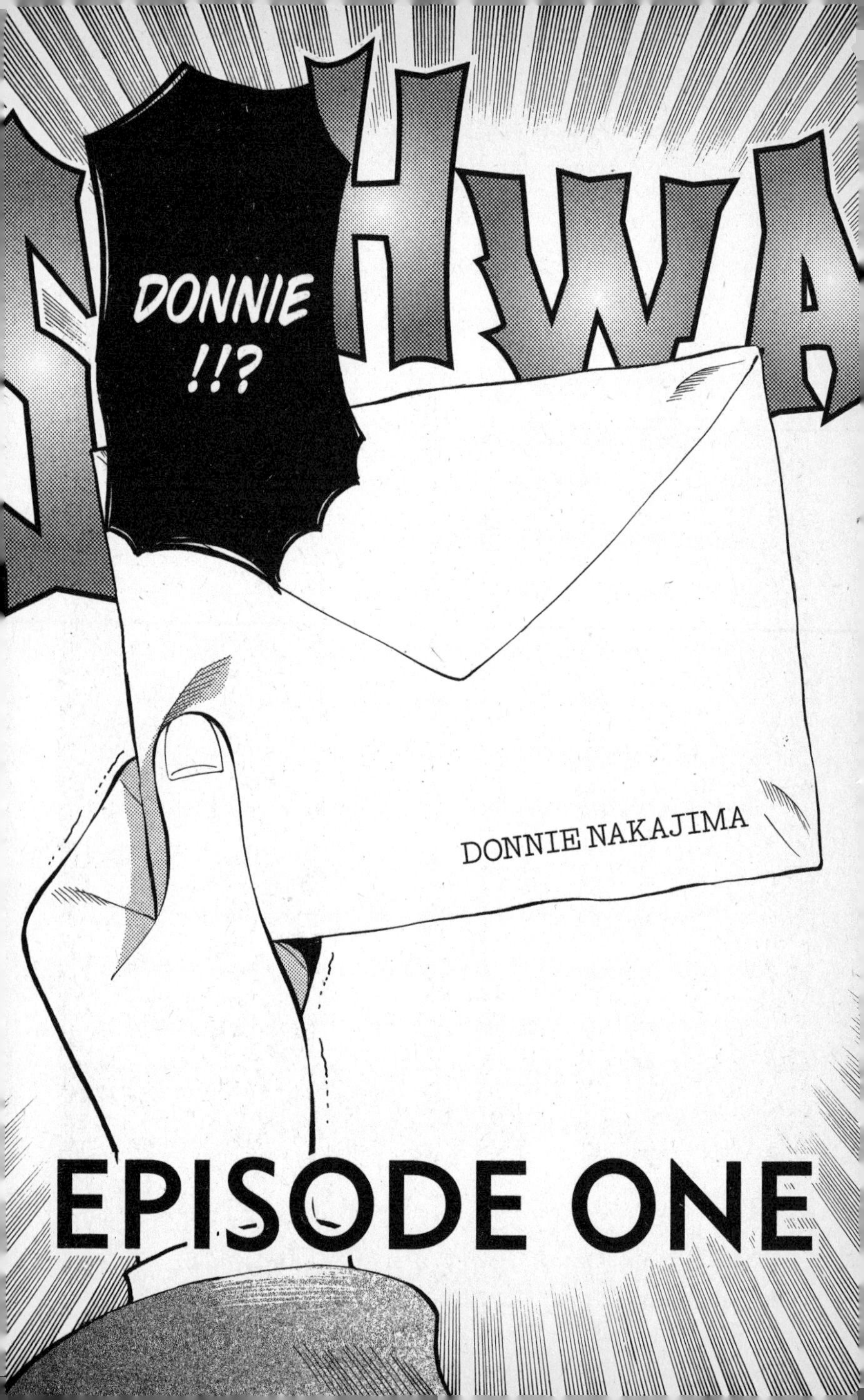

EPISODE ONE

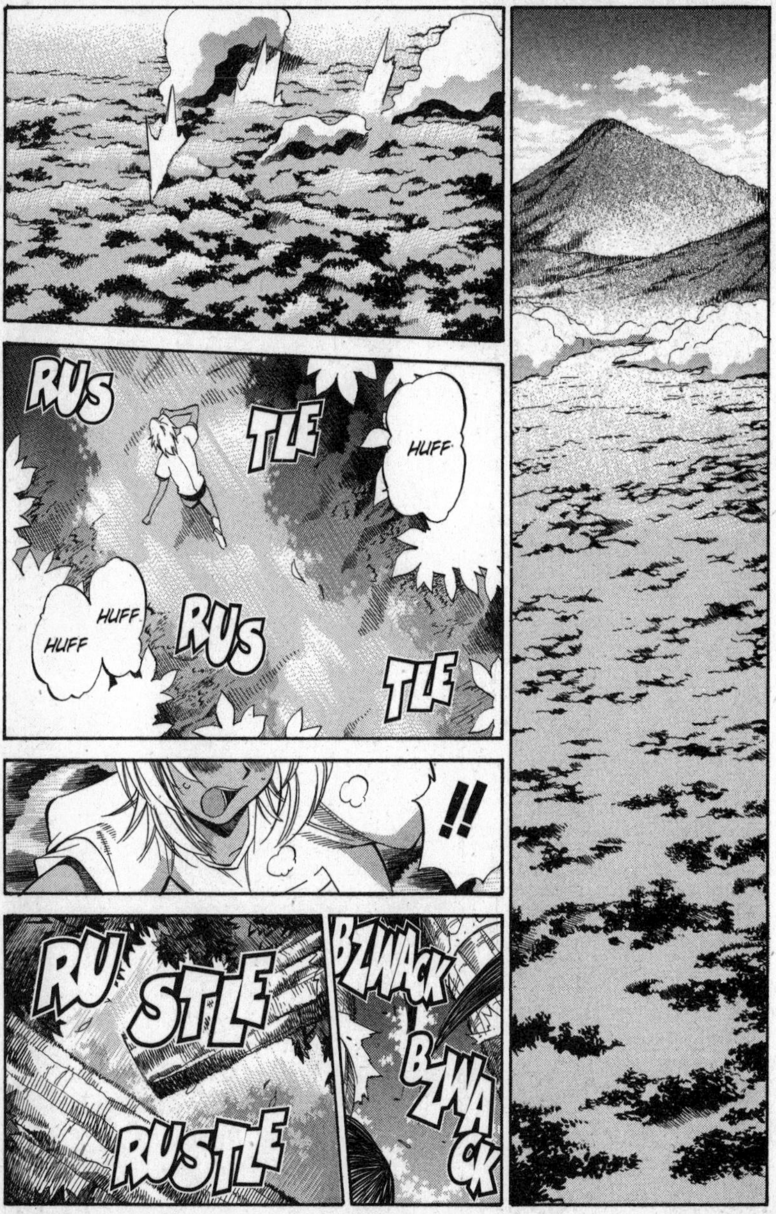
HUFF
RUS
TLE
HUFF
HUFF
RUS
TLE
!!
BZWACK
BZWACK
RU
STLE
RUSTLE

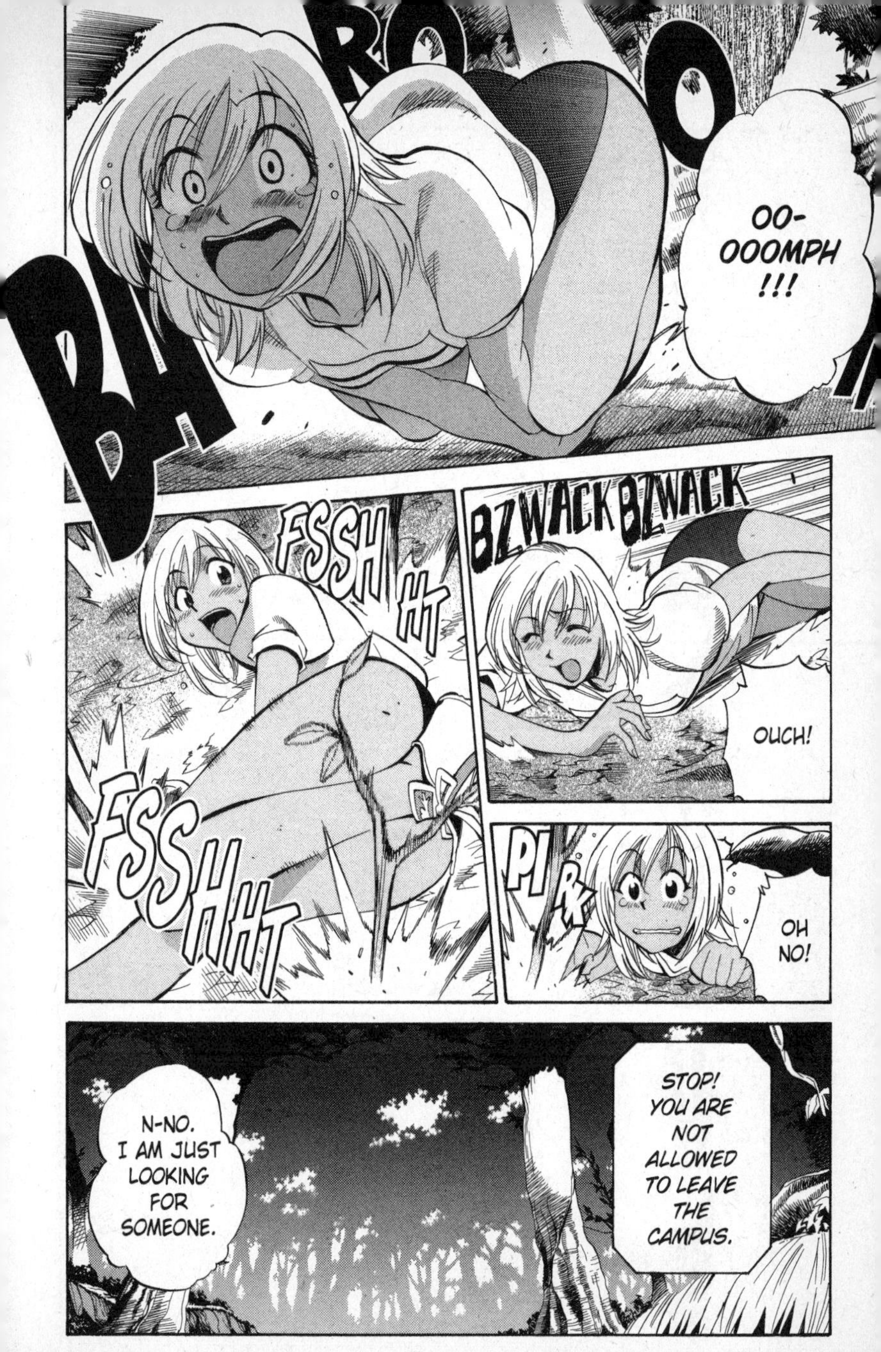
OO-OOOMPH!!!
BZWACK BZWACK
OUCH!
PIRK
OH NO!
FSSHHT
FSSHHT
STOP! YOU ARE NOT ALLOWED TO LEAVE THE CAMPUS.
N-NO. I AM JUST LOOKING FOR SOMEONE.

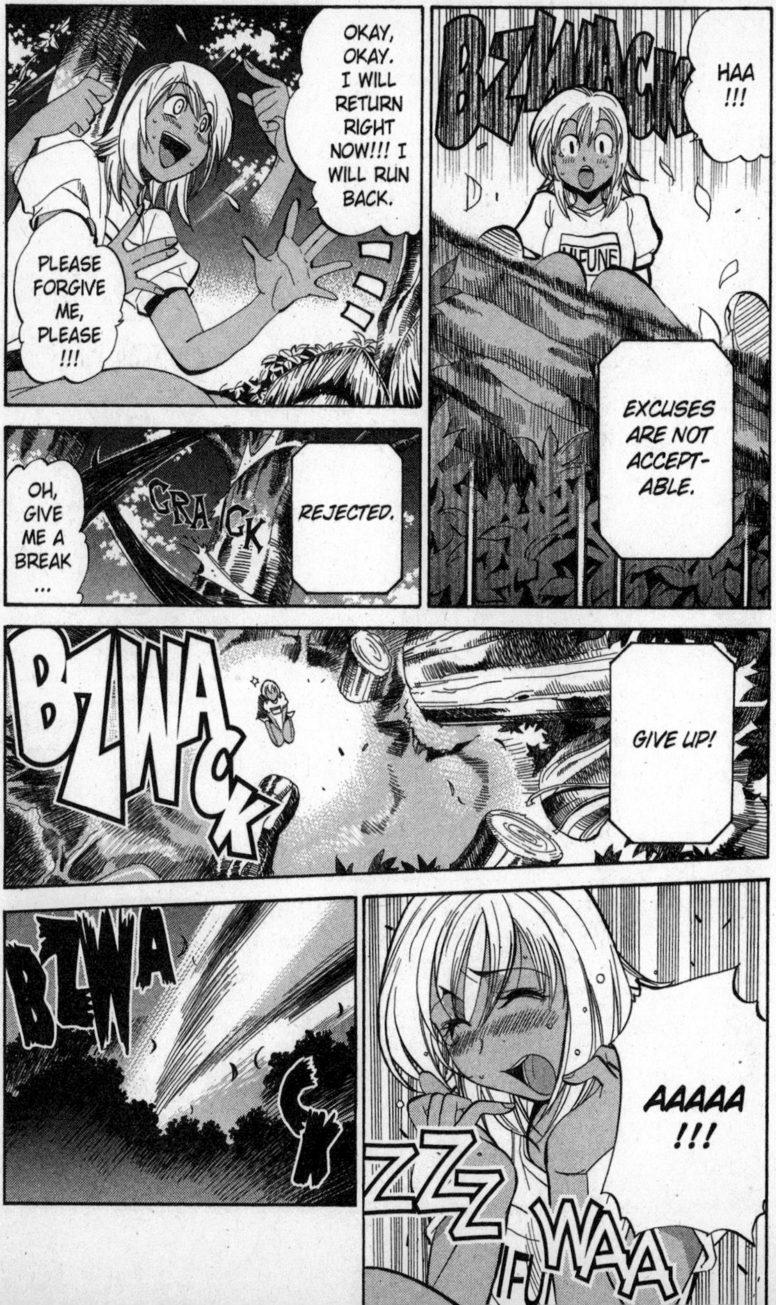
BZWACK
HAA!!!
EXCUSES ARE NOT ACCEPT-ABLE.
OKAY, OKAY. I WILL RETURN RIGHT NOW!!! I WILL RUN BACK.
PLEASE FORGIVE ME, PLEASE!!!
REJECTED.
CRAICK
OH, GIVE ME A BREAK...
GIVE UP!
BZWACK
AAAAA!!!
ZZZ
WAA
BZWACK

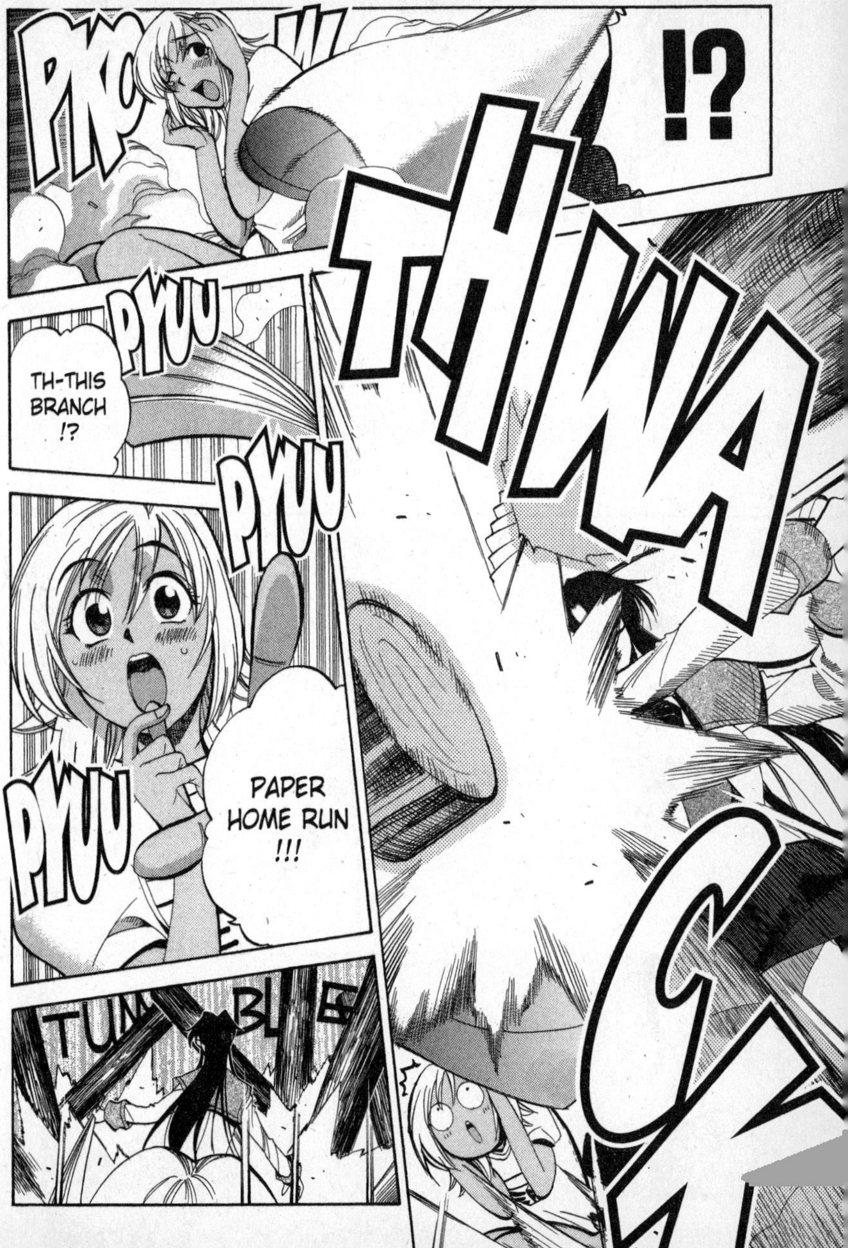
!?
THWA
PYUU
TH-THIS BRANCH !?
PYUU
PYUU
PAPER HOME RUN !!!

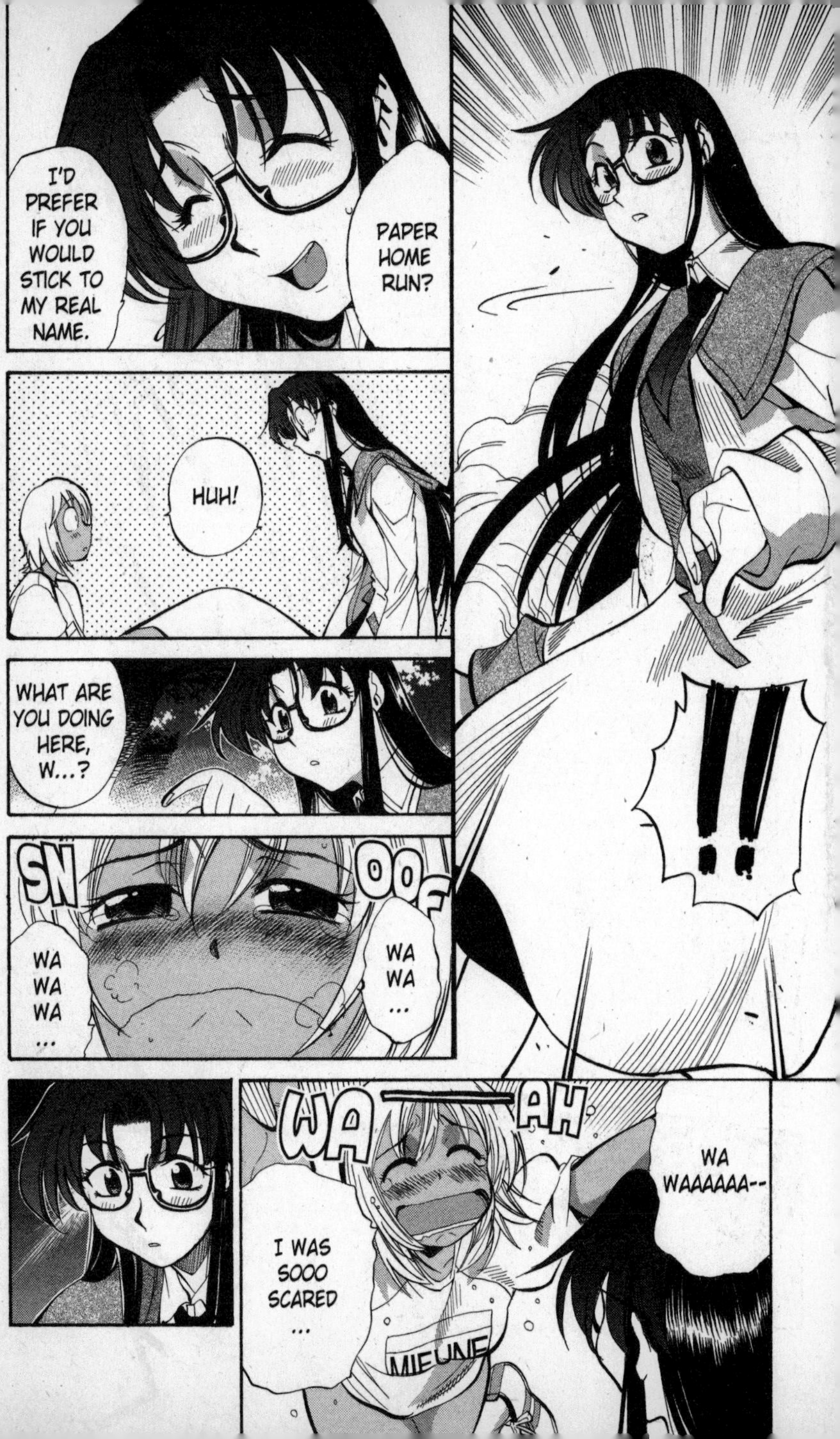
!!
PAPER HOME RUN?
I'D PREFER IF YOU WOULD STICK TO MY REAL NAME.
HUH!
WHAT ARE YOU DOING HERE, W...?
SN OOF
WA WA ...
WA WA WA ...
WAT——AH
WA WAAAAAA--
I WAS SOOO SCARED ...
MIFUNE

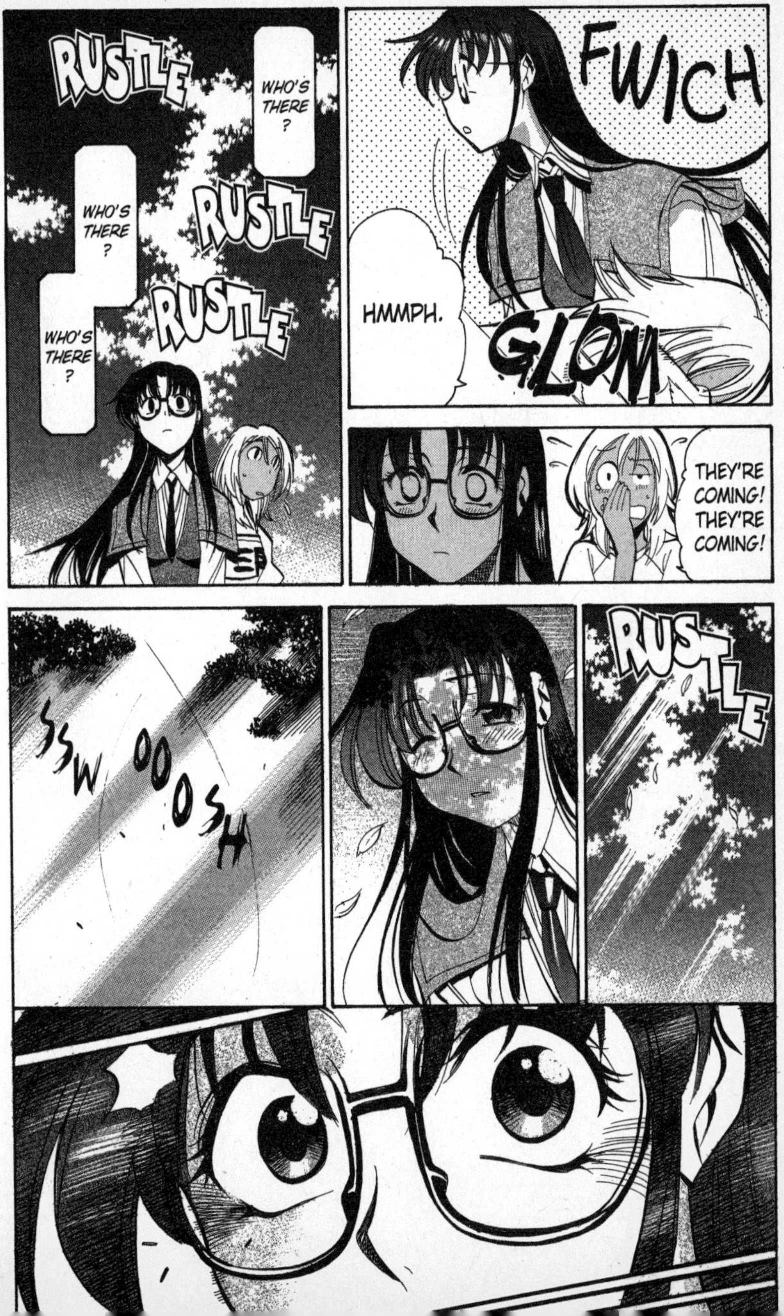
FWICH
HMMPH.
GLOM
RUSTLE
WHO'S THERE ?
RUSTLE
WHO'S THERE ?
RUSTLE
WHO'S THERE ?
THEY'RE COMING! THEY'RE COMING!
RUSTLE
SSWOOOSH

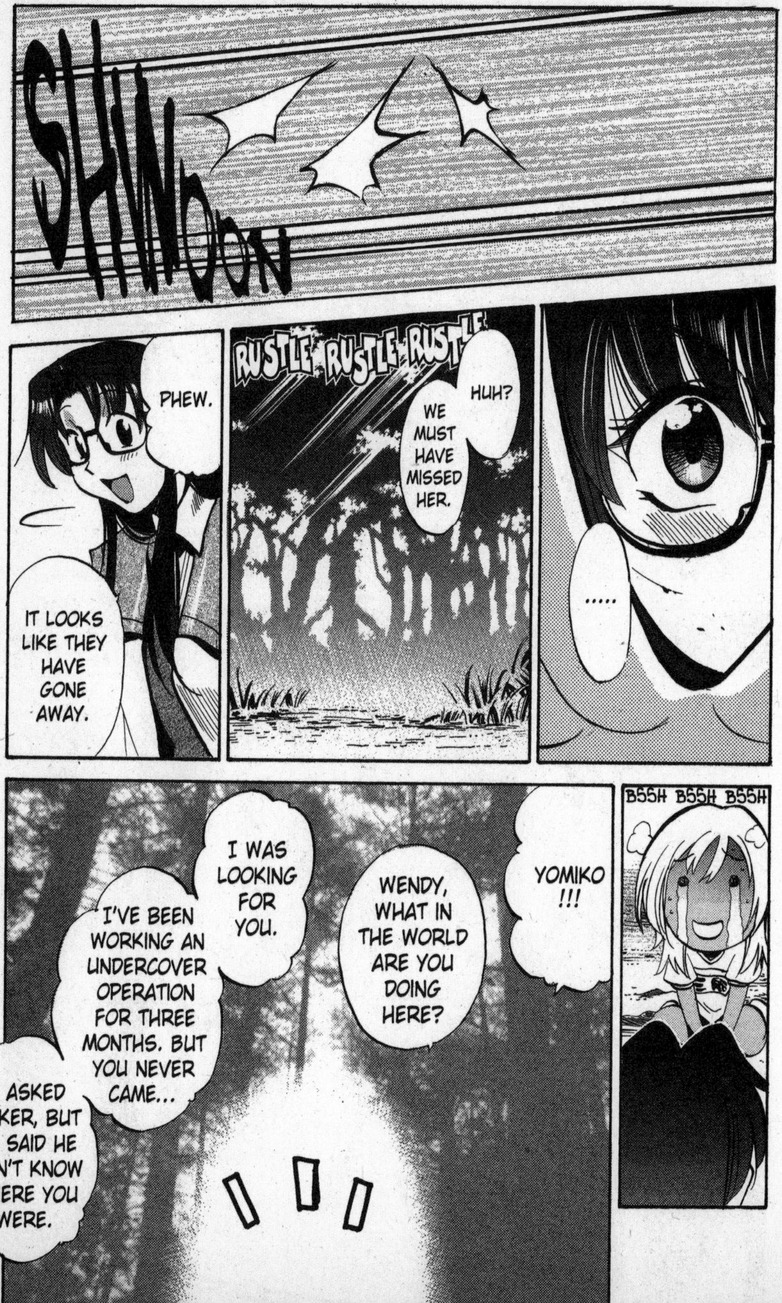
SHINOON
.....
RUSTLE RUSTLE RUSTLE
HUH?
WE MUST HAVE MISSED HER.
PHEW.
IT LOOKS LIKE THEY HAVE GONE AWAY.
BSSH BSSH BSSH
YOMIKO !!!
WENDY, WHAT IN THE WORLD ARE YOU DOING HERE?
I WAS LOOKING FOR YOU.
I'VE BEEN WORKING AN UNDERCOVER OPERATION FOR THREE MONTHS. BUT YOU NEVER CAME...
I ASKED JOKER, BUT HE SAID HE DIDN'T KNOW WHERE YOU WERE.

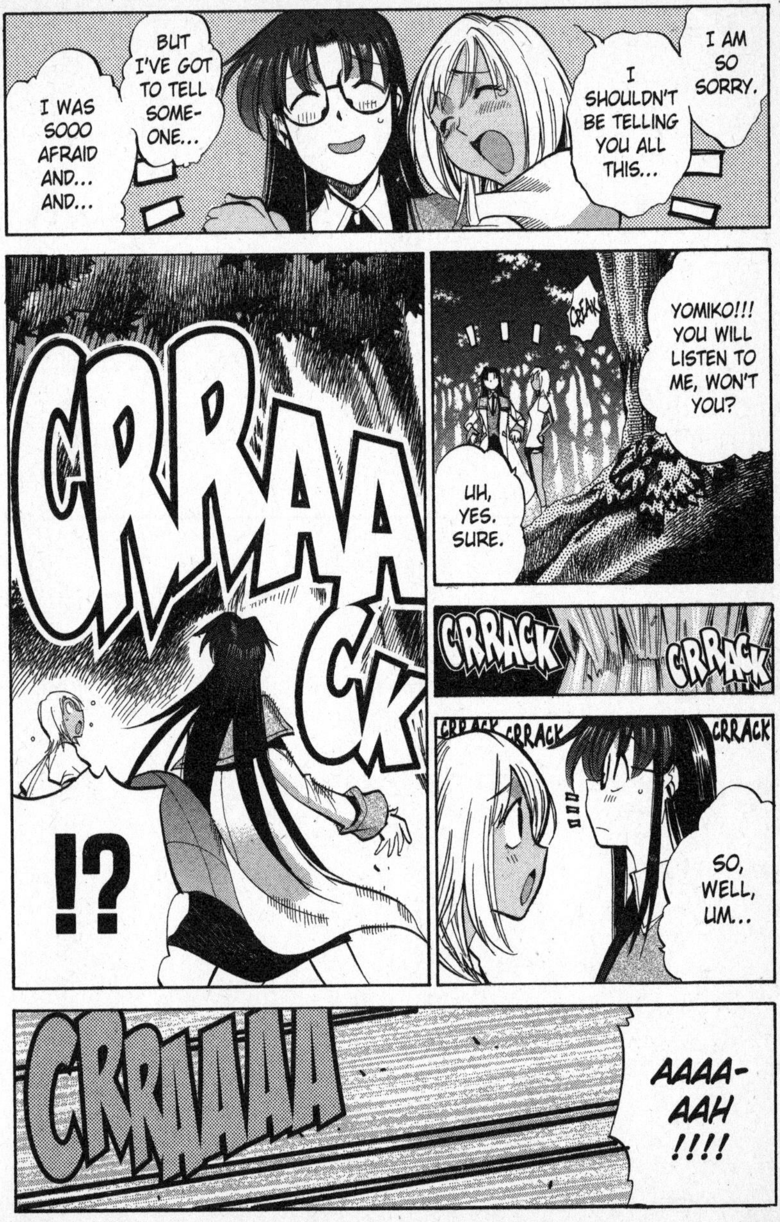
I AM SO SORRY.
I SHOULDN'T BE TELLING YOU ALL THIS...
BUT I'VE GOT TO TELL SOME-ONE...
I WAS SOOO AFRAID AND... AND...
CREAK
YOMIKO!!! YOU WILL LISTEN TO ME, WON'T YOU?
UH, YES. SURE.
CRRACK
CRRACK
CRRACK
CRRACK
CRRACK
SO, WELL, UM...
CRRAACK
!?
AAAA-AAH!!!!
CRRAAAA

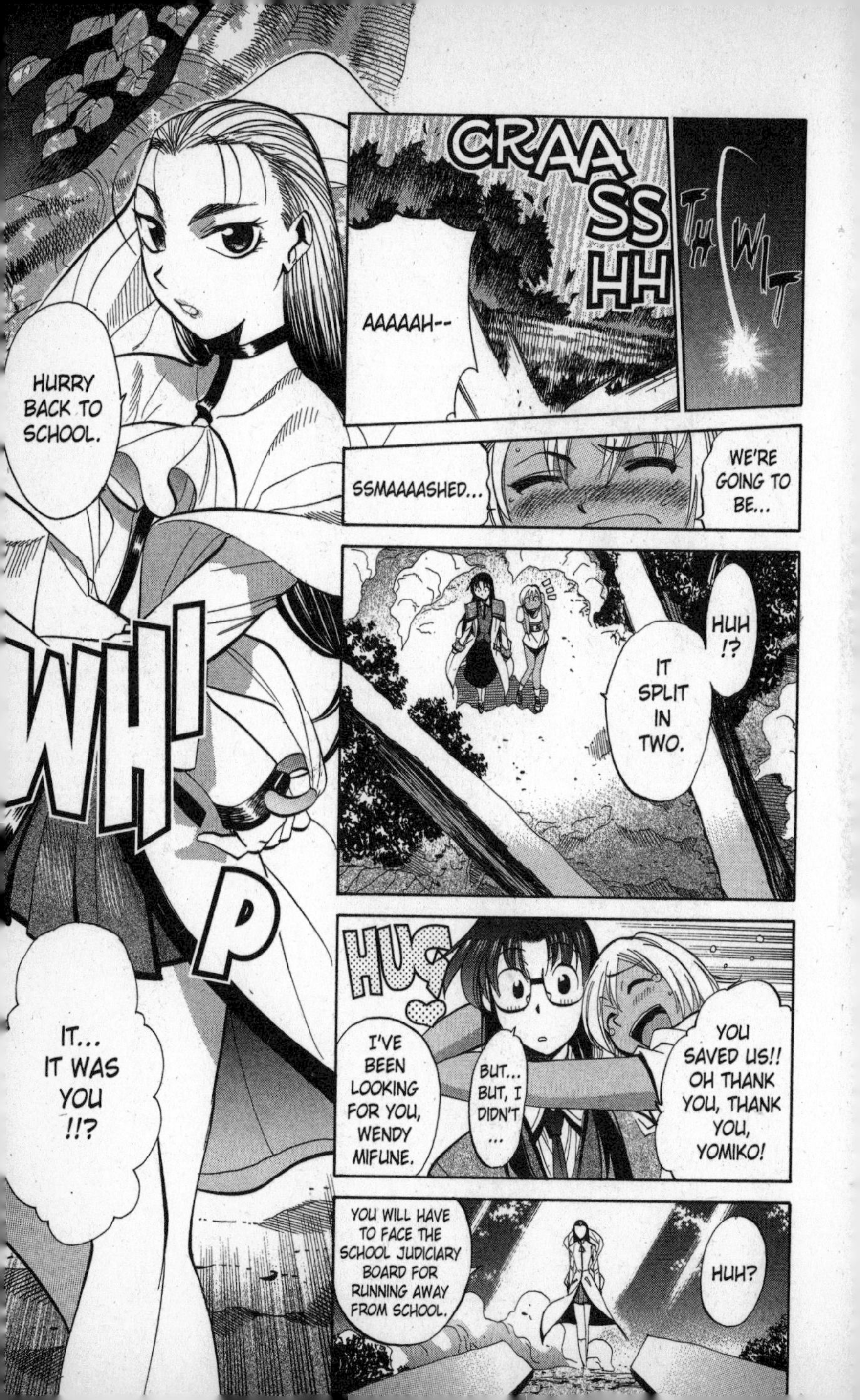
THWIT
CRAASSHH
AAAAAH--
WE'RE GOING TO BE...
SSMAAAASHED...
HUH!?
IT SPLIT IN TWO.
HUG
YOU SAVED US!! OH THANK YOU, THANK YOU, YOMIKO!
BUT... BUT, I DIDN'T...
I'VE BEEN LOOKING FOR YOU, WENDY MIFUNE.
HUH?
YOU WILL HAVE TO FACE THE SCHOOL JUDICIARY BOARD FOR RUNNING AWAY FROM SCHOOL.
HURRY BACK TO SCHOOL.
WHIP
IT... IT WAS YOU!!?

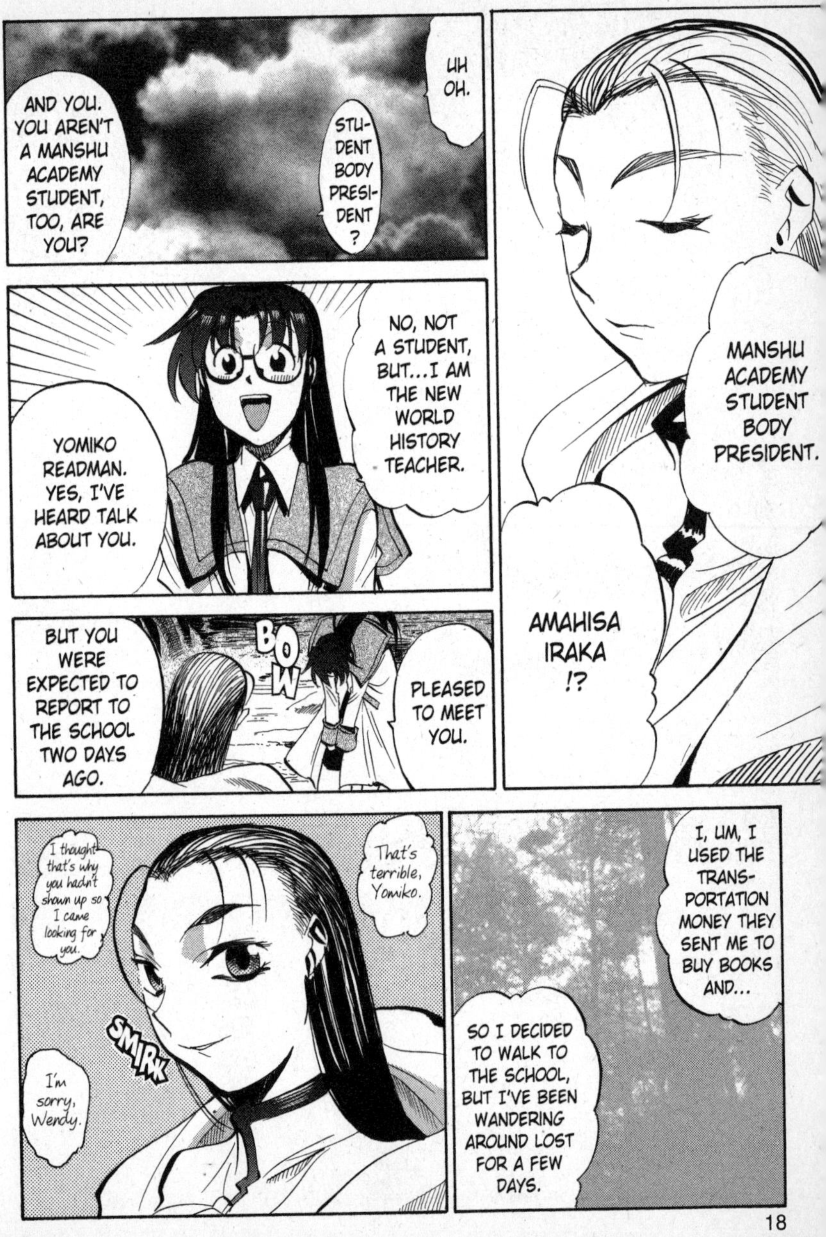
MANSHU ACADEMY STUDENT BODY PRESIDENT.
AMAHISA IRAKA !?
UH OH.
STU-DENT BODY PRESI-DENT ?
AND YOU. YOU AREN'T A MANSHU ACADEMY STUDENT, TOO, ARE YOU?
NO, NOT A STUDENT, BUT...I AM THE NEW WORLD HISTORY TEACHER.
YOMIKO READMAN. YES, I'VE HEARD TALK ABOUT YOU.
PLEASED TO MEET YOU.
BOW
BUT YOU WERE EXPECTED TO REPORT TO THE SCHOOL TWO DAYS AGO.
I, UM, I USED THE TRANS-PORTATION MONEY THEY SENT ME TO BUY BOOKS AND...
SO I DECIDED TO WALK TO THE SCHOOL, BUT I'VE BEEN WANDERING AROUND LOST FOR A FEW DAYS.
That's terrible, Yomiko.
I thought that's why you hadn't shown up so I came looking for you.
SMIRK
I'm sorry, Wendy.

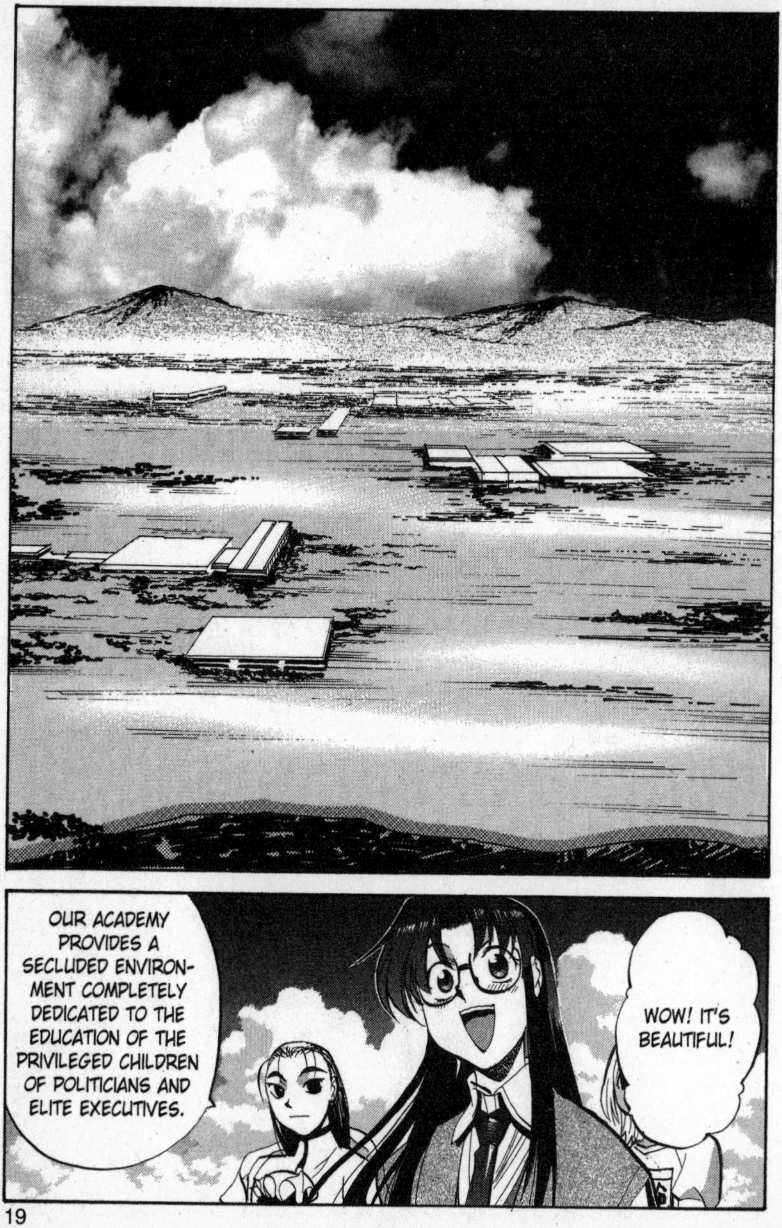
WOW! IT'S BEAUTIFUL!
OUR ACADEMY PROVIDES A SECLUDED ENVIRONMENT COMPLETELY DEDICATED TO THE EDUCATION OF THE PRIVILEGED CHILDREN OF POLITICIANS AND ELITE EXECUTIVES.

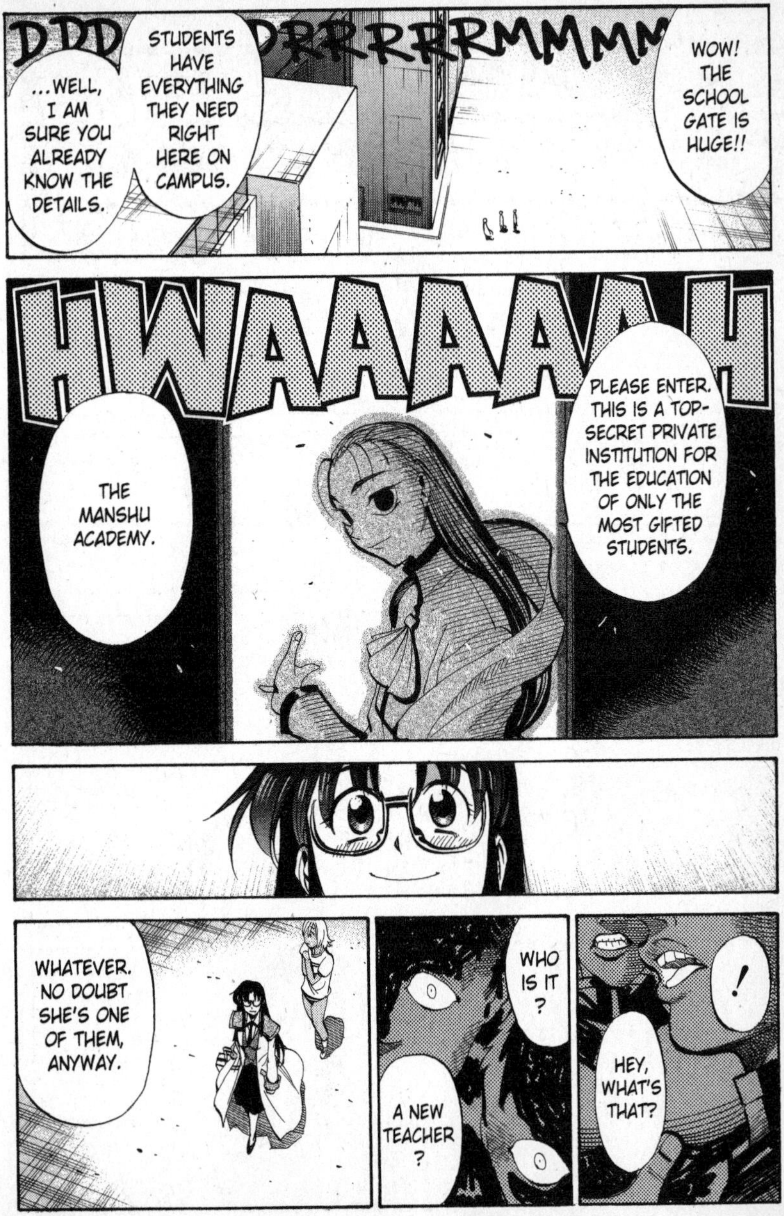
DDDDRRRRRRMMMMM
WOW! THE SCHOOL GATE IS HUGE!!
STUDENTS HAVE EVERYTHING THEY NEED RIGHT HERE ON CAMPUS.
...WELL, I AM SURE YOU ALREADY KNOW THE DETAILS.
HWAAAAAH
PLEASE ENTER. THIS IS A TOP-SECRET PRIVATE INSTITUTION FOR THE EDUCATION OF ONLY THE MOST GIFTED STUDENTS.
THE MANSHU ACADEMY.
!
HEY, WHAT'S THAT?
WHO IS IT?
A NEW TEACHER?
WHATEVER. NO DOUBT SHE'S ONE OF THEM, ANYWAY.

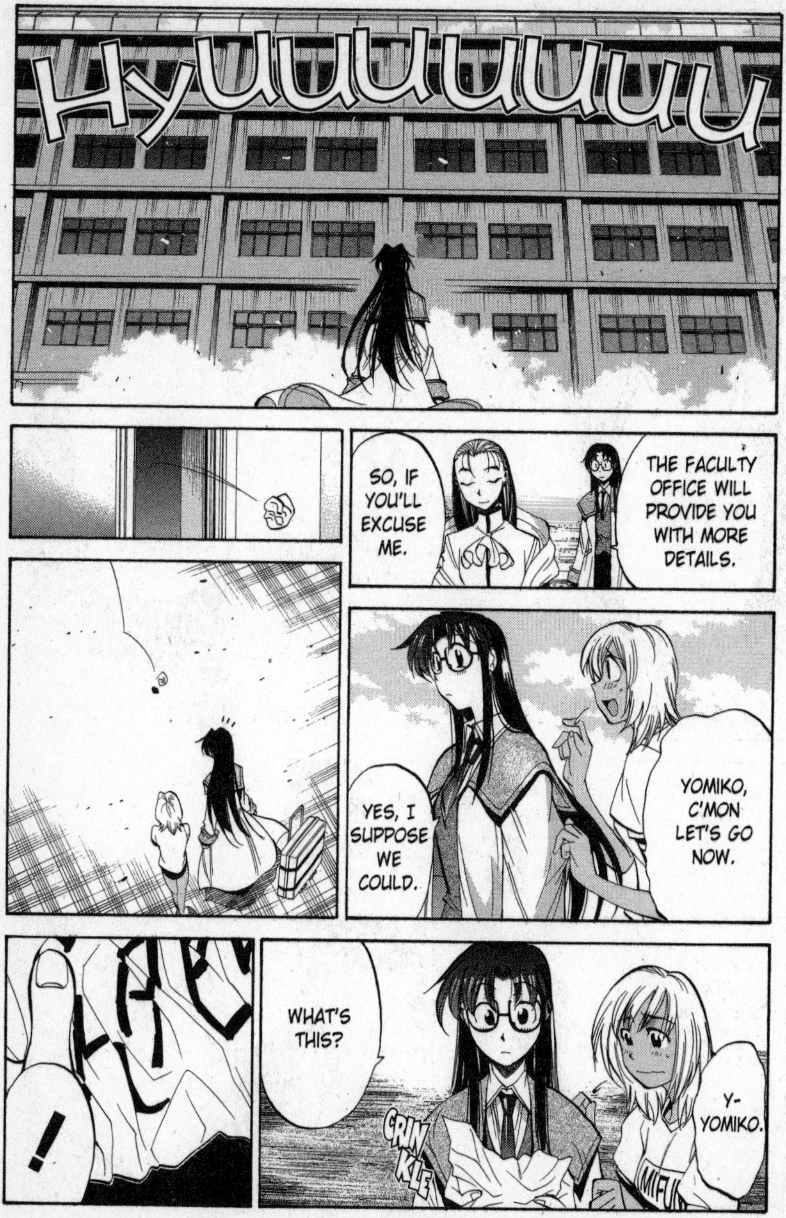
HYUUUUUUUU
THE FACULTY OFFICE WILL PROVIDE YOU WITH MORE DETAILS.
SO, IF YOU'LL EXCUSE ME.
YOMIKO, C'MON LET'S GO NOW.
YES, I SUPPOSE WE COULD.
WHAT'S THIS?
CRINKLE
Y- YOMIKO.
MIFU
!

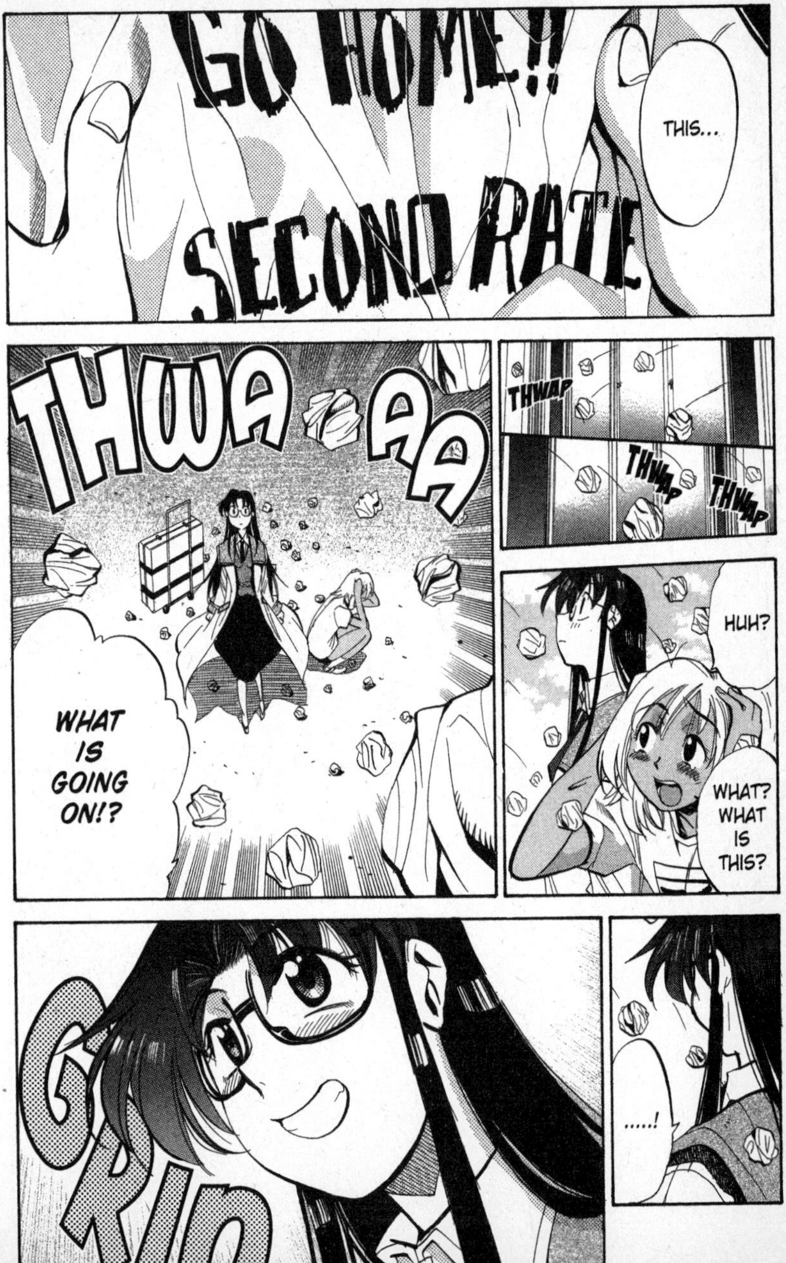
GO HOME!!
THIS...
SECOND RATE
THWAP
THWAP
THWAP
HUH?
WHAT? WHAT IS THIS?
THWAAA
WHAT IS GOING ON!?
......!
GRIN

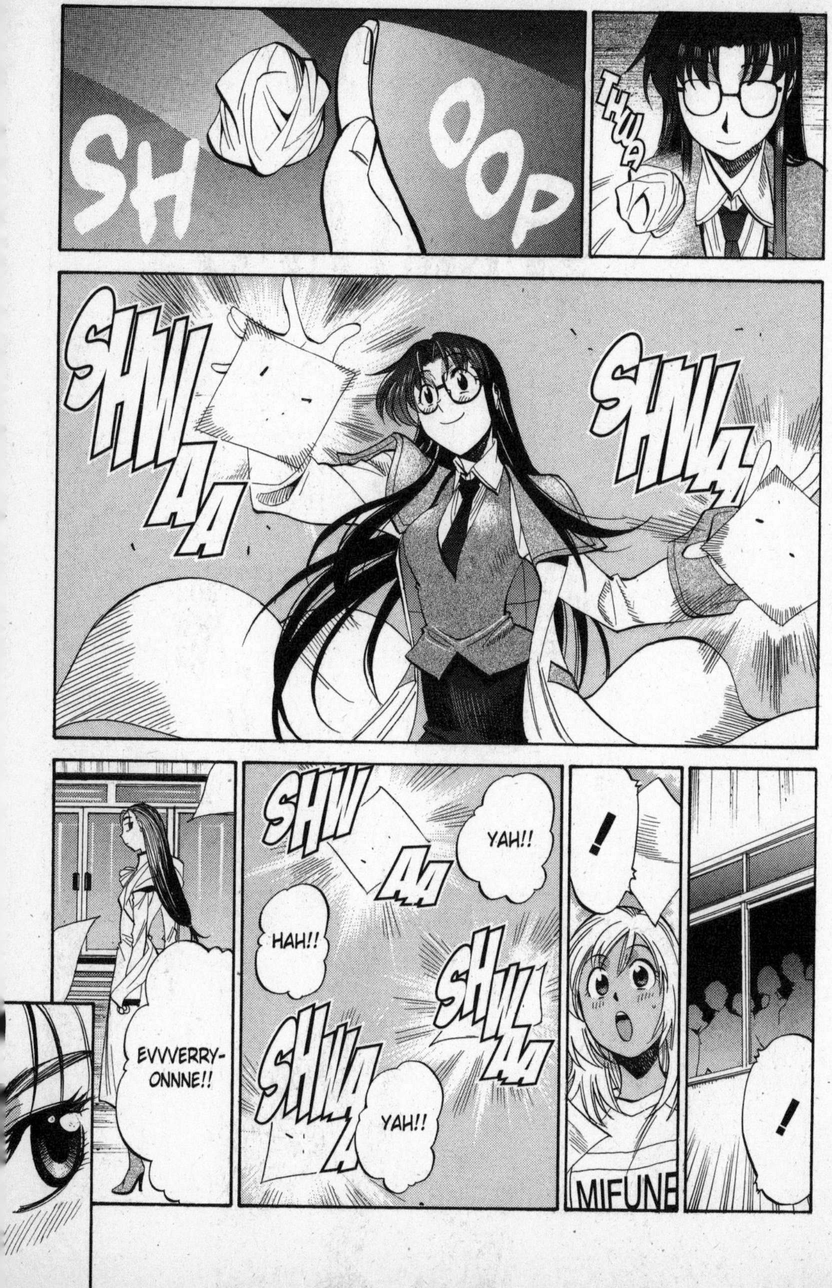
THWA
SH
OOP
SHWA
SHWAA
AA
SHWAA
!
!
MIFUNE
SHW
AA
YAH!!
HAH!!
SHWAA
SHWA
AA
YAH!!
EVVVERRY-ONNNE!!

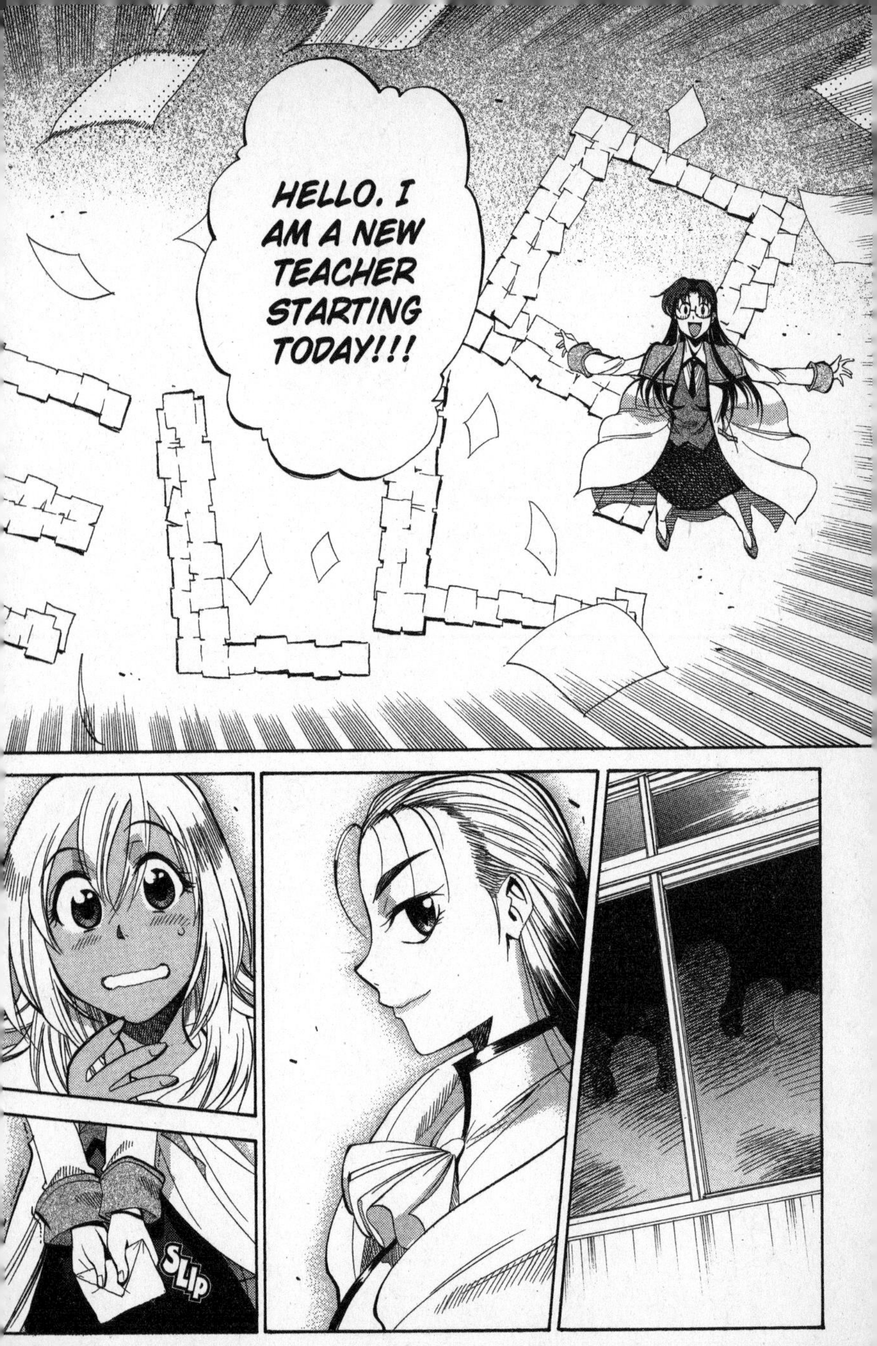
HELLO. I AM A NEW TEACHER STARTING TODAY!!!
SLIP

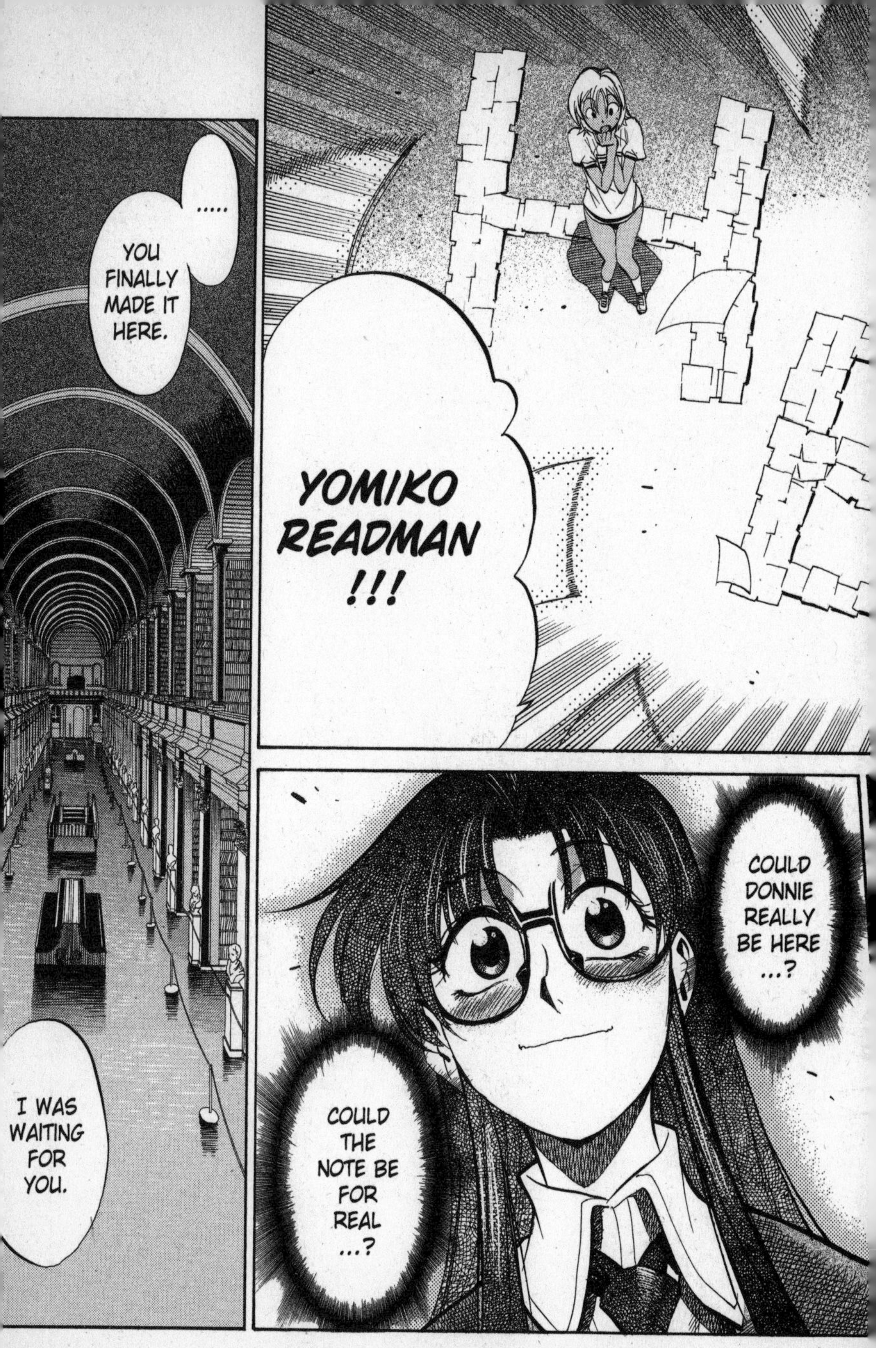
YOMIKO READMAN !!!
COULD DONNIE REALLY BE HERE ...?
COULD THE NOTE BE FOR REAL ...?
.....
YOU FINALLY MADE IT HERE.
I WAS WAITING FOR YOU.

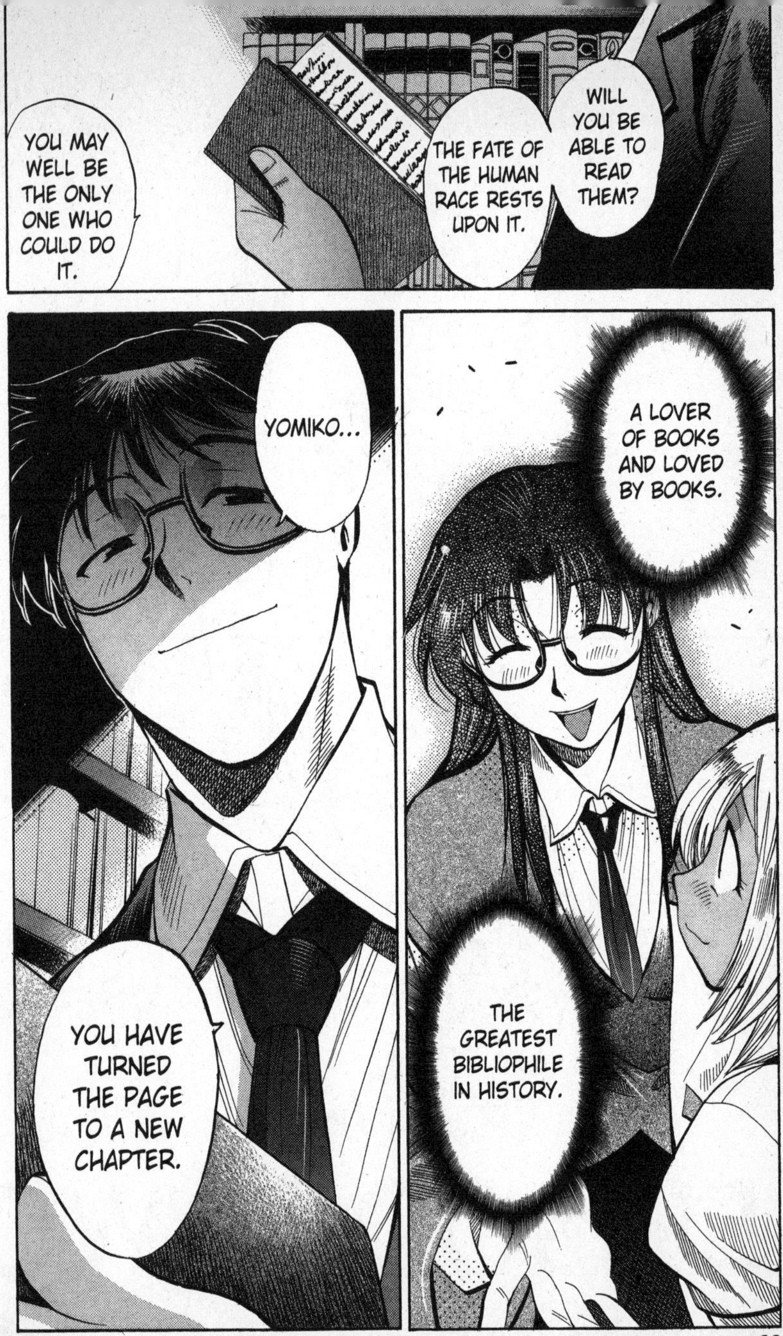
WILL YOU BE ABLE TO READ THEM?
THE FATE OF THE HUMAN RACE RESTS UPON IT.
YOU MAY WELL BE THE ONLY ONE WHO COULD DO IT.
A LOVER OF BOOKS AND LOVED BY BOOKS.
THE GREATEST BIBLIOPHILE IN HISTORY.
YOMIKO...
YOU HAVE TURNED THE PAGE TO A NEW CHAPTER.

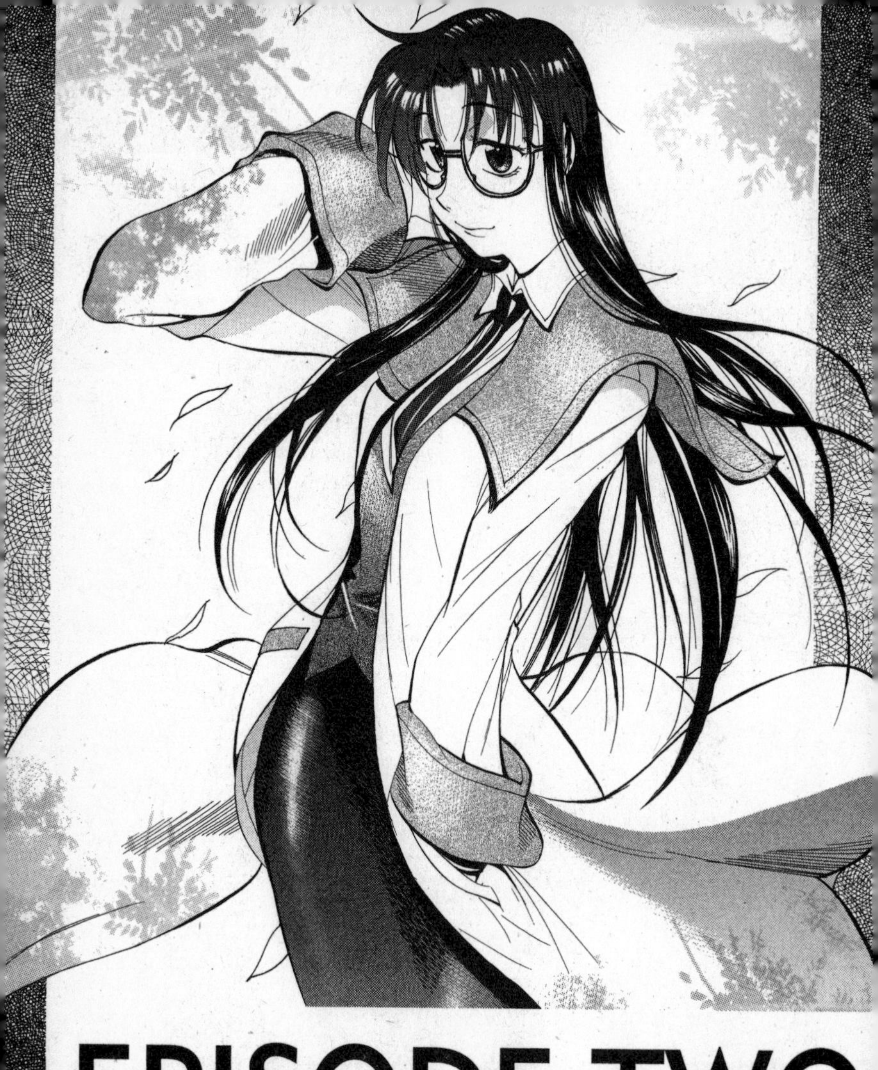

EPISODE TWO

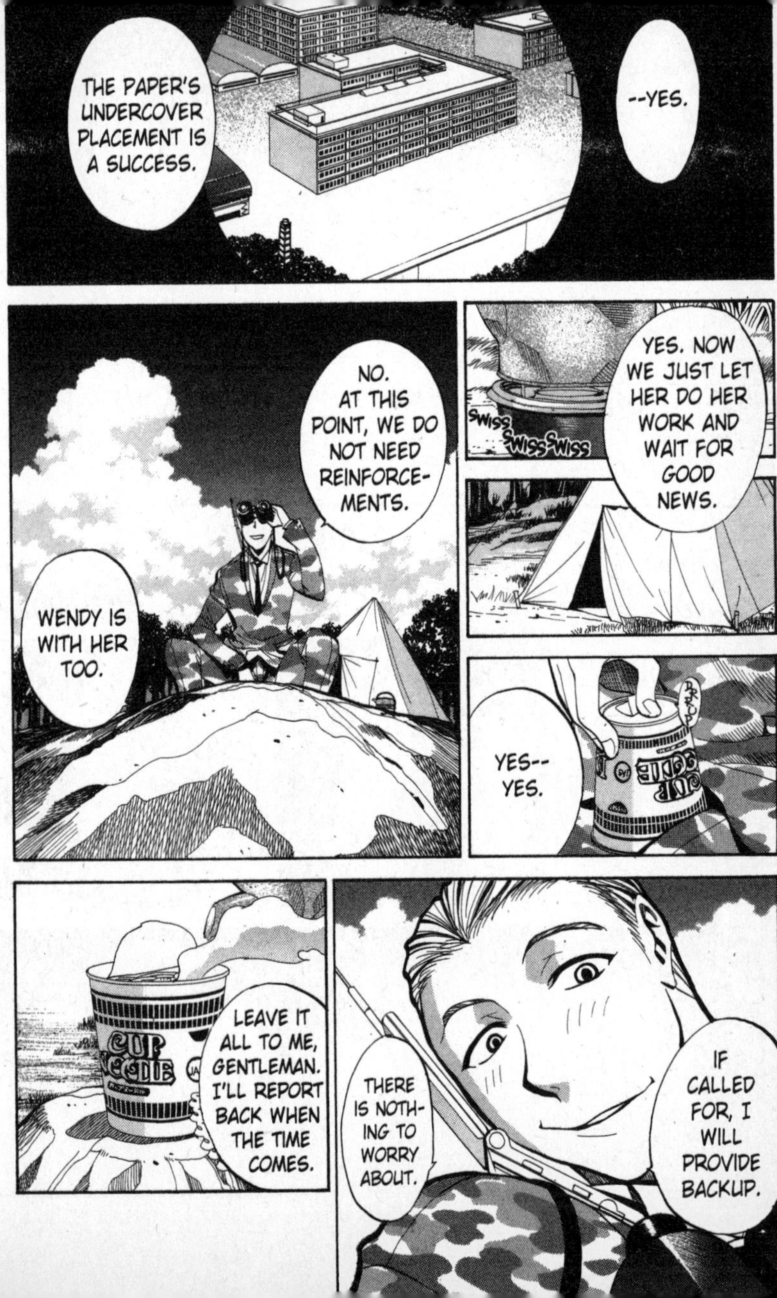
--YES.
THE PAPER'S UNDERCOVER PLACEMENT IS A SUCCESS.
SWISS SWISS SWISS
YES. NOW WE JUST LET HER DO HER WORK AND WAIT FOR GOOD NEWS.
YES-- YES.
NO. AT THIS POINT, WE DO NOT NEED REINFORCE- MENTS.
WENDY IS WITH HER TOO.
IF CALLED FOR, I WILL PROVIDE BACKUP.
THERE IS NOTH- ING TO WORRY ABOUT.
LEAVE IT ALL TO ME, GENTLEMAN. I'LL REPORT BACK WHEN THE TIME COMES.

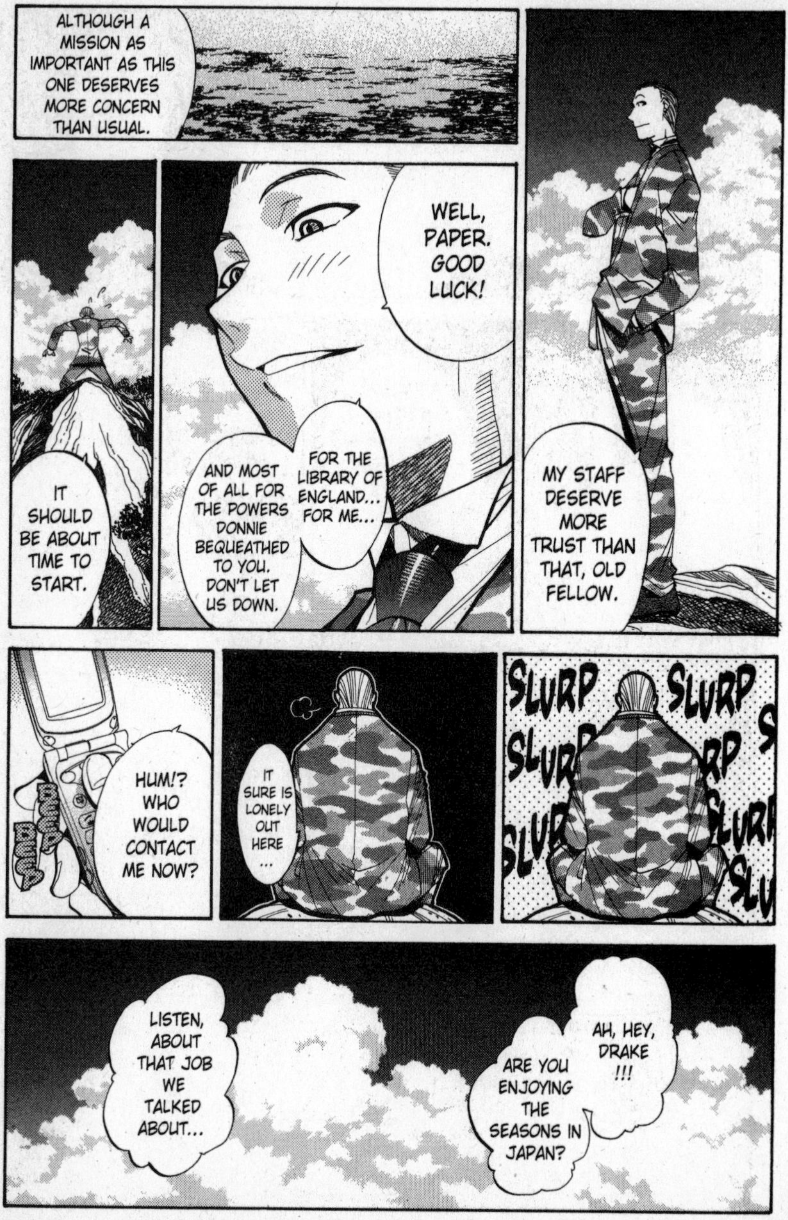
ALTHOUGH A MISSION AS IMPORTANT AS THIS ONE DESERVES MORE CONCERN THAN USUAL.
MY STAFF DESERVE MORE TRUST THAN THAT, OLD FELLOW.
WELL, PAPER. GOOD LUCK!
FOR THE LIBRARY OF ENGLAND... FOR ME...
AND MOST OF ALL FOR THE POWERS DONNIE BEQUEATHED TO YOU. DON'T LET US DOWN.
IT SHOULD BE ABOUT TIME TO START.
SLURP SLURP SLURP
IT SURE IS LONELY OUT HERE...
HUM!? WHO WOULD CONTACT ME NOW?
AH, HEY, DRAKE!!!
ARE YOU ENJOYING THE SEASONS IN JAPAN?
LISTEN, ABOUT THAT JOB WE TALKED ABOUT...

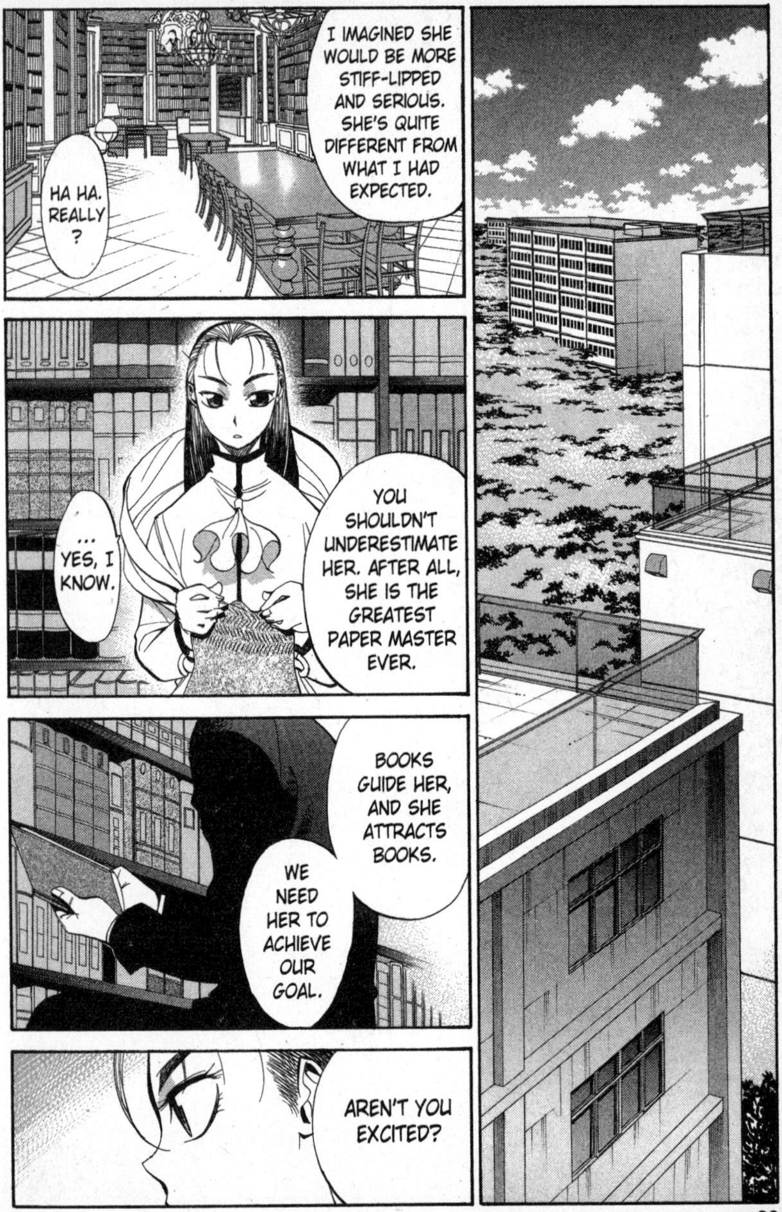
I IMAGINED SHE WOULD BE MORE STIFF-LIPPED AND SERIOUS. SHE'S QUITE DIFFERENT FROM WHAT I HAD EXPECTED.
HA HA. REALLY?
YOU SHOULDN'T UNDERESTIMATE HER. AFTER ALL, SHE IS THE GREATEST PAPER MASTER EVER.
... YES, I KNOW.
BOOKS GUIDE HER, AND SHE ATTRACTS BOOKS.
WE NEED HER TO ACHIEVE OUR GOAL.
AREN'T YOU EXCITED?

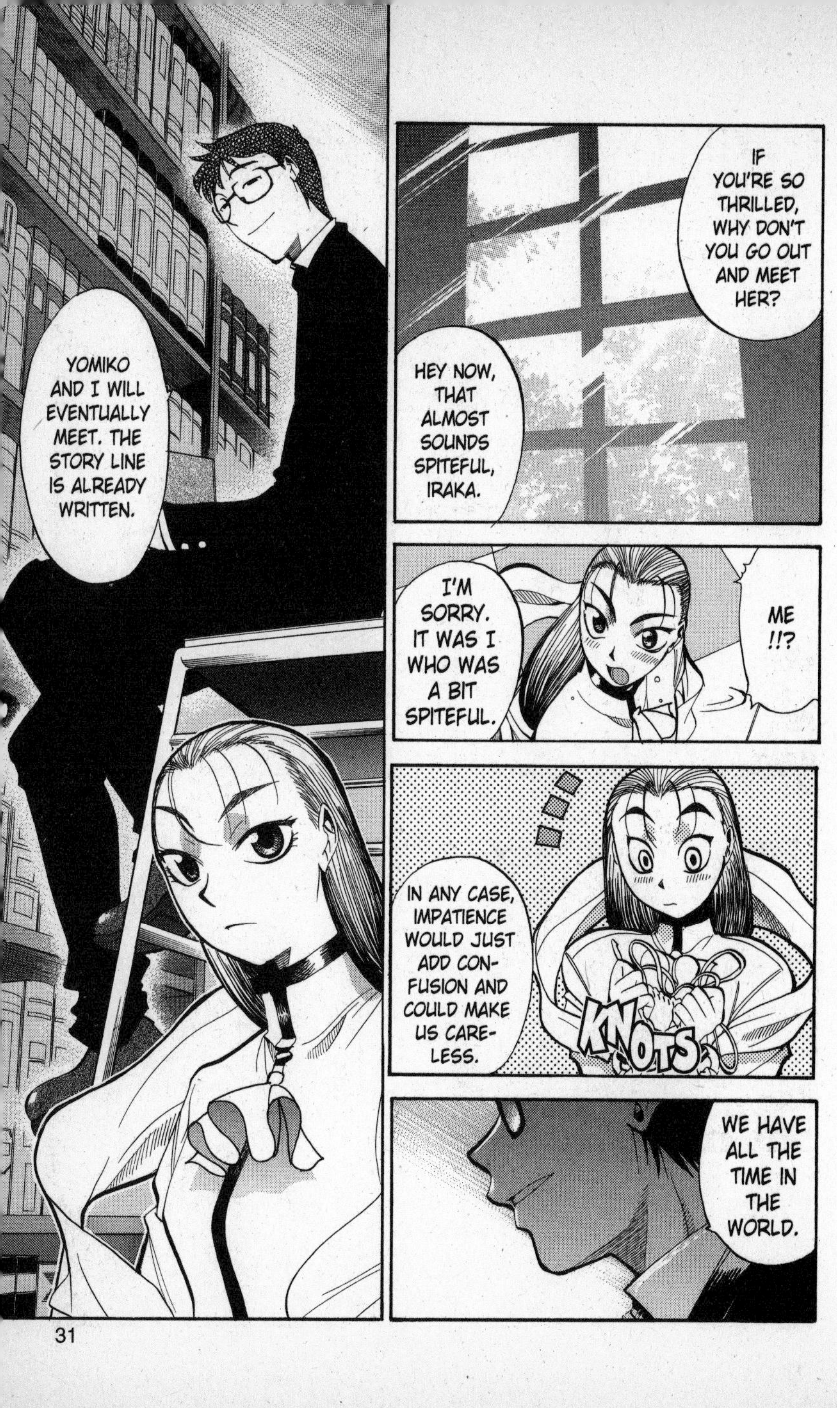
IF YOU'RE SO THRILLED, WHY DON'T YOU GO OUT AND MEET HER?
HEY NOW, THAT ALMOST SOUNDS SPITEFUL, IRAKA.
ME !!?
I'M SORRY. IT WAS I WHO WAS A BIT SPITEFUL.
IN ANY CASE, IMPATIENCE WOULD JUST ADD CON-FUSION AND COULD MAKE US CARE-LESS.
KNOTS
WE HAVE ALL THE TIME IN THE WORLD.
YOMIKO AND I WILL EVENTUALLY MEET. THE STORY LINE IS ALREADY WRITTEN.

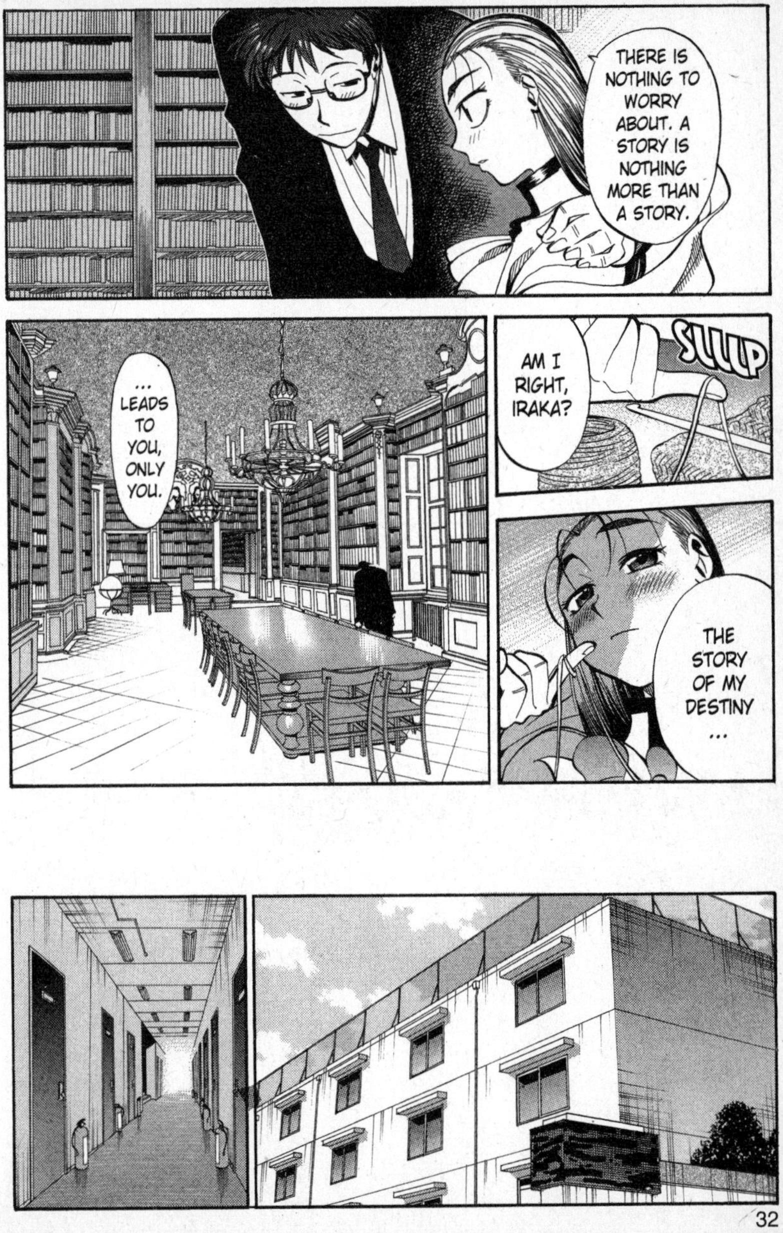
THERE IS NOTHING TO WORRY ABOUT. A STORY IS NOTHING MORE THAN A STORY.
SLLUP
AM I RIGHT, IRAKA?
THE STORY OF MY DESTINY ...
... LEADS TO YOU, ONLY YOU.

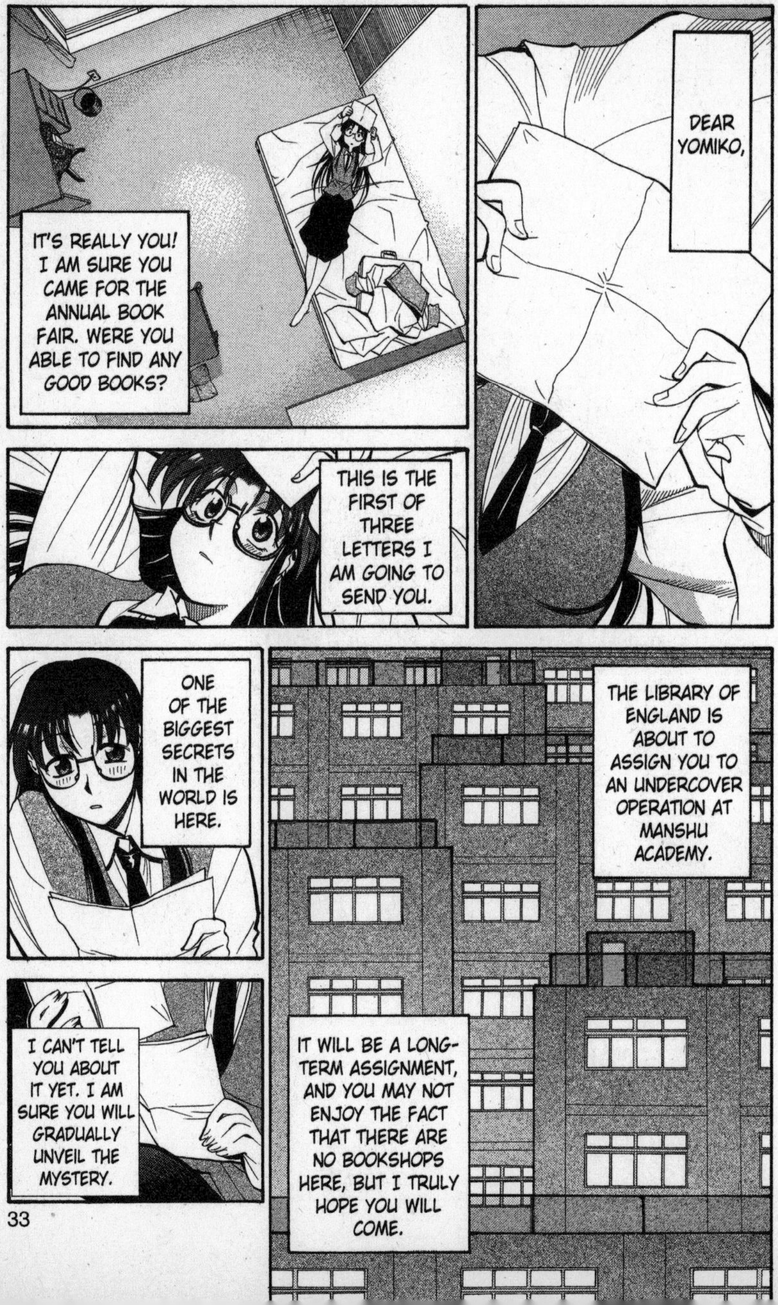
DEAR YOMIKO,
IT'S REALLY YOU! I AM SURE YOU CAME FOR THE ANNUAL BOOK FAIR. WERE YOU ABLE TO FIND ANY GOOD BOOKS?
THIS IS THE FIRST OF THREE LETTERS I AM GOING TO SEND YOU.
THE LIBRARY OF ENGLAND IS ABOUT TO ASSIGN YOU TO AN UNDERCOVER OPERATION AT MANSHU ACADEMY.
IT WILL BE A LONG-TERM ASSIGNMENT, AND YOU MAY NOT ENJOY THE FACT THAT THERE ARE NO BOOKSHOPS HERE, BUT I TRULY HOPE YOU WILL COME.
ONE OF THE BIGGEST SECRETS IN THE WORLD IS HERE.
I CAN'T TELL YOU ABOUT IT YET. I AM SURE YOU WILL GRADUALLY UNVEIL THE MYSTERY.

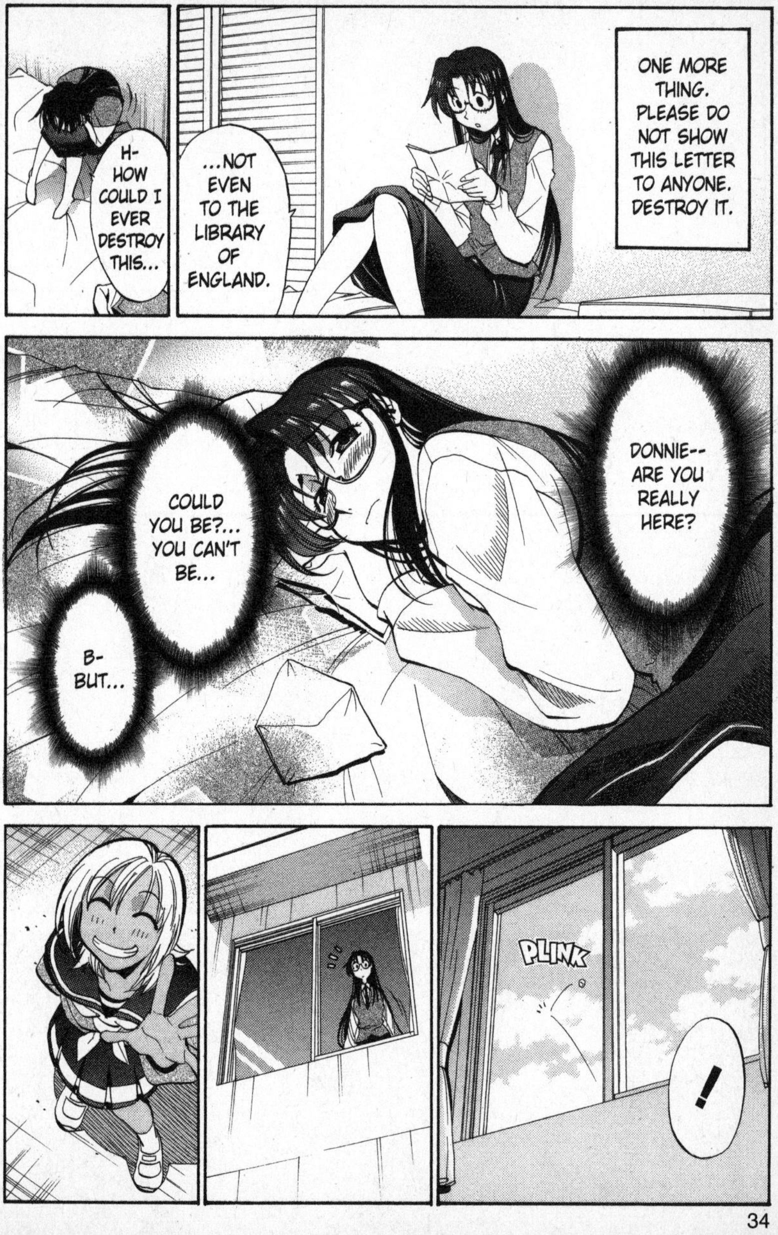
ONE MORE THING. PLEASE DO NOT SHOW THIS LETTER TO ANYONE. DESTROY IT.
...NOT EVEN TO THE LIBRARY OF ENGLAND.
H-HOW COULD I EVER DESTROY THIS...
DONNIE-- ARE YOU REALLY HERE?
COULD YOU BE?... YOU CAN'T BE...
B-BUT...
PLINK
!

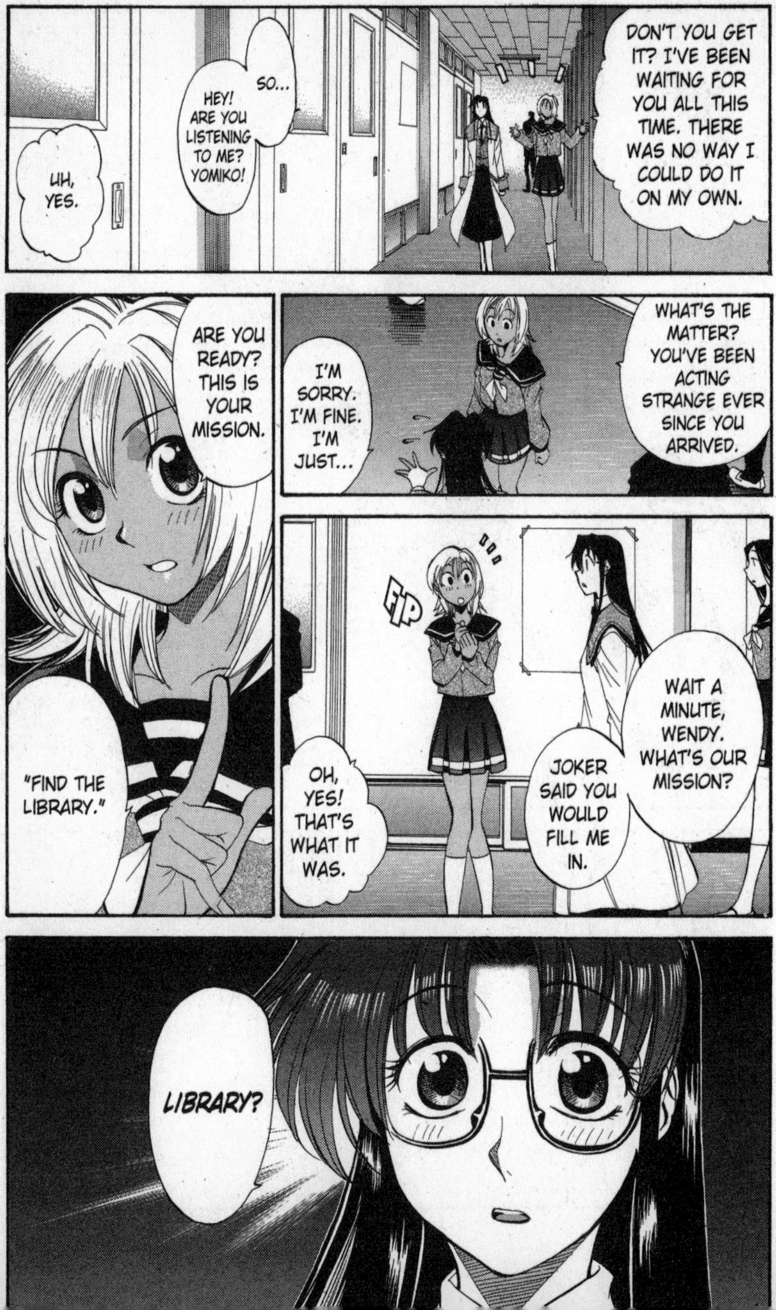
DON'T YOU GET IT? I'VE BEEN WAITING FOR YOU ALL THIS TIME. THERE WAS NO WAY I COULD DO IT ON MY OWN.
SO...
HEY! ARE YOU LISTENING TO ME? YOMIKO!
UH, YES.
WHAT'S THE MATTER? YOU'VE BEEN ACTING STRANGE EVER SINCE YOU ARRIVED.
I'M SORRY. I'M FINE. I'M JUST...
FIP
WAIT A MINUTE, WENDY. WHAT'S OUR MISSION?
JOKER SAID YOU WOULD FILL ME IN.
OH, YES! THAT'S WHAT IT WAS.
ARE YOU READY? THIS IS YOUR MISSION.
"FIND THE LIBRARY."
LIBRARY?

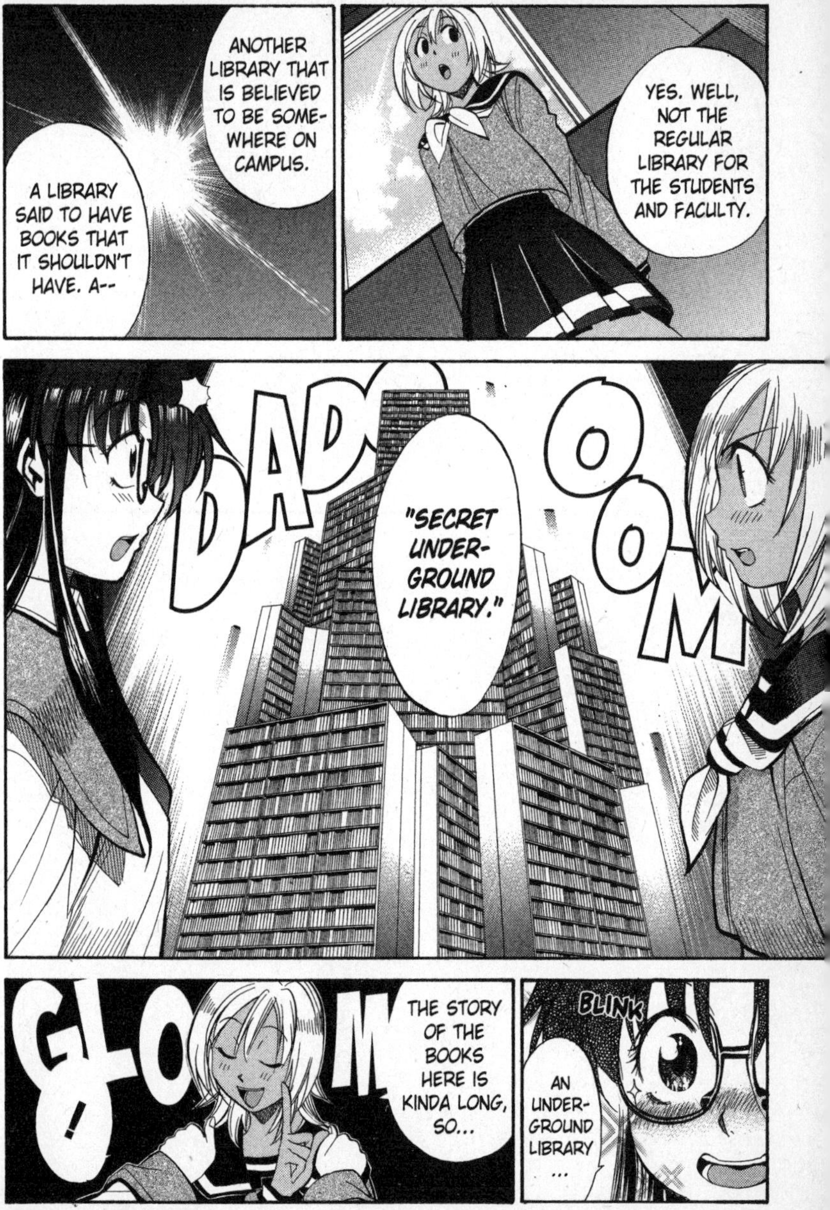
YES. WELL, NOT THE REGULAR LIBRARY FOR THE STUDENTS AND FACULTY.
ANOTHER LIBRARY THAT IS BELIEVED TO BE SOME-WHERE ON CAMPUS.
A LIBRARY SAID TO HAVE BOOKS THAT IT SHOULDN'T HAVE. A--
DADOOOM
"SECRET UNDER-GROUND LIBRARY."
BLINK
AN UNDER-GROUND LIBRARY ...
GLOOM
!
THE STORY OF THE BOOKS HERE IS KINDA LONG, SO...

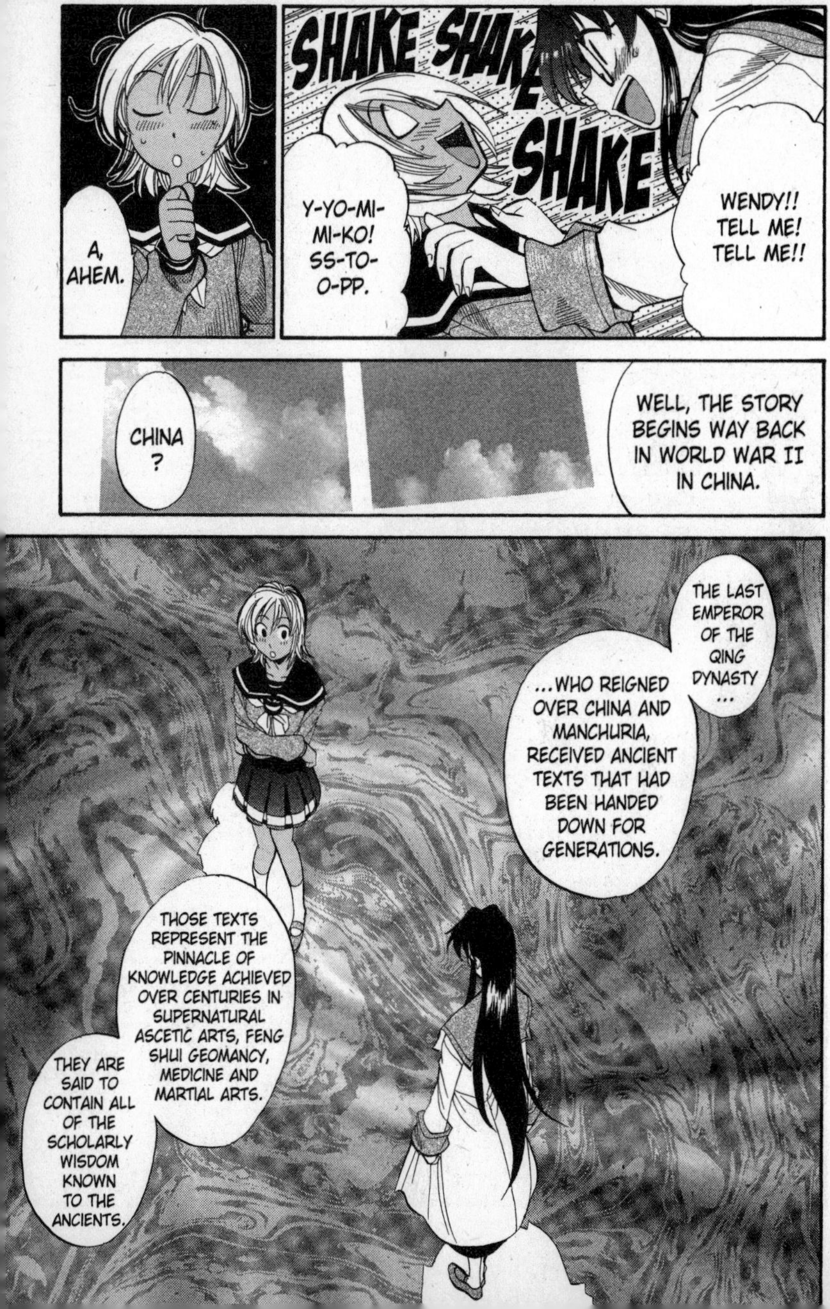
WENDY!! TELL ME! TELL ME!!
SHAKE SHAKE SHAKE
Y-YO-MI-MI-KO! SS-TO-O-PP.
A, AHEM.
WELL, THE STORY BEGINS WAY BACK IN WORLD WAR II IN CHINA.
CHINA ?
THE LAST EMPEROR OF THE QING DYNASTY ...
...WHO REIGNED OVER CHINA AND MANCHURIA, RECEIVED ANCIENT TEXTS THAT HAD BEEN HANDED DOWN FOR GENERATIONS.
THOSE TEXTS REPRESENT THE PINNACLE OF KNOWLEDGE ACHIEVED OVER CENTURIES IN SUPERNATURAL ASCETIC ARTS, FENG SHUI GEOMANCY, MEDICINE AND MARTIAL ARTS.
THEY ARE SAID TO CONTAIN ALL OF THE SCHOLARLY WISDOM KNOWN TO THE ANCIENTS.

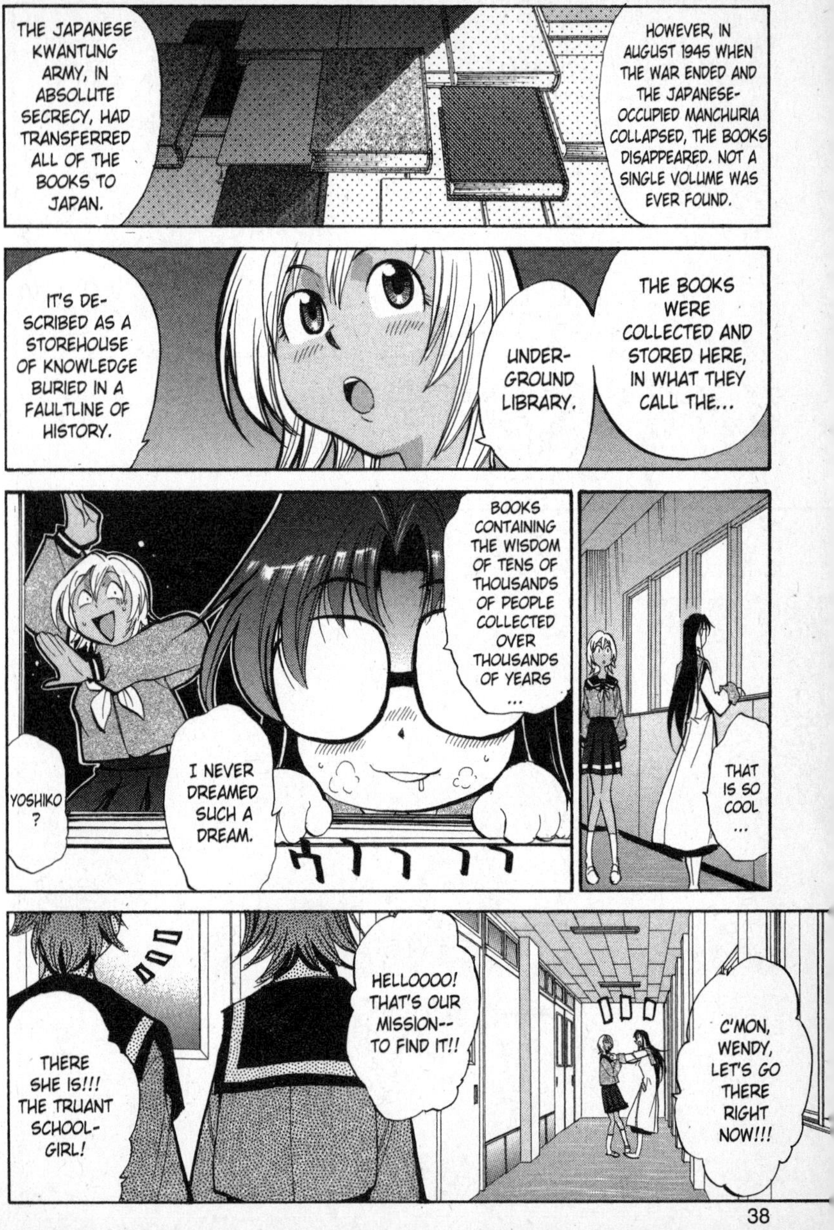
HOWEVER, IN AUGUST 1945 WHEN THE WAR ENDED AND THE JAPANESE-OCCUPIED MANCHURIA COLLAPSED, THE BOOKS DISAPPEARED. NOT A SINGLE VOLUME WAS EVER FOUND.
THE JAPANESE KWANTUNG ARMY, IN ABSOLUTE SECRECY, HAD TRANSFERRED ALL OF THE BOOKS TO JAPAN.
THE BOOKS WERE COLLECTED AND STORED HERE, IN WHAT THEY CALL THE...
UNDER-GROUND LIBRARY.
IT'S DE-SCRIBED AS A STOREHOUSE OF KNOWLEDGE BURIED IN A FAULTLINE OF HISTORY.
THAT IS SO COOL ...
BOOKS CONTAINING THE WISDOM OF TENS OF THOUSANDS OF PEOPLE COLLECTED OVER THOUSANDS OF YEARS ...
I NEVER DREAMED SUCH A DREAM.
YOSHIKO ?
C'MON, WENDY, LET'S GO THERE RIGHT NOW!!!
HELLOOOO! THAT'S OUR MISSION-- TO FIND IT!!
THERE SHE IS!!! THE TRUANT SCHOOL-GIRL!

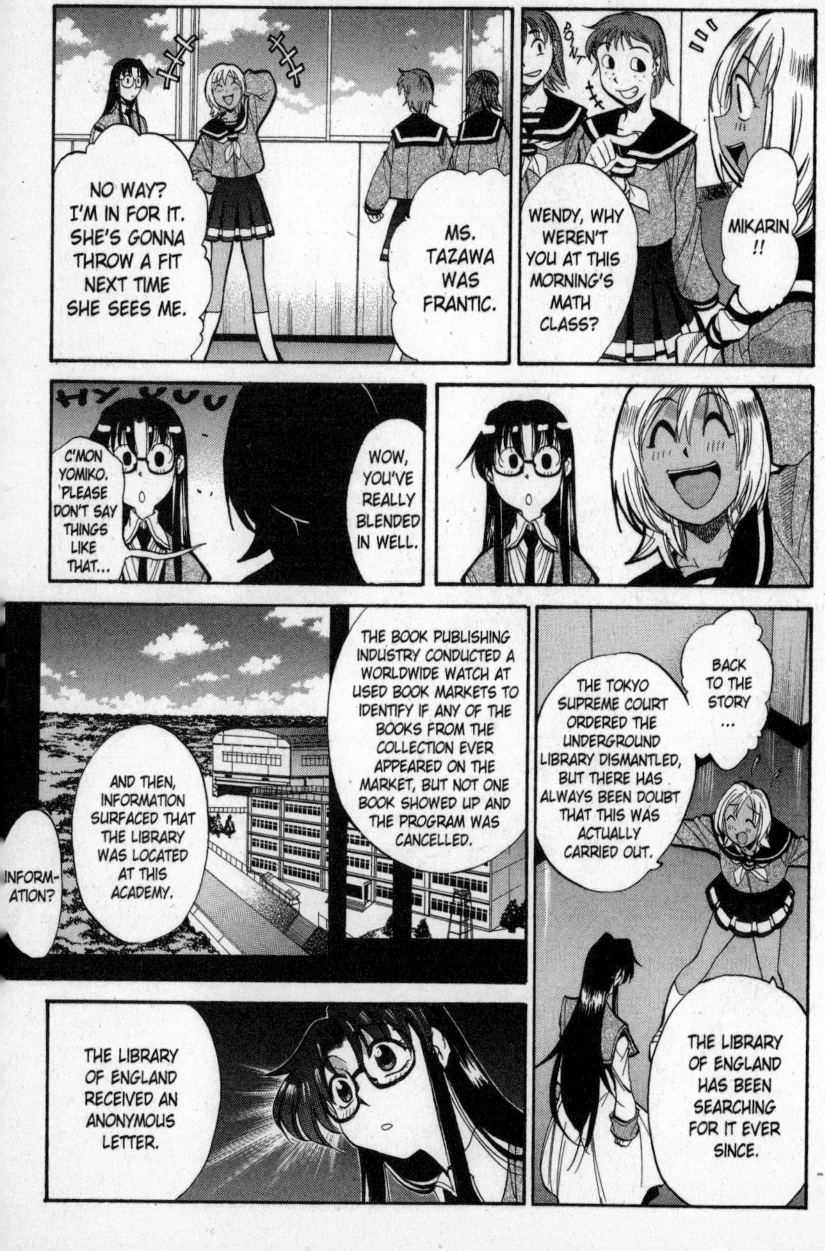
POINT
MIKARIN !!
WENDY, WHY WEREN'T YOU AT THIS MORNING'S MATH CLASS?
MS. TAZAWA WAS FRANTIC.
NO WAY? I'M IN FOR IT. SHE'S GONNA THROW A FIT NEXT TIME SHE SEES ME.
WOW, YOU'VE REALLY BLENDED IN WELL.
C'MON YOMIKO. PLEASE DON'T SAY THINGS LIKE THAT...
BACK TO THE STORY ...
THE TOKYO SUPREME COURT ORDERED THE UNDERGROUND LIBRARY DISMANTLED, BUT THERE HAS ALWAYS BEEN DOUBT THAT THIS WAS ACTUALLY CARRIED OUT.
THE LIBRARY OF ENGLAND HAS BEEN SEARCHING FOR IT EVER SINCE.
THE BOOK PUBLISHING INDUSTRY CONDUCTED A WORLDWIDE WATCH AT USED BOOK MARKETS TO IDENTIFY IF ANY OF THE BOOKS FROM THE COLLECTION EVER APPEARED ON THE MARKET, BUT NOT ONE BOOK SHOWED UP AND THE PROGRAM WAS CANCELLED.
AND THEN, INFORMATION SURFACED THAT THE LIBRARY WAS LOCATED AT THIS ACADEMY.
INFORM-ATION?
THE LIBRARY OF ENGLAND RECEIVED AN ANONYMOUS LETTER.

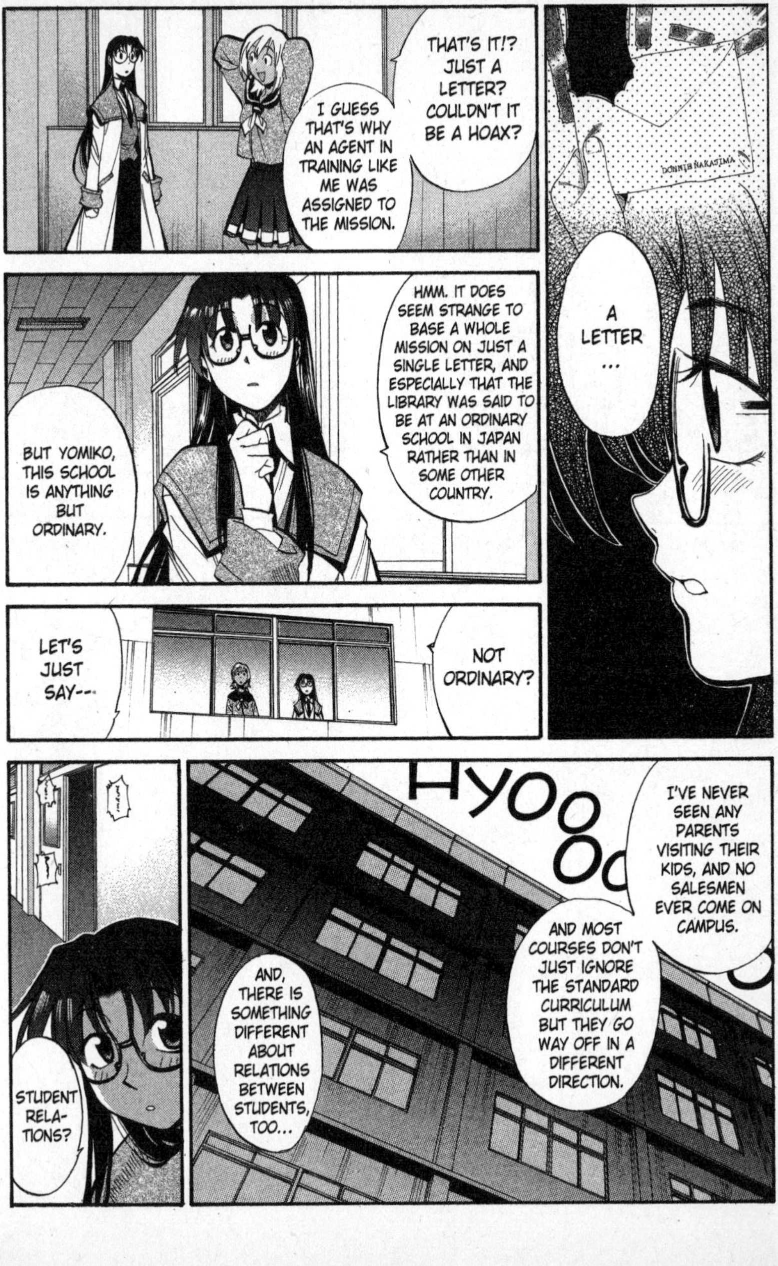
DONNIE NAKAJIMA
A LETTER ...
THAT'S IT!? JUST A LETTER? COULDN'T IT BE A HOAX?
I GUESS THAT'S WHY AN AGENT IN TRAINING LIKE ME WAS ASSIGNED TO THE MISSION.
HMM. IT DOES SEEM STRANGE TO BASE A WHOLE MISSION ON JUST A SINGLE LETTER, AND ESPECIALLY THAT THE LIBRARY WAS SAID TO BE AT AN ORDINARY SCHOOL IN JAPAN RATHER THAN IN SOME OTHER COUNTRY.
BUT YOMIKO, THIS SCHOOL IS ANYTHING BUT ORDINARY.
NOT ORDINARY?
LET'S JUST SAY--
HYOOOO
I'VE NEVER SEEN ANY PARENTS VISITING THEIR KIDS, AND NO SALESMEN EVER COME ON CAMPUS.
AND MOST COURSES DON'T JUST IGNORE THE STANDARD CURRICULUM BUT THEY GO WAY OFF IN A DIFFERENT DIRECTION.
AND, THERE IS SOMETHING DIFFERENT ABOUT RELATIONS BETWEEN STUDENTS, TOO...
STUDENT RELA-TIONS?

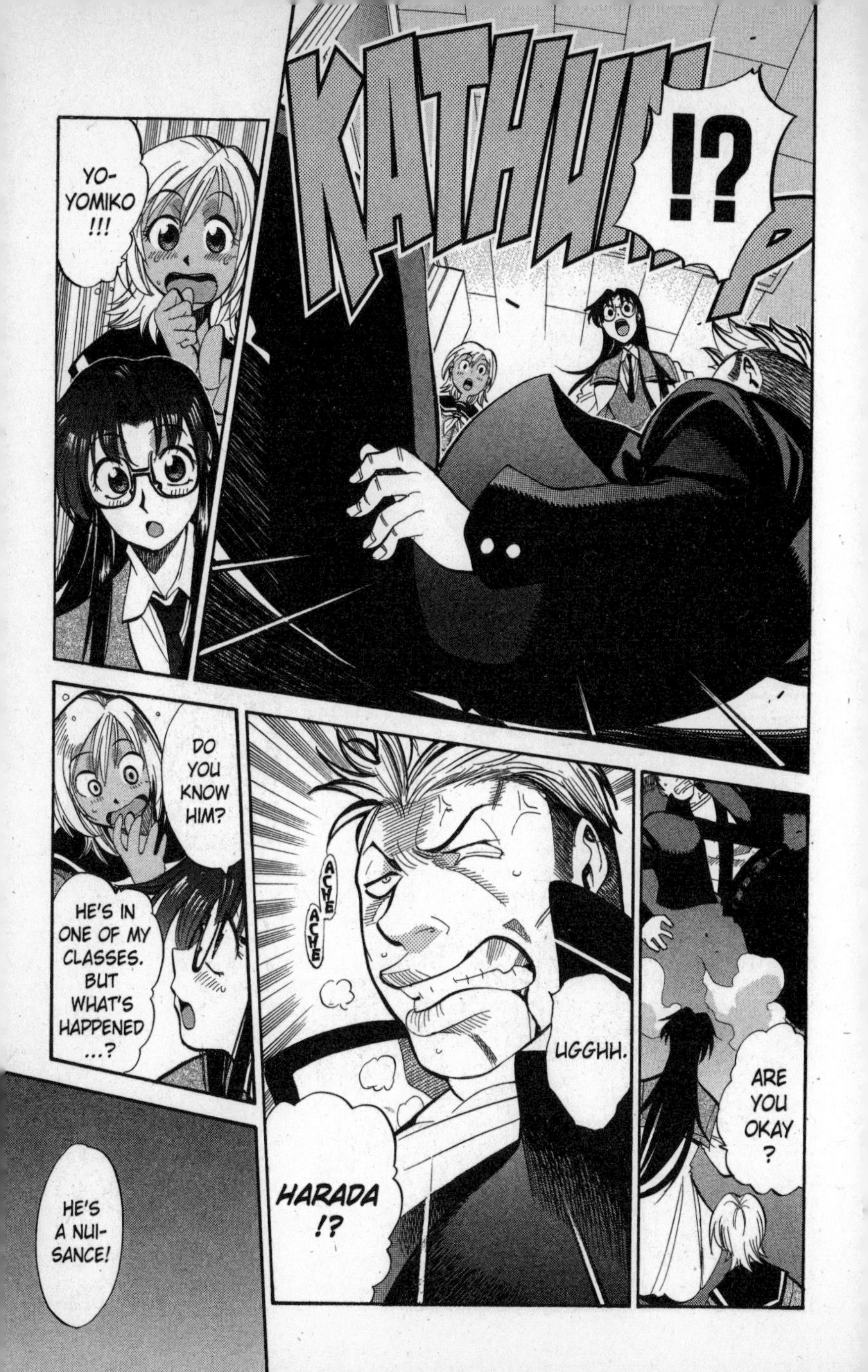
KATHU...P
!?
YO-YOMIKO!!!
ARE YOU OKAY?
UGGHH.
ACHE ACHE
HARADA!?
DO YOU KNOW HIM?
HE'S IN ONE OF MY CLASSES. BUT WHAT'S HAPPENED...?
HE'S A NUISANCE!

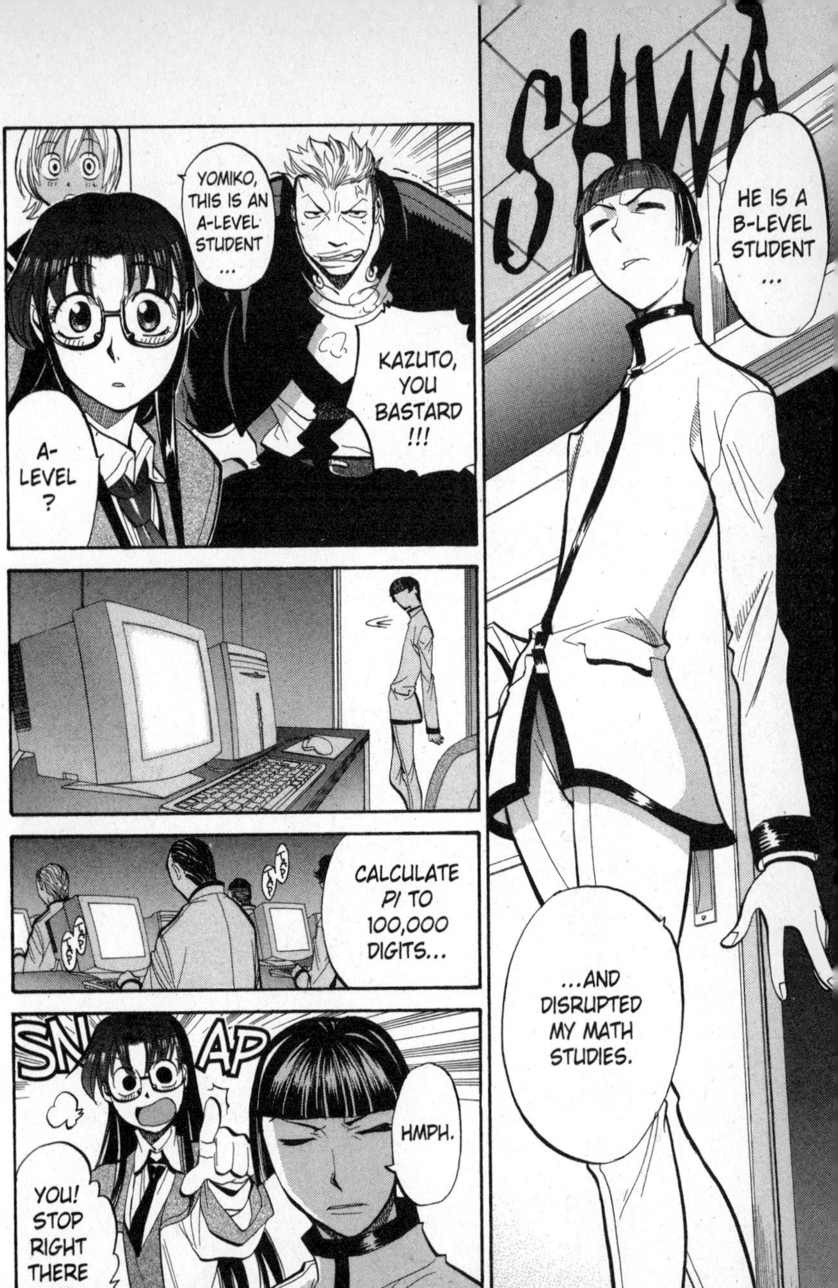
SHWA
HE IS A B-LEVEL STUDENT ...
...AND DISRUPTED MY MATH STUDIES.
YOMIKO, THIS IS AN A-LEVEL STUDENT ...
KAZUTO, YOU BASTARD !!!
A-LEVEL ?
TAP TAP
TAP TAP
CALCULATE PI TO 100,000 DIGITS...
SNAP
HMPH.
YOU! STOP RIGHT THERE !!!

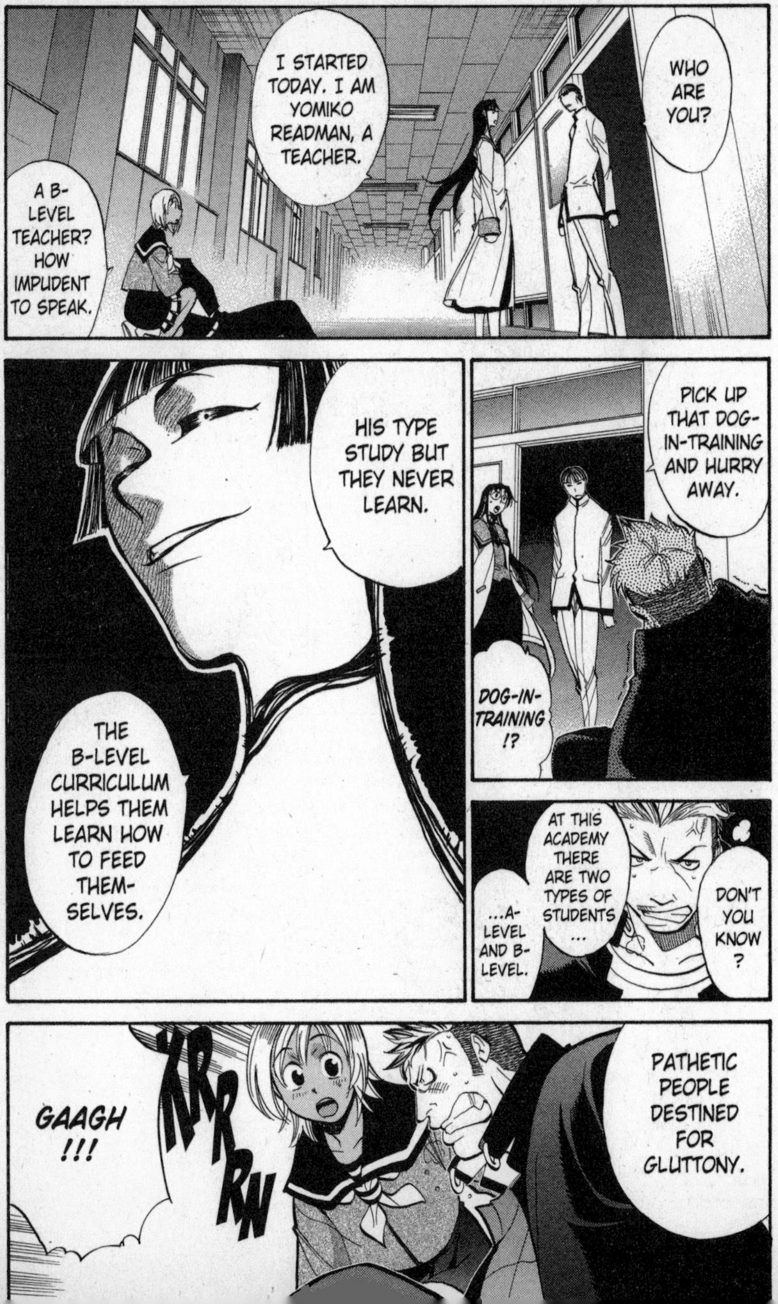
WHO ARE YOU?
I STARTED TODAY. I AM YOMIKO READMAN, A TEACHER.
A B-LEVEL TEACHER? HOW IMPUDENT TO SPEAK.
PICK UP THAT DOG-IN-TRAINING AND HURRY AWAY.
DOG-IN-TRAINING!?
DON'T YOU KNOW?
AT THIS ACADEMY THERE ARE TWO TYPES OF STUDENTS...
...A-LEVEL AND B-LEVEL.
HIS TYPE STUDY BUT THEY NEVER LEARN.
THE B-LEVEL CURRICULUM HELPS THEM LEARN HOW TO FEED THEM-SELVES.
PATHETIC PEOPLE DESTINED FOR GLUTTONY.
KRRRRN
GAAGH!!!

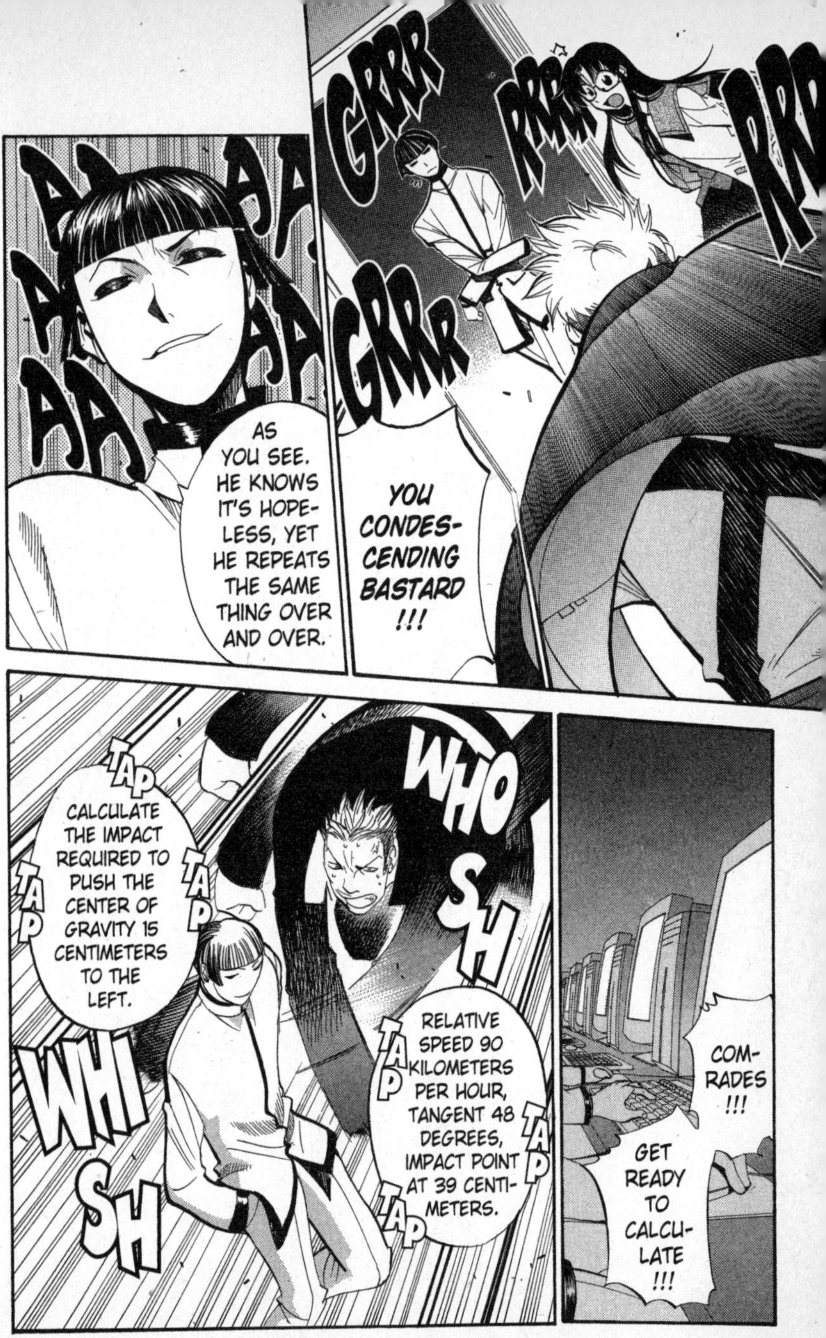
GRRR
RRRR
RRRR
GRRR
YOU CONDESCENDING BASTARD!!!
AAAAAAAA
AS YOU SEE. HE KNOWS IT'S HOPELESS, YET HE REPEATS THE SAME THING OVER AND OVER.
COMRADES!!!
GET READY TO CALCULATE!!!
WHOOSH
TAP
TAP
RELATIVE SPEED 90 KILOMETERS PER HOUR, TANGENT 48 DEGREES, IMPACT POINT AT 39 CENTIMETERS.
TAP
TAP
TAP
CALCULATE THE IMPACT REQUIRED TO PUSH THE CENTER OF GRAVITY 15 CENTIMETERS TO THE LEFT.
TAP
WHISH

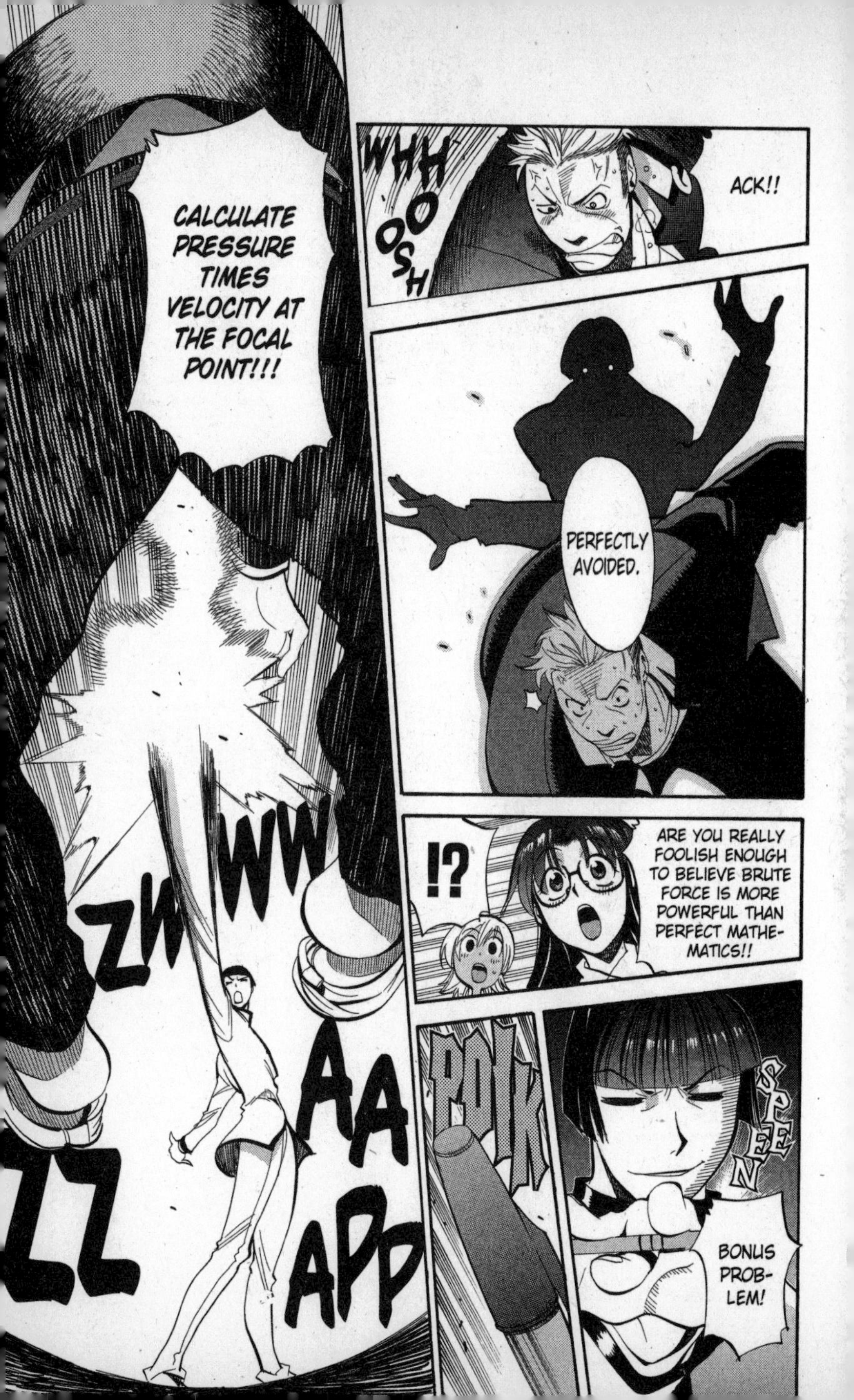
WHOOSH
ACK!!
PERFECTLY AVOIDED.
!?
ARE YOU REALLY FOOLISH ENOUGH TO BELIEVE BRUTE FORCE IS MORE POWERFUL THAN PERFECT MATHE-MATICS!!
SPEEN
BONUS PROB-LEM!
POIK
CALCULATE PRESSURE TIMES VELOCITY AT THE FOCAL POINT!!!
ZWWW
AA
APP
ZZ

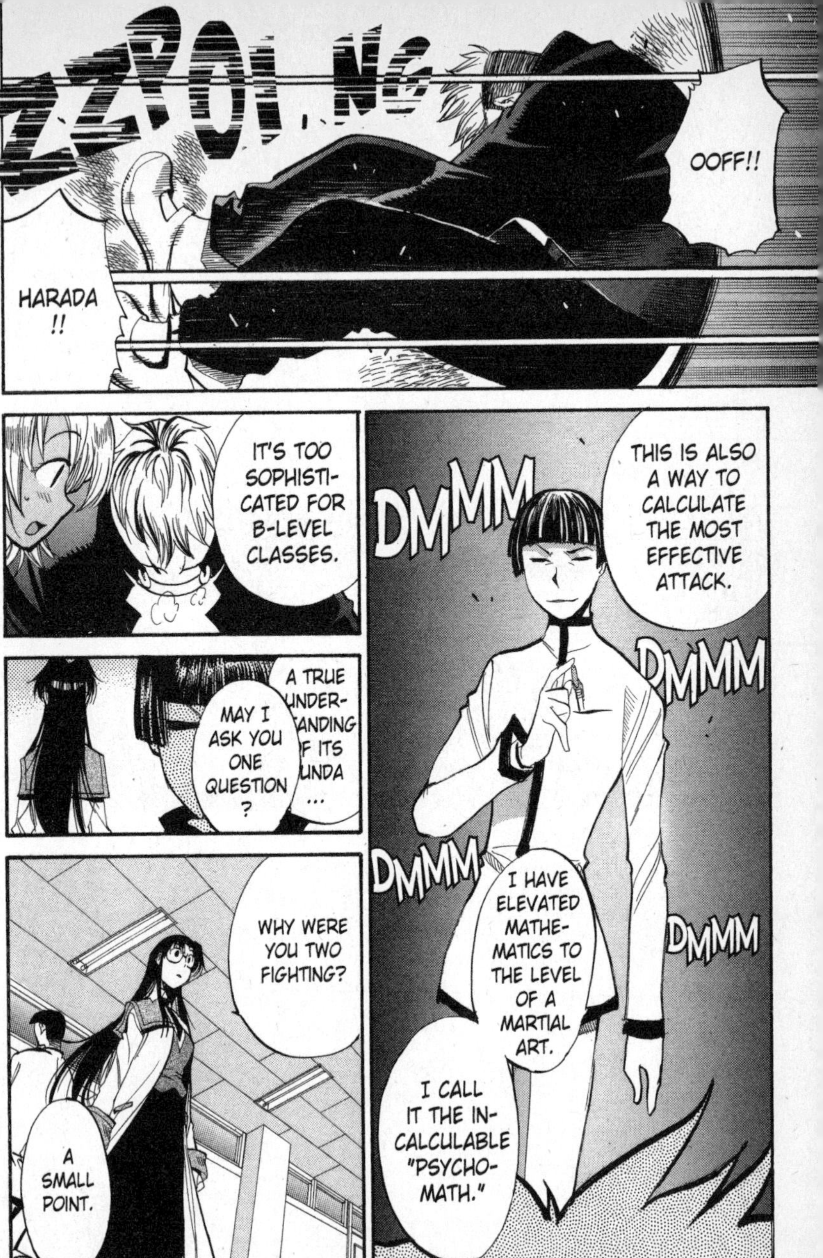
OOFF!!
ZZPOING
HARADA!!
THIS IS ALSO A WAY TO CALCULATE THE MOST EFFECTIVE ATTACK.
DMMMM
DMMM
I HAVE ELEVATED MATHEMATICS TO THE LEVEL OF A MARTIAL ART.
DMMM
DMMM
I CALL IT THE INCALCULABLE "PSYCHO-MATH."
IT'S TOO SOPHISTICATED FOR B-LEVEL CLASSES.
A TRUE UNDER- ANDING F ITS UNDA ...
MAY I ASK YOU ONE QUESTION?
WHY WERE YOU TWO FIGHTING?
A SMALL POINT.

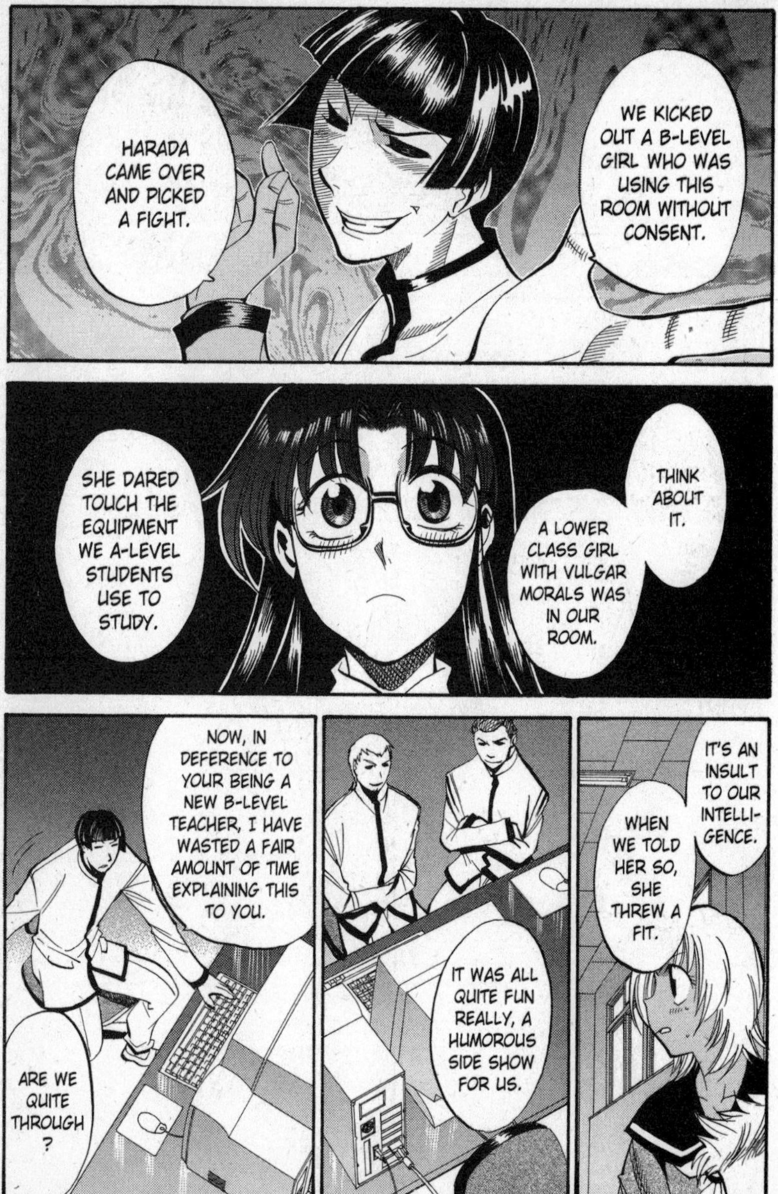
WE KICKED OUT A B-LEVEL GIRL WHO WAS USING THIS ROOM WITHOUT CONSENT.
HARADA CAME OVER AND PICKED A FIGHT.
THINK ABOUT IT.
A LOWER CLASS GIRL WITH VULGAR MORALS WAS IN OUR ROOM.
SHE DARED TOUCH THE EQUIPMENT WE A-LEVEL STUDENTS USE TO STUDY.
IT'S AN INSULT TO OUR INTELLIGENCE.
WHEN WE TOLD HER SO, SHE THREW A FIT.
IT WAS ALL QUITE FUN REALLY, A HUMOROUS SIDE SHOW FOR US.
NOW, IN DEFERENCE TO YOUR BEING A NEW B-LEVEL TEACHER, I HAVE WASTED A FAIR AMOUNT OF TIME EXPLAINING THIS TO YOU.
ARE WE QUITE THROUGH?

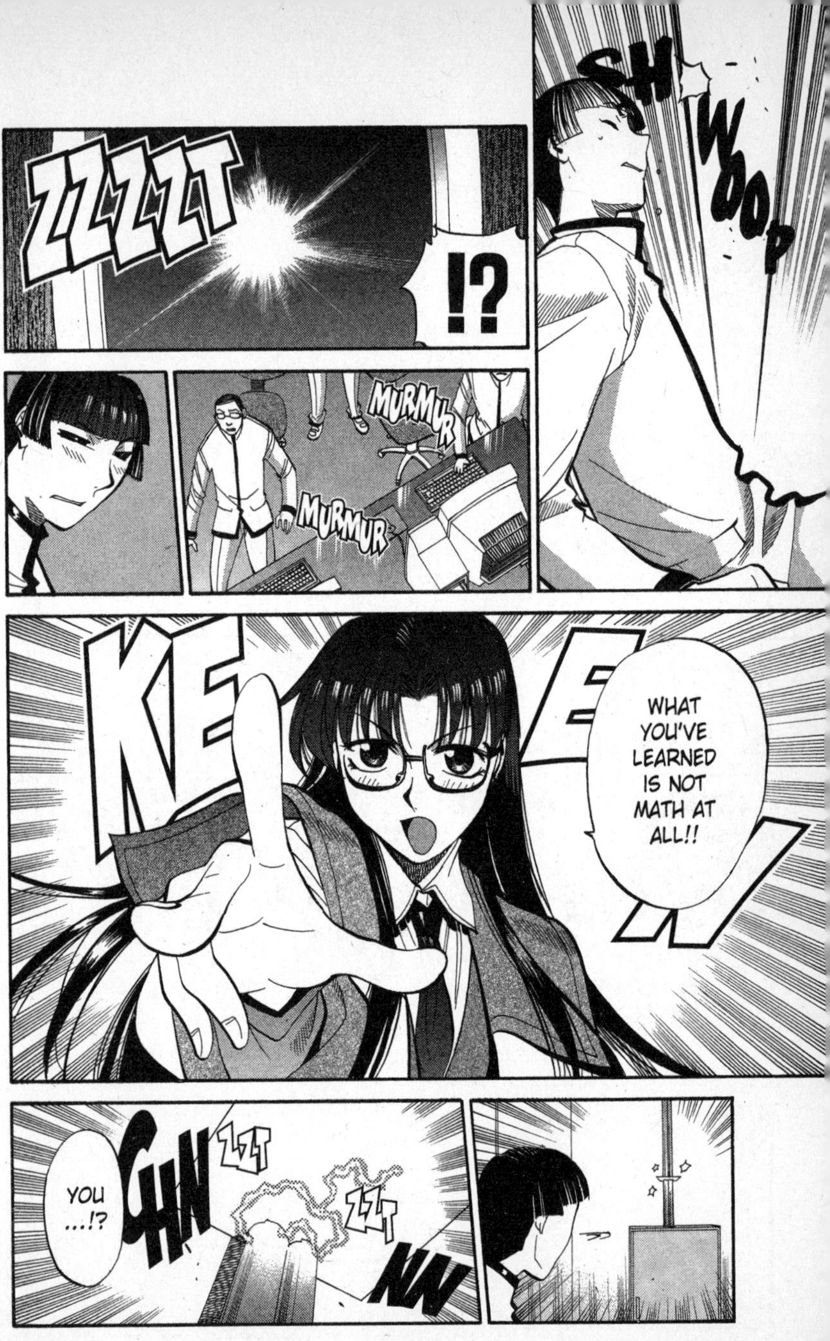
SHWOOP
ZZZZZT
!?
MURMUR
MURMUR
WHAT YOU'VE LEARNED IS NOT MATH AT ALL!!
ZZT
ZZT
CHINNN
YOU ...!?

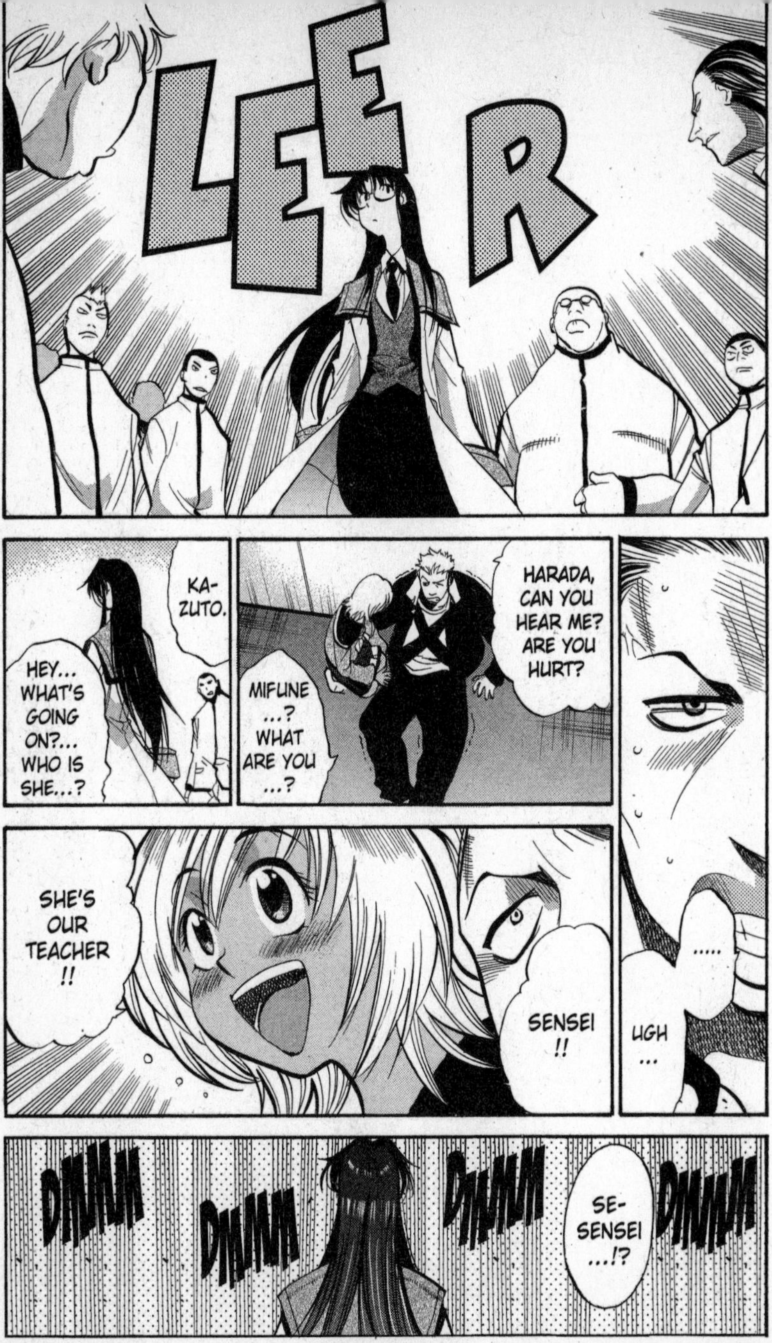
LEER
.....
UGH ...
HARADA, CAN YOU HEAR ME? ARE YOU HURT?
MIFUNE ...? WHAT ARE YOU ...?
KA-ZUTO.
HEY... WHAT'S GOING ON?... WHO IS SHE...?
SENSEI !!
SHE'S OUR TEACHER !!
DMMM
SE-SENSEI ...!?
DMMM
DMMM
DMMM

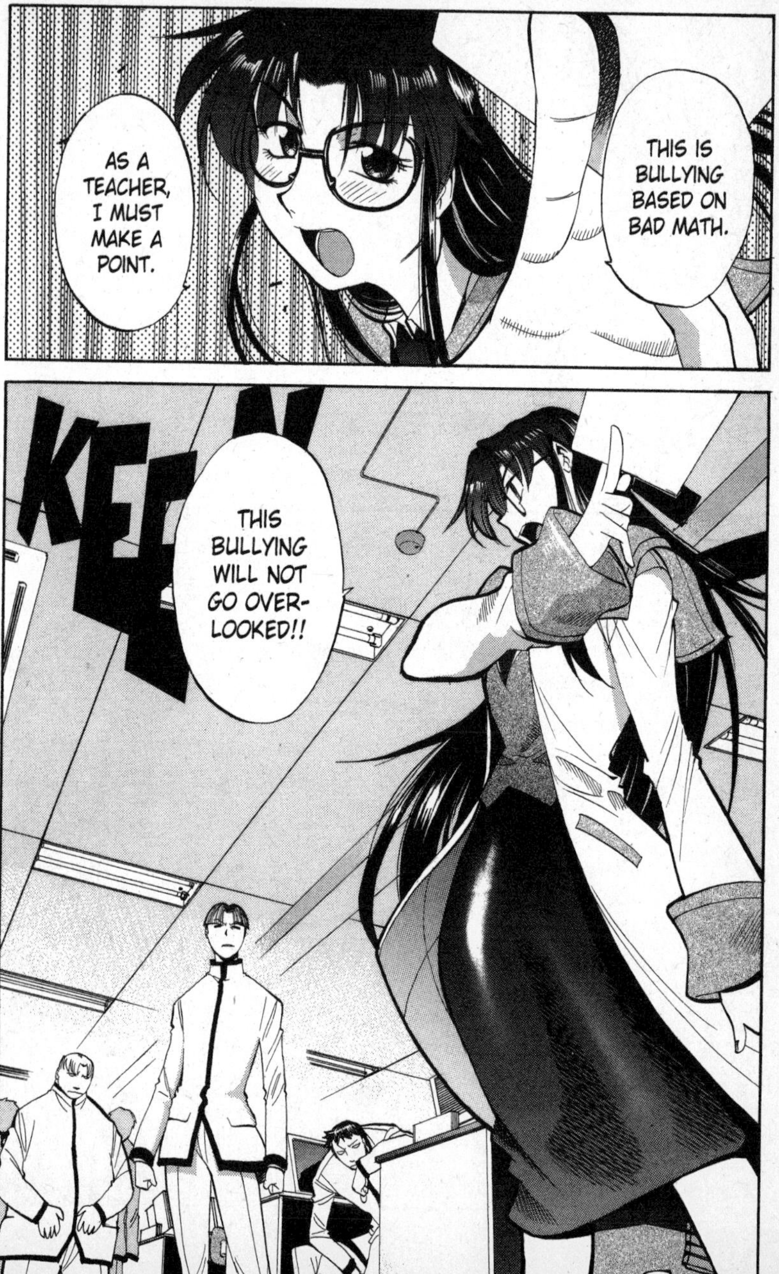
THIS IS BULLYING BASED ON BAD MATH.
AS A TEACHER, I MUST MAKE A POINT.
THIS BULLYING WILL NOT GO OVER-LOOKED!!

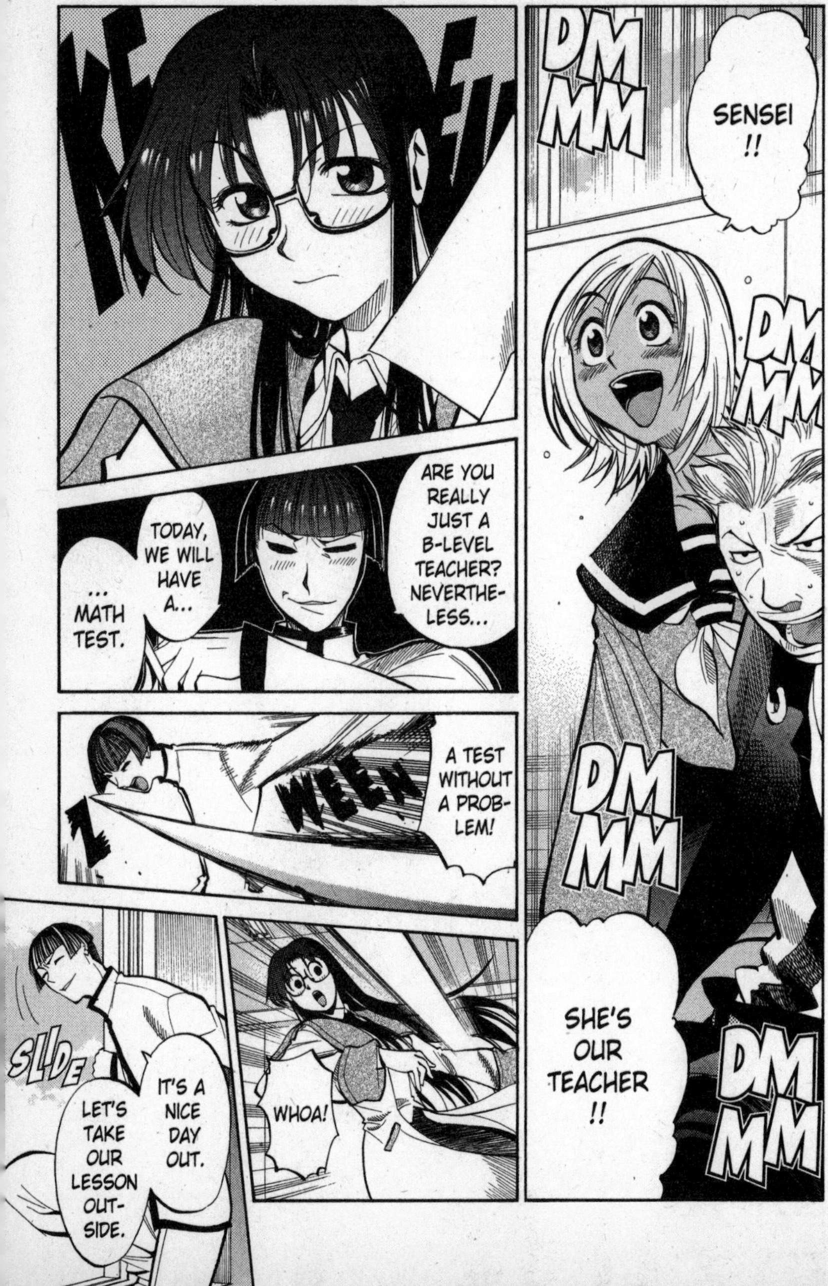
DM MM
SENSEI !!
DM MM
DM MM
SHE'S OUR TEACHER !!
DM MM
ARE YOU REALLY JUST A B-LEVEL TEACHER? NEVERTHELESS...
TODAY, WE WILL HAVE A...
... MATH TEST.
A TEST WITHOUT A PROBLEM!
WEEN
WHOA!
SLIDE
IT'S A NICE DAY OUT.
LET'S TAKE OUR LESSON OUT-SIDE.

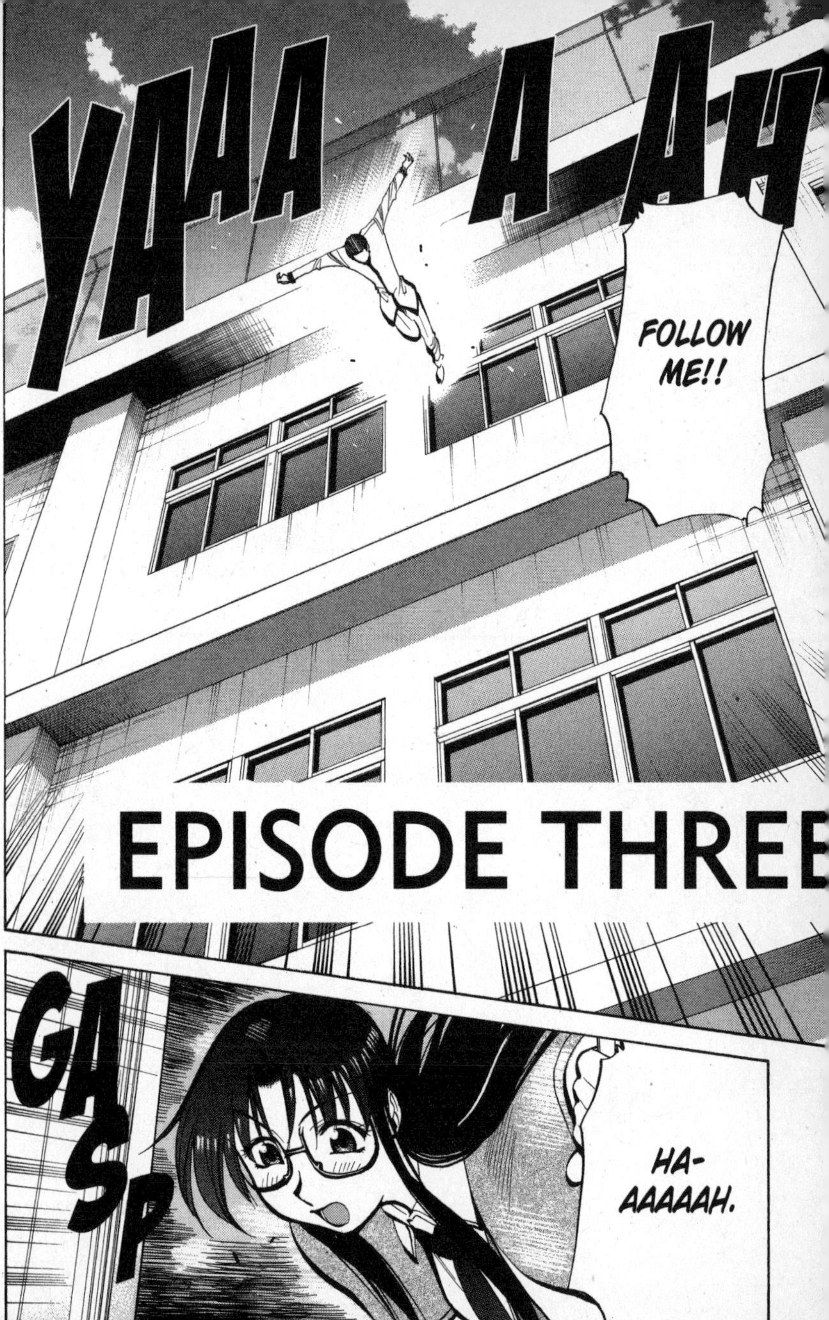
YAAAA-A-AH
FOLLOW ME!!
EPISODE THREE
HA-AAAAAH.
GASP

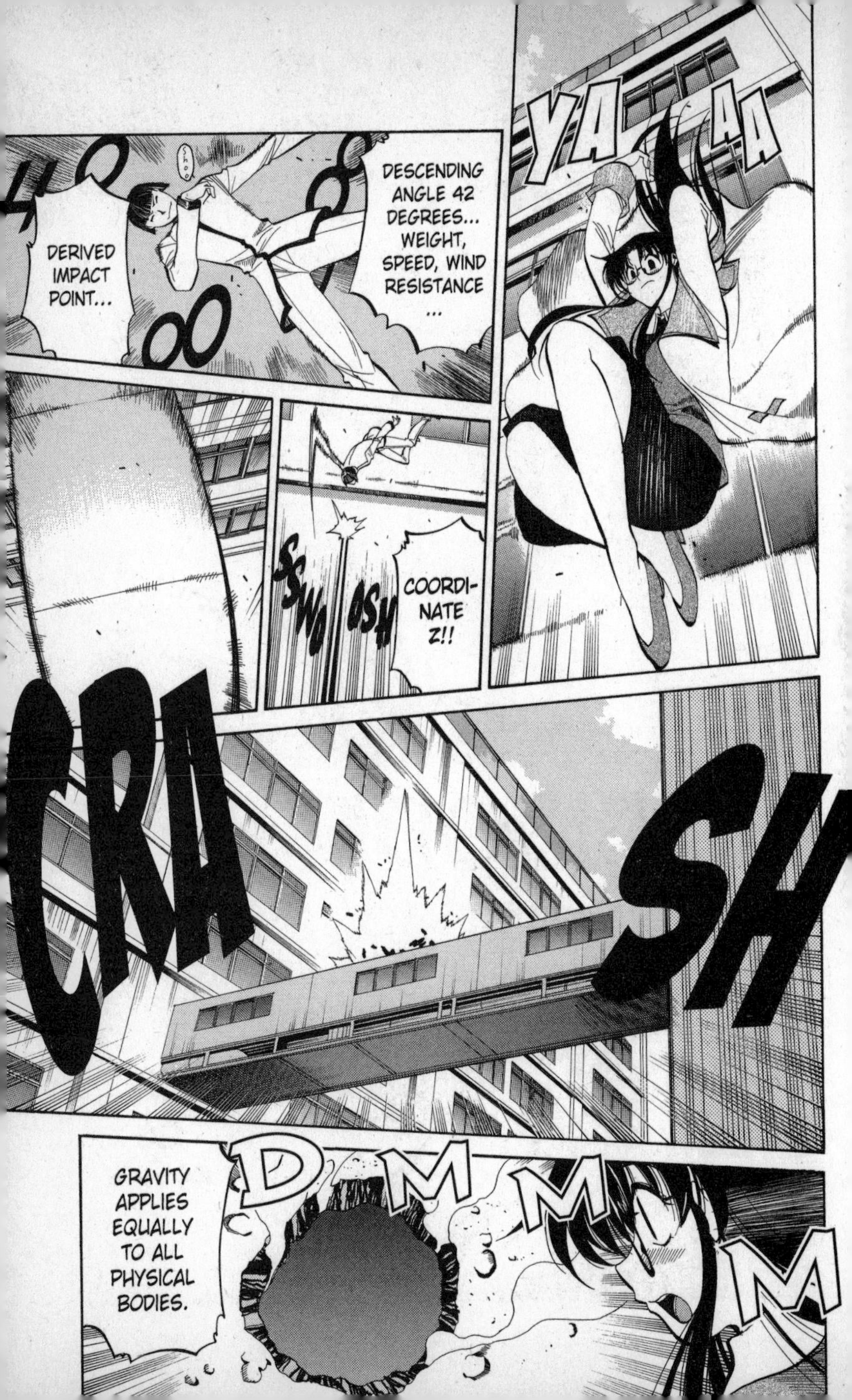

YAAA
shoo
DESCENDING ANGLE 42 DEGREES... WEIGHT, SPEED, WIND RESISTANCE ...
DERIVED IMPACT POINT...
SSWOOSH
COORDINATE Z!!
CRASH
DMMMM
GRAVITY APPLIES EQUALLY TO ALL PHYSICAL BODIES.

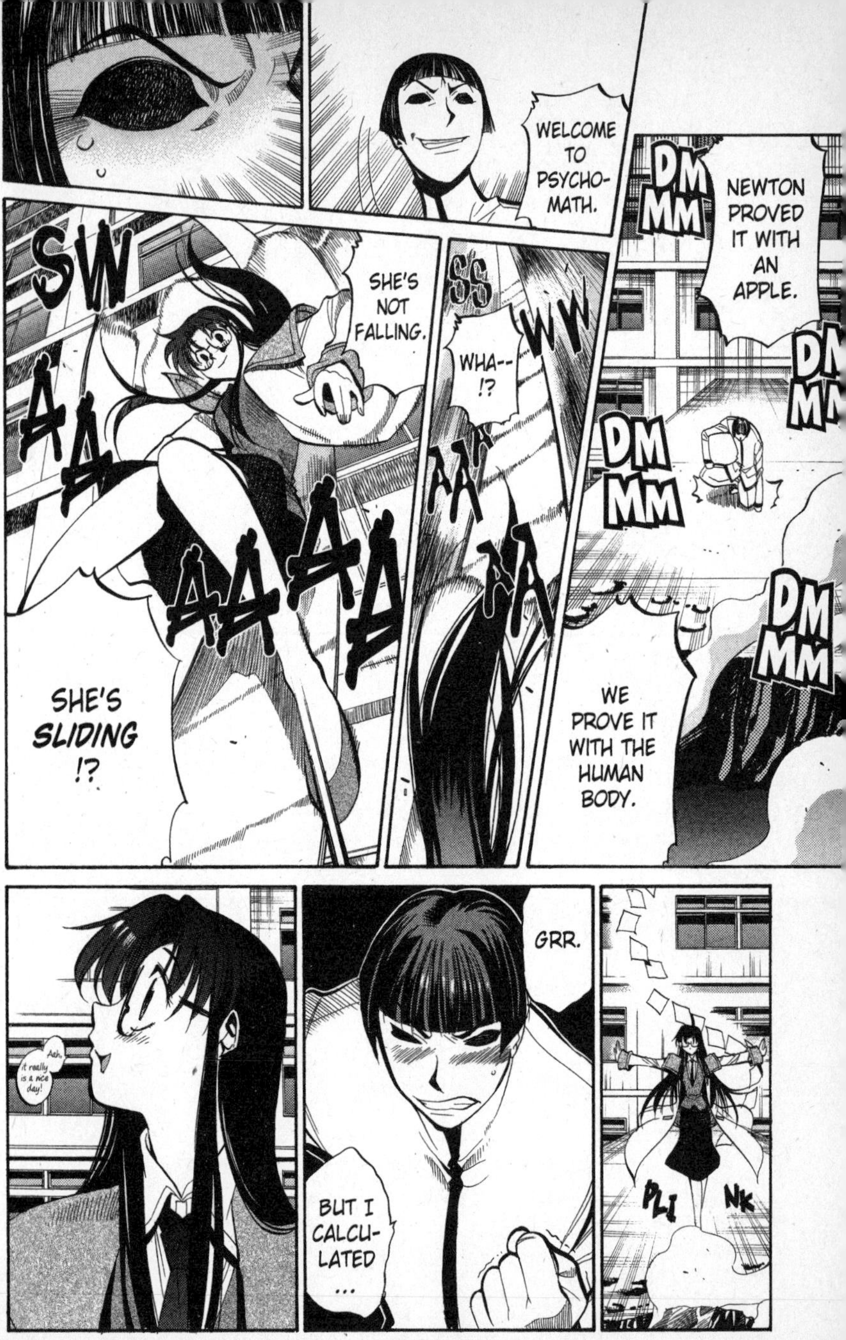
WELCOME TO PSYCHO-MATH.
DMMM
NEWTON PROVED IT WITH AN APPLE.
DMMM
DMMM
DMMM
WE PROVE IT WITH THE HUMAN BODY.
SSWW
WHA--!?
AAAA
SW
SHE'S NOT FALLING.
AAAAA
SHE'S SLIDING!?
PLINK
GRR.
BUT I CALCULATED...
Aah, it really is a nice day!

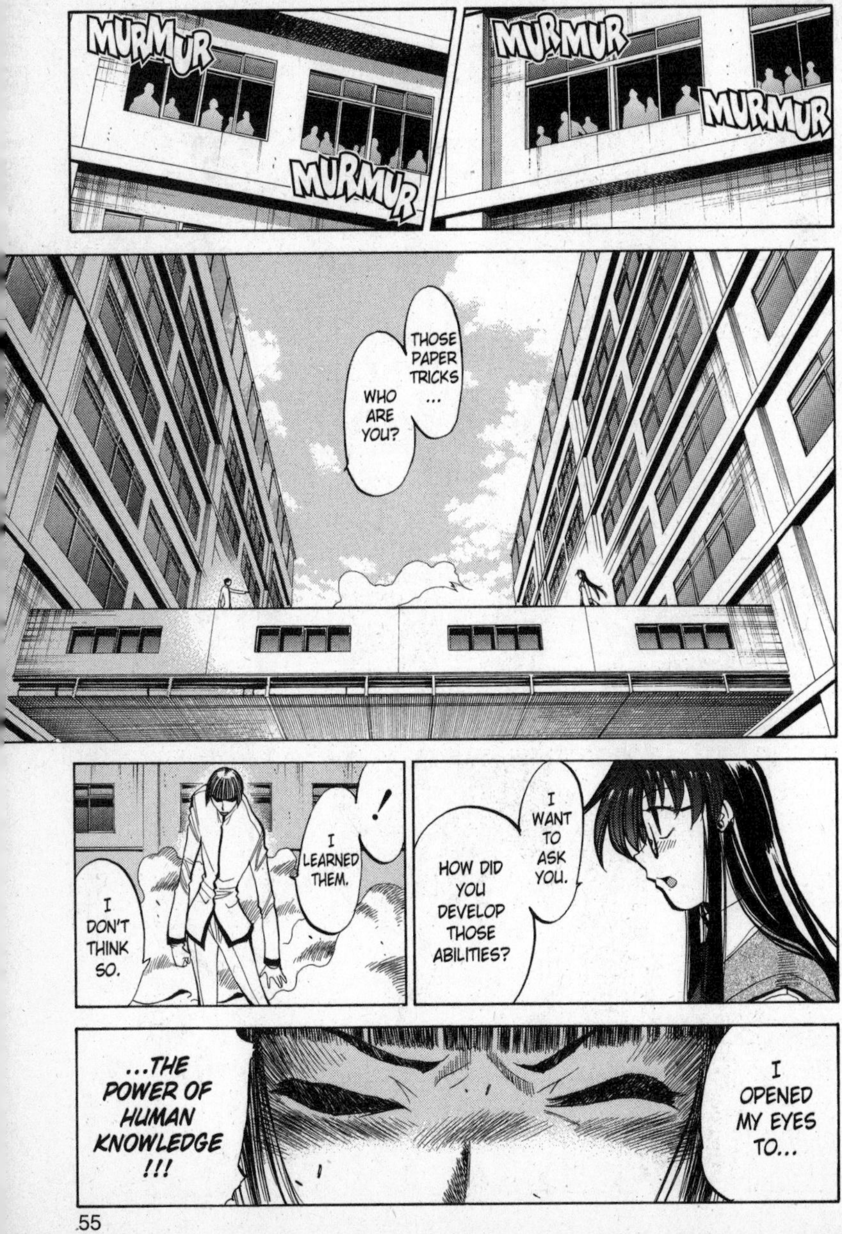
MURMUR
MURMUR
MURMUR
MURMUR
THOSE PAPER TRICKS...
WHO ARE YOU?
I WANT TO ASK YOU.
HOW DID YOU DEVELOP THOSE ABILITIES?
!
I LEARNED THEM.
I DON'T THINK SO.
I OPENED MY EYES TO...
...THE POWER OF HUMAN KNOWLEDGE!!!

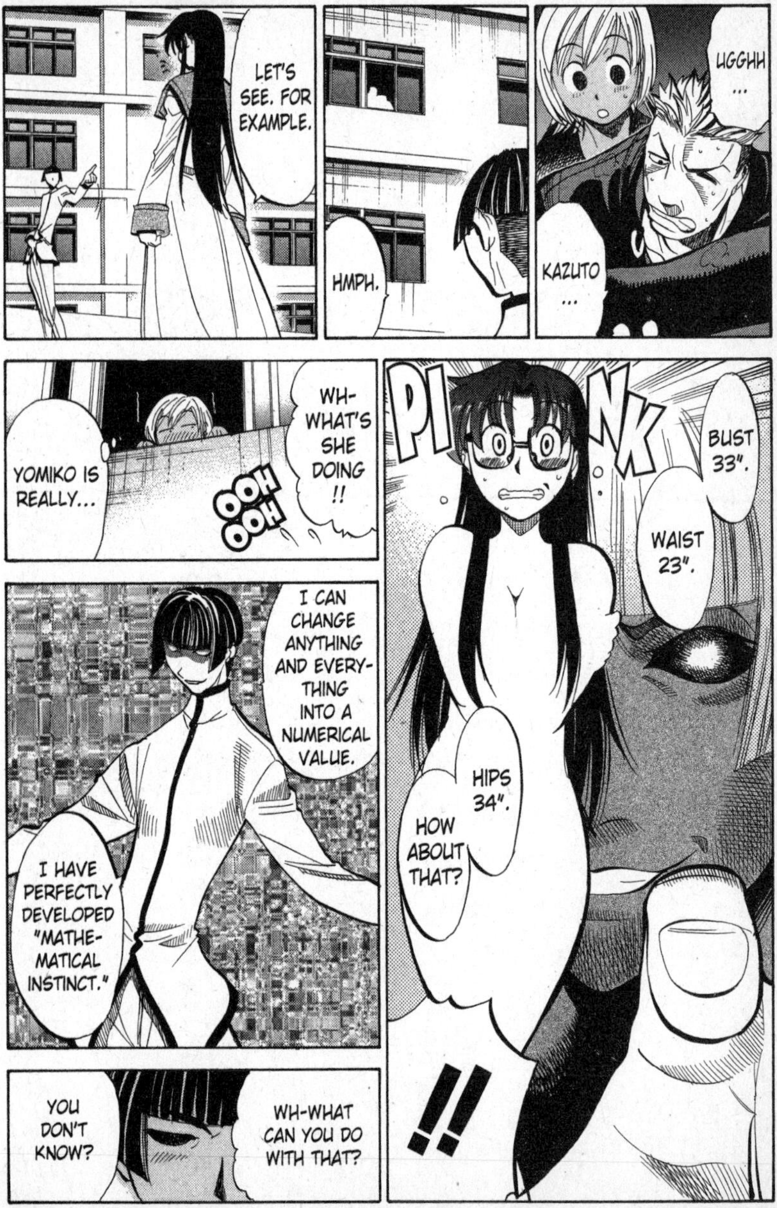
UGGHH ...
KAZUTO ...
HMPH.
LET'S SEE. FOR EXAMPLE.
PINK
BUST 33".
WAIST 23".
HIPS 34".
HOW ABOUT THAT?
!!
WH-WHAT'S SHE DOING !!
OOH OOH
YOMIKO IS REALLY...
I CAN CHANGE ANYTHING AND EVERY-THING INTO A NUMERICAL VALUE.
I HAVE PERFECTLY DEVELOPED "MATHE-MATICAL INSTINCT."
WH-WHAT CAN YOU DO WITH THAT?
YOU DON'T KNOW?

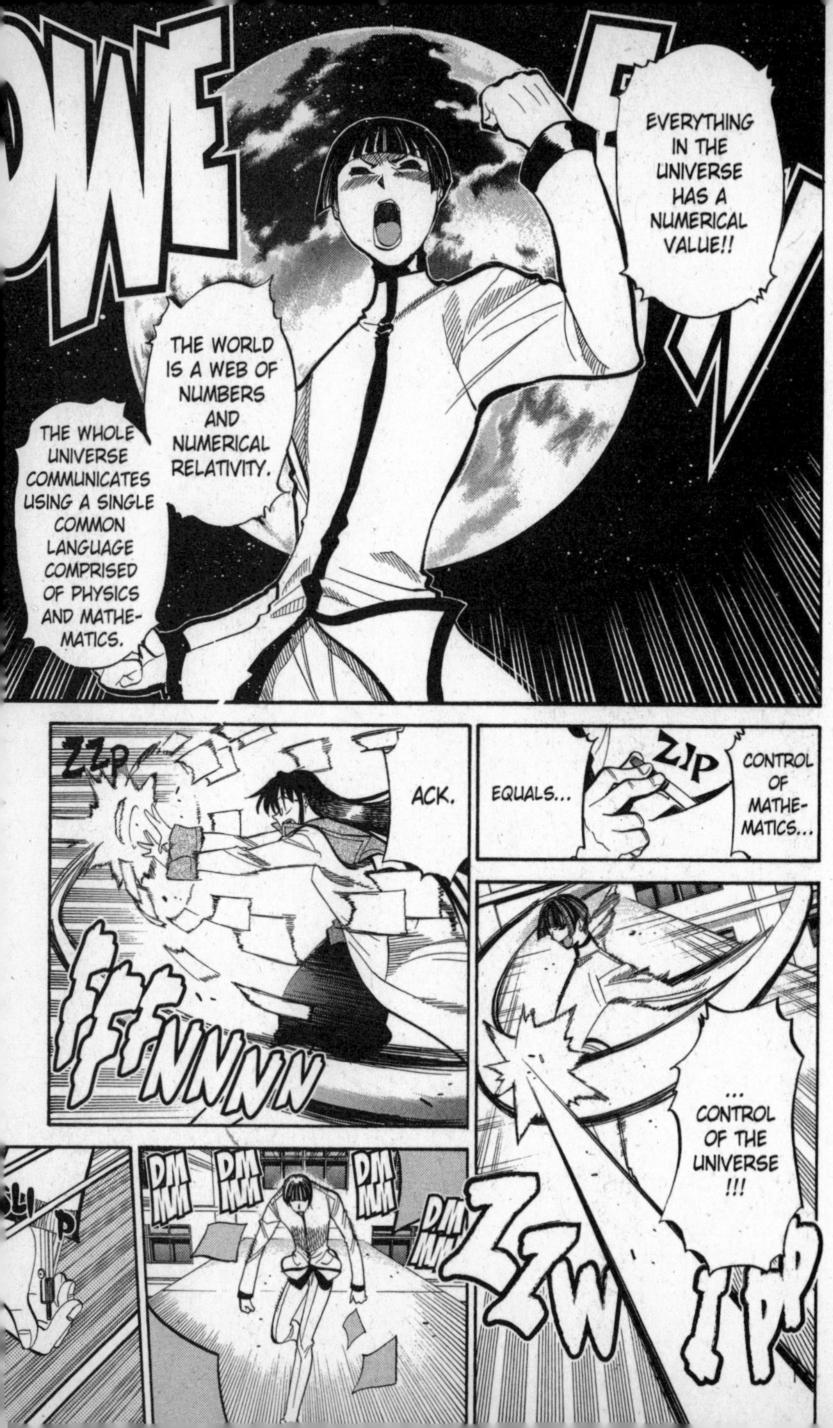
EVERYTHING IN THE UNIVERSE HAS A NUMERICAL VALUE!!
THE WORLD IS A WEB OF NUMBERS AND NUMERICAL RELATIVITY.
THE WHOLE UNIVERSE COMMUNICATES USING A SINGLE COMMON LANGUAGE COMPRISED OF PHYSICS AND MATHE-MATICS.
CONTROL OF MATHE-MATICS...
ZIP
EQUALS...
... CONTROL OF THE UNIVERSE !!!
ACK.
ZZP
FFNNNNN
DM MM
DM MM
DM MM
DM MM

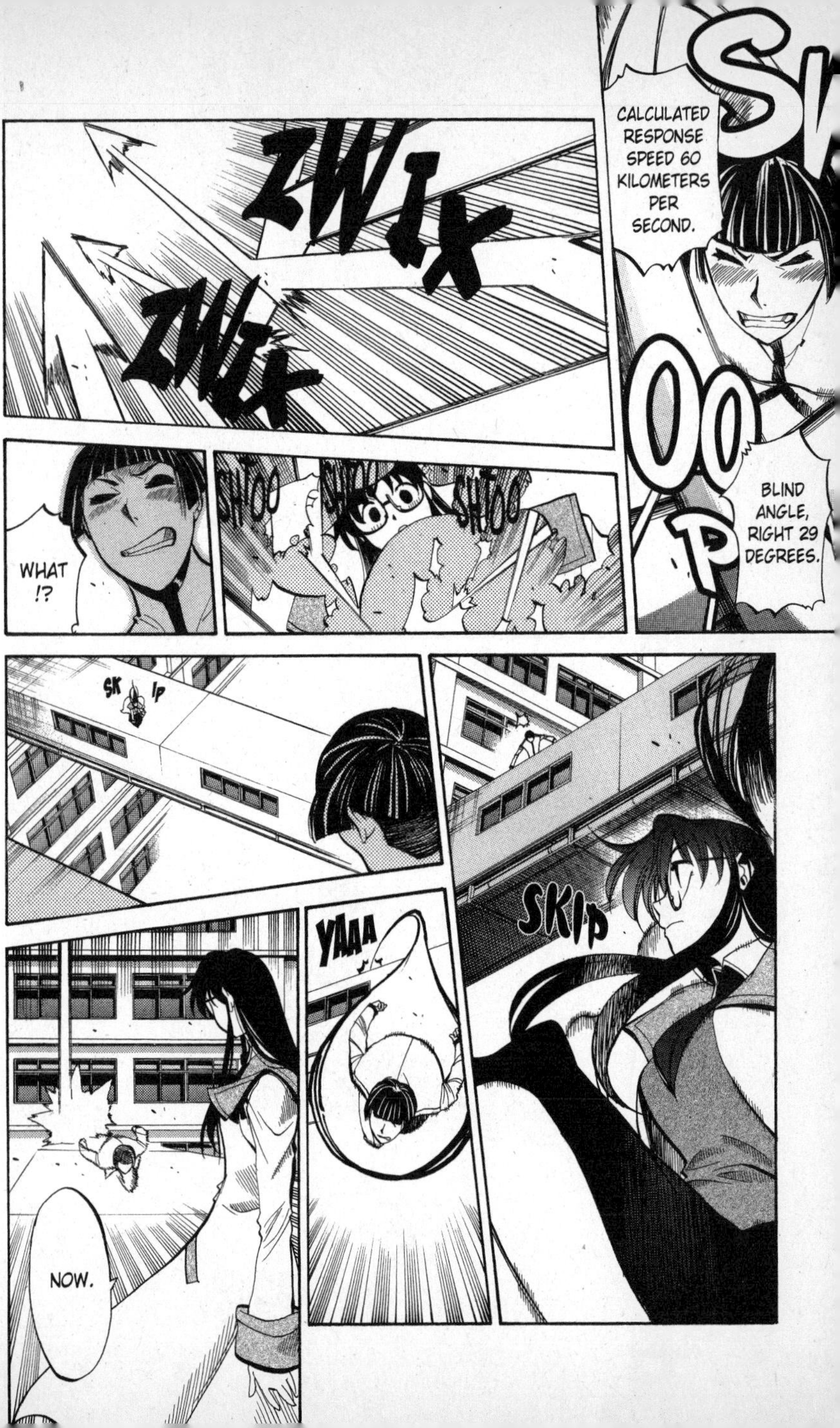

CALCULATED RESPONSE SPEED 60 KILOMETERS PER SECOND.
OOP
BLIND ANGLE, RIGHT 29 DEGREES.
ZWIX
ZWIX
SHOO
SHOO
SHOO
WHAT !?
SKIP
SK IP
YAAA
NOW.

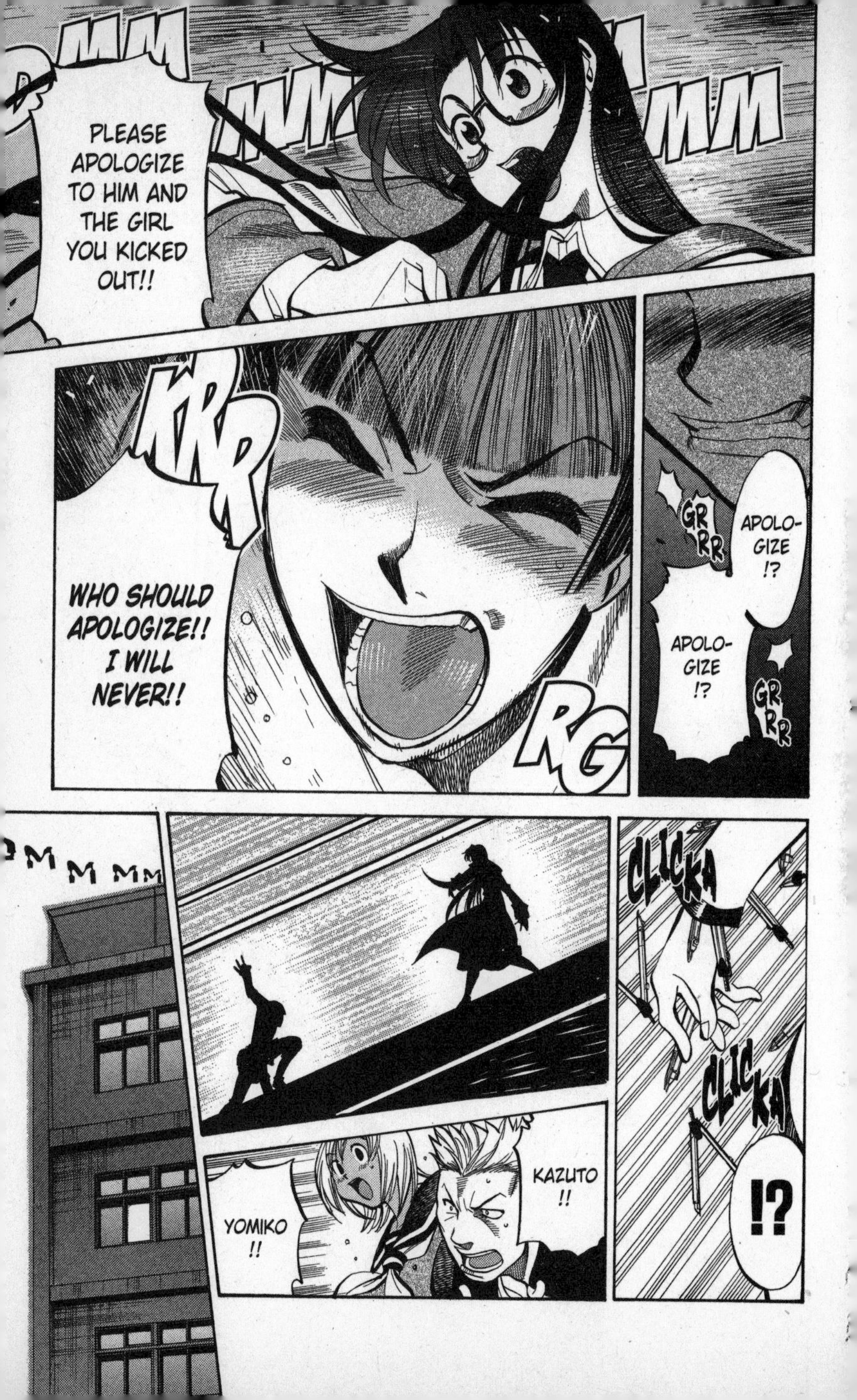

MMM
PLEASE APOLOGIZE TO HIM AND THE GIRL YOU KICKED OUT!!
APOLO-GIZE !?
GRRR
APOLO-GIZE !?
GRRR
KRRG
WHO SHOULD APOLOGIZE!! I WILL NEVER!!
CLICKA
CLICKA
!?
KAZUTO !!
YOMIKO !!
MMMMM

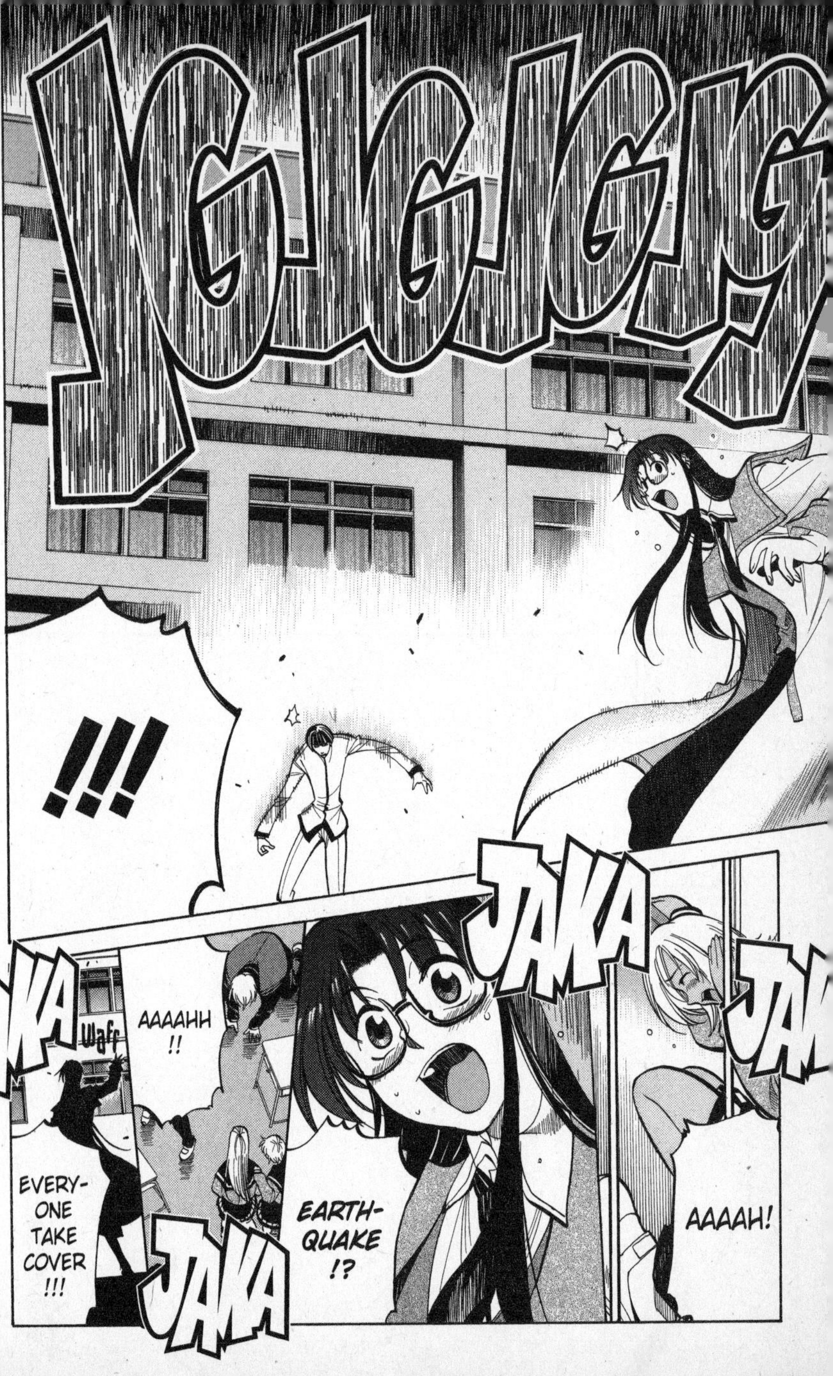
!!!
JAKA
AAAAH!
EARTH-QUAKE !?
AAAAHH !!
EVERY-ONE TAKE COVER !!!
JAKA

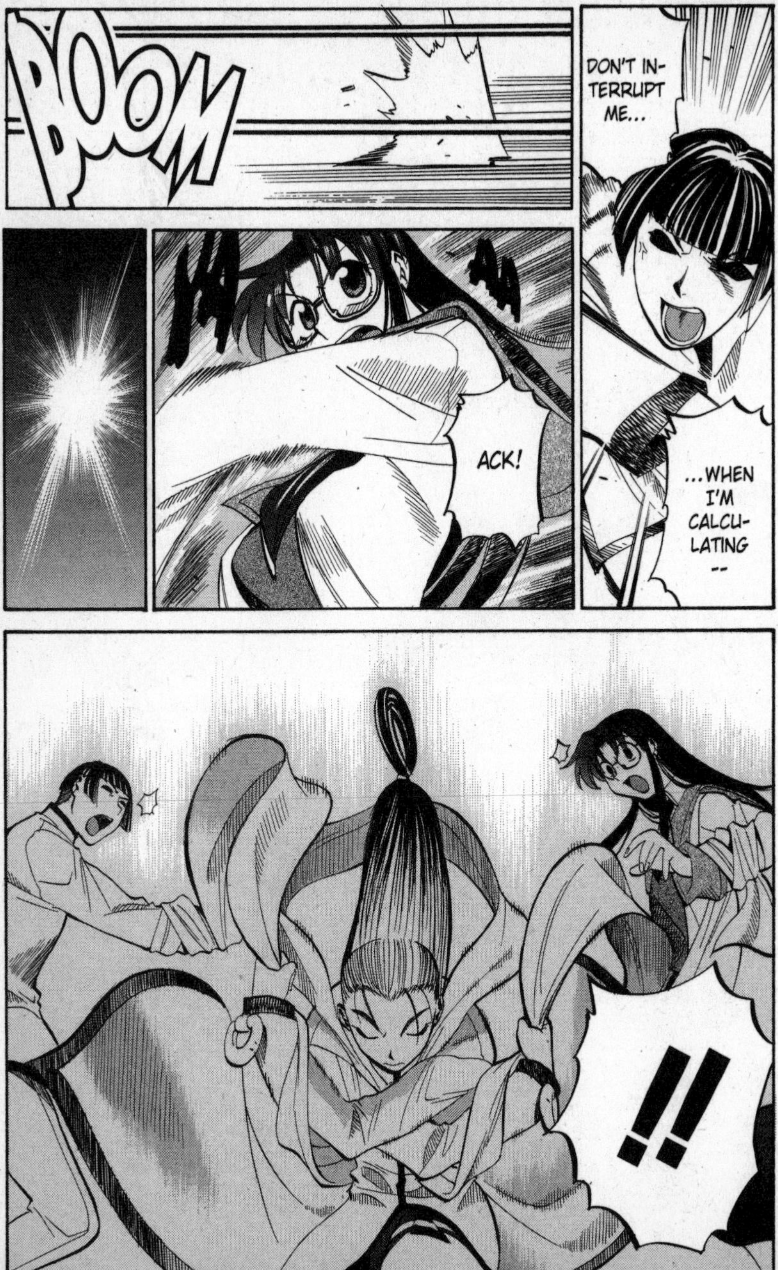
DON'T IN-TERRUPT ME...
...WHEN I'M CALCULATING --
BOOM
HA
AA
ACK!
!!

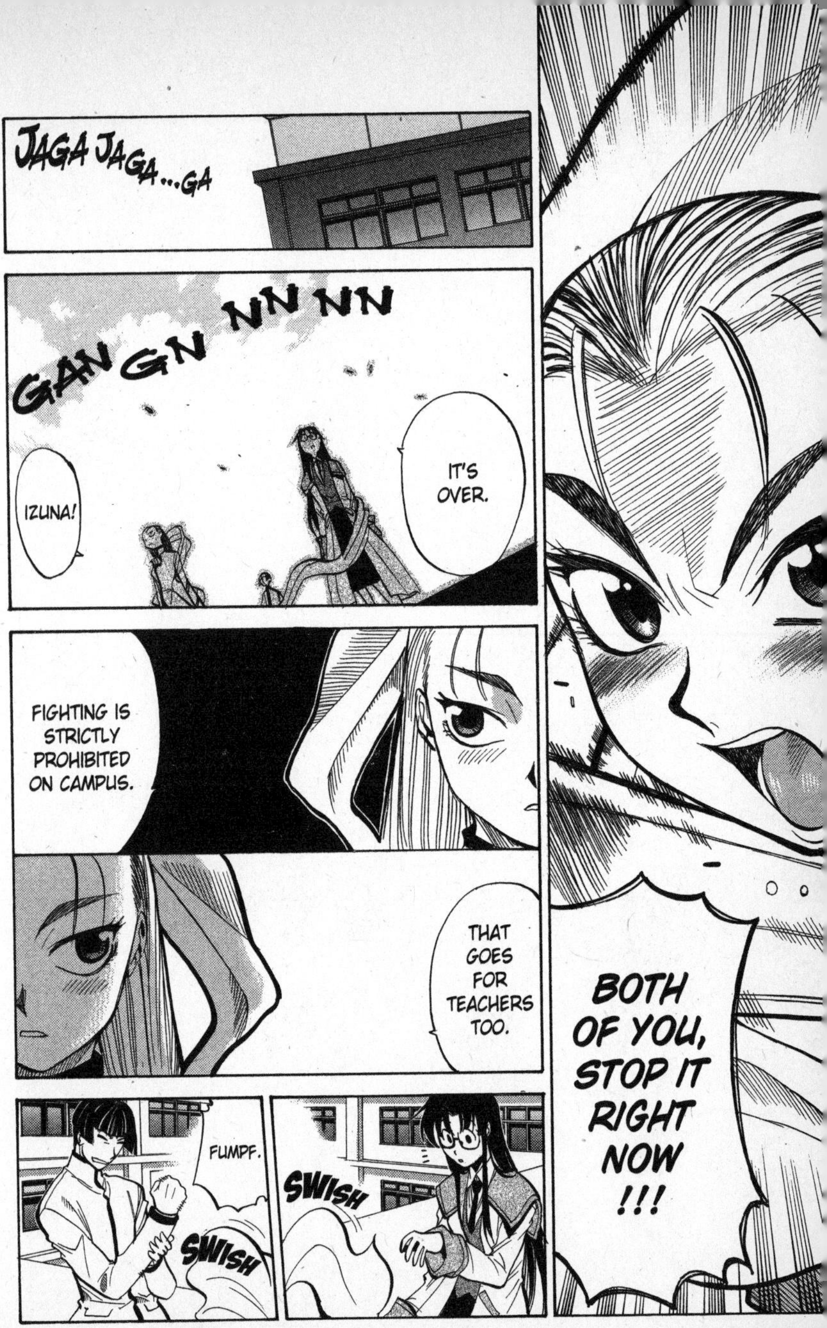
BOTH OF YOU, STOP IT RIGHT NOW!!!
JAGA JAGA...GA
GAN GN NN NN
IT'S OVER.
IZUNA!
FIGHTING IS STRICTLY PROHIBITED ON CAMPUS.
THAT GOES FOR TEACHERS TOO.
SWISH
FUMPF.
SWISH

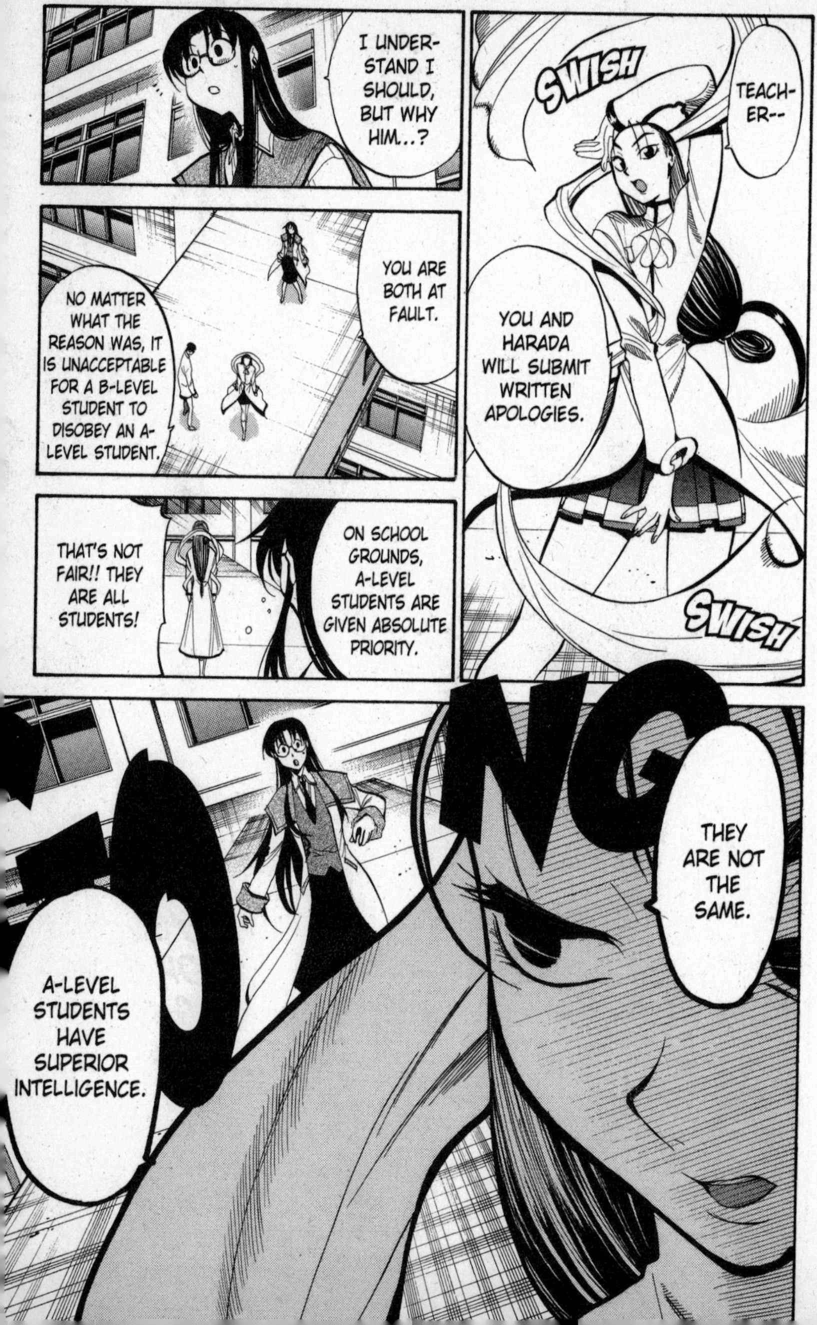
SWISH
TEACHER--
YOU AND HARADA WILL SUBMIT WRITTEN APOLOGIES.
SWISH
I UNDERSTAND I SHOULD, BUT WHY HIM...?
YOU ARE BOTH AT FAULT.
NO MATTER WHAT THE REASON WAS, IT IS UNACCEPTABLE FOR A B-LEVEL STUDENT TO DISOBEY AN A-LEVEL STUDENT.
ON SCHOOL GROUNDS, A-LEVEL STUDENTS ARE GIVEN ABSOLUTE PRIORITY.
THAT'S NOT FAIR!! THEY ARE ALL STUDENTS!
NG
THEY ARE NOT THE SAME.
A-LEVEL STUDENTS HAVE SUPERIOR INTELLIGENCE.

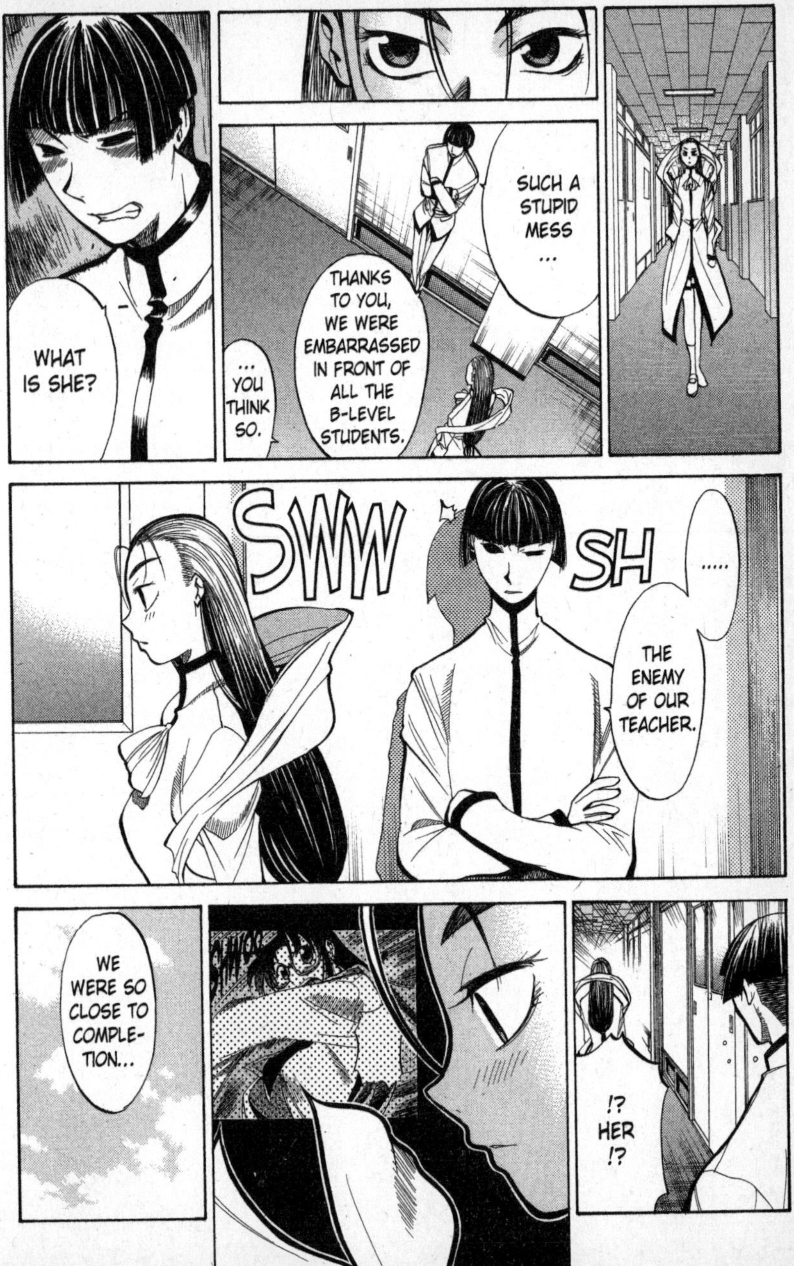
SUCH A STUPID MESS ...
THANKS TO YOU, WE WERE EMBARRASSED IN FRONT OF ALL THE B-LEVEL STUDENTS.
... YOU THINK SO.
WHAT IS SHE?
.....
THE ENEMY OF OUR TEACHER.
SWWSH
!? HER !?
WE WERE SO CLOSE TO COMPLE-TION...

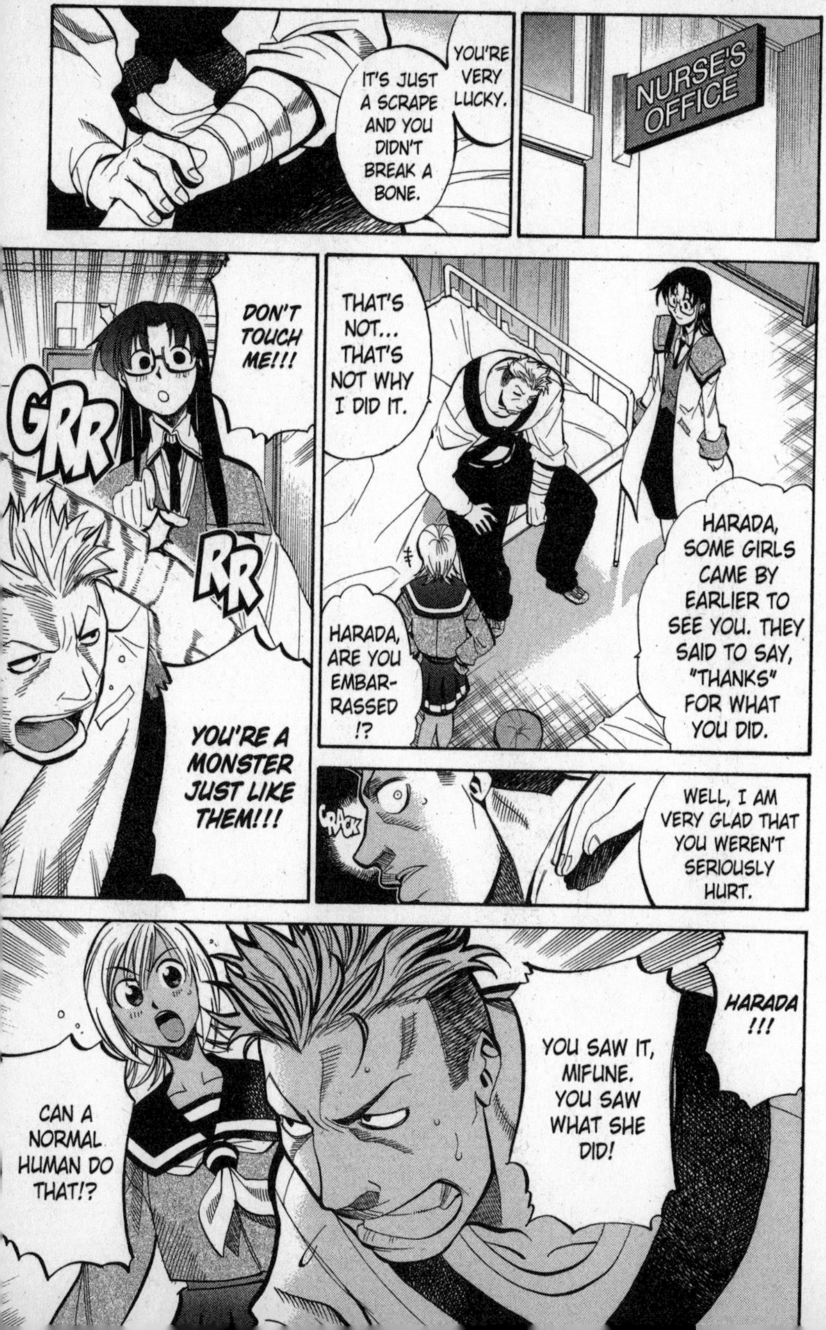
NURSE'S OFFICE
YOU'RE VERY LUCKY.
IT'S JUST A SCRAPE AND YOU DIDN'T BREAK A BONE.
HARADA, SOME GIRLS CAME BY EARLIER TO SEE YOU. THEY SAID TO SAY, "THANKS" FOR WHAT YOU DID.
THAT'S NOT... THAT'S NOT WHY I DID IT.
HARADA, ARE YOU EMBARRASSED !?
WELL, I AM VERY GLAD THAT YOU WEREN'T SERIOUSLY HURT.
CRACK
DON'T TOUCH ME!!!
GRR
RR
YOU'RE A MONSTER JUST LIKE THEM!!!
HARADA !!!
YOU SAW IT, MIFUNE. YOU SAW WHAT SHE DID!
CAN A NORMAL HUMAN DO THAT!?

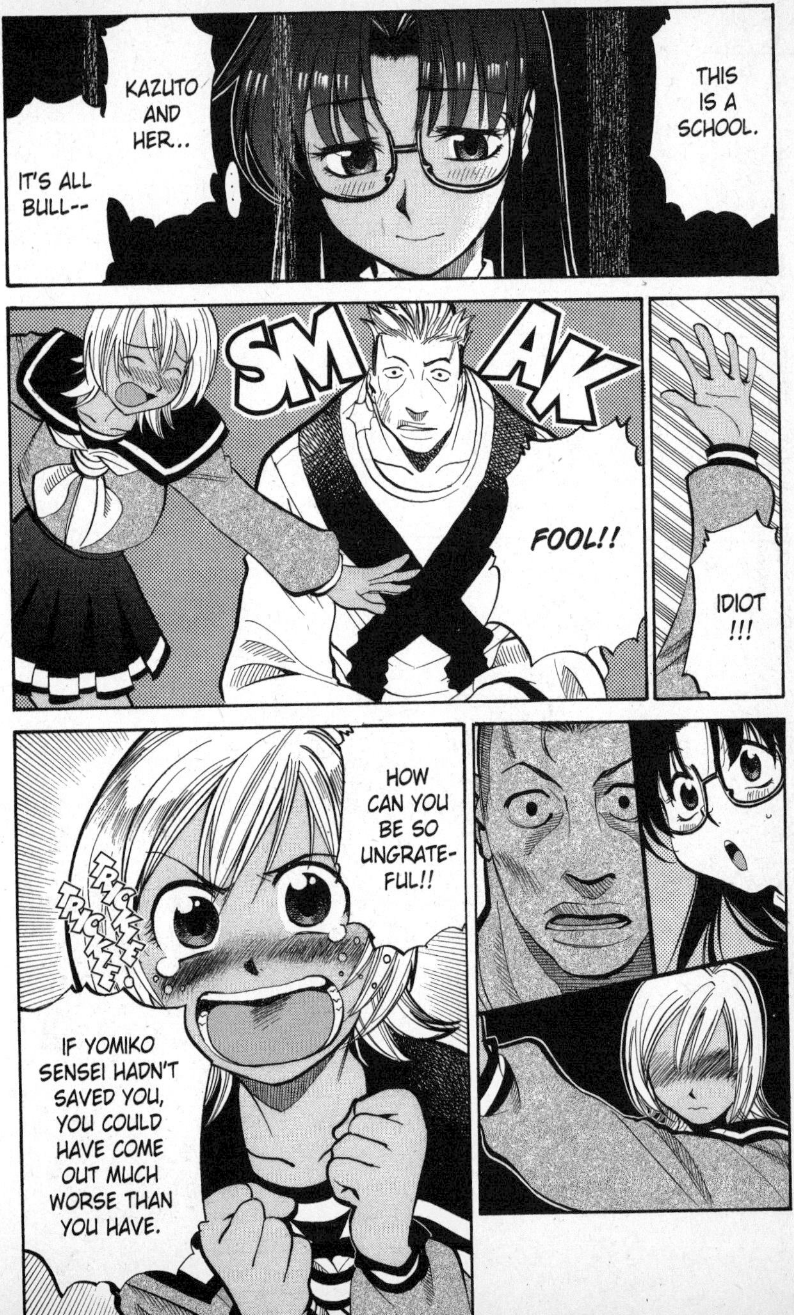
THIS IS A SCHOOL.
KAZUTO AND HER...
IT'S ALL BULL--
IDIOT !!!
SMAK
FOOL!!
HOW CAN YOU BE SO UNGRATE-FUL!!
TRICKLE TRICKLE
IF YOMIKO SENSEI HADN'T SAVED YOU, YOU COULD HAVE COME OUT MUCH WORSE THAN YOU HAVE.

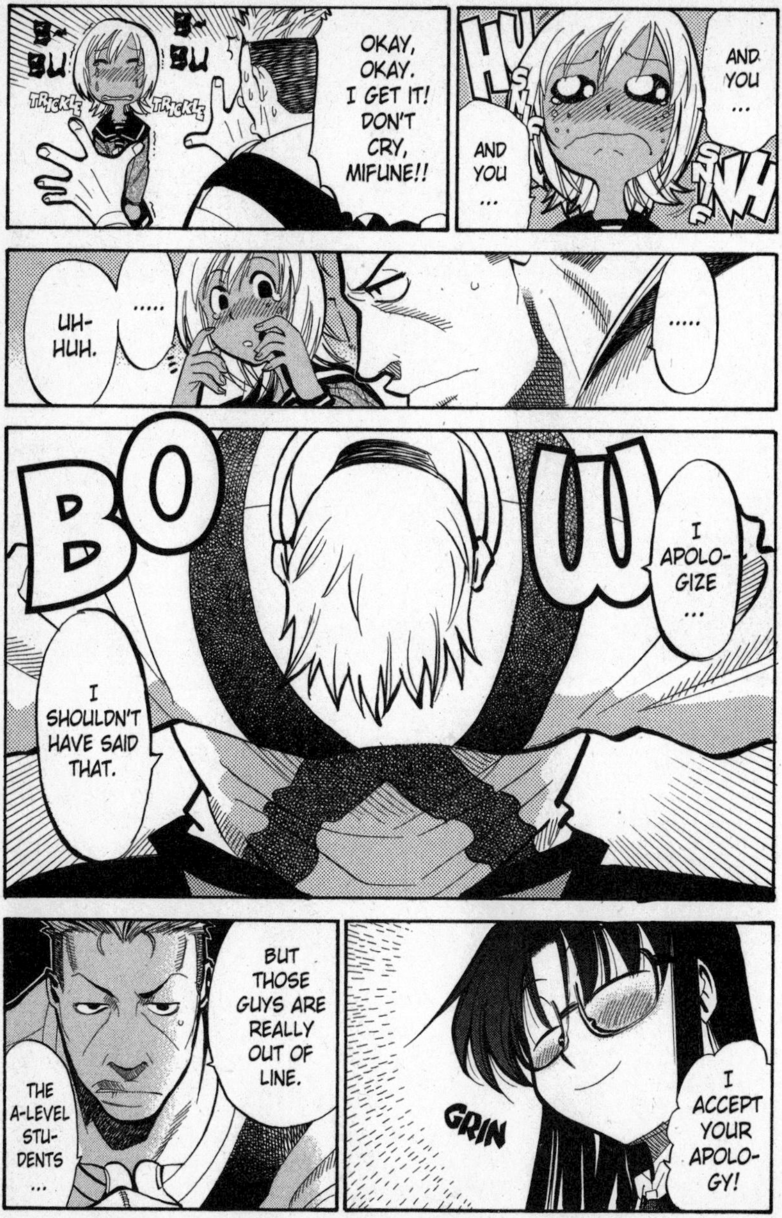
HUH
SNIFF
AND YOU ...
AND YOU ...
SNIFF
OKAY, OKAY. I GET IT! DON'T CRY, MIFUNE!!
BU
BU
TRICKLE
TRICKLE
.....
.....
UH-HUH.
BOW
I APOLOGIZE ...
I SHOULDN'T HAVE SAID THAT.
I ACCEPT YOUR APOLOGY!
GRIN
BUT THOSE GUYS ARE REALLY OUT OF LINE.
THE A-LEVEL STUDENTS ...

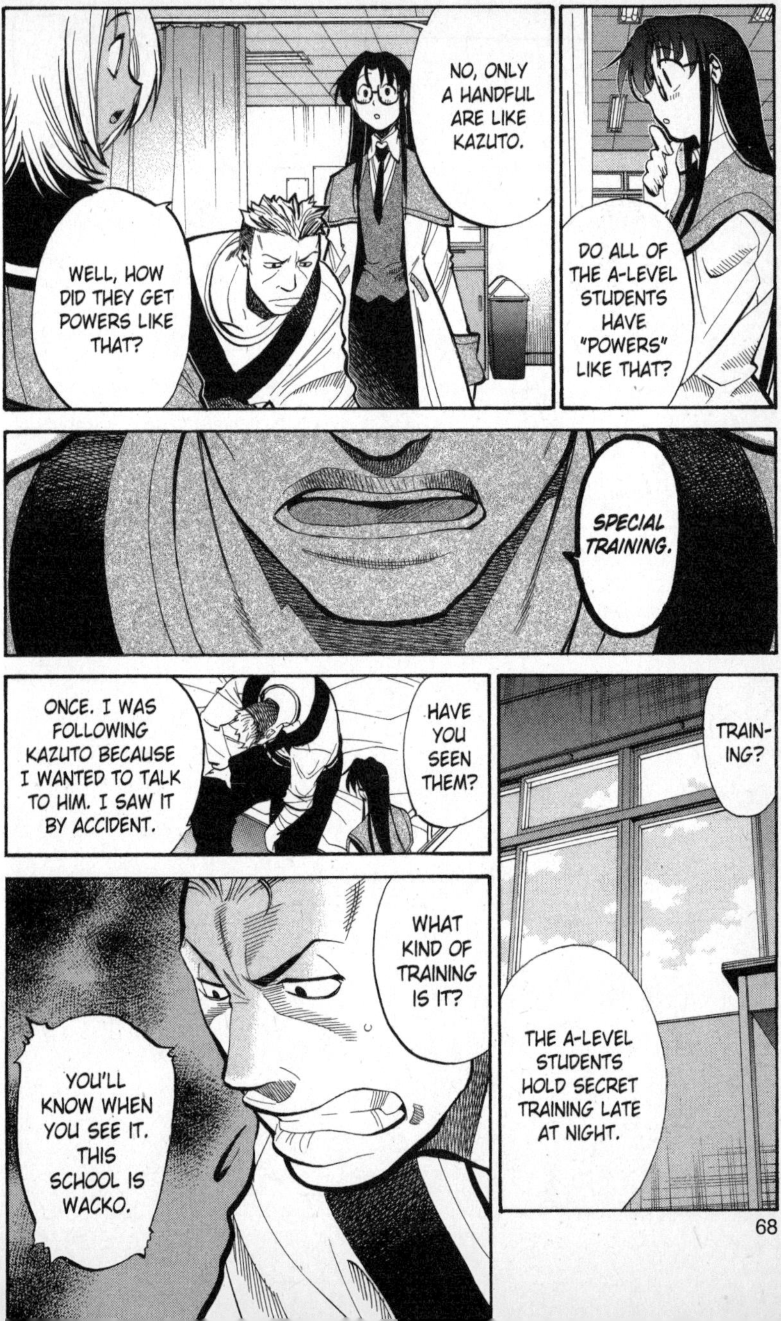
DO ALL OF THE A-LEVEL STUDENTS HAVE "POWERS" LIKE THAT?
NO, ONLY A HANDFUL ARE LIKE KAZUTO.
WELL, HOW DID THEY GET POWERS LIKE THAT?
SPECIAL TRAINING.
TRAIN-ING?
THE A-LEVEL STUDENTS HOLD SECRET TRAINING LATE AT NIGHT.
HAVE YOU SEEN THEM?
ONCE. I WAS FOLLOWING KAZUTO BECAUSE I WANTED TO TALK TO HIM. I SAW IT BY ACCIDENT.
WHAT KIND OF TRAINING IS IT?
YOU'LL KNOW WHEN YOU SEE IT. THIS SCHOOL IS WACKO.

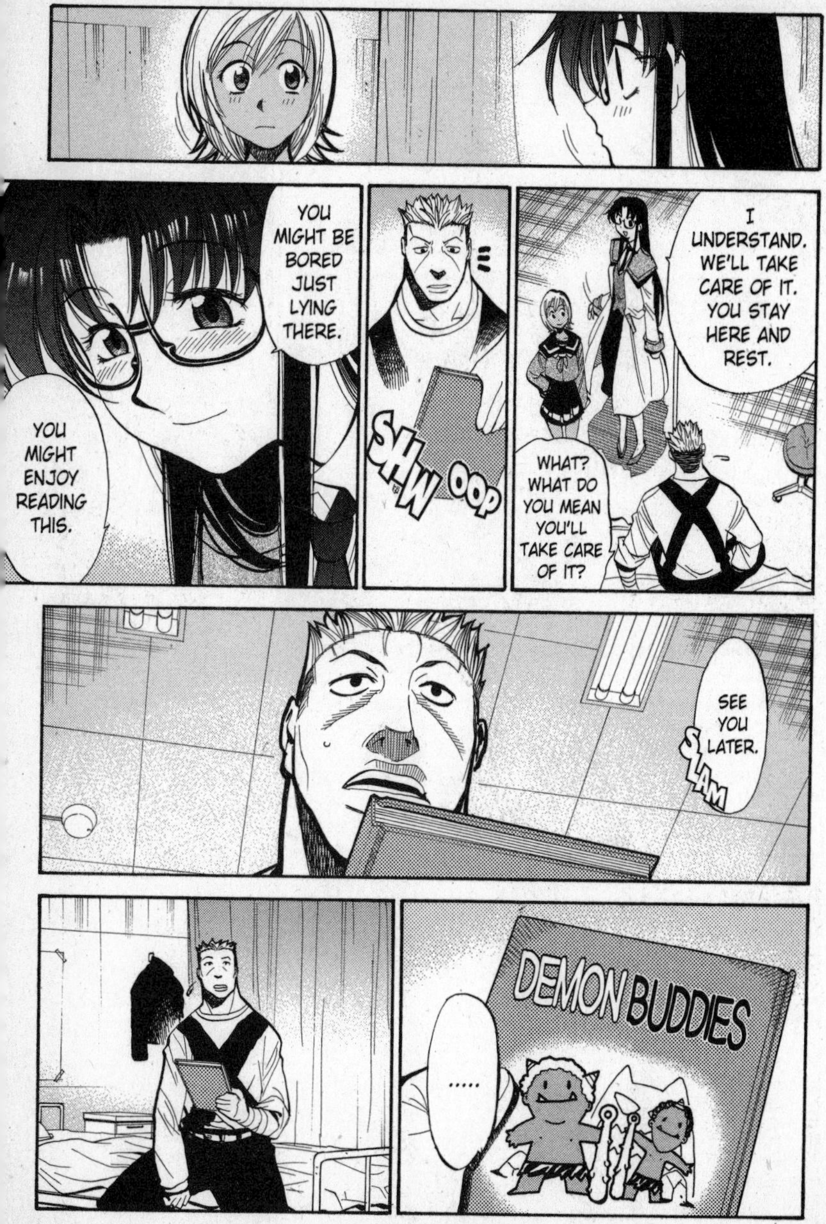
I UNDERSTAND. WE'LL TAKE CARE OF IT. YOU STAY HERE AND REST.
WHAT? WHAT DO YOU MEAN YOU'LL TAKE CARE OF IT?
SHWOOP
YOU MIGHT BE BORED JUST LYING THERE.
YOU MIGHT ENJOY READING THIS.
SEE YOU LATER.
SLAM
DEMON BUDDIES
.....

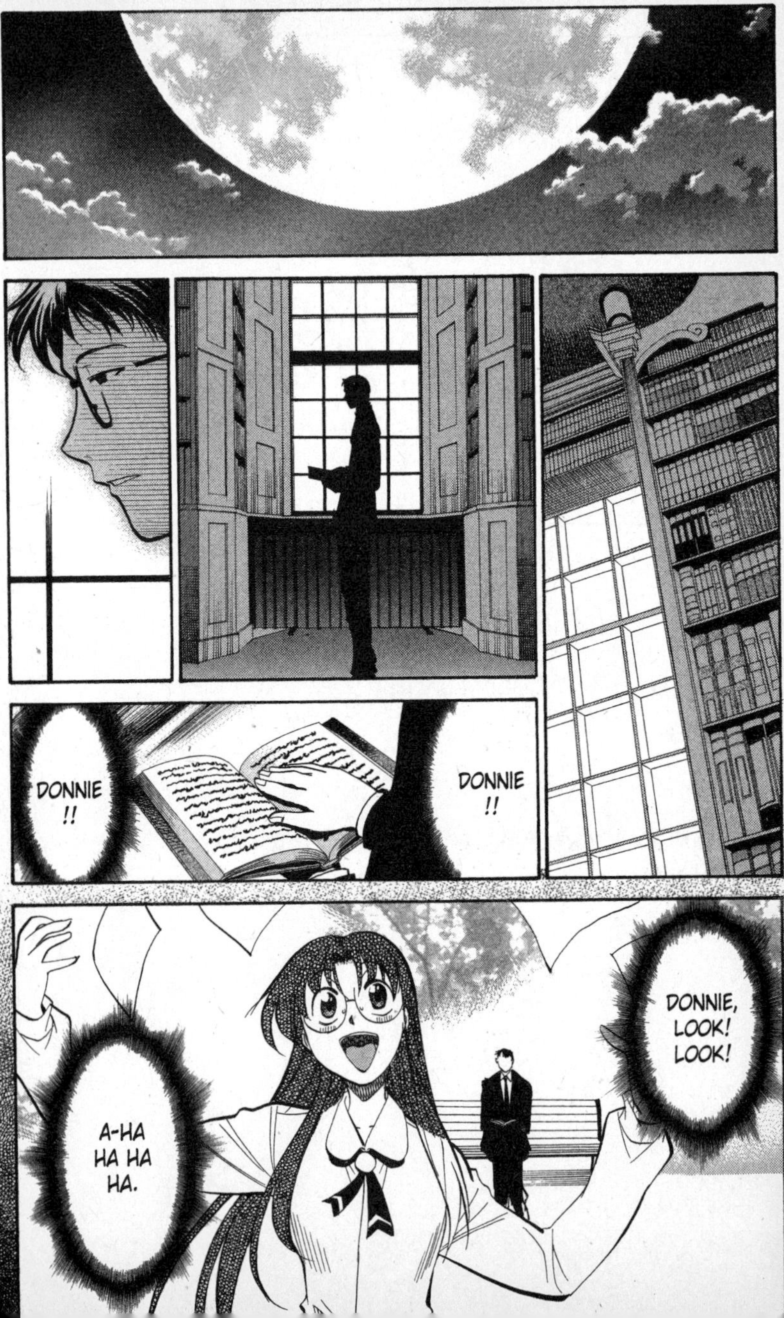
DONNIE !!
DONNIE !!
DONNIE, LOOK! LOOK!
A-HA HA HA HA.

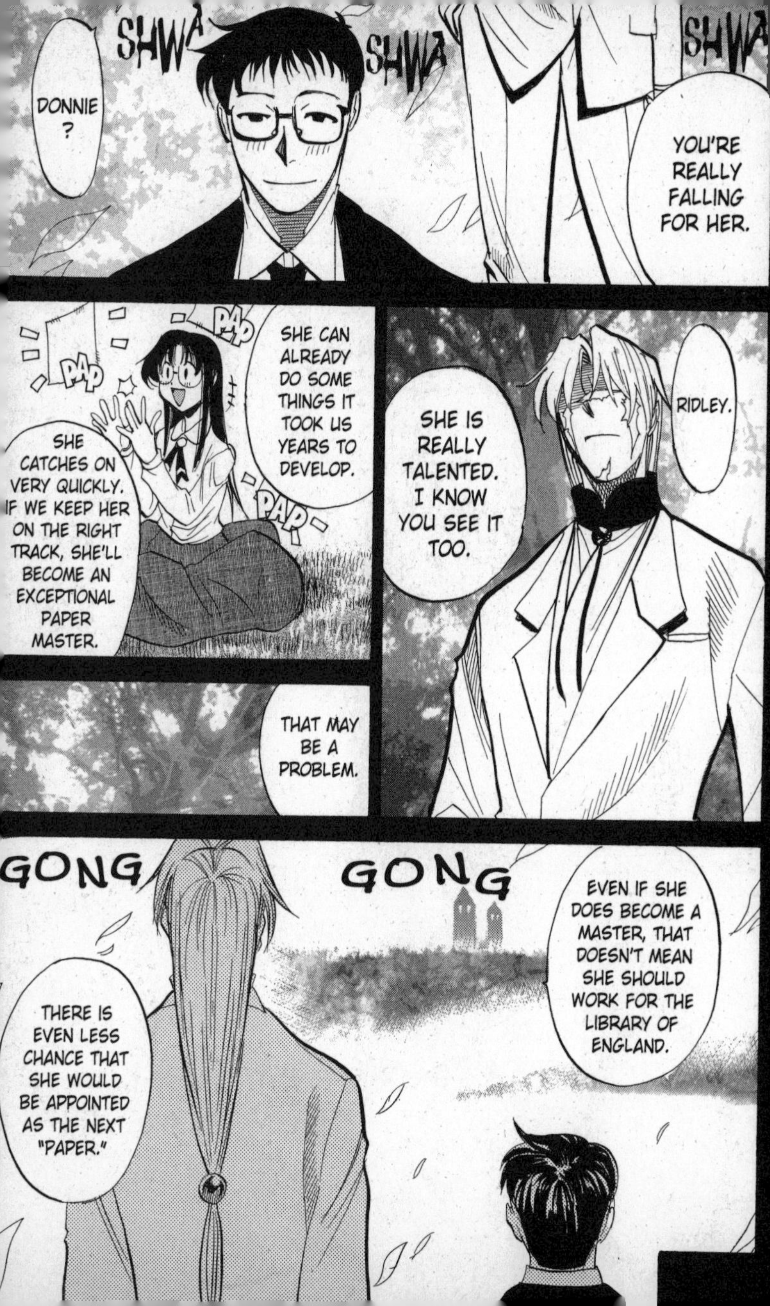

SHWA
YOU'RE REALLY FALLING FOR HER.
SHWA
SHWA
DONNIE?
RIDLEY.
SHE IS REALLY TALENTED. I KNOW YOU SEE IT TOO.
PAP
SHE CAN ALREADY DO SOME THINGS IT TOOK US YEARS TO DEVELOP.
PAP
PAP
SHE CATCHES ON VERY QUICKLY. IF WE KEEP HER ON THE RIGHT TRACK, SHE'LL BECOME AN EXCEPTIONAL PAPER MASTER.
THAT MAY BE A PROBLEM.
EVEN IF SHE DOES BECOME A MASTER, THAT DOESN'T MEAN SHE SHOULD WORK FOR THE LIBRARY OF ENGLAND.
GONG
GONG
THERE IS EVEN LESS CHANCE THAT SHE WOULD BE APPOINTED AS THE NEXT "PAPER."

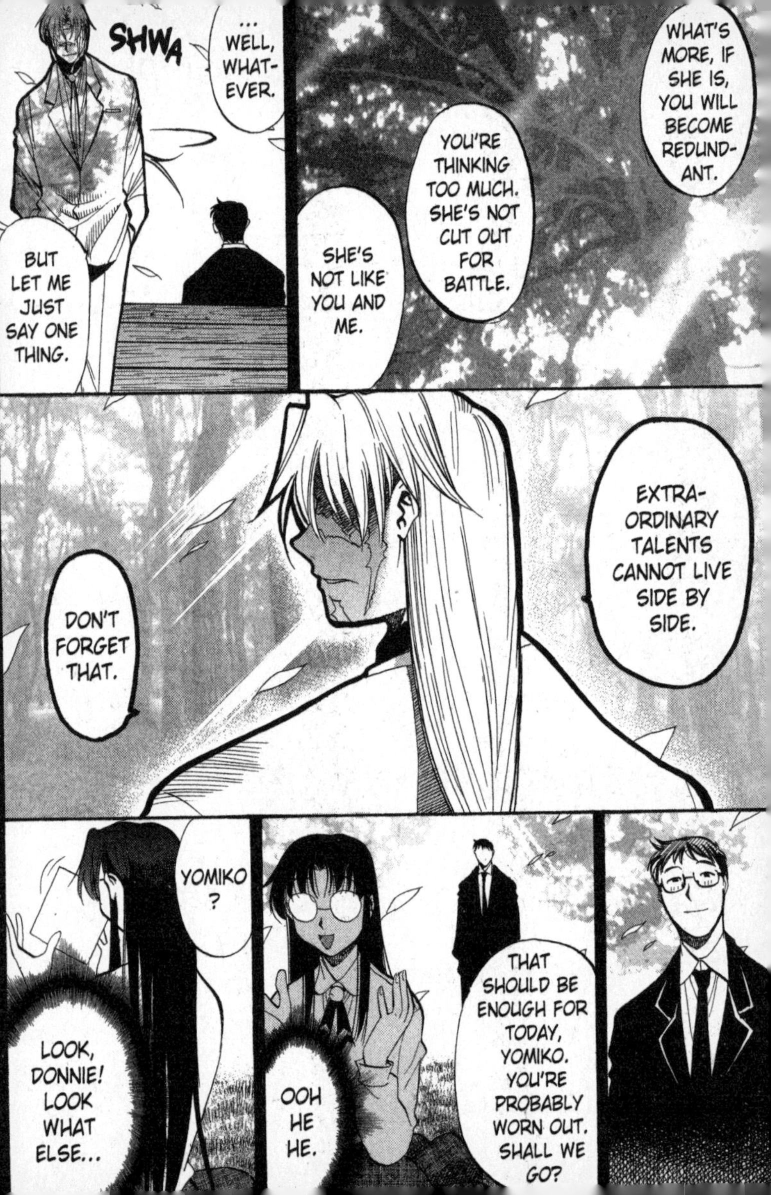
WHAT'S MORE, IF SHE IS, YOU WILL BECOME REDUND-ANT.
YOU'RE THINKING TOO MUCH. SHE'S NOT CUT OUT FOR BATTLE.
SHE'S NOT LIKE YOU AND ME.
SHWA
... WELL, WHAT-EVER.
BUT LET ME JUST SAY ONE THING.
EXTRA-ORDINARY TALENTS CANNOT LIVE SIDE BY SIDE.
DON'T FORGET THAT.
THAT SHOULD BE ENOUGH FOR TODAY, YOMIKO. YOU'RE PROBABLY WORN OUT. SHALL WE GO?
YOMIKO ?
OOH HE HE.
LOOK, DONNIE! LOOK WHAT ELSE...

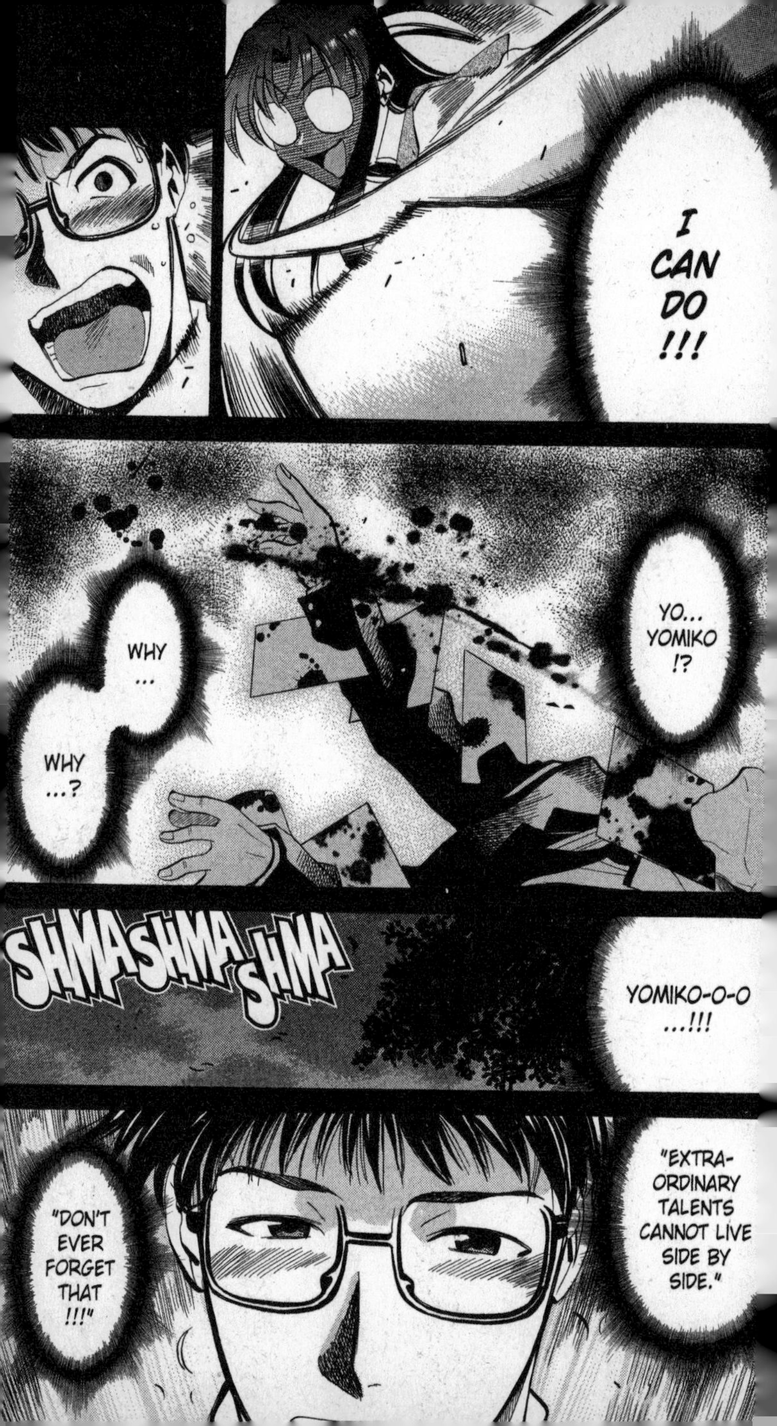
I CAN DO!!!
YO... YOMIKO!?
WHY... WHY...?
YOMIKO-O-O...!!!
SHMA SHMA SHMA
"EXTRA-ORDINARY TALENTS CANNOT LIVE SIDE BY SIDE."
"DON'T EVER FORGET THAT!!!"

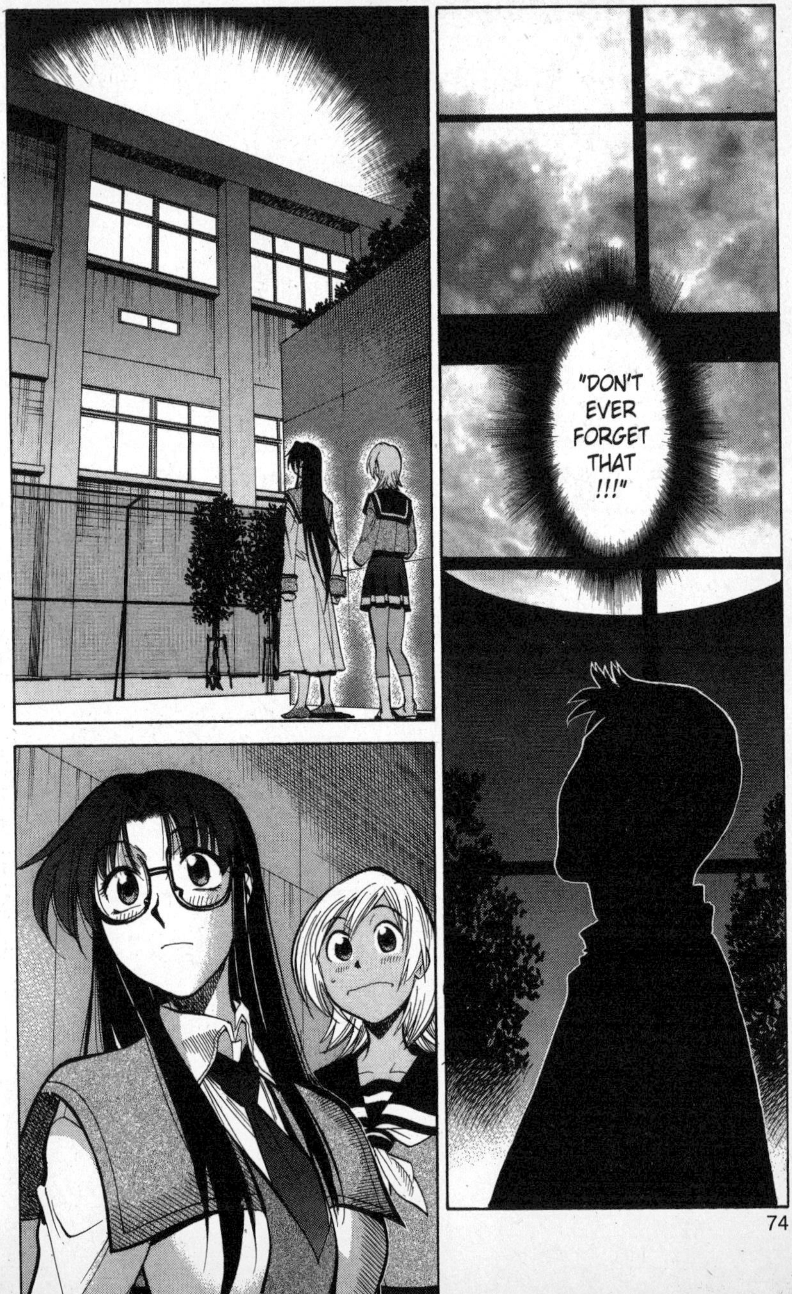
"DON'T EVER FORGET THAT !!!"

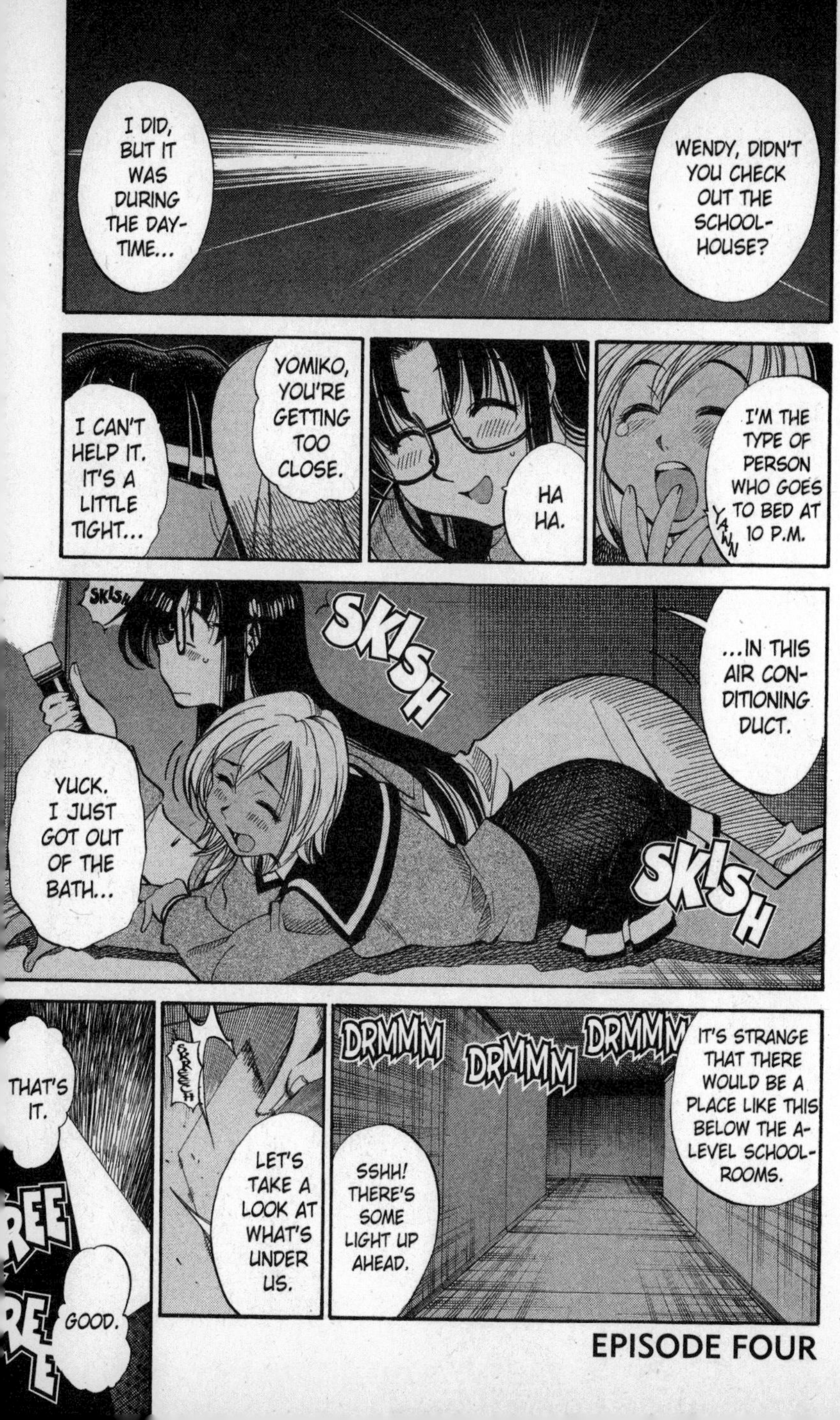
WENDY, DIDN'T YOU CHECK OUT THE SCHOOL-HOUSE?
I DID, BUT IT WAS DURING THE DAY-TIME...
I'M THE TYPE OF PERSON WHO GOES TO BED AT 10 P.M.
YAWN
HA HA.
YOMIKO, YOU'RE GETTING TOO CLOSE.
I CAN'T HELP IT. IT'S A LITTLE TIGHT...
...IN THIS AIR CON-DITIONING DUCT.
SKISH
SKISH
SKISH
YUCK. I JUST GOT OUT OF THE BATH...
IT'S STRANGE THAT THERE WOULD BE A PLACE LIKE THIS BELOW THE A-LEVEL SCHOOL-ROOMS.
DRMMM
DRMMM
DRMMM
SSHH! THERE'S SOME LIGHT UP AHEAD.
SKREECH
LET'S TAKE A LOOK AT WHAT'S UNDER US.
THAT'S IT.
GOOD.

EPISODE FOUR

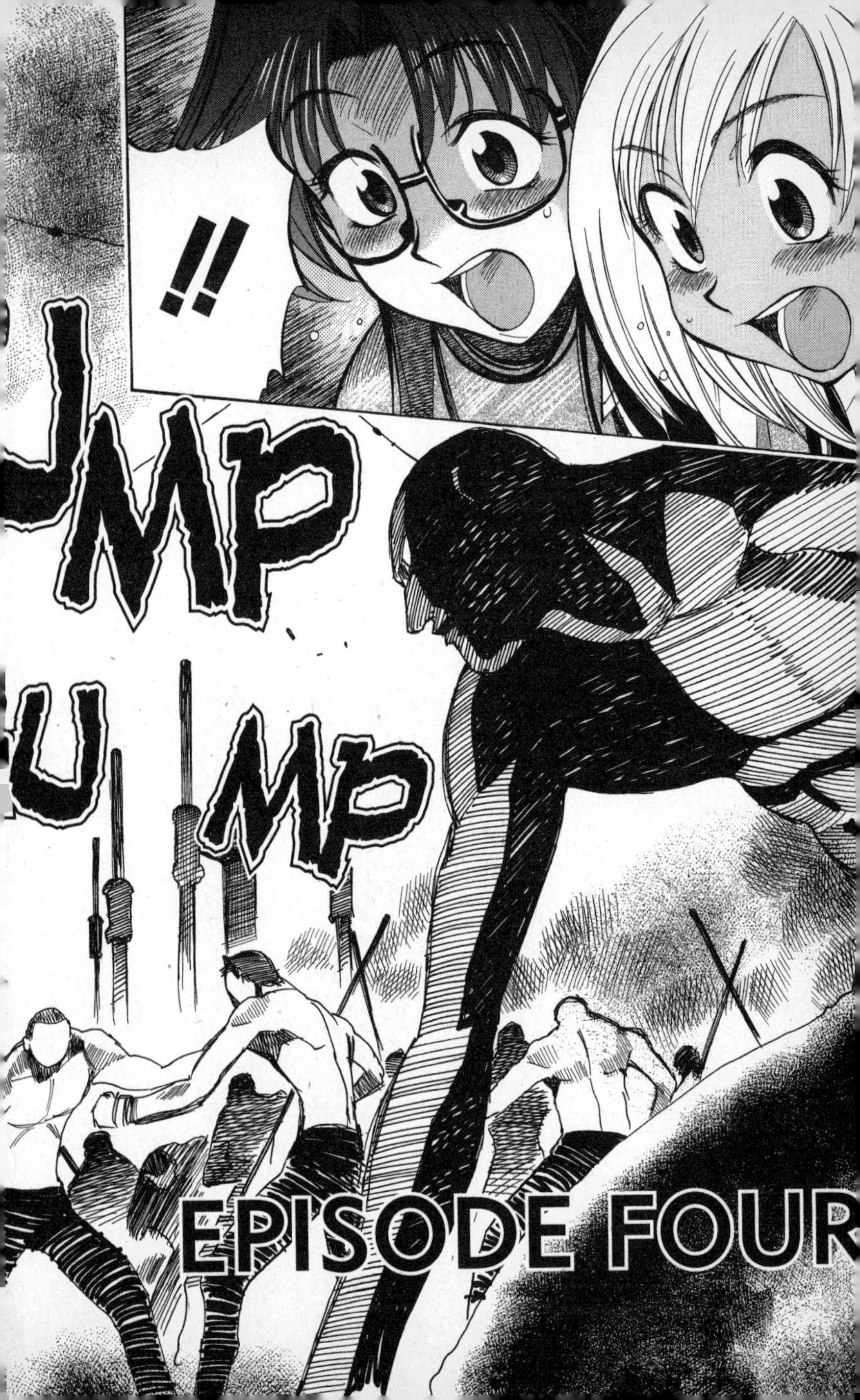
!!
UMP
UMP
EPISODE FOUR

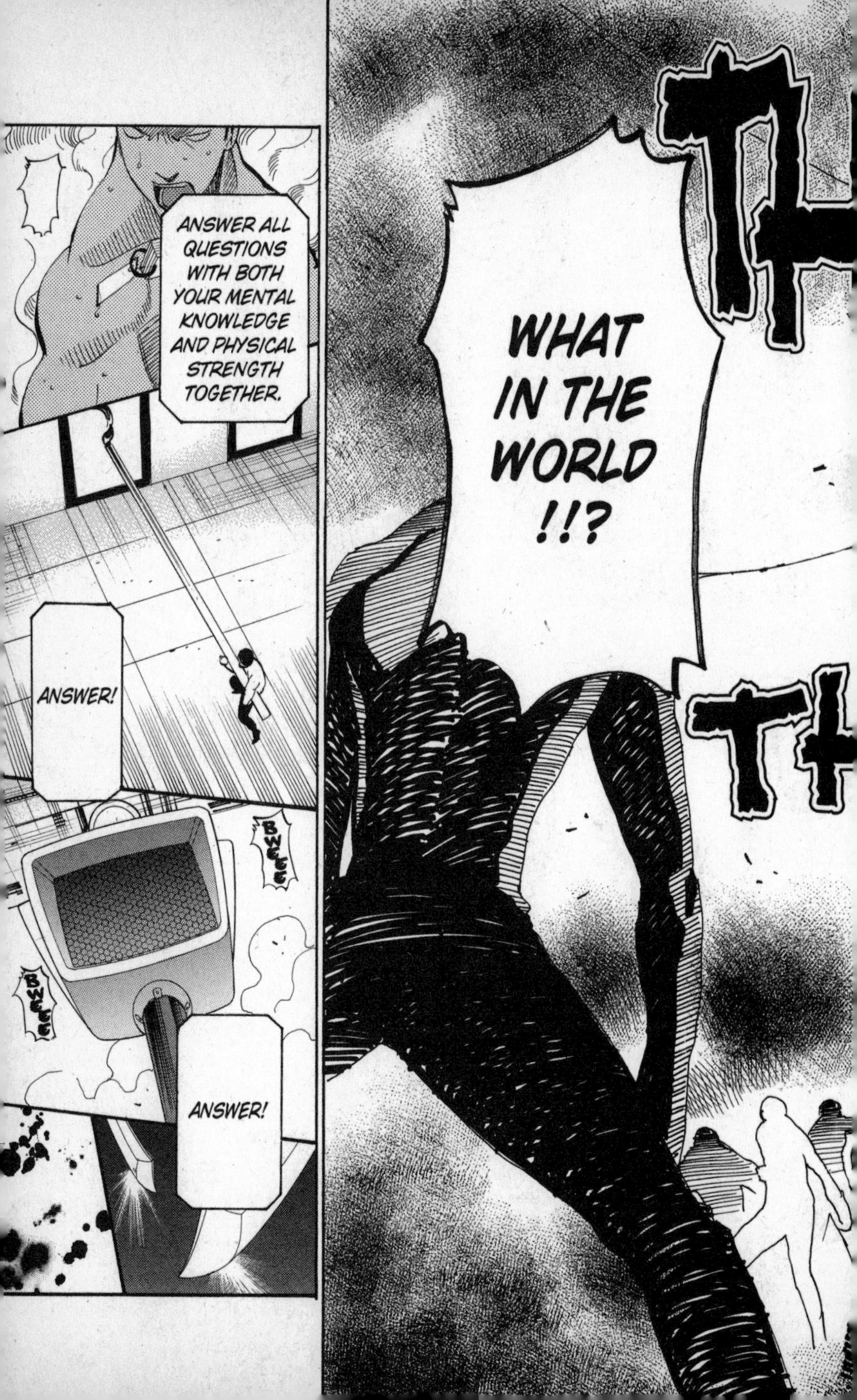
WHAT IN THE WORLD !!?
ANSWER ALL QUESTIONS WITH BOTH YOUR MENTAL KNOWLEDGE AND PHYSICAL STRENGTH TOGETHER.
ANSWER!
BWEEE
BWEEE
ANSWER!

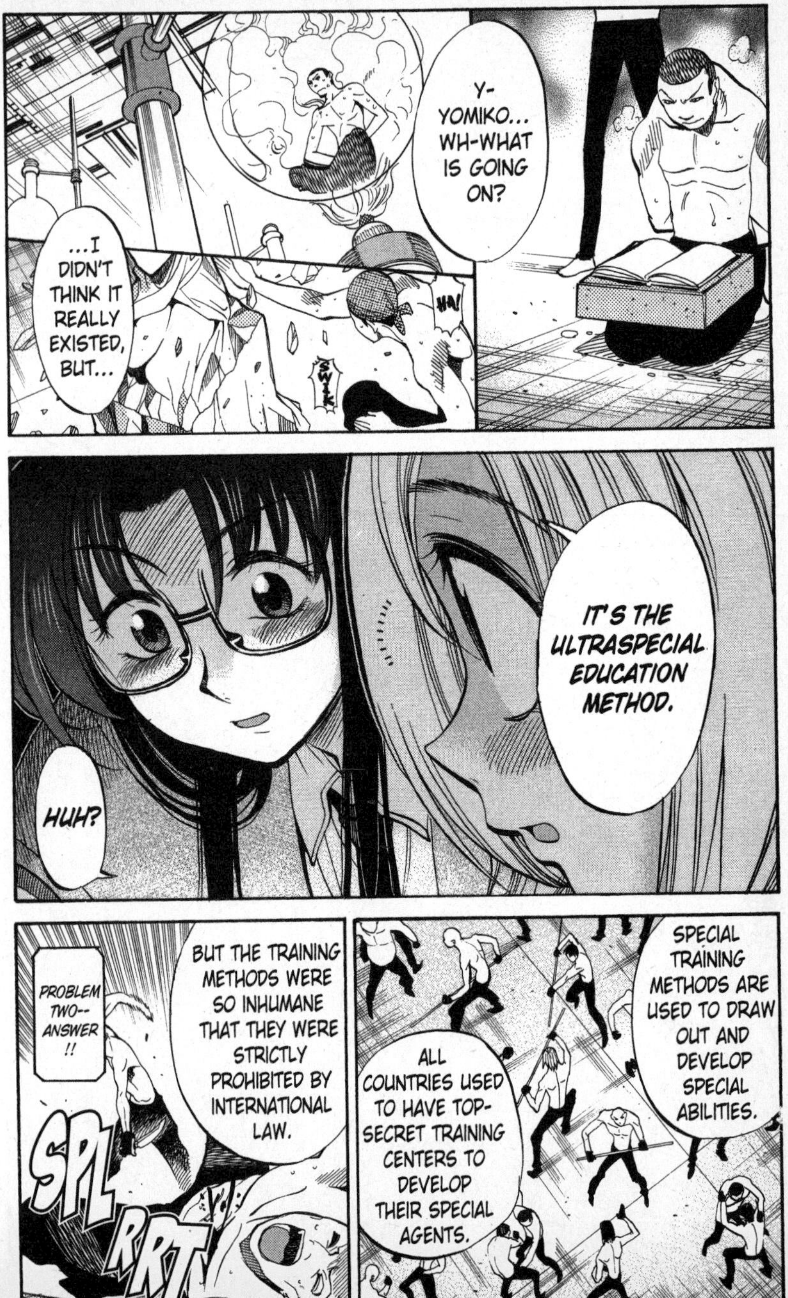
Y-YOMIKO... WH-WHAT IS GOING ON?
...I DIDN'T THINK IT REALLY EXISTED, BUT...
HA!
SWISH
IT'S THE ULTRASPECIAL EDUCATION METHOD.
HUH?
SPECIAL TRAINING METHODS ARE USED TO DRAW OUT AND DEVELOP SPECIAL ABILITIES.
ALL COUNTRIES USED TO HAVE TOP-SECRET TRAINING CENTERS TO DEVELOP THEIR SPECIAL AGENTS.
BUT THE TRAINING METHODS WERE SO INHUMANE THAT THEY WERE STRICTLY PROHIBITED BY INTERNATIONAL LAW.
PROBLEM TWO-- ANSWER !!
SPLRRT

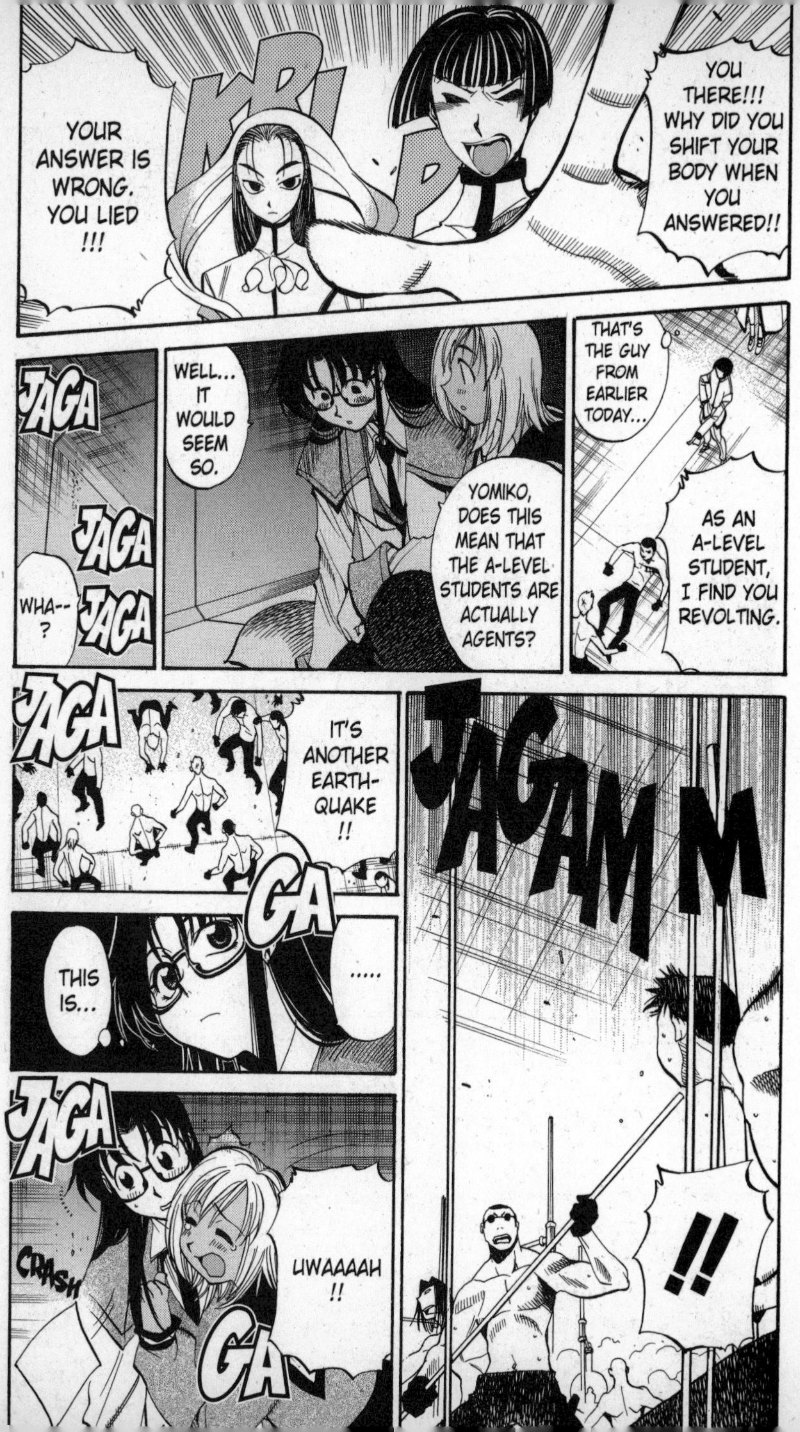
YOU THERE!!! WHY DID YOU SHIFT YOUR BODY WHEN YOU ANSWERED!!
YOUR ANSWER IS WRONG. YOU LIED !!!
THAT'S THE GUY FROM EARLIER TODAY...
AS AN A-LEVEL STUDENT, I FIND YOU REVOLTING.
YOMIKO, DOES THIS MEAN THAT THE A-LEVEL STUDENTS ARE ACTUALLY AGENTS?
WELL... IT WOULD SEEM SO.
JAGA
JAGA
JAGA
WHA-- ?
JAGAM M
!!
JAGA
IT'S ANOTHER EARTH-QUAKE !!
GA
.....
THIS IS...
JAGA
CRASH
UWAAAAH !!
GA

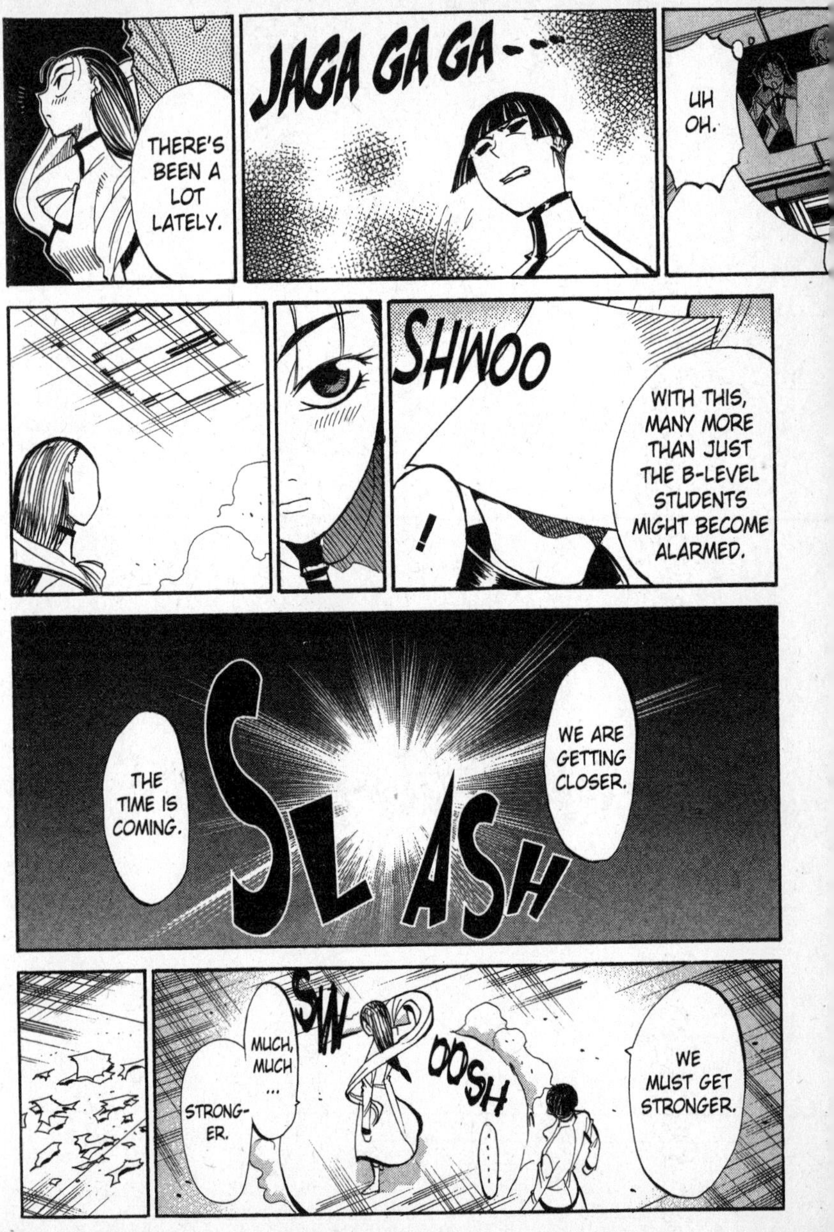
UH OH.
JAGA GA GA...
THERE'S BEEN A LOT LATELY.
SHWOO
WITH THIS, MANY MORE THAN JUST THE B-LEVEL STUDENTS MIGHT BECOME ALARMED.
!
WE ARE GETTING CLOSER.
SLASH
THE TIME IS COMING.
WE MUST GET STRONGER.
SWOOSH
...
MUCH, MUCH ...
STRONG-ER.

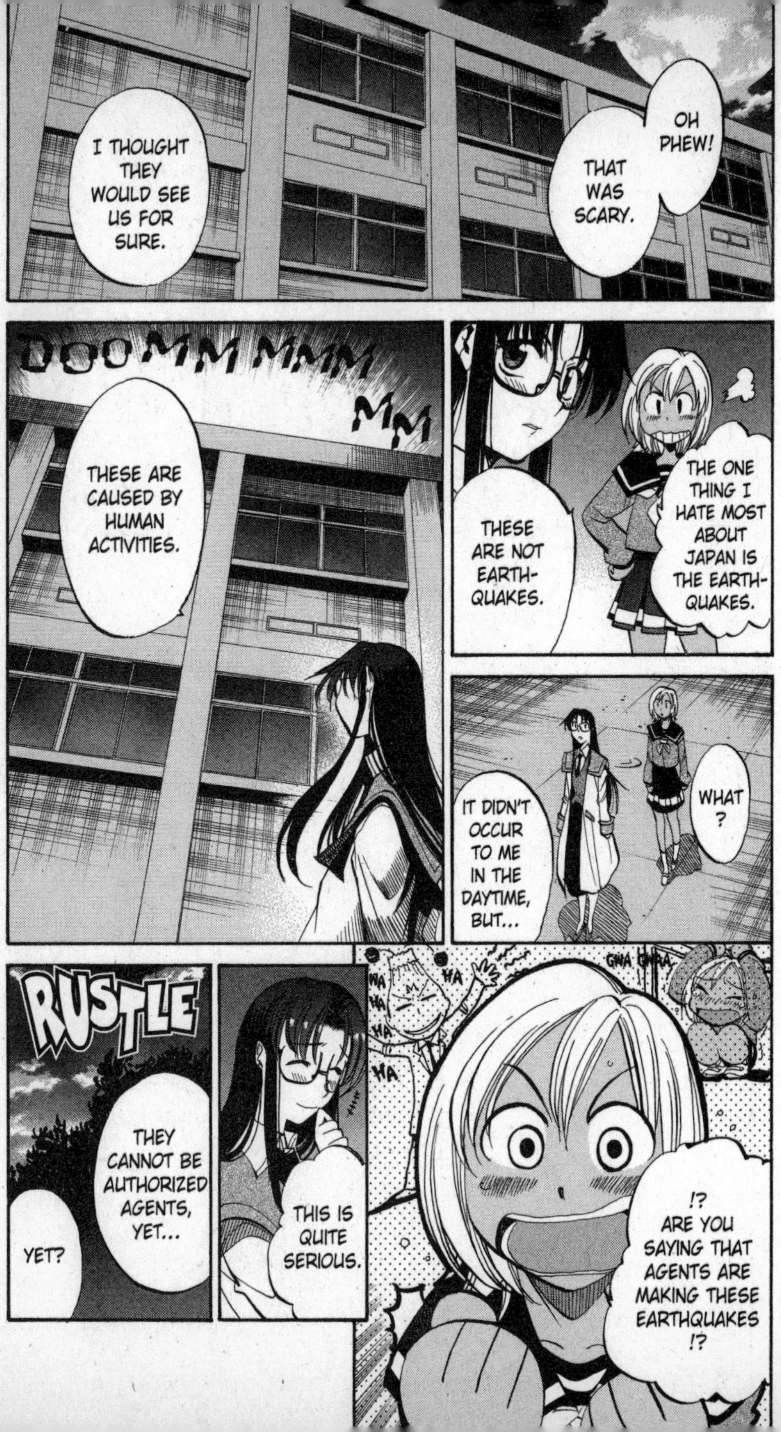
OH PHEW!
THAT WAS SCARY.
I THOUGHT THEY WOULD SEE US FOR SURE.
THE ONE THING I HATE MOST ABOUT JAPAN IS THE EARTH-QUAKES.
THESE ARE NOT EARTH-QUAKES.
WHAT?
IT DIDN'T OCCUR TO ME IN THE DAYTIME, BUT...
DOOMMMMMMMMM
THESE ARE CAUSED BY HUMAN ACTIVITIES.
GWA GWAA
!? ARE YOU SAYING THAT AGENTS ARE MAKING THESE EARTHQUAKES!?
THIS IS QUITE SERIOUS.
RUSTLE
THEY CANNOT BE AUTHORIZED AGENTS, YET...
YET?

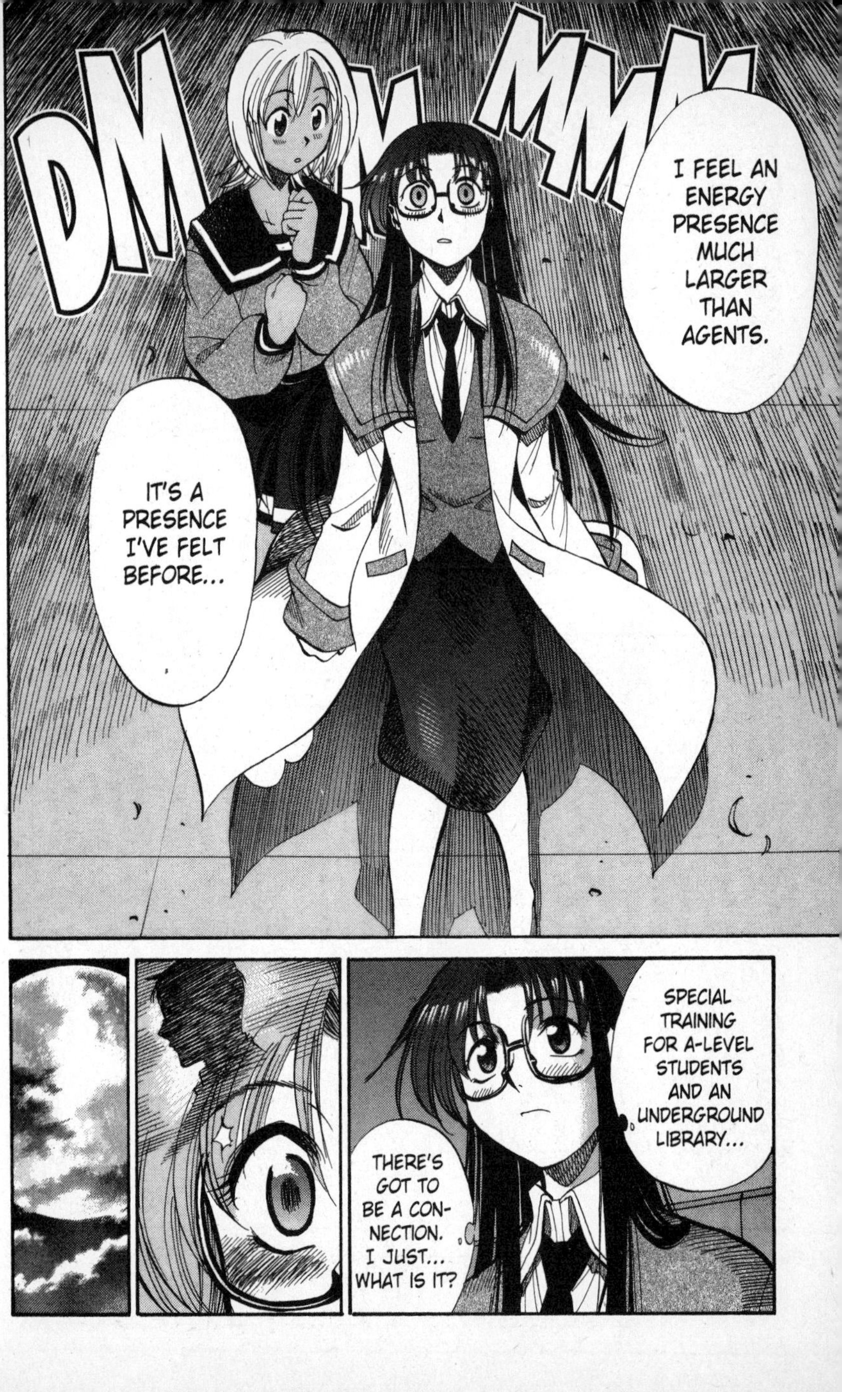
DM M MMM
I FEEL AN ENERGY PRESENCE MUCH LARGER THAN AGENTS.
IT'S A PRESENCE I'VE FELT BEFORE...
SPECIAL TRAINING FOR A-LEVEL STUDENTS AND AN UNDERGROUND LIBRARY...
THERE'S GOT TO BE A CON-NECTION. I JUST... WHAT IS IT?

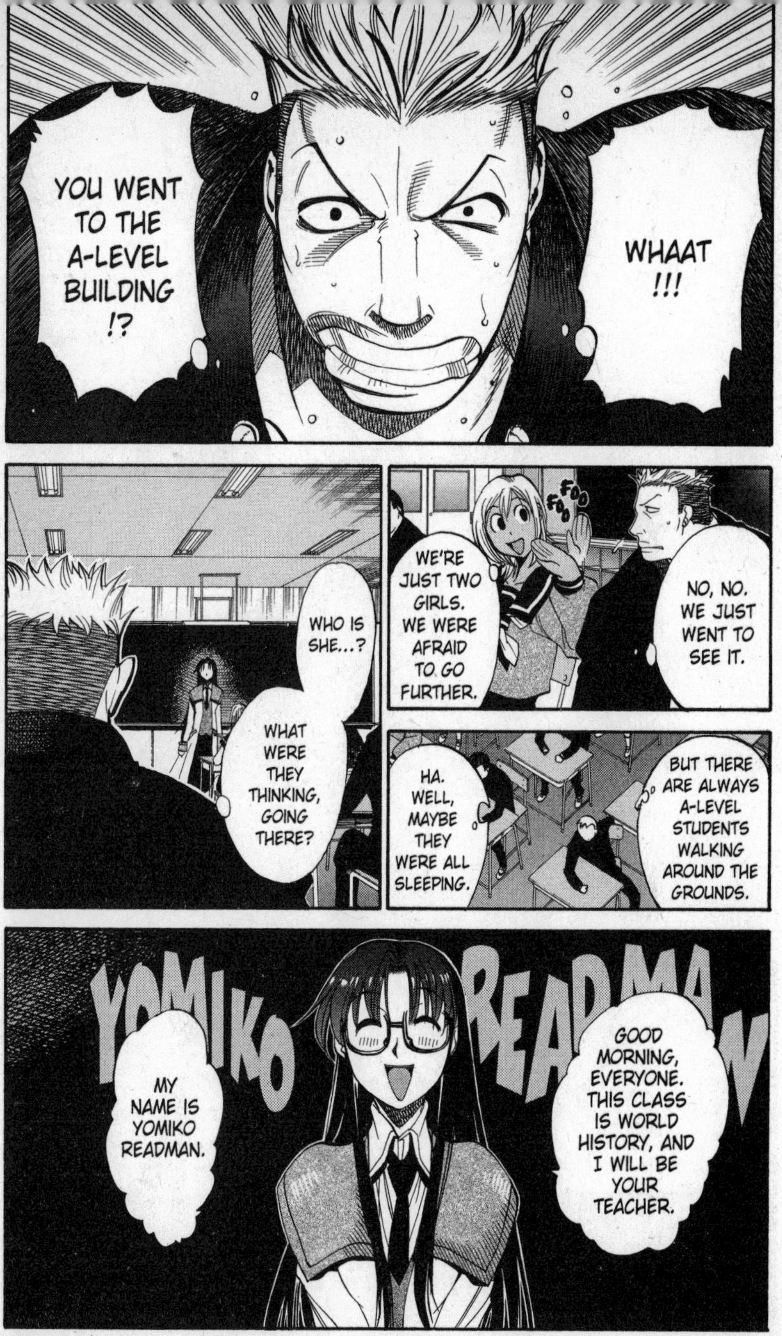
WHAAT !!!
YOU WENT TO THE A-LEVEL BUILDING !?
NO, NO. WE JUST WENT TO SEE IT.
FOO FOO
WE'RE JUST TWO GIRLS. WE WERE AFRAID TO GO FURTHER.
BUT THERE ARE ALWAYS A-LEVEL STUDENTS WALKING AROUND THE GROUNDS.
HA. WELL, MAYBE THEY WERE ALL SLEEPING.
WHO IS SHE...?
WHAT WERE THEY THINKING, GOING THERE?
YOMIKO READMAN
GOOD MORNING, EVERYONE. THIS CLASS IS WORLD HISTORY, AND I WILL BE YOUR TEACHER.
MY NAME IS YOMIKO READMAN.

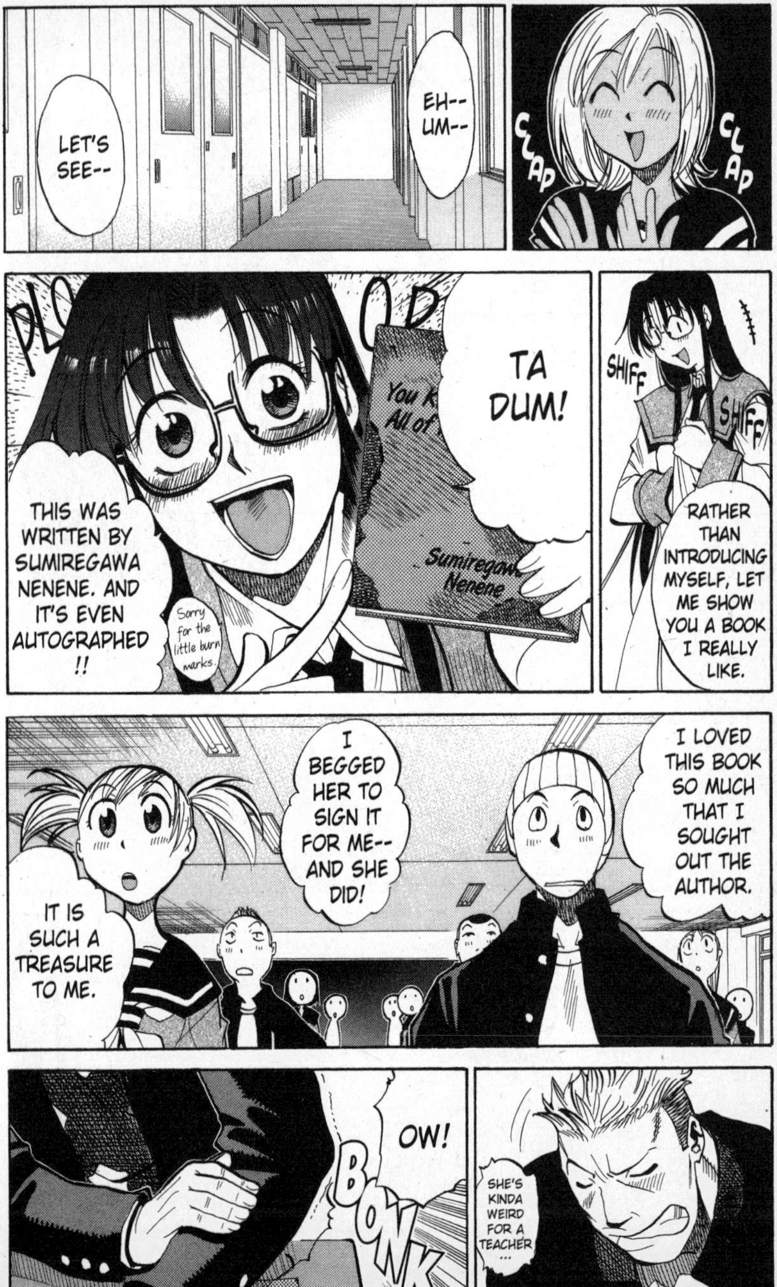
CLAP
CLAP
EH-- UM--
LET'S SEE--
SHIFF
SHIFF
RATHER THAN INTRODUCING MYSELF, LET ME SHOW YOU A BOOK I REALLY LIKE.
TA DUM!
Sumiregawa Nenene
THIS WAS WRITTEN BY SUMIREGAWA NENENE. AND IT'S EVEN AUTOGRAPHED !!
Sorry for the little burn marks.
I LOVED THIS BOOK SO MUCH THAT I SOUGHT OUT THE AUTHOR.
I BEGGED HER TO SIGN IT FOR ME-- AND SHE DID!
IT IS SUCH A TREASURE TO ME.
SHE'S KINDA WEIRD FOR A TEACHER...
OW!
BONK

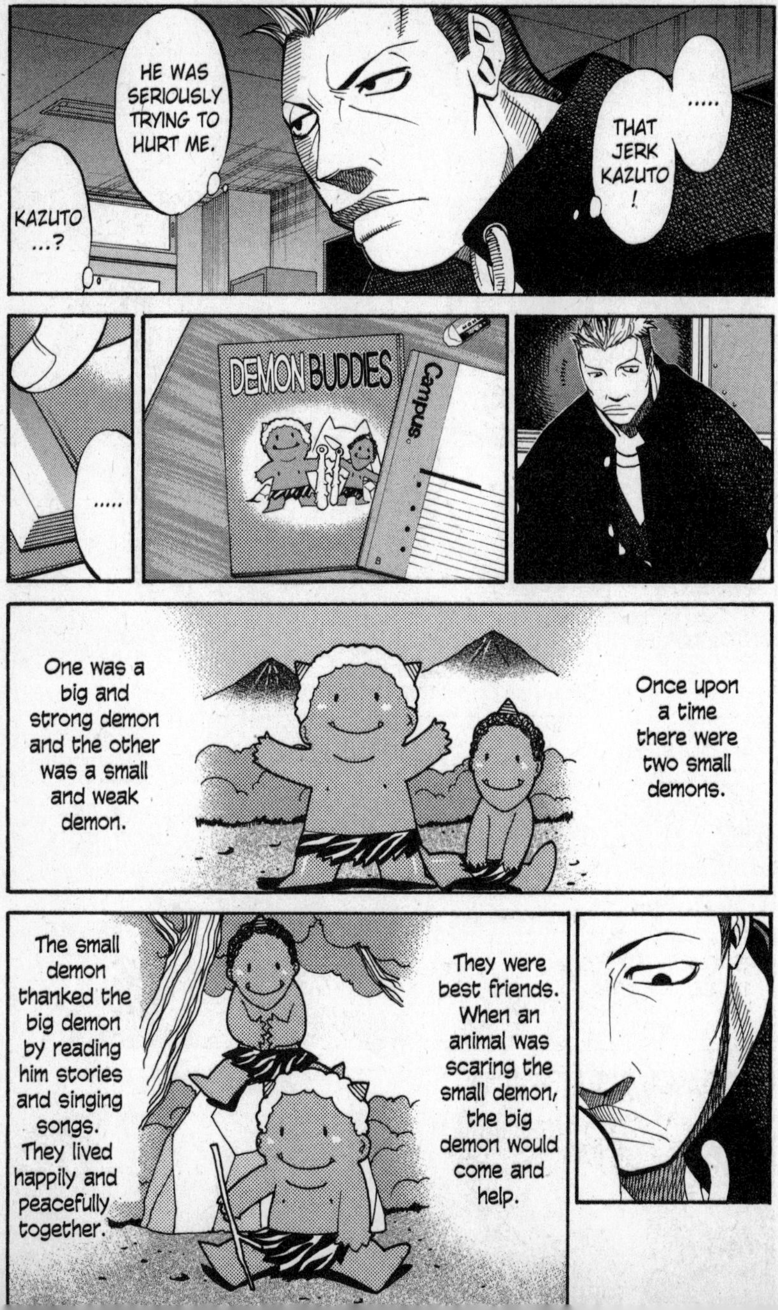
.....
THAT JERK KAZUTO!
HE WAS SERIOUSLY TRYING TO HURT ME.
KAZUTO ...?
DEMON BUDDIES
Campus
.....
Once upon a time there were two small demons.
One was a big and strong demon and the other was a small and weak demon.
They were best friends. When an animal was scaring the small demon, the big demon would come and help.
The small demon thanked the big demon by reading him stories and singing songs. They lived happily and peacefully together.

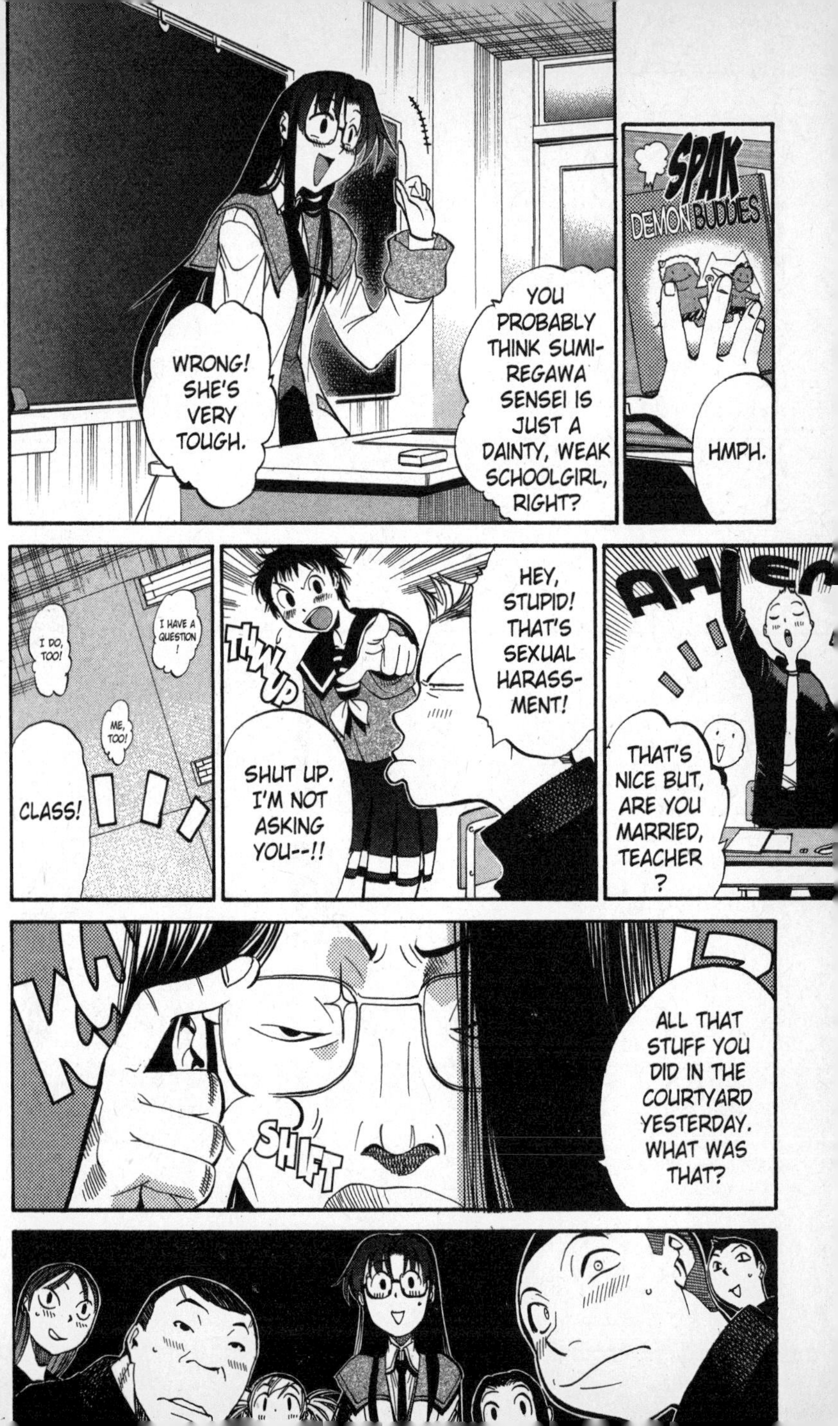
SPAK
DEMON BUDDIES
HMPH.
YOU PROBABLY THINK SUMIREGAWA SENSEI IS JUST A DAINTY, WEAK SCHOOLGIRL, RIGHT?
WRONG! SHE'S VERY TOUGH.
AHEM
THAT'S NICE BUT, ARE YOU MARRIED, TEACHER?
HEY, STUPID! THAT'S SEXUAL HARASSMENT!
THWUP
SHUT UP. I'M NOT ASKING YOU--!!
I HAVE A QUESTION!
I DO, TOO!
ME, TOO!
CLASS!
ALL THAT STUFF YOU DID IN THE COURTYARD YESTERDAY. WHAT WAS THAT?
SHIFT

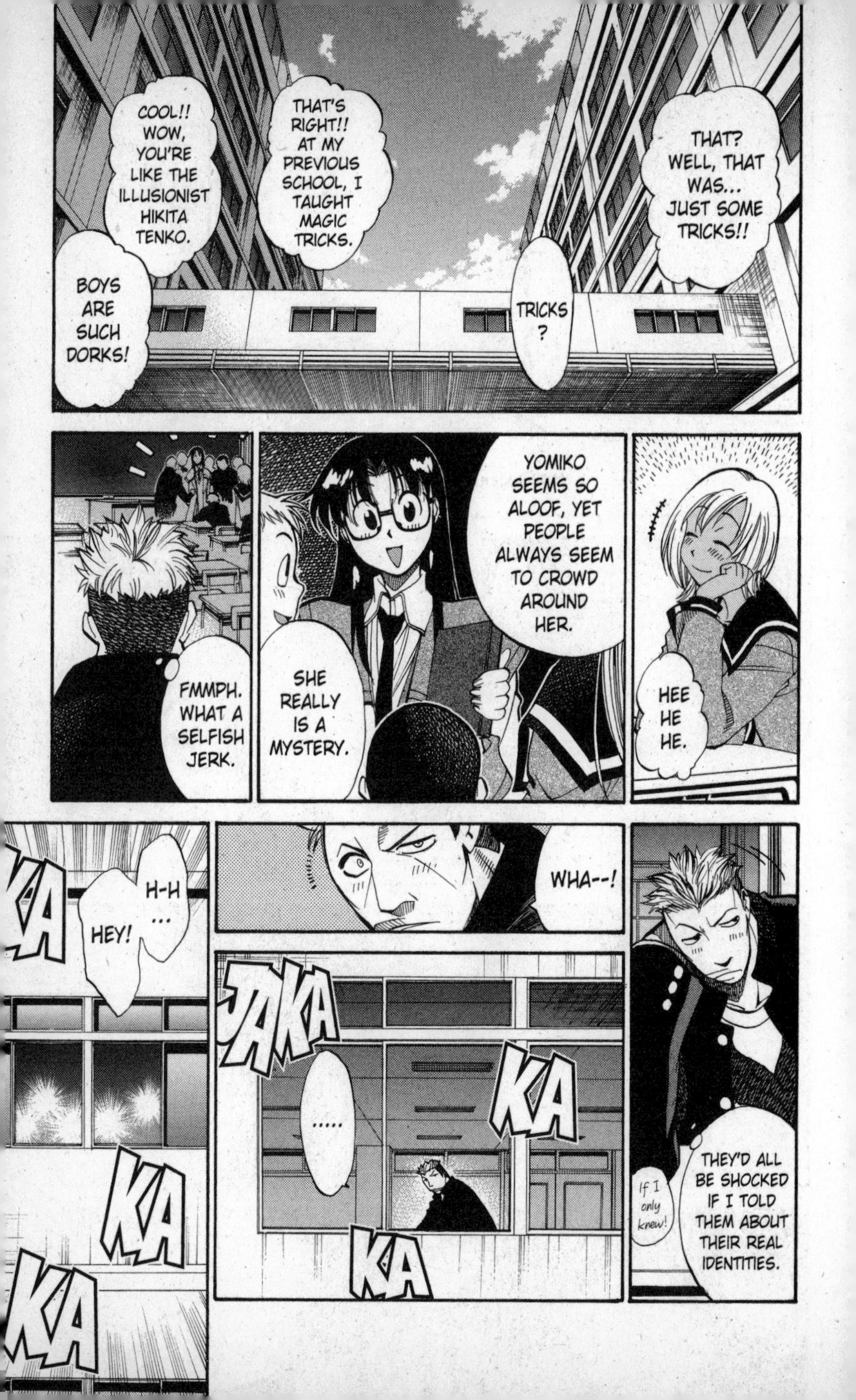
THAT? WELL, THAT WAS... JUST SOME TRICKS!!
TRICKS?
THAT'S RIGHT!! AT MY PREVIOUS SCHOOL, I TAUGHT MAGIC TRICKS.
COOL!! WOW, YOU'RE LIKE THE ILLUSIONIST HIKITA TENKO.
BOYS ARE SUCH DORKS!
HEE HE HE.
YOMIKO SEEMS SO ALOOF, YET PEOPLE ALWAYS SEEM TO CROWD AROUND HER.
SHE REALLY IS A MYSTERY.
FMMPH. WHAT A SELFISH JERK.
THEY'D ALL BE SHOCKED IF I TOLD THEM ABOUT THEIR REAL IDENTITIES.
If I only knew!
WHA--!
JAKA
KA
.....
KA
H-H ...
HEY!
KA
KA

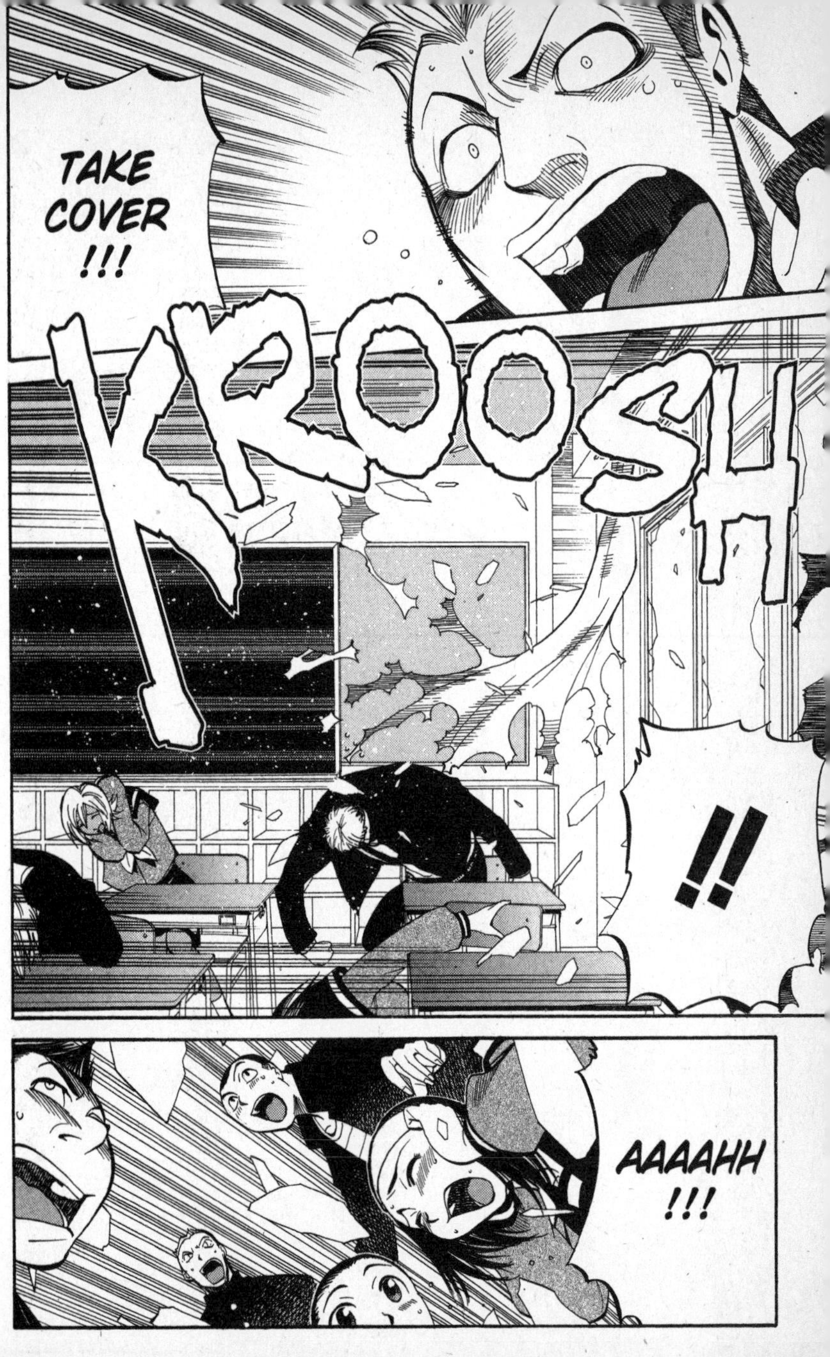
TAKE COVER !!!
KROOSH
!!
AAAAHH !!!

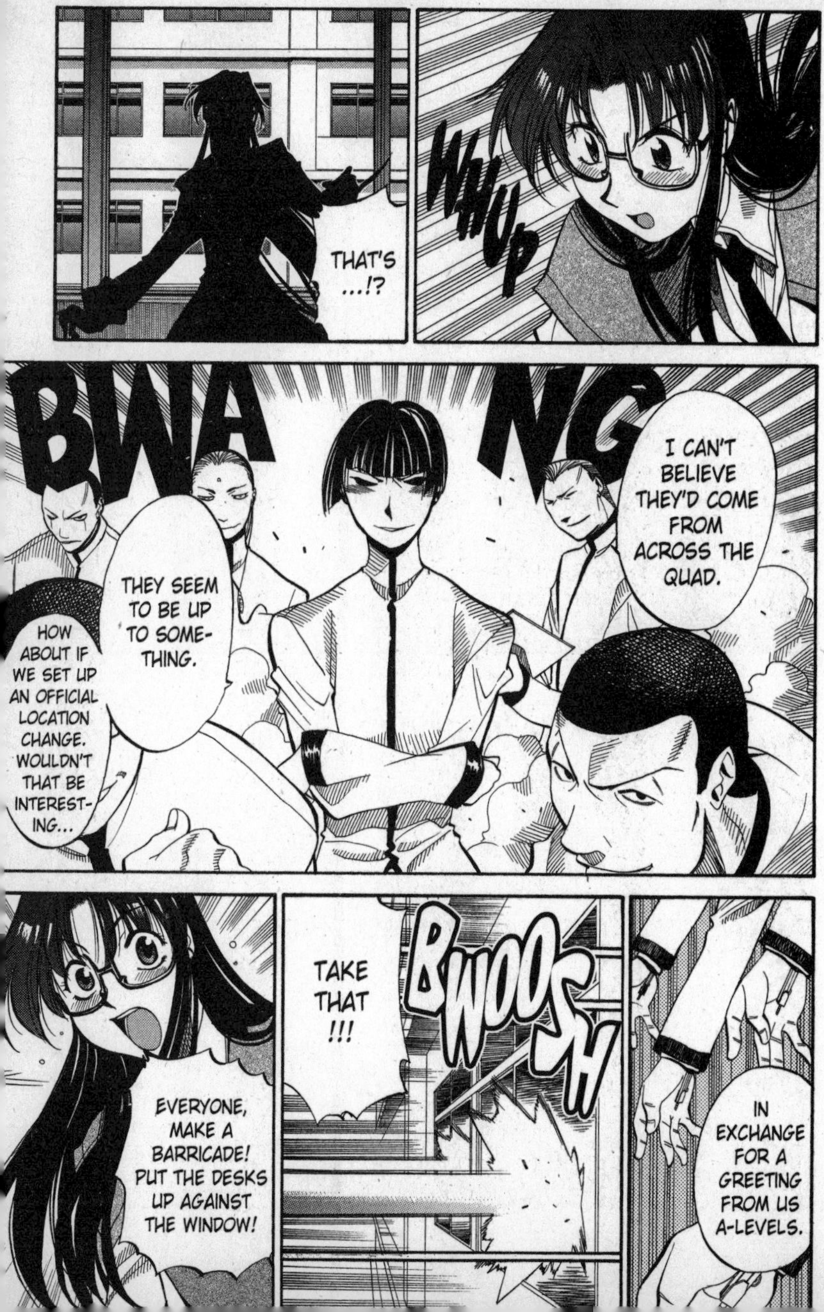
WHUP
THAT'S ...!?
BWANG
I CAN'T BELIEVE THEY'D COME FROM ACROSS THE QUAD.
THEY SEEM TO BE UP TO SOMETHING.
HOW ABOUT IF WE SET UP AN OFFICIAL LOCATION CHANGE. WOULDN'T THAT BE INTERESTING...
IN EXCHANGE FOR A GREETING FROM US A-LEVELS.
BWOOSH
TAKE THAT !!!
EVERYONE, MAKE A BARRICADE! PUT THE DESKS UP AGAINST THE WINDOW!

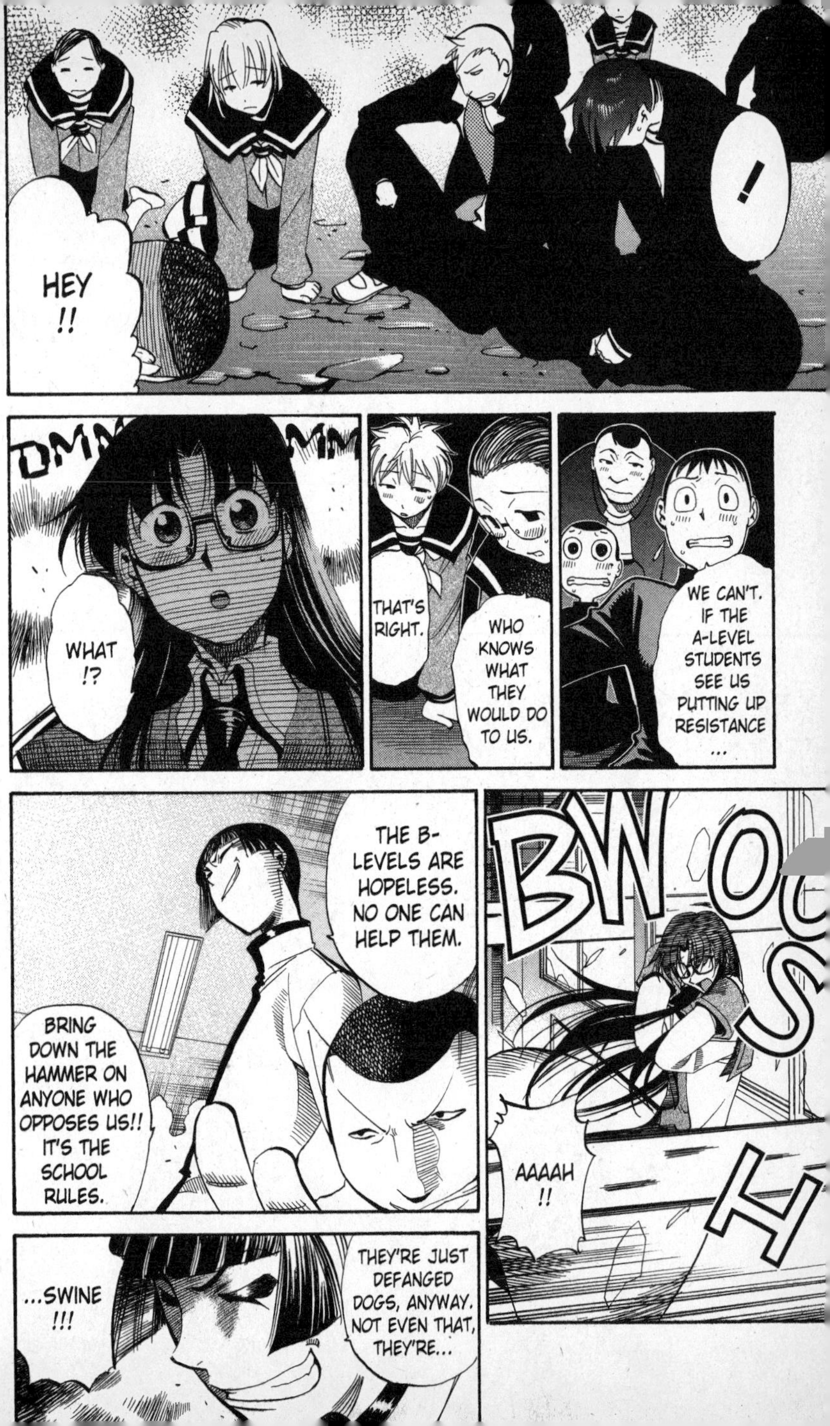
!
HEY !!
WE CAN'T. IF THE A-LEVEL STUDENTS SEE US PUTTING UP RESISTANCE ...
WHO KNOWS WHAT THEY WOULD DO TO US.
THAT'S RIGHT.
DMMMMM
WHAT !?
BWOOSH
AAAAH !!
THE B-LEVELS ARE HOPELESS. NO ONE CAN HELP THEM.
BRING DOWN THE HAMMER ON ANYONE WHO OPPOSES US!! IT'S THE SCHOOL RULES.
THEY'RE JUST DEFANGED DOGS, ANYWAY. NOT EVEN THAT, THEY'RE...
...SWINE !!!

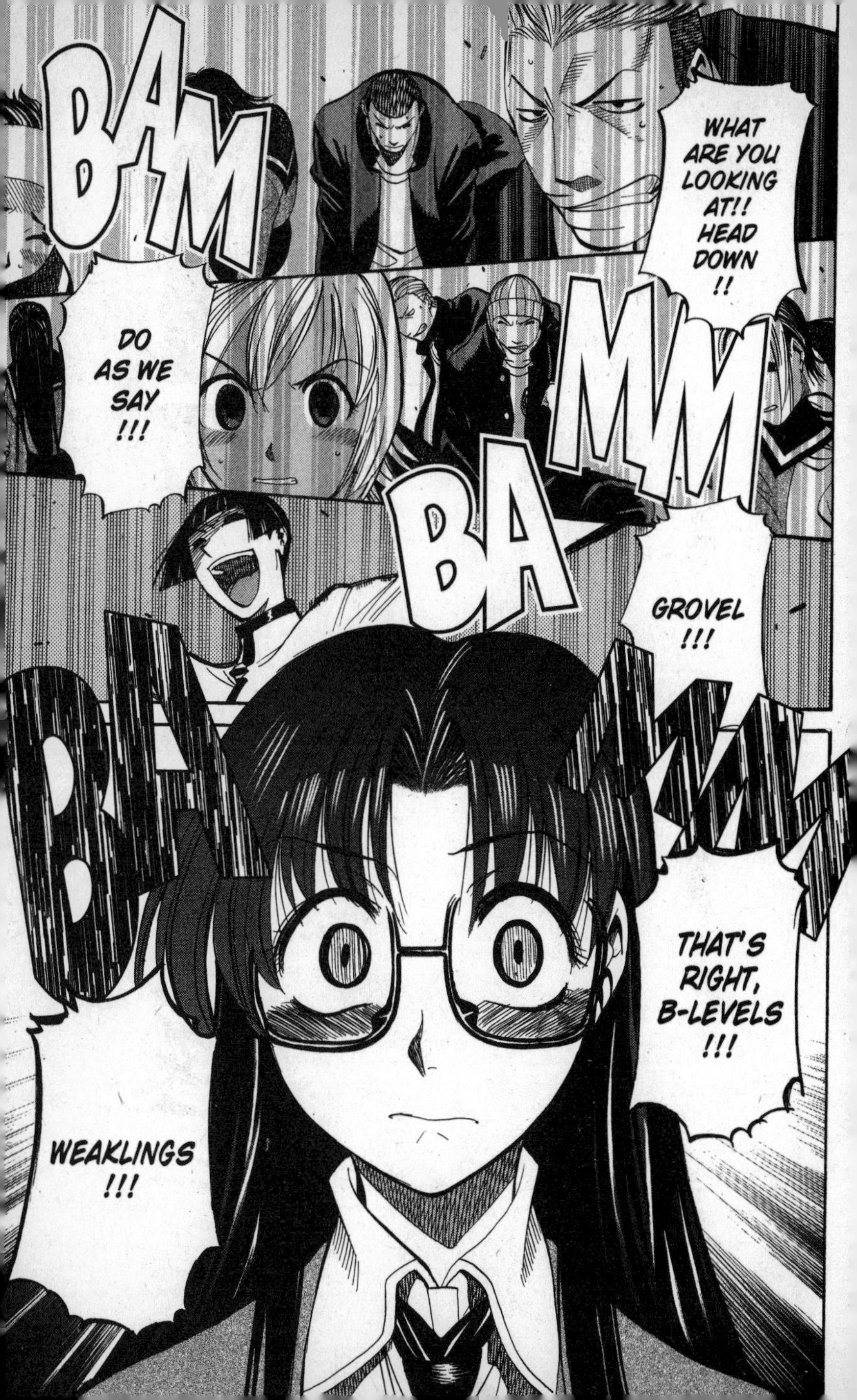
WHAT ARE YOU LOOKING AT!! HEAD DOWN !!
BAM
BAMM
DO AS WE SAY !!!
GROVEL !!!
BA
THAT'S RIGHT, B-LEVELS !!!
WEAKLINGS !!!

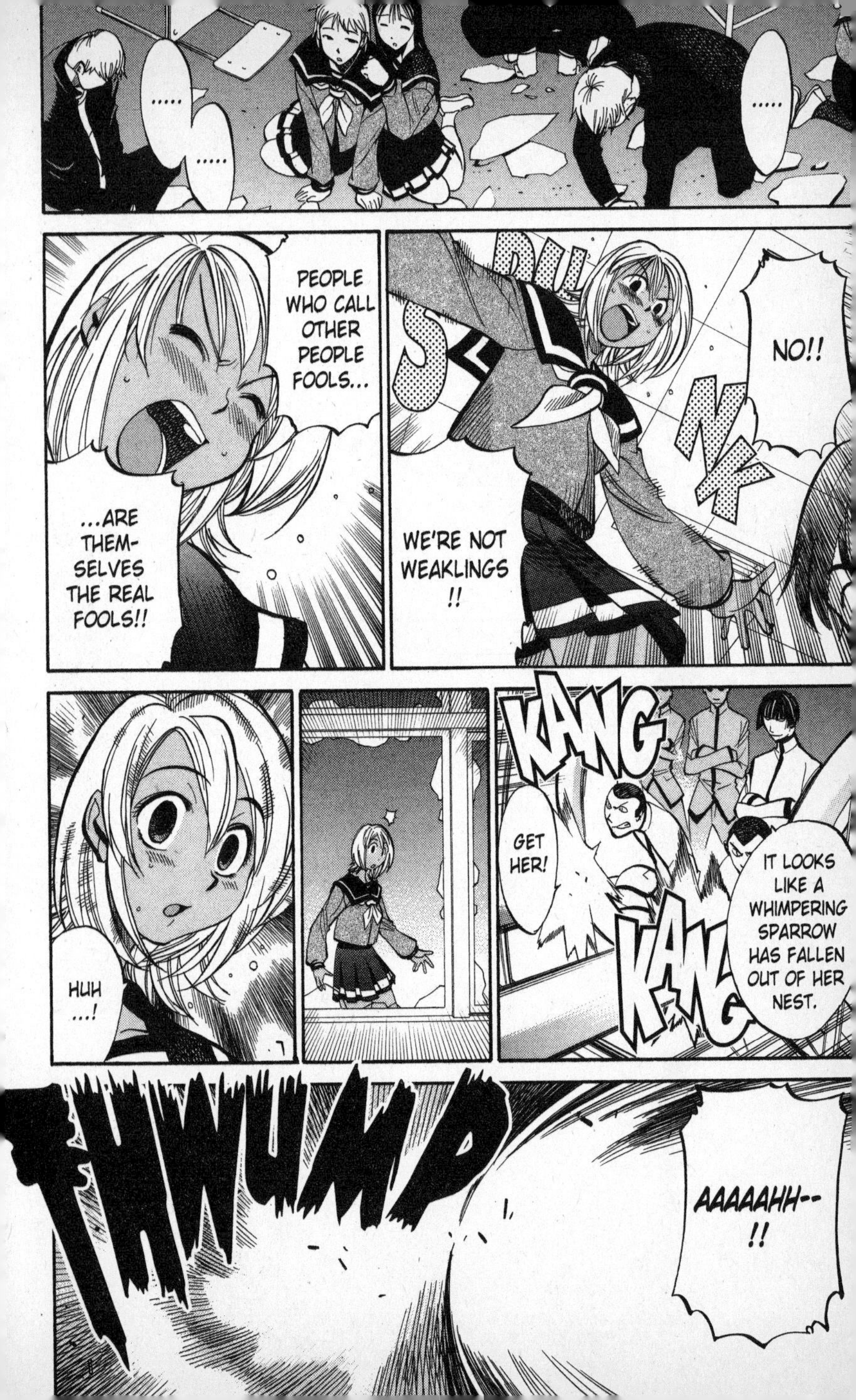
.....
.....
.....
NO!!
WE'RE NOT WEAKLINGS !!
PEOPLE WHO CALL OTHER PEOPLE FOOLS...
...ARE THEM-SELVES THE REAL FOOLS!!
KANG
IT LOOKS LIKE A WHIMPERING SPARROW HAS FALLEN OUT OF HER NEST.
GET HER!
HUH ...!
AAAAAHH-- !!
THWUMP

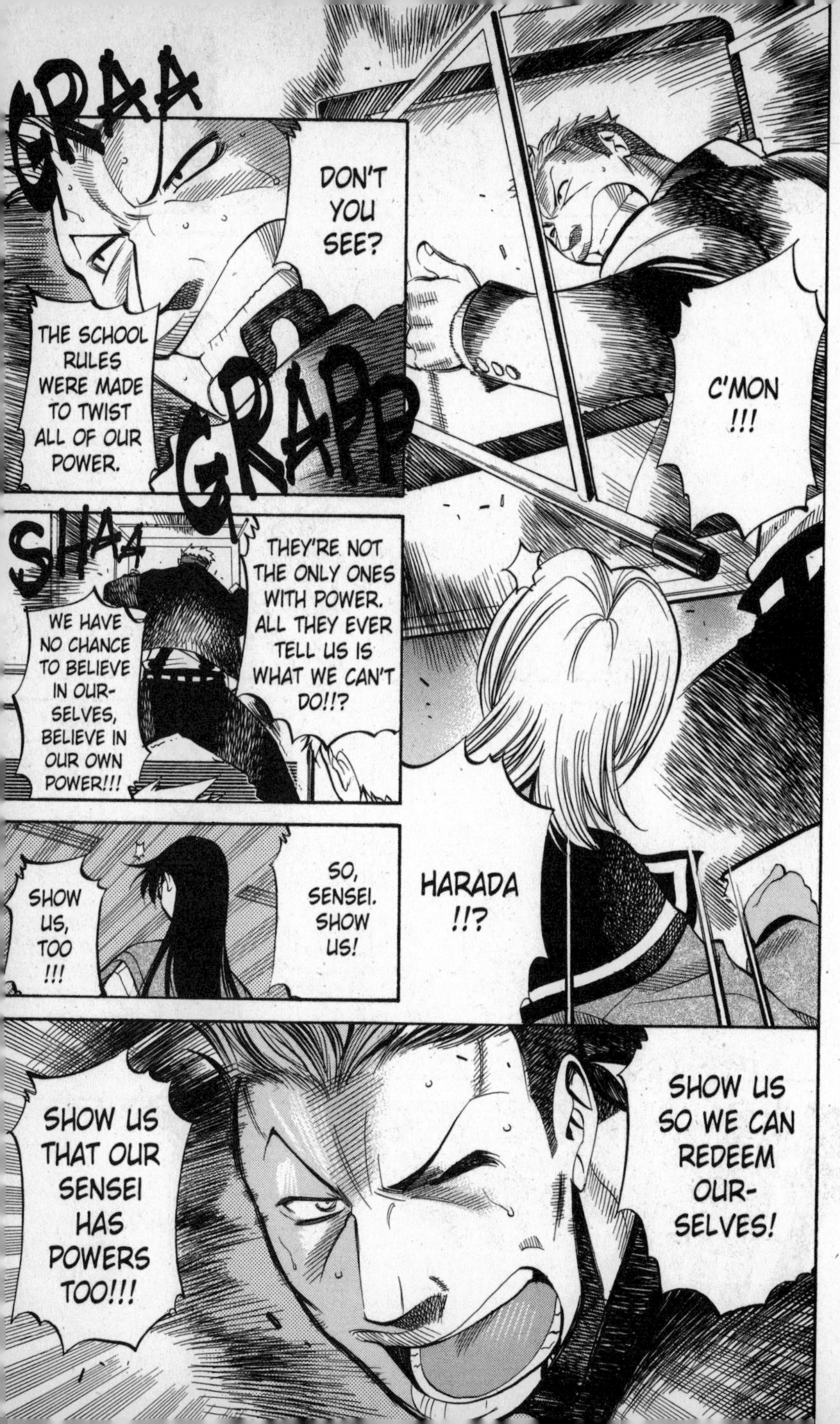
C'MON !!!
GRAA
DON'T YOU SEE?
THE SCHOOL RULES WERE MADE TO TWIST ALL OF OUR POWER.
GRAPP
HARADA !!?
SHAA
THEY'RE NOT THE ONLY ONES WITH POWER. ALL THEY EVER TELL US IS WHAT WE CAN'T DO!!?
WE HAVE NO CHANCE TO BELIEVE IN OURSELVES, BELIEVE IN OUR OWN POWER!!!
SO, SENSEI. SHOW US!
SHOW US, TOO !!!
SHOW US SO WE CAN REDEEM OURSELVES!
SHOW US THAT OUR SENSEI HAS POWERS TOO!!!

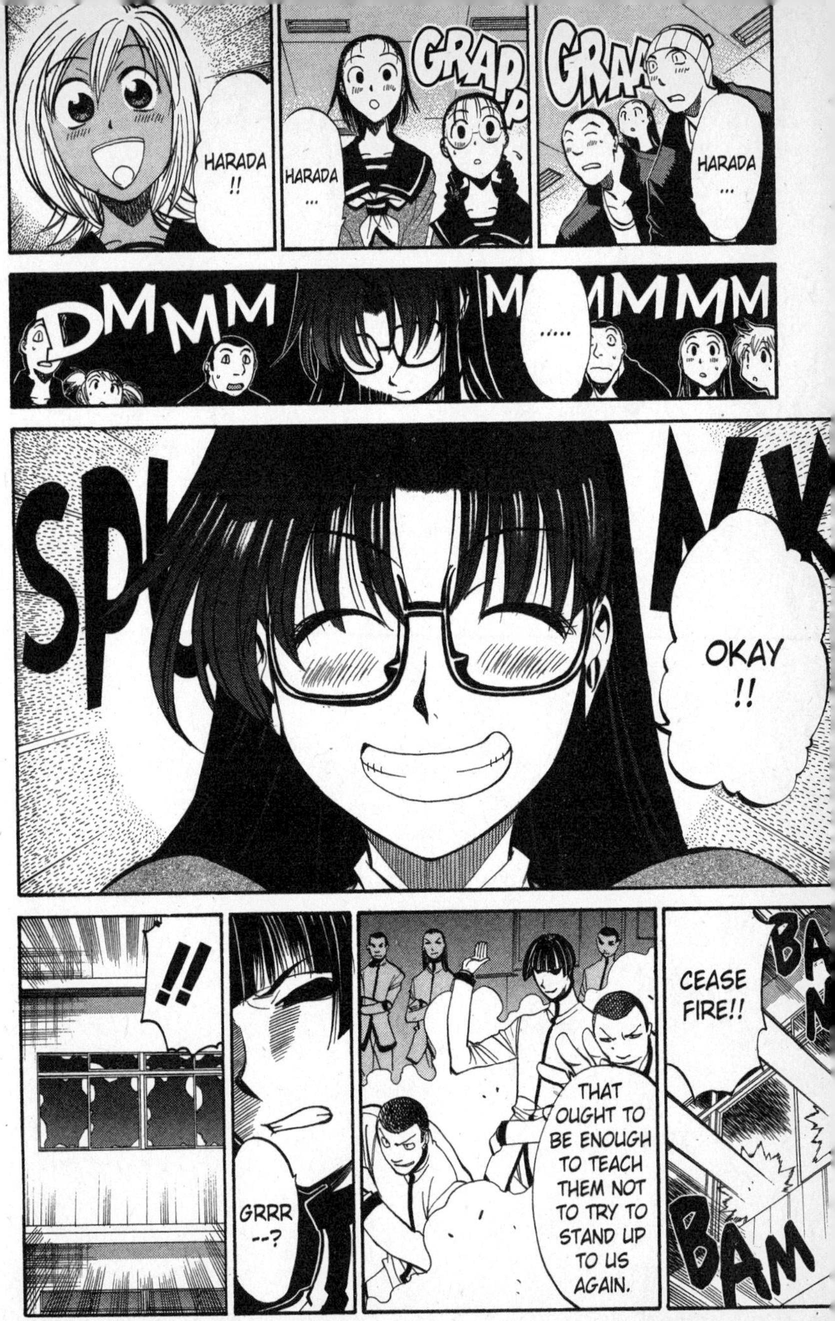
GRAA
HARADA ...
GRAPP
HARADA ...
HARADA !!
MMMMMM
.....
DMMM
OKAY !!
CEASE FIRE!!
BAM
THAT OUGHT TO BE ENOUGH TO TEACH THEM NOT TO TRY TO STAND UP TO US AGAIN.
GRRR --?
!!

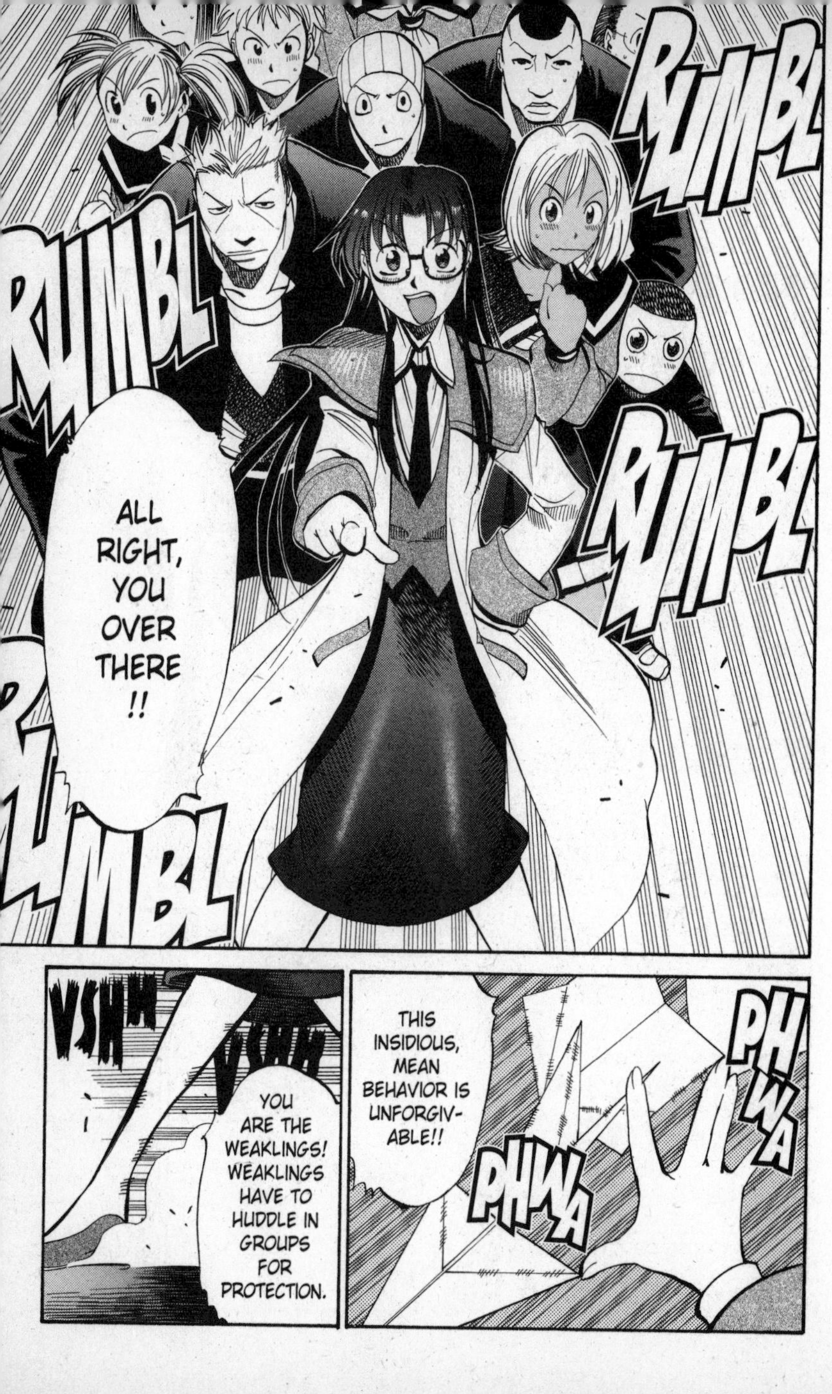
RUMBL
RUMBL
ALL RIGHT, YOU OVER THERE!!
RUMBL
RUMBL
PHWA
THIS INSIDIOUS, MEAN BEHAVIOR IS UNFORGIVABLE!!
PHWA
VSHN
VSHN
YOU ARE THE WEAKLINGS! WEAKLINGS HAVE TO HUDDLE IN GROUPS FOR PROTECTION.

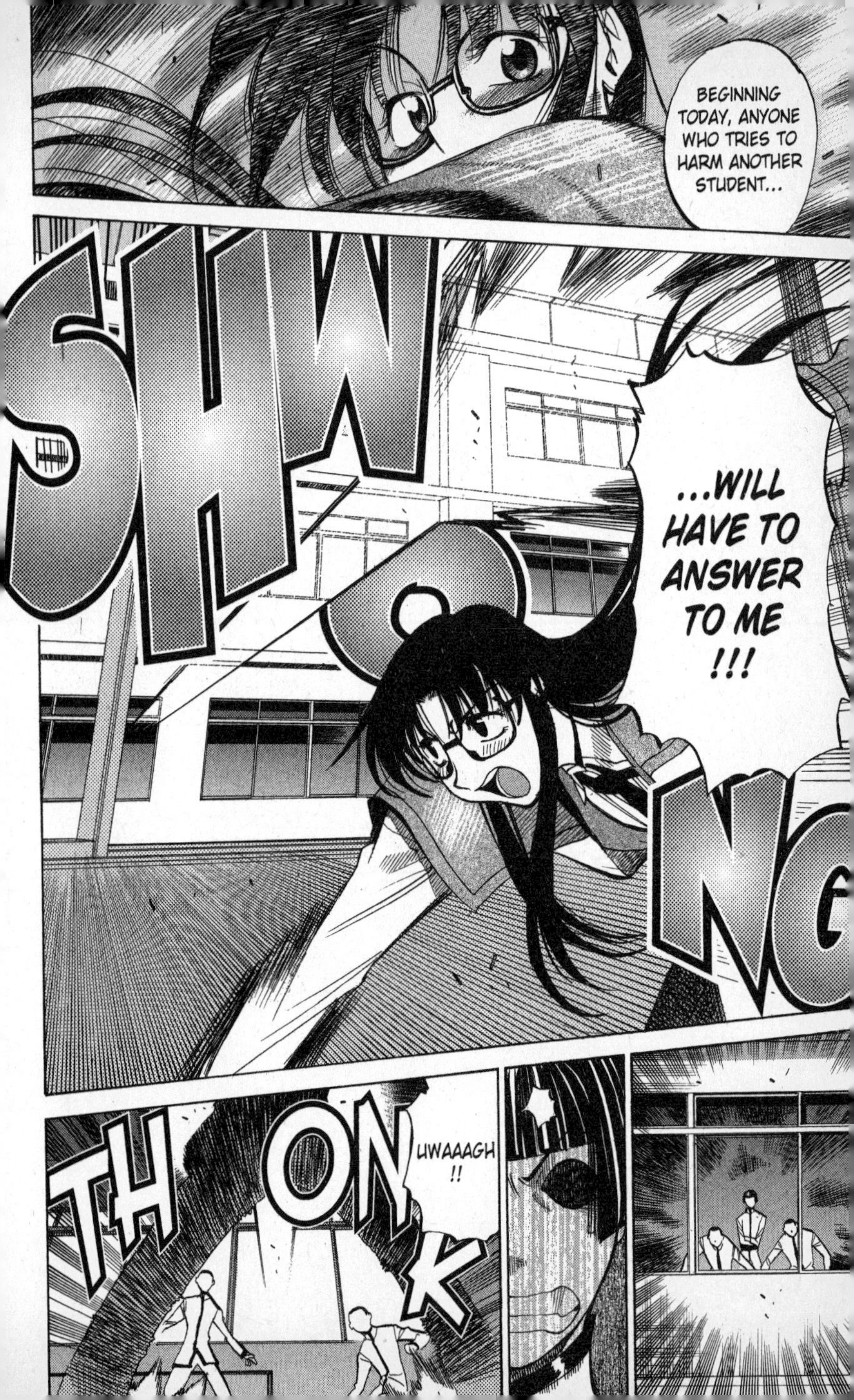
BEGINNING TODAY, ANYONE WHO TRIES TO HARM ANOTHER STUDENT...
SHWING
...WILL HAVE TO ANSWER TO ME !!!
UWAAAGH !!
THONK

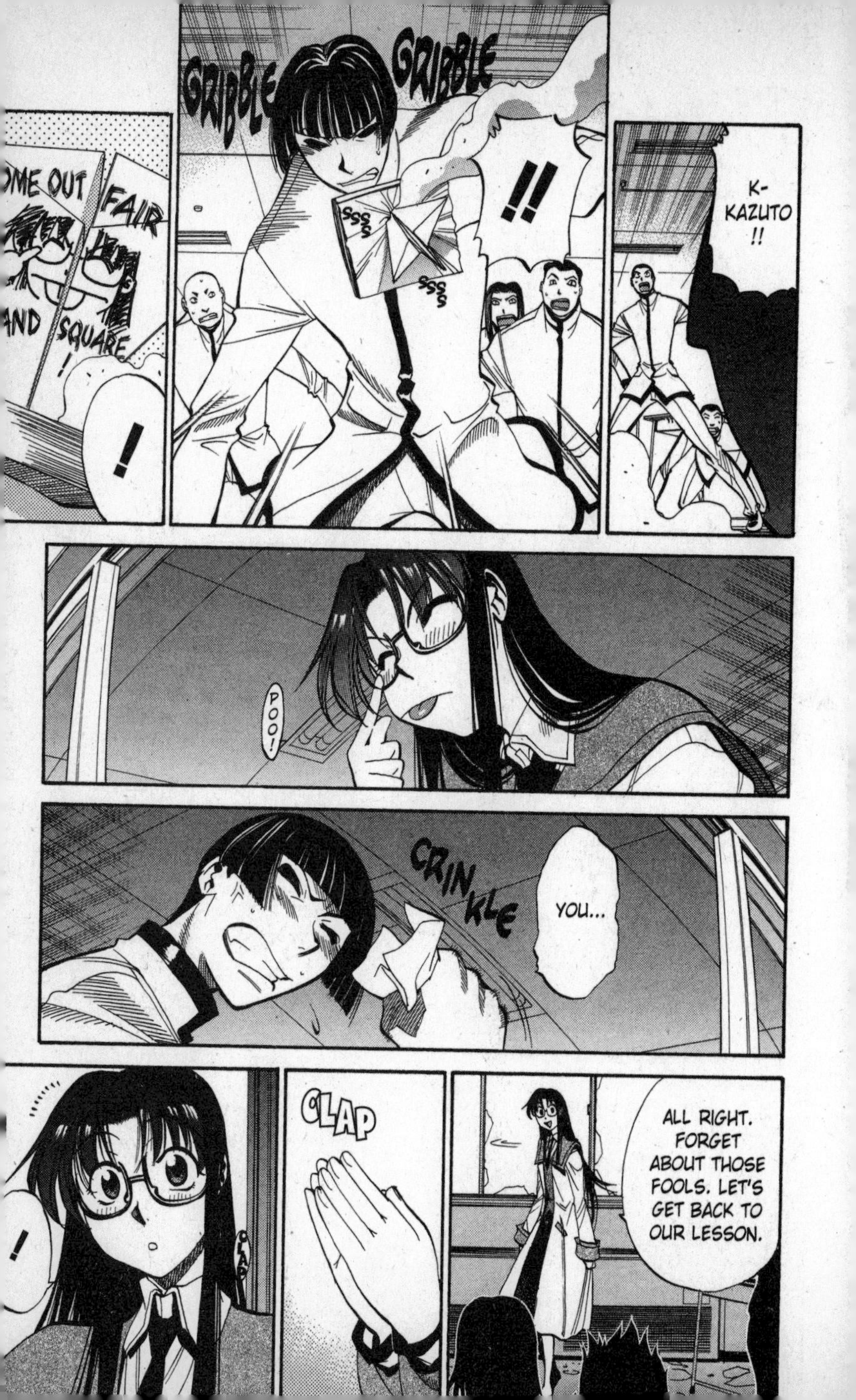
K-KAZUTO !!
GRIBBLE GRIBBLE
!!
SSSS
SSSS
!
OME OUT FAIR AND SQUARE !
POO!
CRINKLE
YOU...
ALL RIGHT. FORGET ABOUT THOSE FOOLS. LET'S GET BACK TO OUR LESSON.
CLAP
!
CLAP

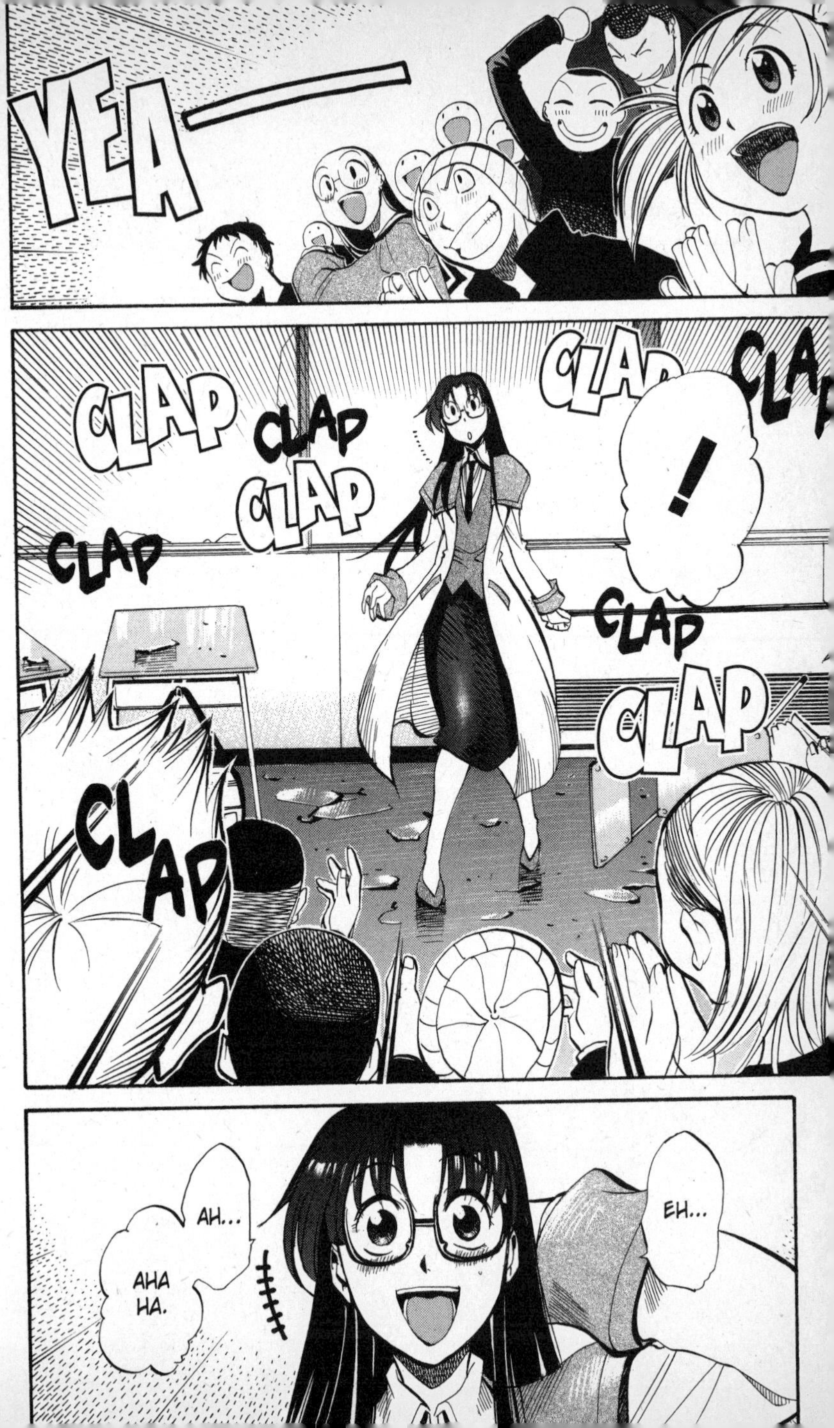
YEA—
CLAP
CLAP
!
CLAP
CLAP
CLAP
CLAP
CLAP
CLAP
CLAP
EH...
AH...
AHA HA.

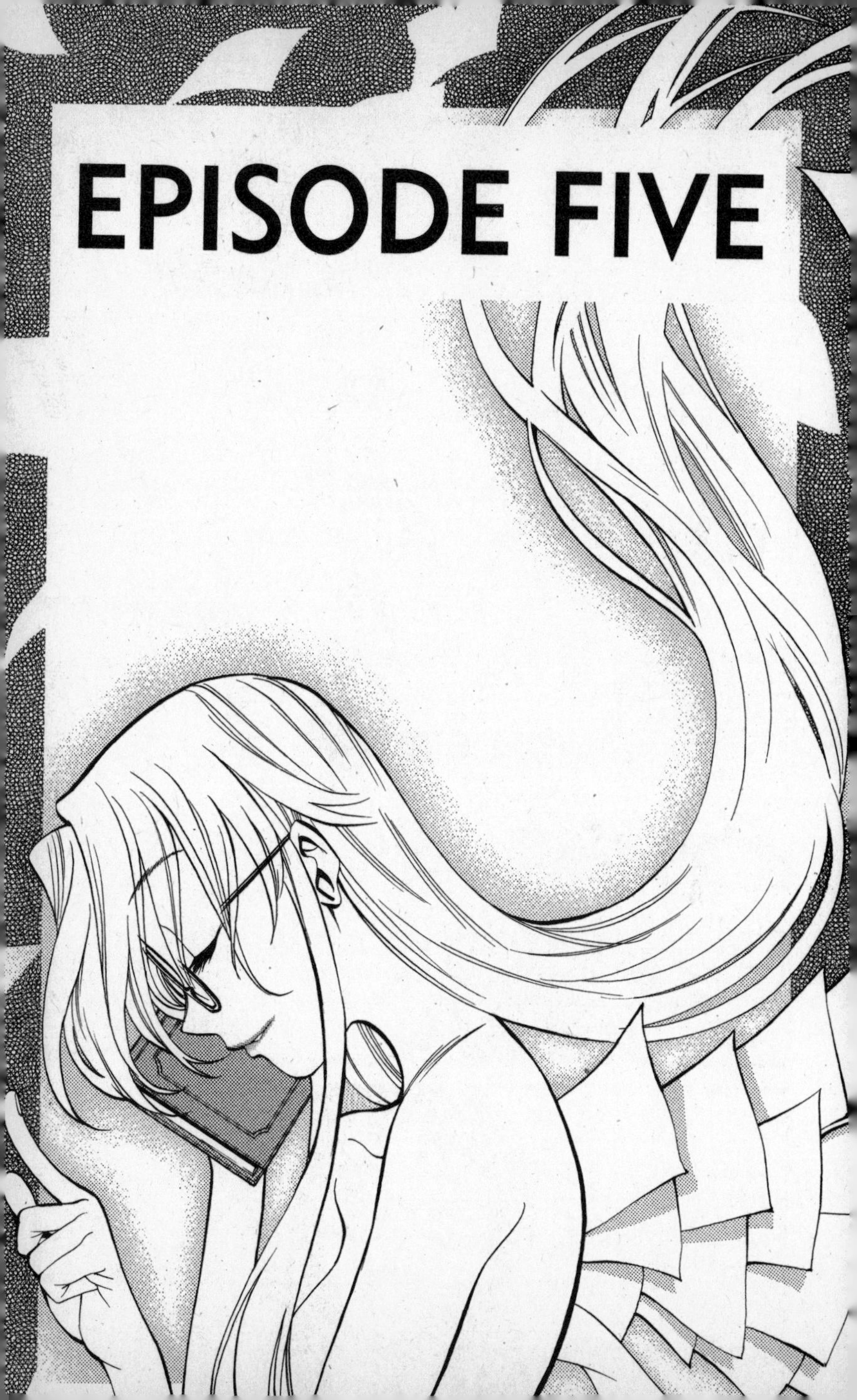
EPISODE FIVE

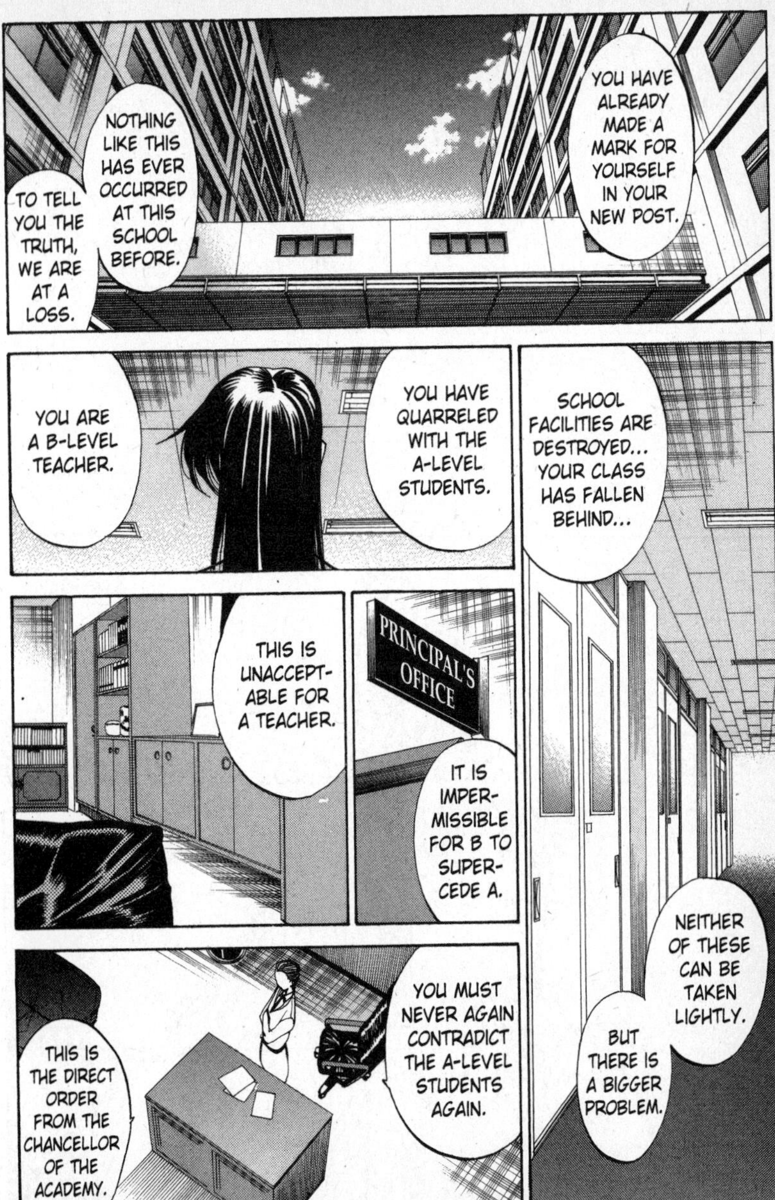
YOU HAVE ALREADY MADE A MARK FOR YOURSELF IN YOUR NEW POST.
NOTHING LIKE THIS HAS EVER OCCURRED AT THIS SCHOOL BEFORE.
TO TELL YOU THE TRUTH, WE ARE AT A LOSS.
SCHOOL FACILITIES ARE DESTROYED... YOUR CLASS HAS FALLEN BEHIND...
NEITHER OF THESE CAN BE TAKEN LIGHTLY.
BUT THERE IS A BIGGER PROBLEM.
YOU HAVE QUARRELED WITH THE A-LEVEL STUDENTS.
YOU ARE A B-LEVEL TEACHER.
PRINCIPAL'S OFFICE
IT IS IMPERMISSIBLE FOR B TO SUPERCEDE A.
THIS IS UNACCEPTABLE FOR A TEACHER.
YOU MUST NEVER AGAIN CONTRADICT THE A-LEVEL STUDENTS AGAIN.
THIS IS THE DIRECT ORDER FROM THE CHANCELLOR OF THE ACADEMY.

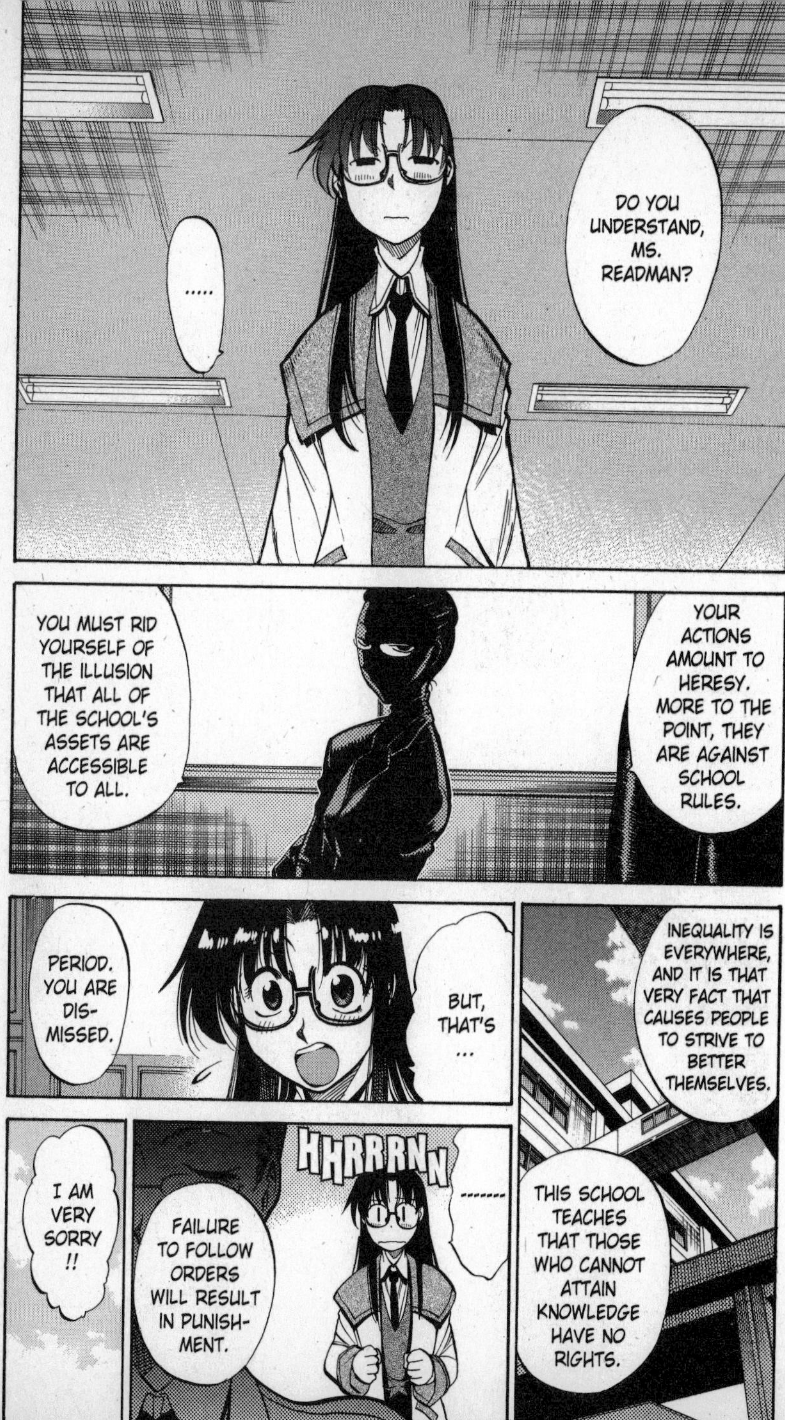
DO YOU UNDERSTAND, MS. READMAN?
.....
YOUR ACTIONS AMOUNT TO HERESY. MORE TO THE POINT, THEY ARE AGAINST SCHOOL RULES.
YOU MUST RID YOURSELF OF THE ILLUSION THAT ALL OF THE SCHOOL'S ASSETS ARE ACCESSIBLE TO ALL.
INEQUALITY IS EVERYWHERE, AND IT IS THAT VERY FACT THAT CAUSES PEOPLE TO STRIVE TO BETTER THEMSELVES.
THIS SCHOOL TEACHES THAT THOSE WHO CANNOT ATTAIN KNOWLEDGE HAVE NO RIGHTS.
BUT, THAT'S ...
PERIOD. YOU ARE DIS-MISSED.
HHRRRNN

FAILURE TO FOLLOW ORDERS WILL RESULT IN PUNISH-MENT.
I AM VERY SORRY !!

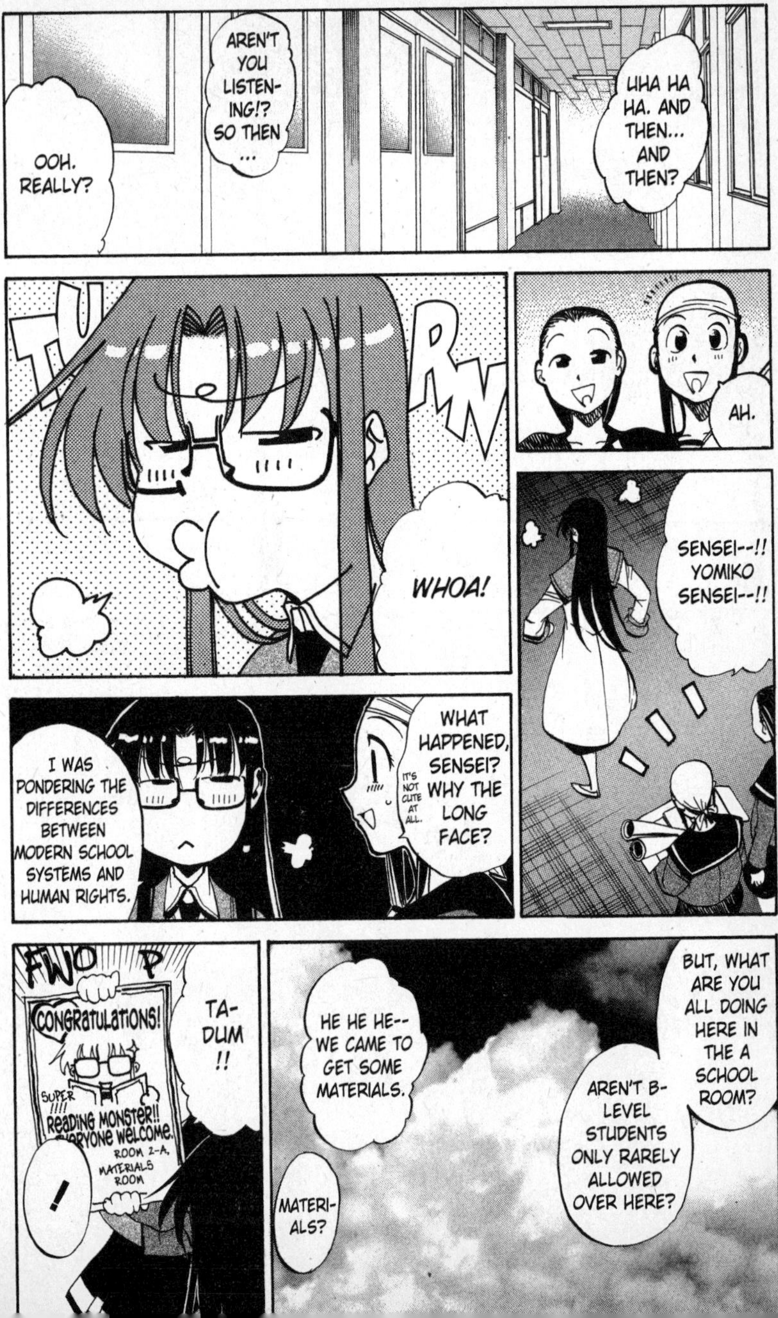
UHA HA HA. AND THEN... AND THEN?
AREN'T YOU LISTEN-ING!? SO THEN ...
OOH. REALLY?
AH.
TURN
WHOA!
SENSEI--!! YOMIKO SENSEI--!!
WHAT HAPPENED, SENSEI? WHY THE LONG FACE?
IT'S NOT CUTE AT ALL.
I WAS PONDERING THE DIFFERENCES BETWEEN MODERN SCHOOL SYSTEMS AND HUMAN RIGHTS.
BUT, WHAT ARE YOU ALL DOING HERE IN THE A SCHOOL ROOM?
AREN'T B-LEVEL STUDENTS ONLY RARELY ALLOWED OVER HERE?
HE HE HE-- WE CAME TO GET SOME MATERIALS.
MATERI-ALS?
FWOP
TA-DUM !!
CONGRATULATIONS!
SUPER !!!!
READING MONSTER!!
EVERYONE WELCOME.
ROOM 2-A, MATERIALS ROOM
!

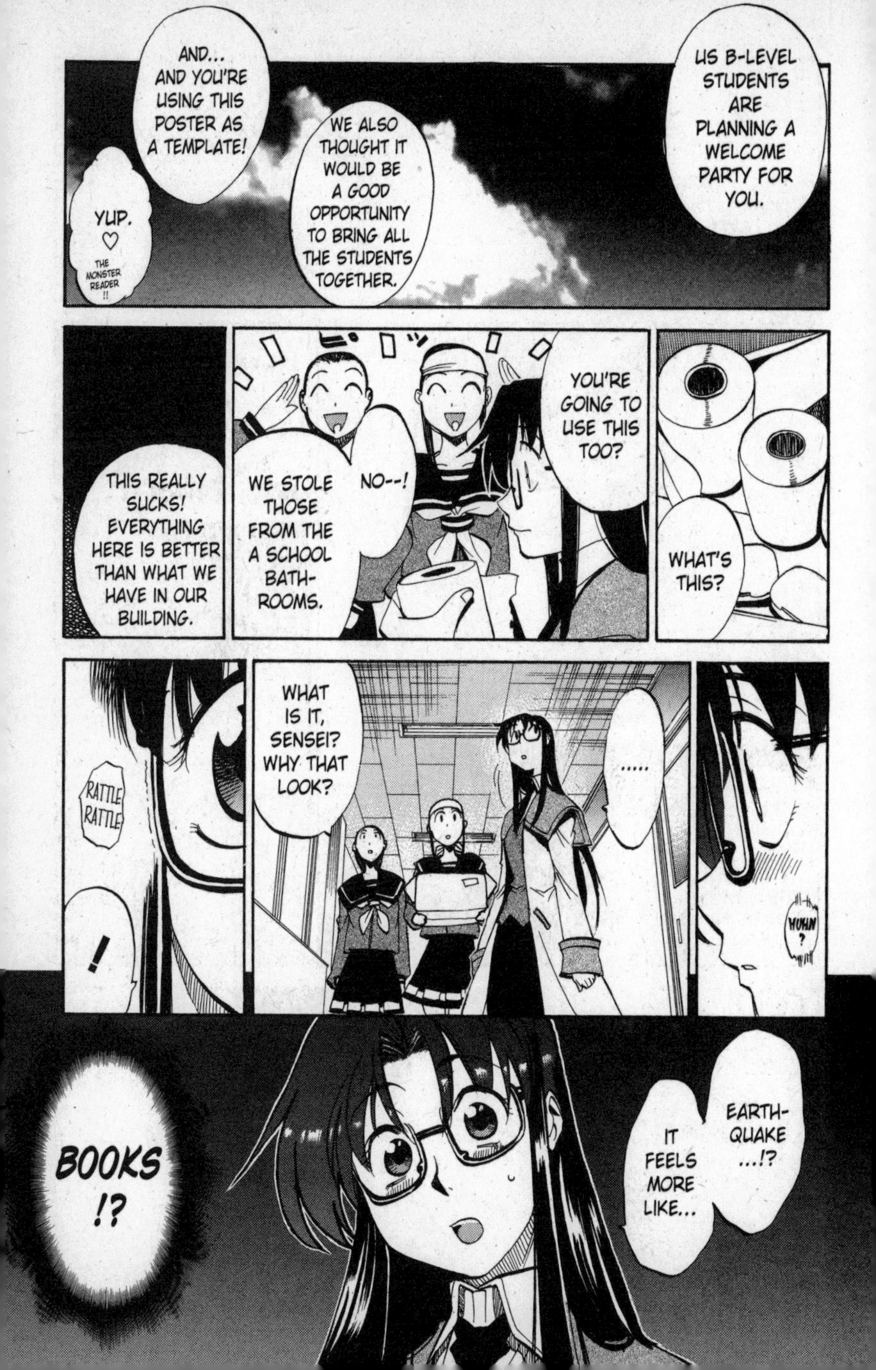

US B-LEVEL STUDENTS ARE PLANNING A WELCOME PARTY FOR YOU.
WE ALSO THOUGHT IT WOULD BE A GOOD OPPORTUNITY TO BRING ALL THE STUDENTS TOGETHER.
AND... AND YOU'RE USING THIS POSTER AS A TEMPLATE!
YUP. ♡
THE MONSTER READER !!
WHAT'S THIS?
YOU'RE GOING TO USE THIS TOO?
NO--!
WE STOLE THOSE FROM THE A SCHOOL BATH-ROOMS.
THIS REALLY SUCKS! EVERYTHING HERE IS BETTER THAN WHAT WE HAVE IN OUR BUILDING.
WUHN ?
.....
WHAT IS IT, SENSEI? WHY THAT LOOK?
RATTLE RATTLE
!
EARTH-QUAKE ...!?
IT FEELS MORE LIKE...
BOOKS !?

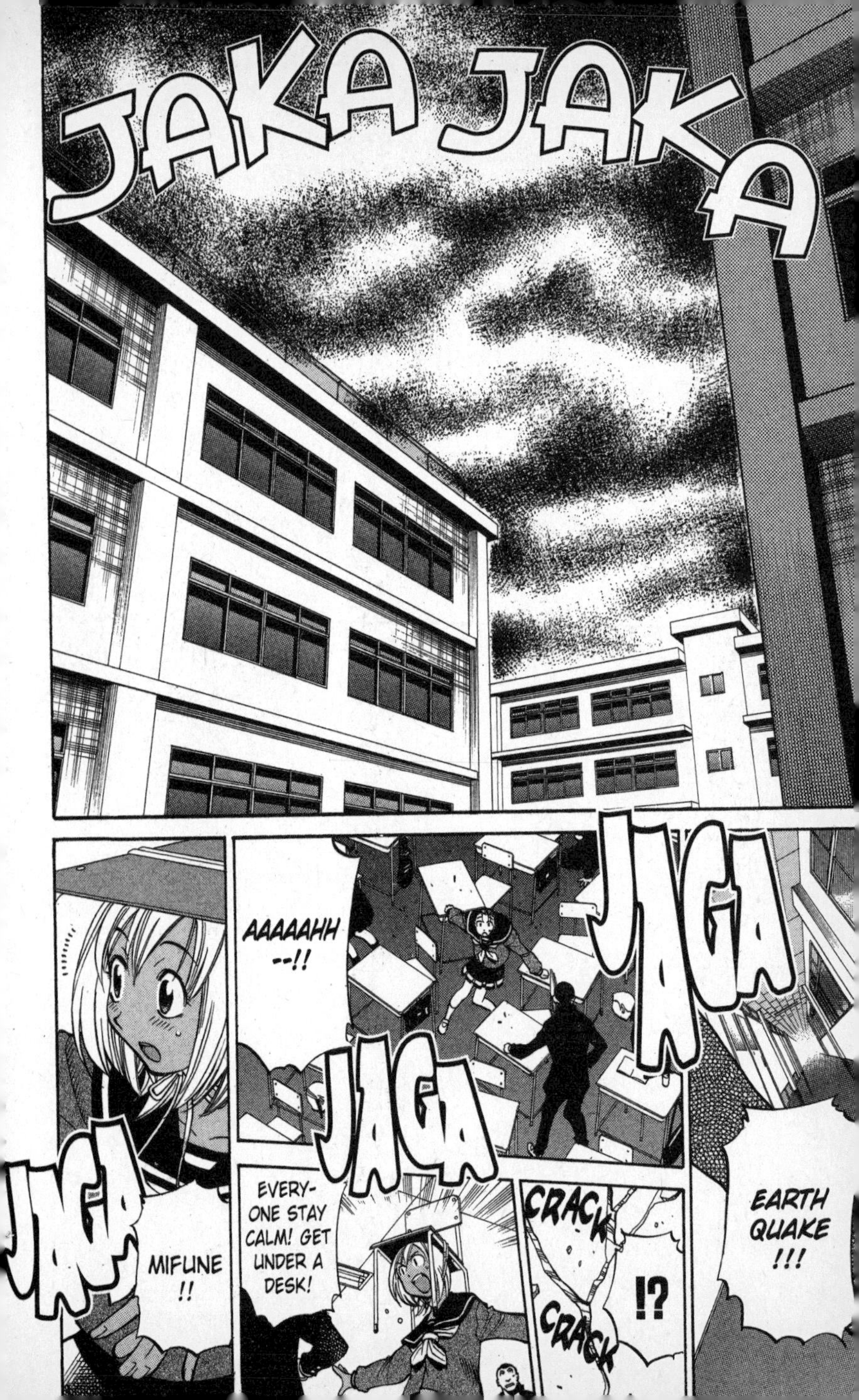
JAKA JAKA
JAGA
AAAAAHH--!!
JAGA
EARTH QUAKE!!!
CRACK
!?
CRACK
EVERY-ONE STAY CALM! GET UNDER A DESK!
MIFUNE!!
JAGA

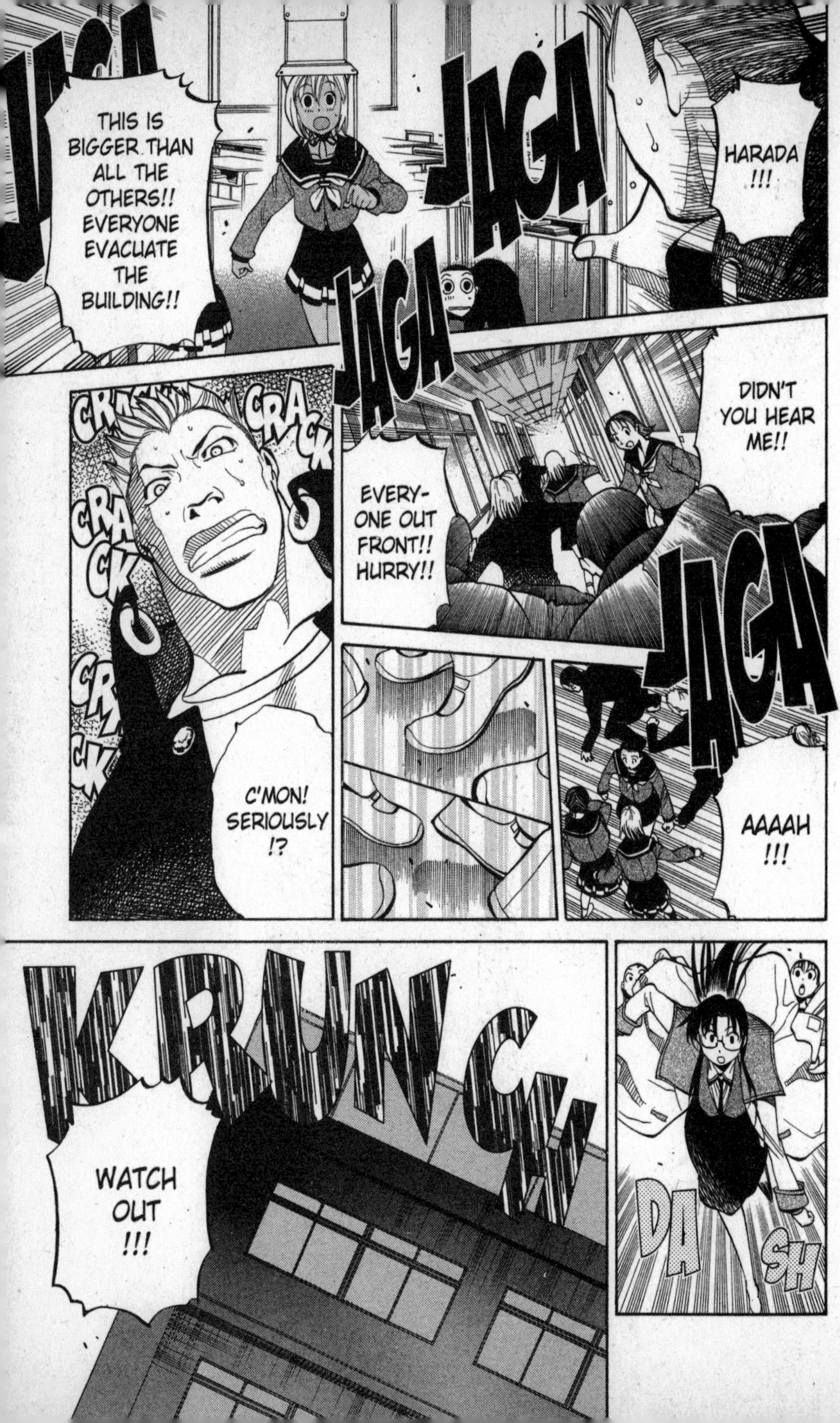
HARADA!!!
JAGA
JAGA
JAGA
THIS IS BIGGER THAN ALL THE OTHERS!! EVERYONE EVACUATE THE BUILDING!!
JAGA
DIDN'T YOU HEAR ME!!
EVERY-ONE OUT FRONT!! HURRY!!
JAGA
AAAAH!!!
CRACK
CRACK
CRACK
CRACK
C'MON! SERIOUSLY!?
DASH
KRUNCH
WATCH OUT!!!

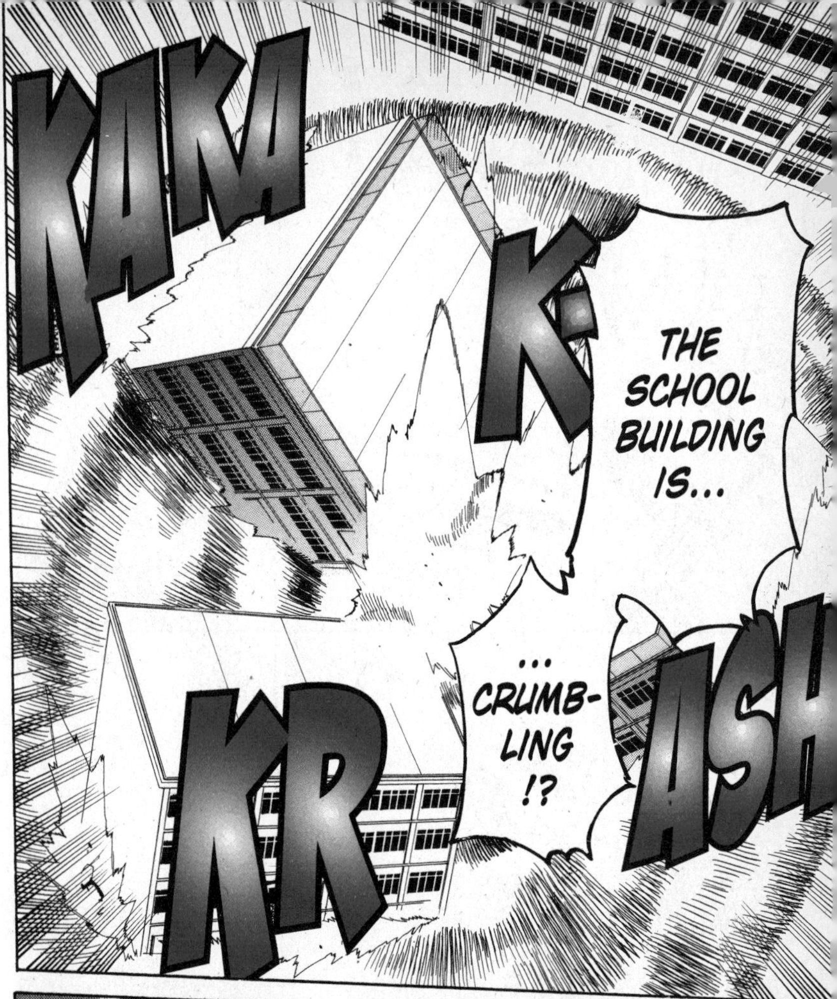
THE SCHOOL BUILDING IS...
... CRÜMB-LING !?
KAKA
K-
KR
ASH

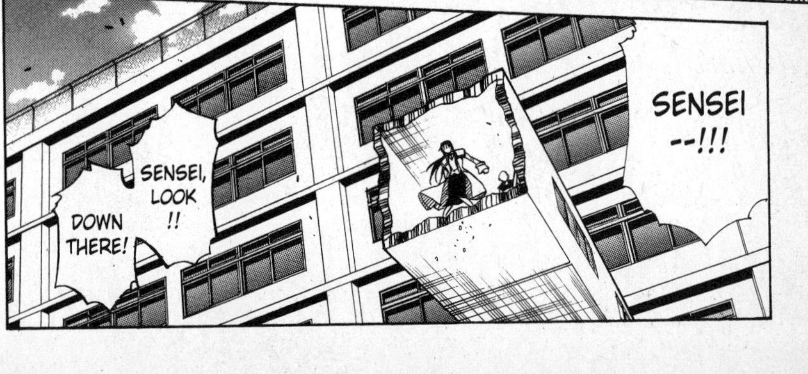
SENSEI --!!!
SENSEI, LOOK !!
DOWN THERE!

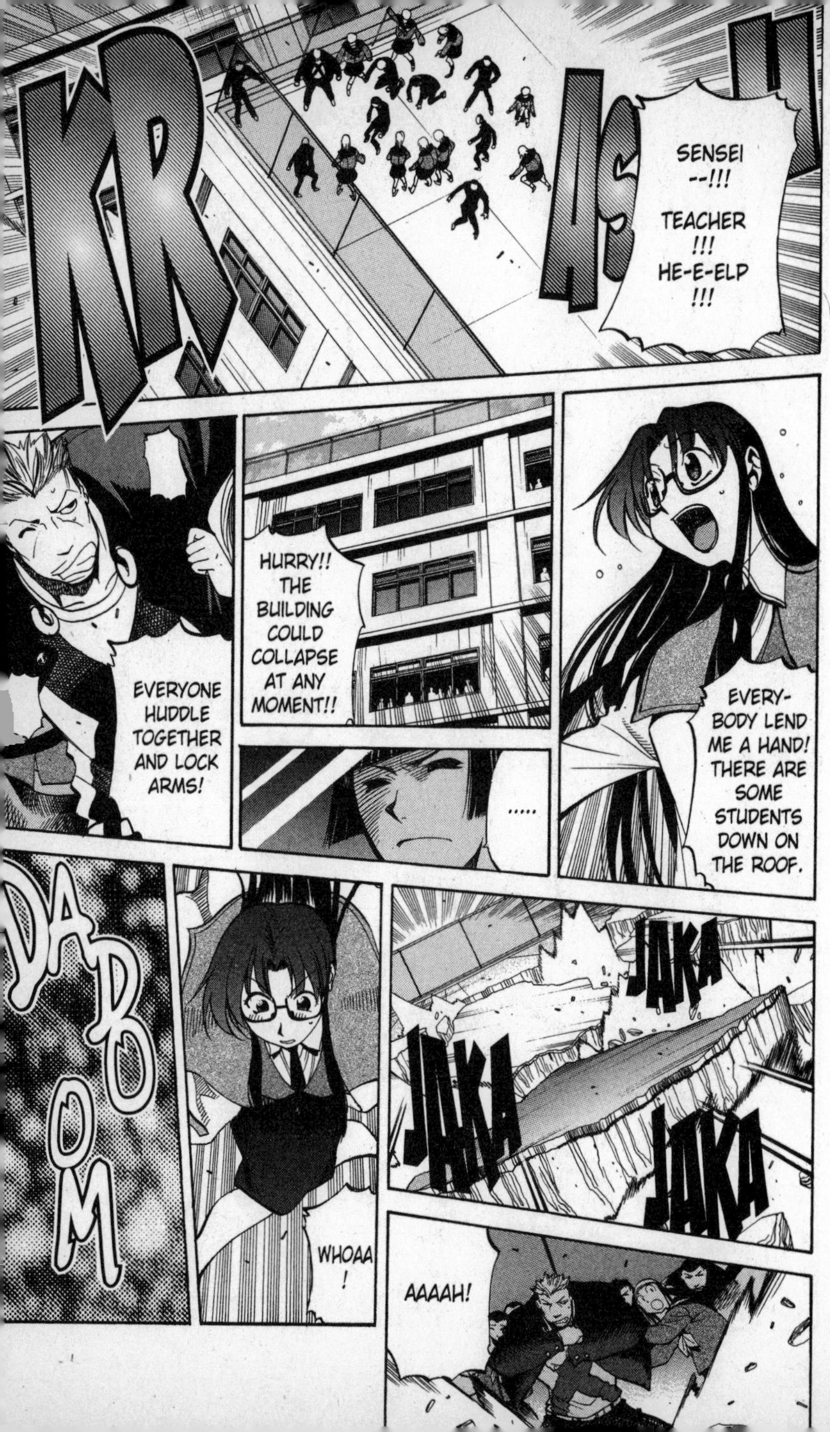
KRASH
SENSEI --!!! TEACHER !!! HE-E-ELP !!!
EVERY-BODY LEND ME A HAND! THERE ARE SOME STUDENTS DOWN ON THE ROOF.
HURRY!! THE BUILDING COULD COLLAPSE AT ANY MOMENT!!
.....
EVERYONE HUDDLE TOGETHER AND LOCK ARMS!
JAKA
JAKA
JAKA
AAAAH!
WHOAA !
DABOOM

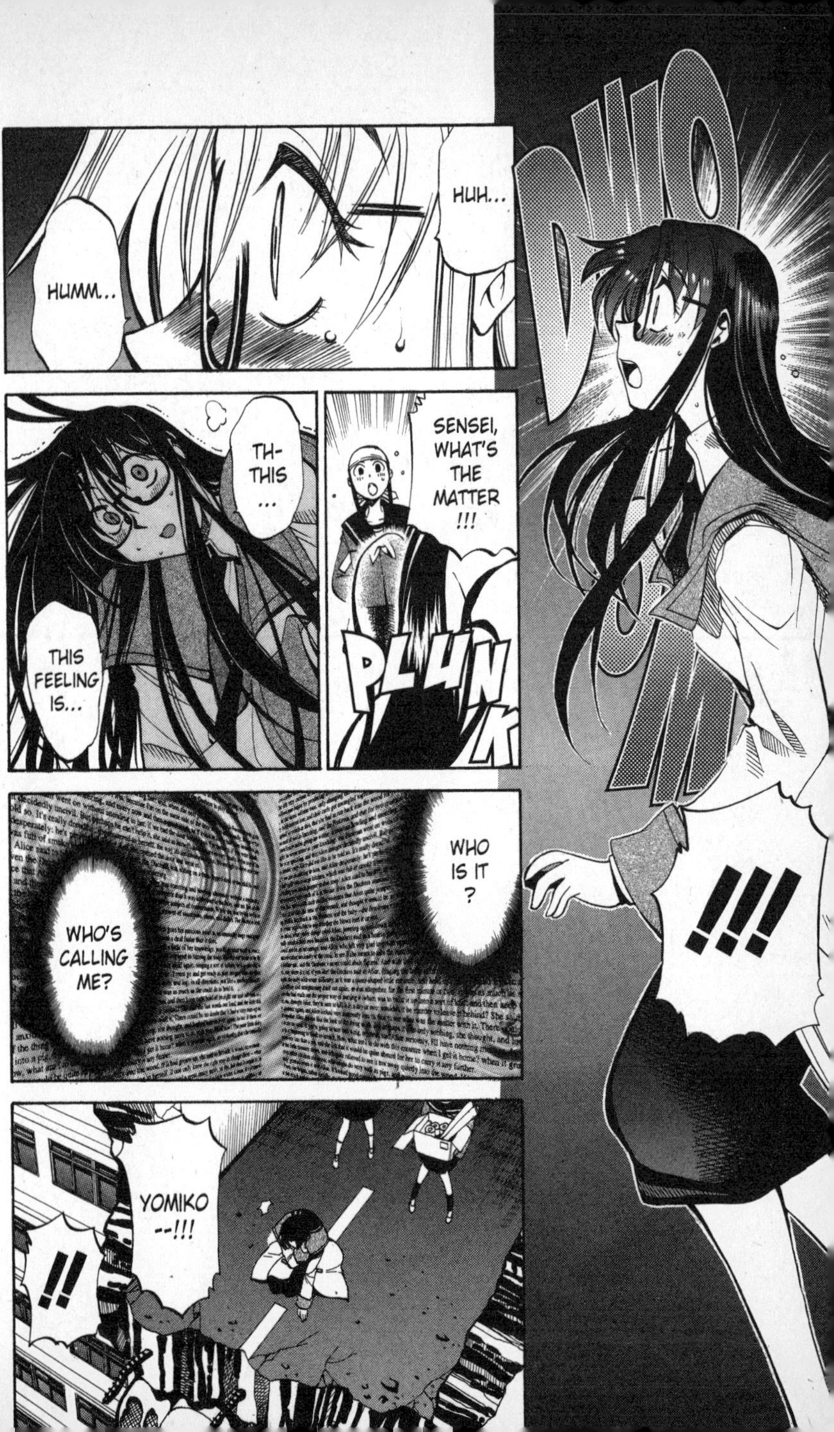
!!!
HUH...
HUMM...
SENSEI, WHAT'S THE MATTER !!!
PLUNK
TH- THIS ...
THIS FEELING IS...
WHO IS IT ?
WHO'S CALLING ME?
YOMIKO --!!!
!!

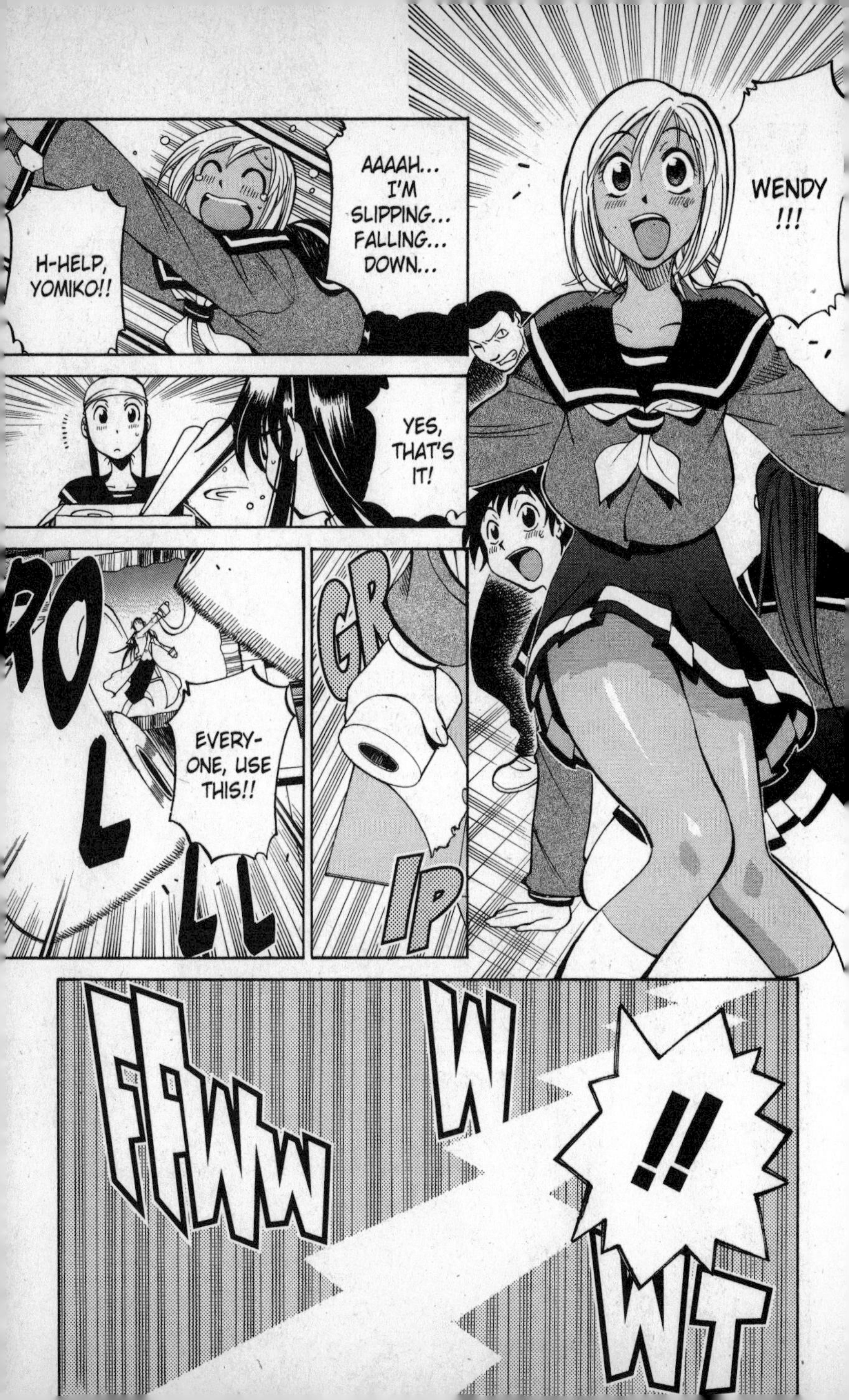
WENDY !!!
AAAAH... I'M SLIPPING... FALLING... DOWN...
H-HELP, YOMIKO!!
YES, THAT'S IT!
GR IP
EVERY-ONE, USE THIS!!
ROLL L L
FFWW
W
!!
WT

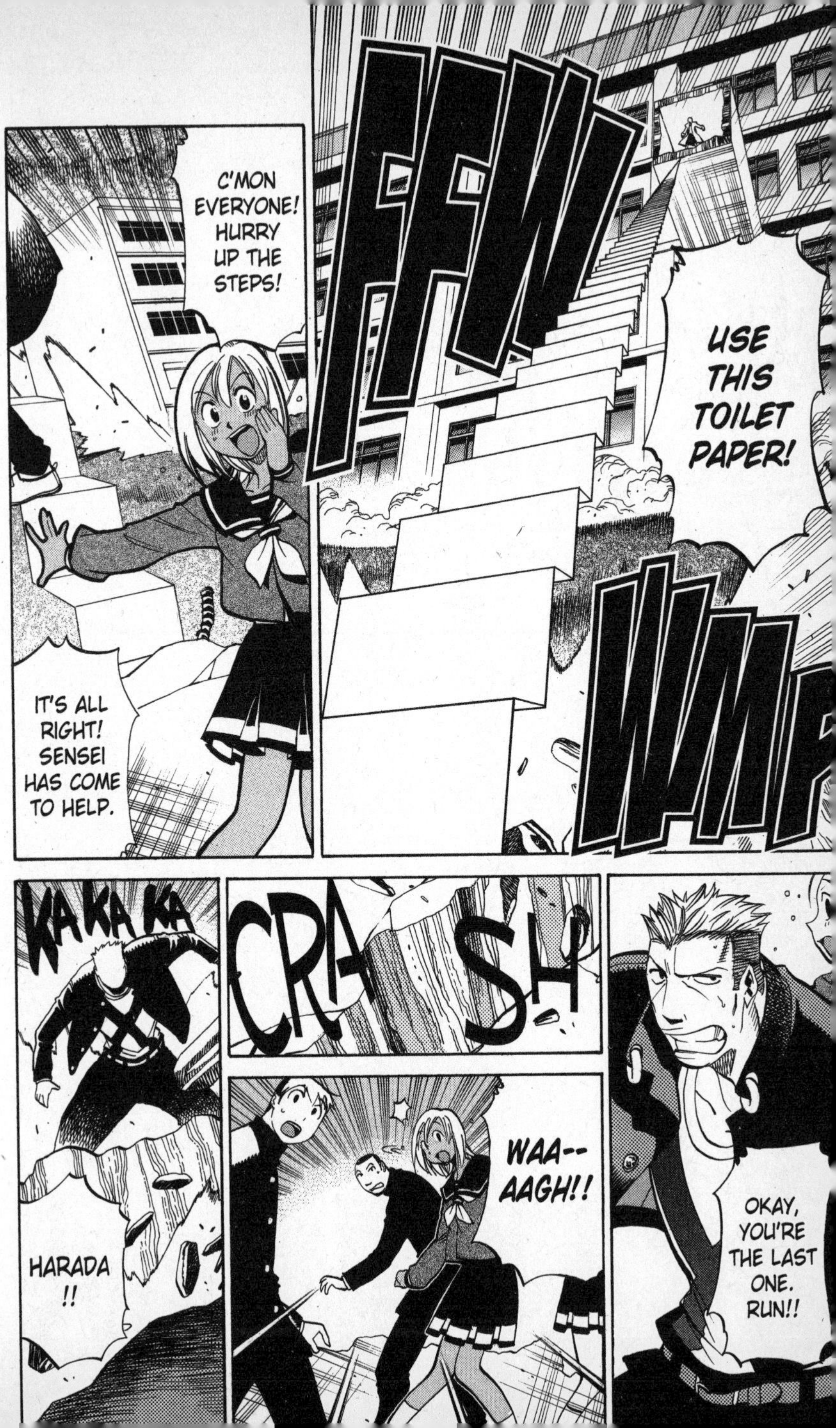
USE THIS TOILET PAPER!
C'MON EVERYONE! HURRY UP THE STEPS!
IT'S ALL RIGHT! SENSEI HAS COME TO HELP.
OKAY, YOU'RE THE LAST ONE. RUN!!
CRASH
WAA-- AAGH!!
KA KA KA
HARADA !!

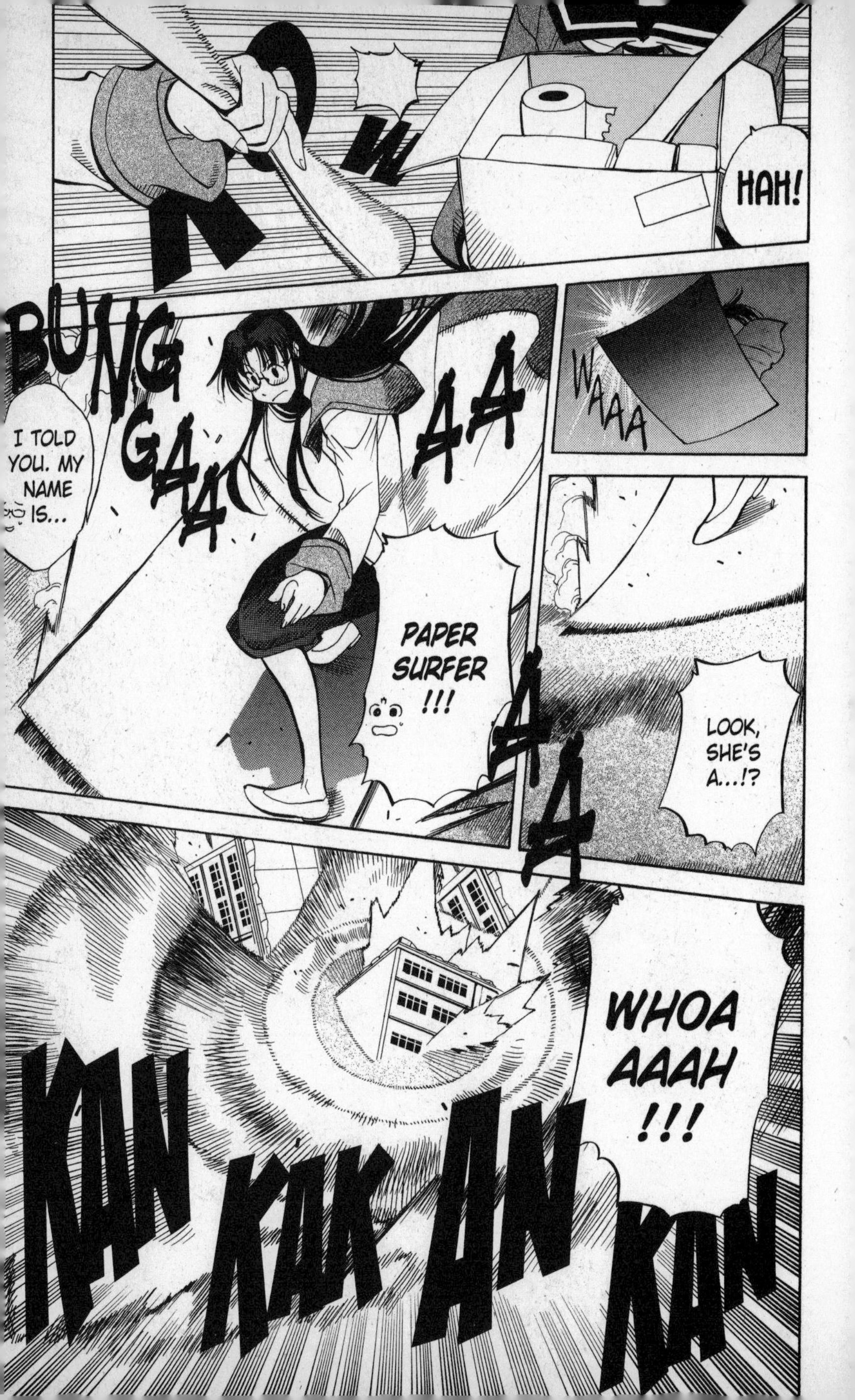
HAH!
WAAAA
LOOK, SHE'S A...!?
BUNG GA44
44
44
I TOLD YOU. MY NAME IS...
PAPER SURFER!!!
WHOA AAAH!!!
KAN KAK AN KAN

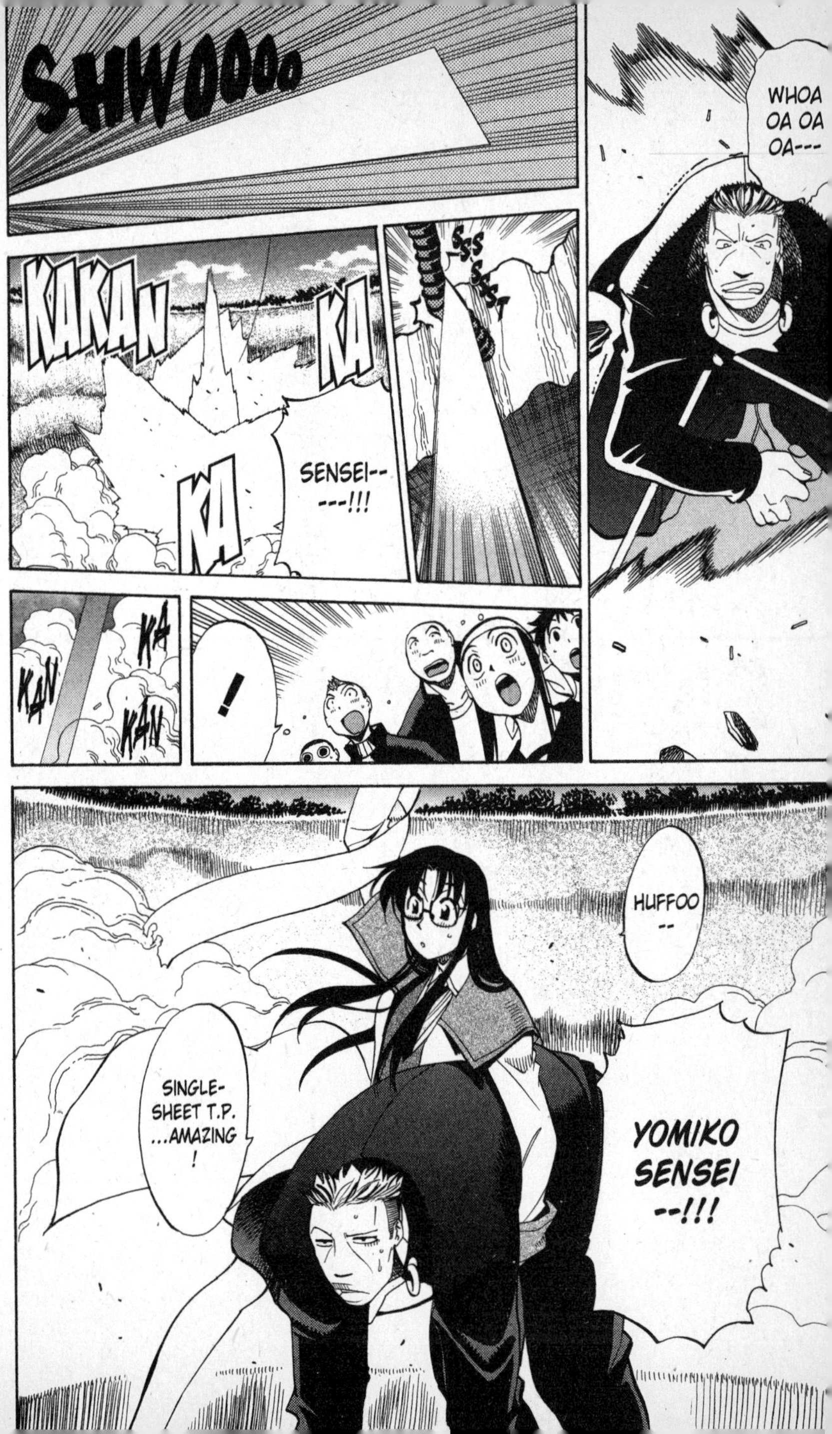
WHOA OA OA OA---
SHWOOOO
SSS SSSS
KAKAN KA
SENSEI-----!!!
KA
!
KA
KAN
KAN
HUFFOO --
YOMIKO SENSEI --!!!
SINGLE-SHEET T.P. ...AMAZING!

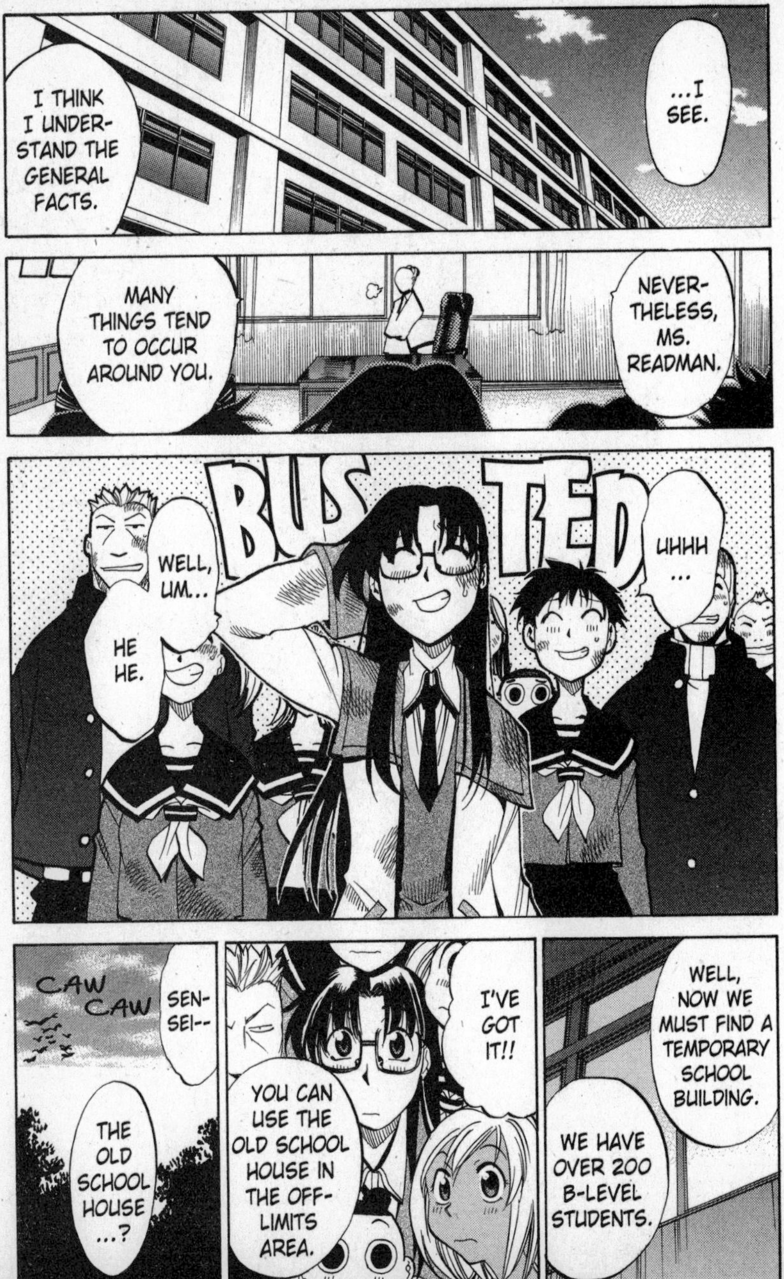
...I SEE.
I THINK I UNDERSTAND THE GENERAL FACTS.
NEVERTHELESS, MS. READMAN.
MANY THINGS TEND TO OCCUR AROUND YOU.
BUSTED
UHHH...
WELL, UM...
HE HE.
WELL, NOW WE MUST FIND A TEMPORARY SCHOOL BUILDING.
WE HAVE OVER 200 B-LEVEL STUDENTS.
I'VE GOT IT!!
YOU CAN USE THE OLD SCHOOL HOUSE IN THE OFF-LIMITS AREA.
CAW CAW
SEN-SEI--
THE OLD SCHOOL HOUSE...?

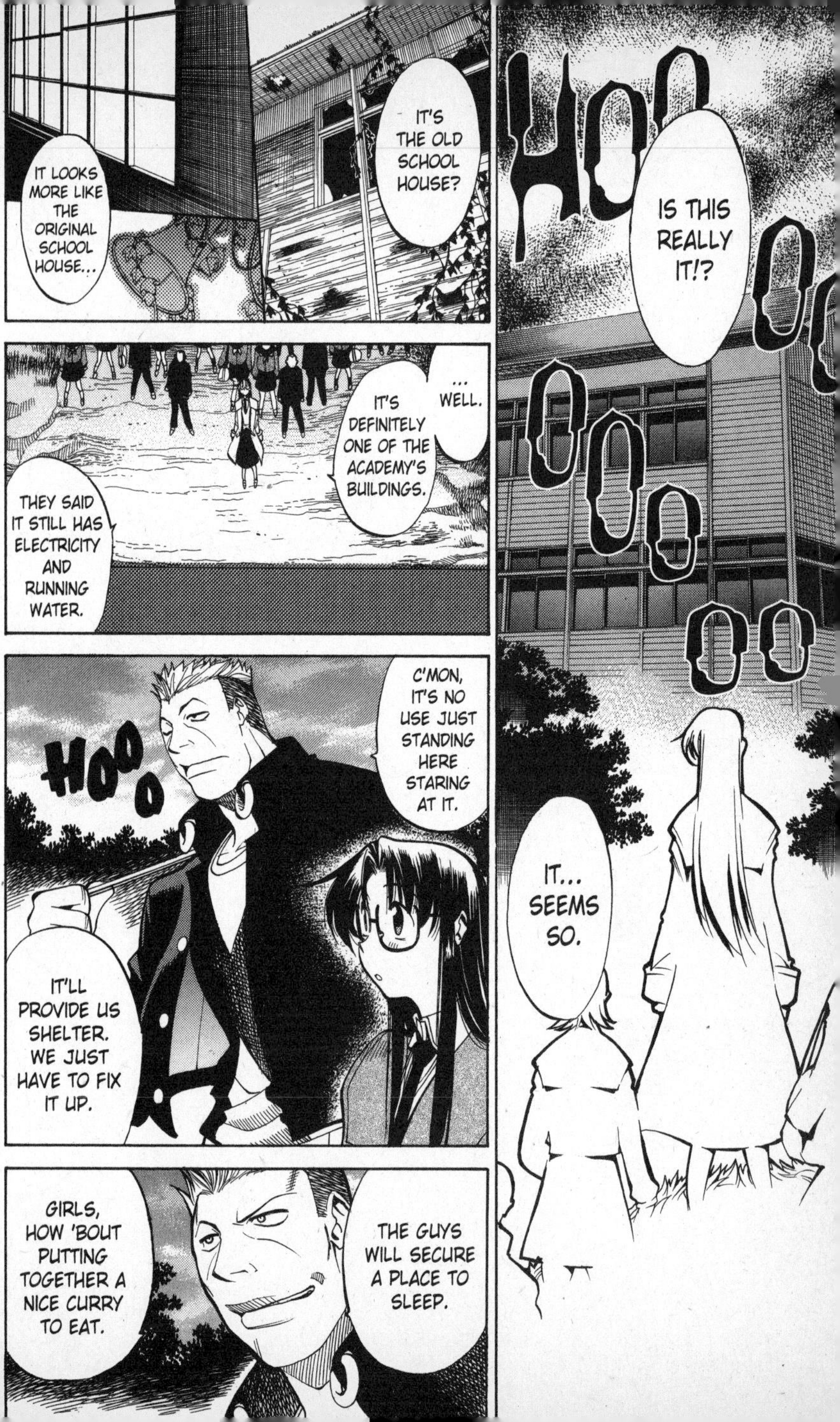
HOOOOOOOOOO
IS THIS REALLY IT!?
IT... SEEMS SO.
IT'S THE OLD SCHOOL HOUSE?
IT LOOKS MORE LIKE THE ORIGINAL SCHOOL HOUSE...
... WELL.
IT'S DEFINITELY ONE OF THE ACADEMY'S BUILDINGS.
THEY SAID IT STILL HAS ELECTRICITY AND RUNNING WATER.
C'MON, IT'S NO USE JUST STANDING HERE STARING AT IT.
HOOO
IT'LL PROVIDE US SHELTER. WE JUST HAVE TO FIX IT UP.
THE GUYS WILL SECURE A PLACE TO SLEEP.
GIRLS, HOW 'BOUT PUTTING TOGETHER A NICE CURRY TO EAT.

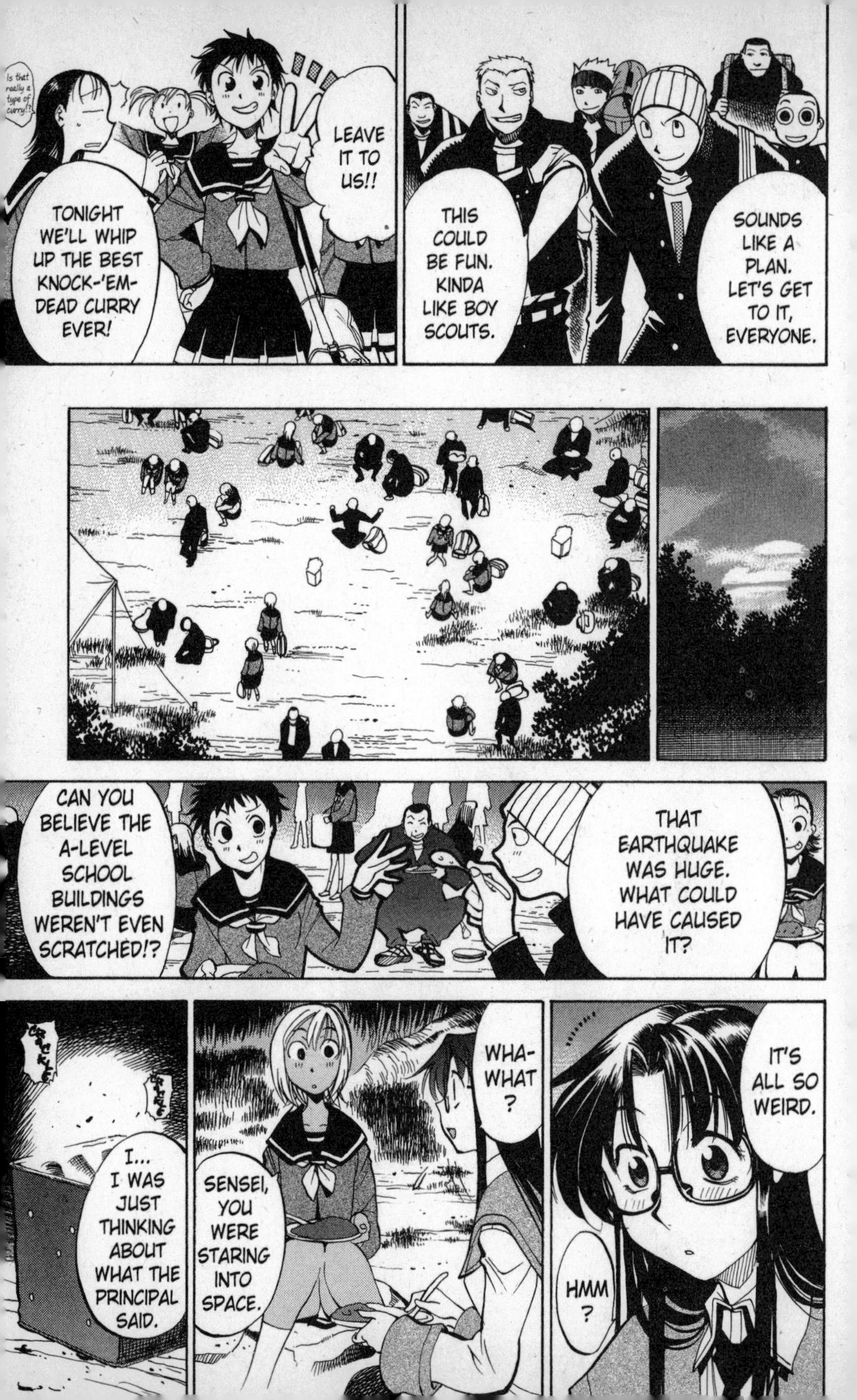
SOUNDS LIKE A PLAN. LET'S GET TO IT, EVERYONE.
THIS COULD BE FUN. KINDA LIKE BOY SCOUTS.
TONIGHT WE'LL WHIP UP THE BEST KNOCK-'EM-DEAD CURRY EVER!
LEAVE IT TO US!!
Is that really a type of curry!?
THAT EARTHQUAKE WAS HUGE. WHAT COULD HAVE CAUSED IT?
CAN YOU BELIEVE THE A-LEVEL SCHOOL BUILDINGS WEREN'T EVEN SCRATCHED!?
IT'S ALL SO WEIRD.
HMM?
SENSEI, YOU WERE STARING INTO SPACE.
WHA-WHAT?
CRACKLE
CRACKLE
I... I WAS JUST THINKING ABOUT WHAT THE PRINCIPAL SAID.

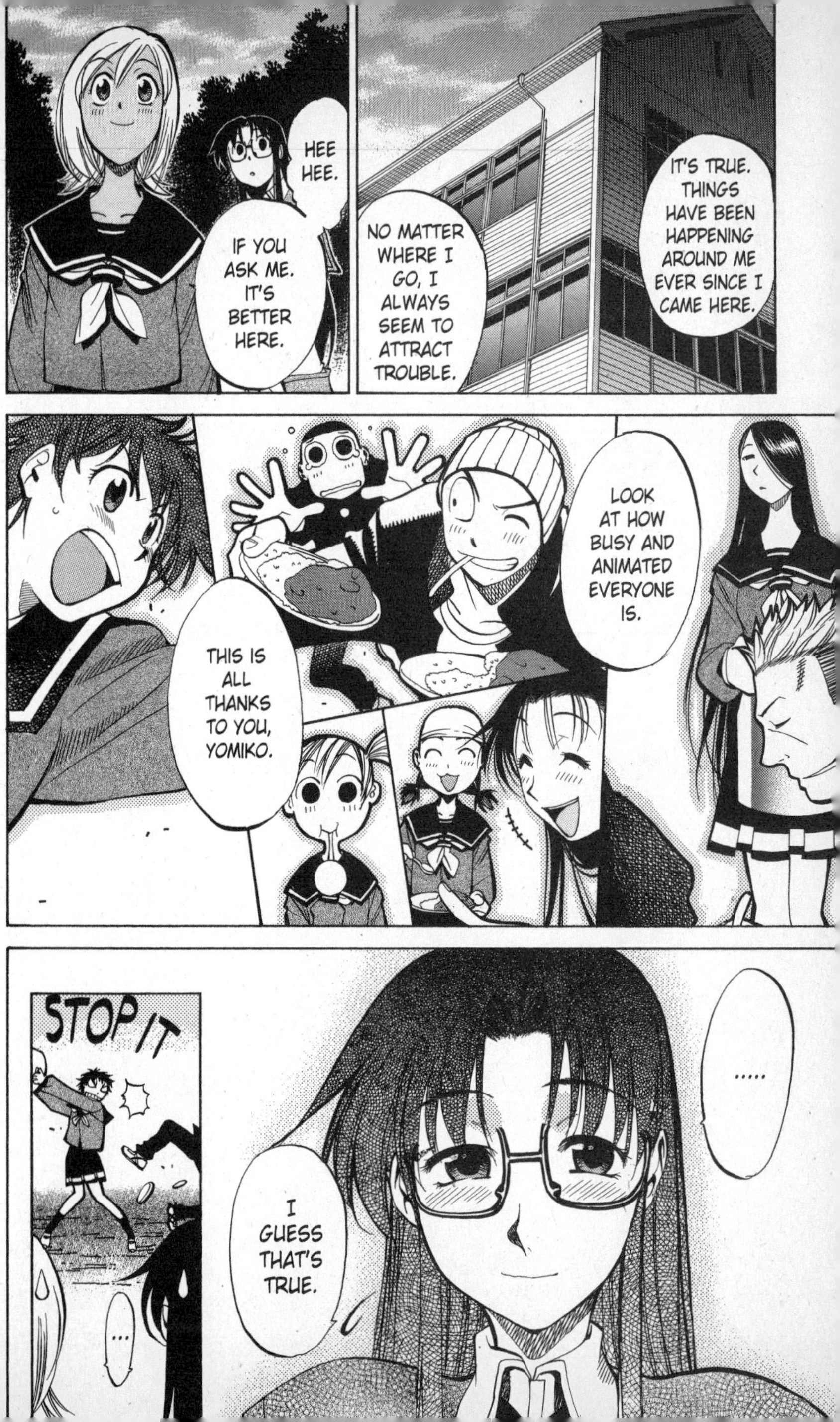
IT'S TRUE. THINGS HAVE BEEN HAPPENING AROUND ME EVER SINCE I CAME HERE.
NO MATTER WHERE I GO, I ALWAYS SEEM TO ATTRACT TROUBLE.
HEE HEE.
IF YOU ASK ME. IT'S BETTER HERE.
LOOK AT HOW BUSY AND ANIMATED EVERYONE IS.
THIS IS ALL THANKS TO YOU, YOMIKO.
.....
I GUESS THAT'S TRUE.
STOP IT
...

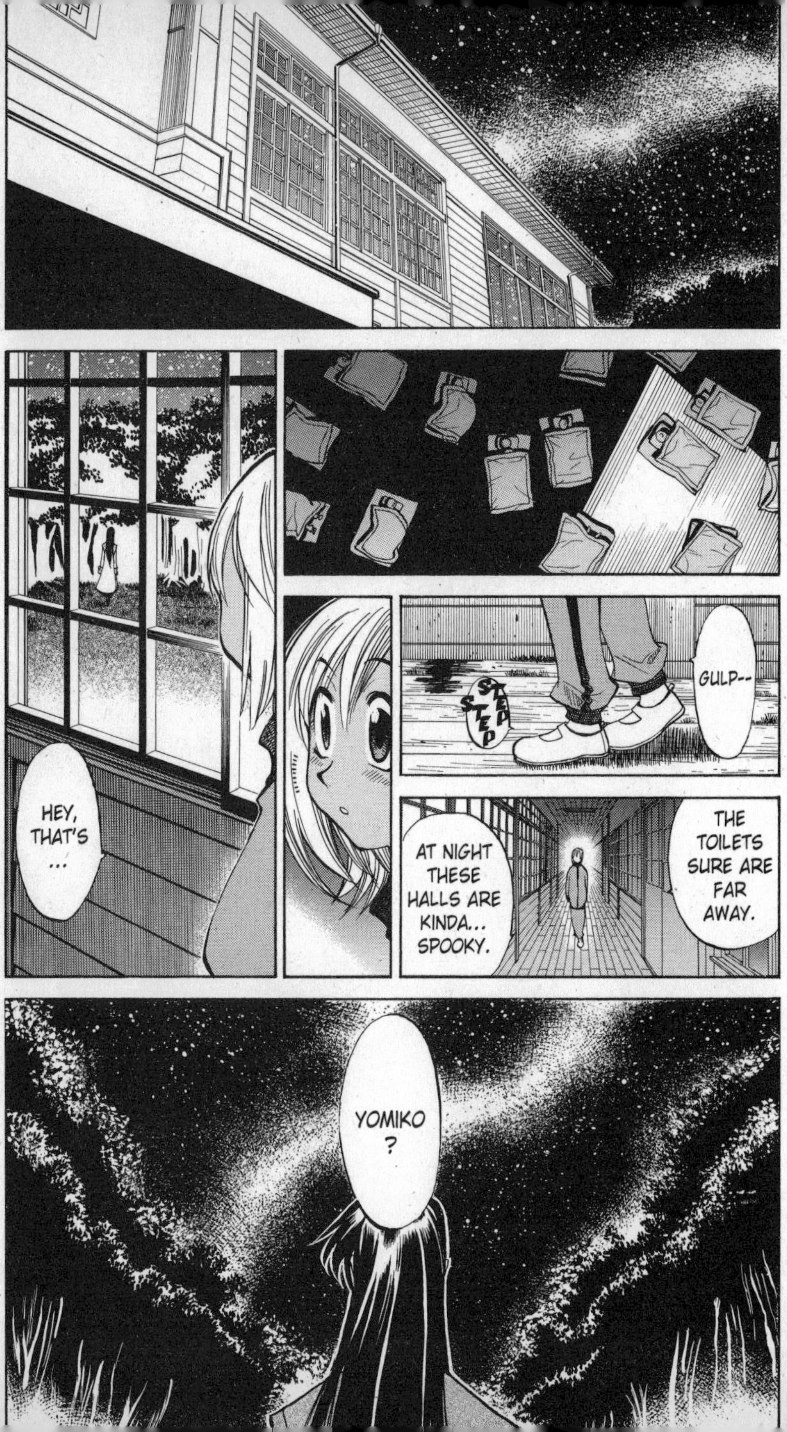
GULP--
STEP STEP
THE TOILETS SURE ARE FAR AWAY.
AT NIGHT THESE HALLS ARE KINDA... SPOOKY.
HEY, THAT'S ...
YOMIKO ?

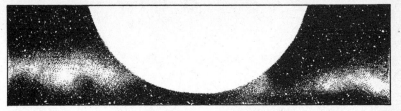

IT'S GONE. I DON'T FEEL IT ANYMORE.

WHAT COULD IT HAVE BEEN?

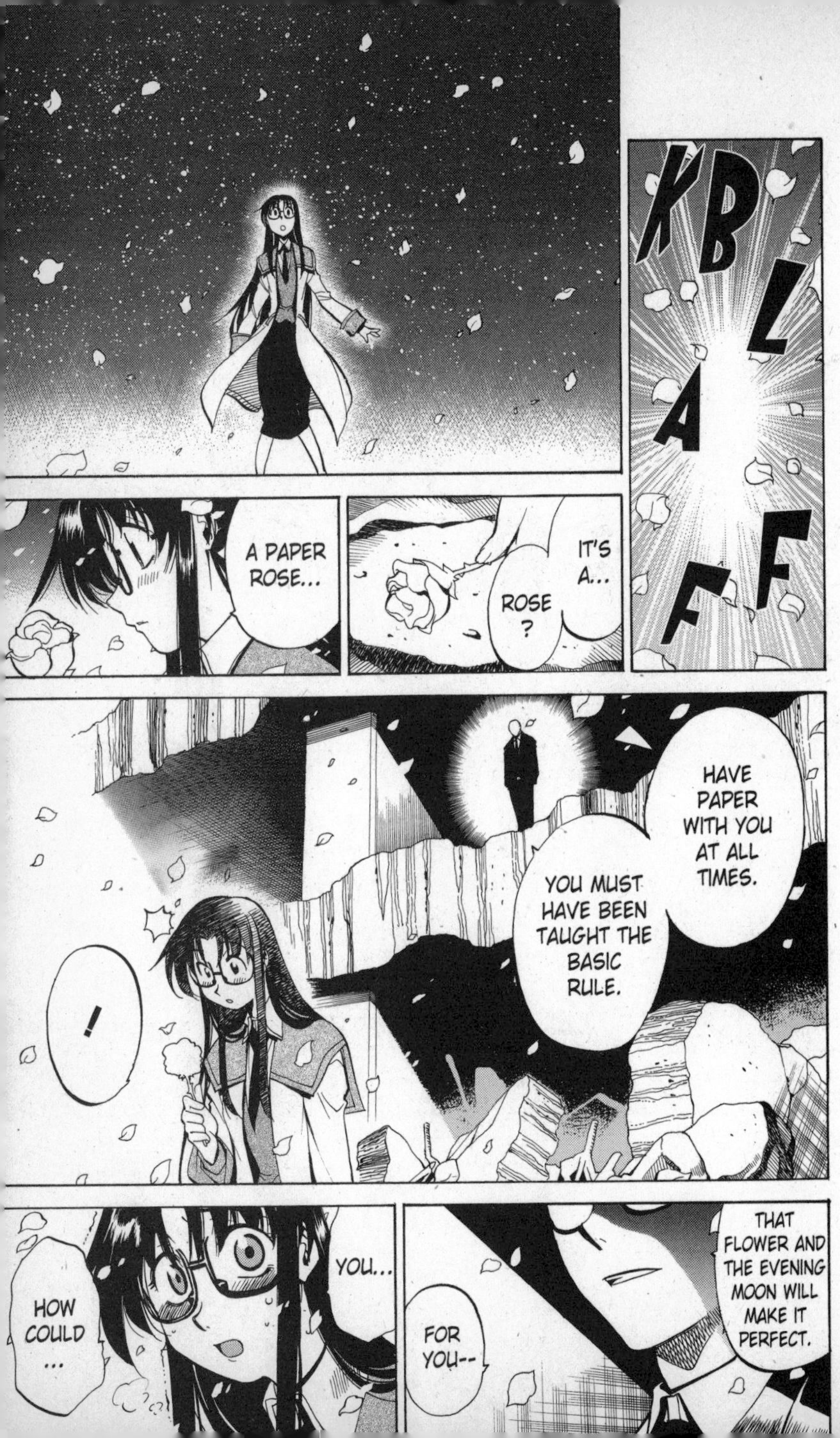
KBLAFF
IT'S A... ROSE?
A PAPER ROSE...
HAVE PAPER WITH YOU AT ALL TIMES.
YOU MUST HAVE BEEN TAUGHT THE BASIC RULE.
!
THAT FLOWER AND THE EVENING MOON WILL MAKE IT PERFECT.
FOR YOU--
YOU...
HOW COULD ...

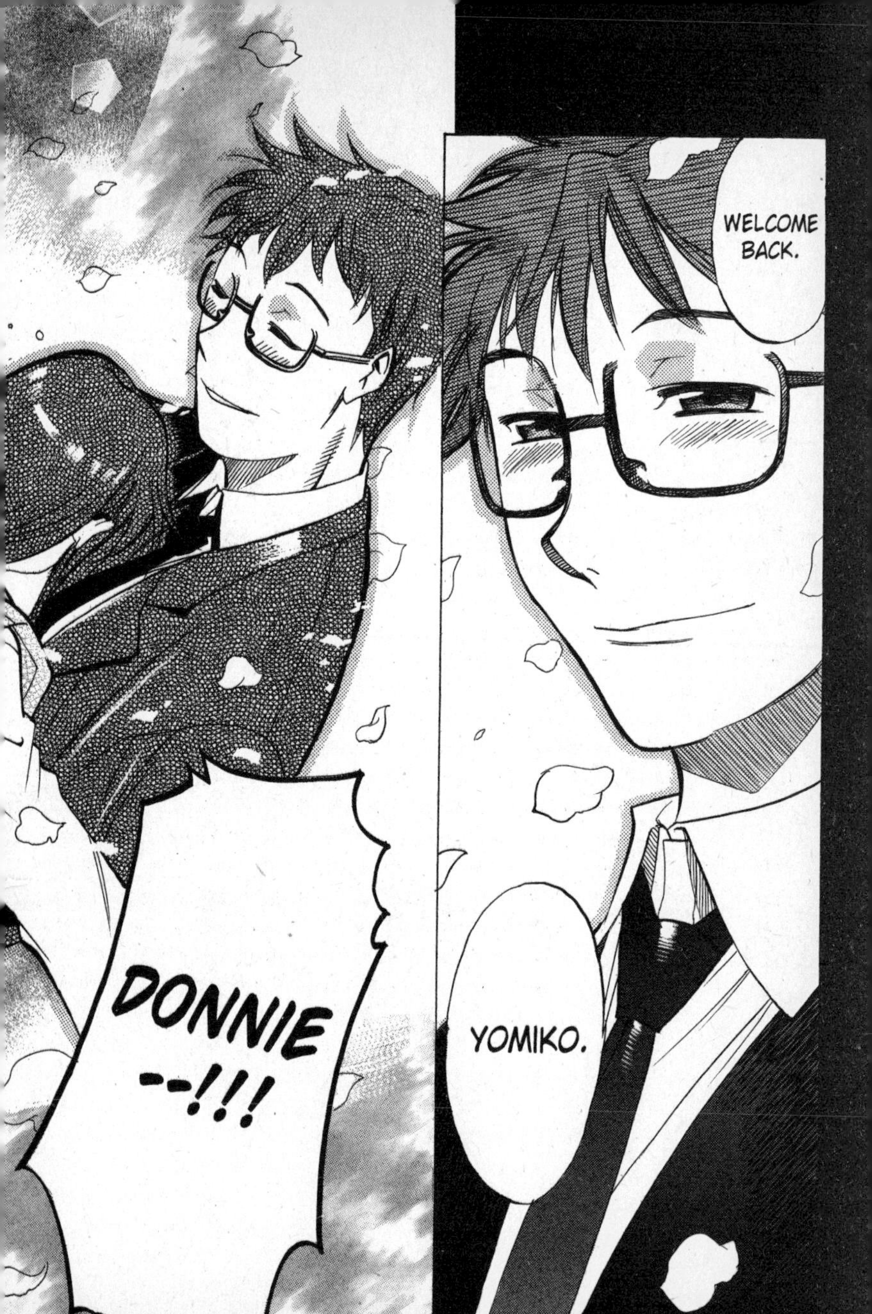
WELCOME BACK.
YOMIKO.
DONNIE --!!!

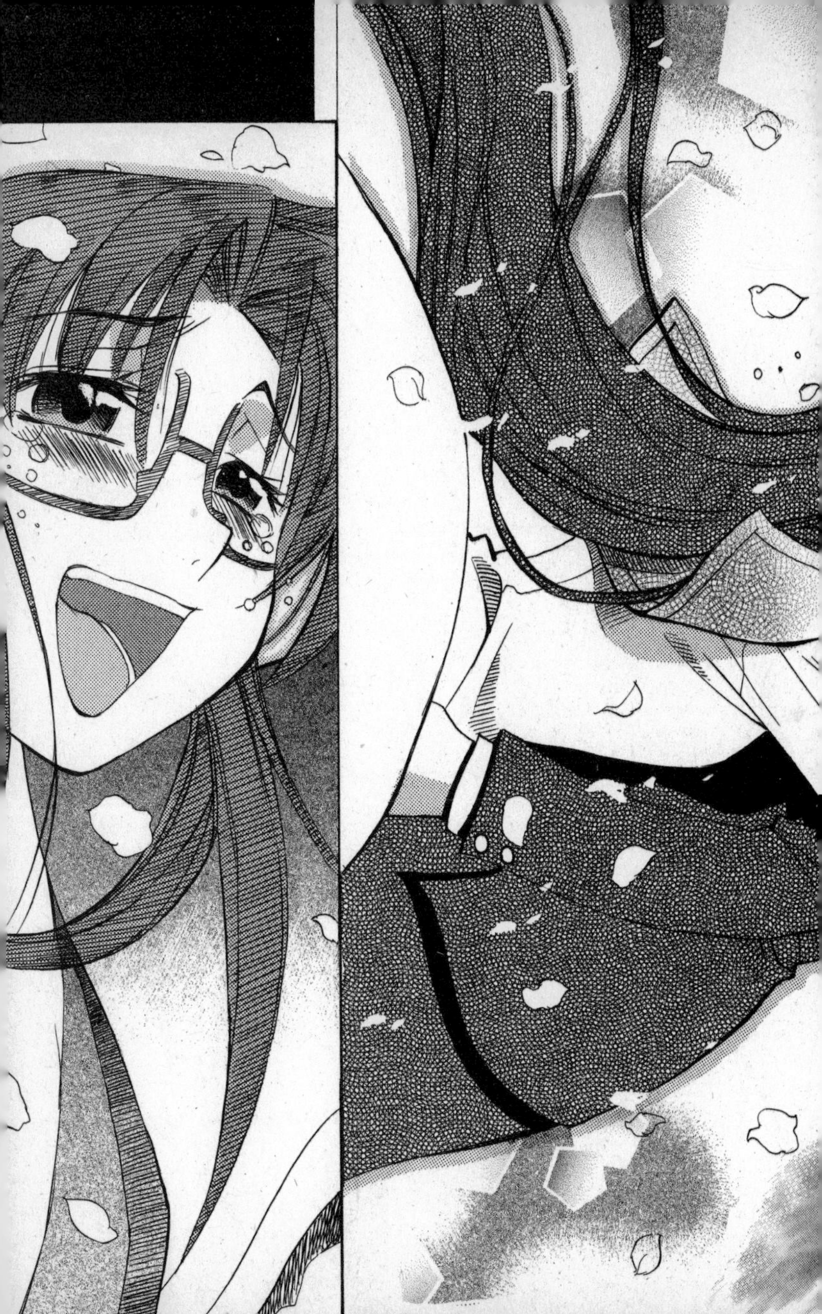

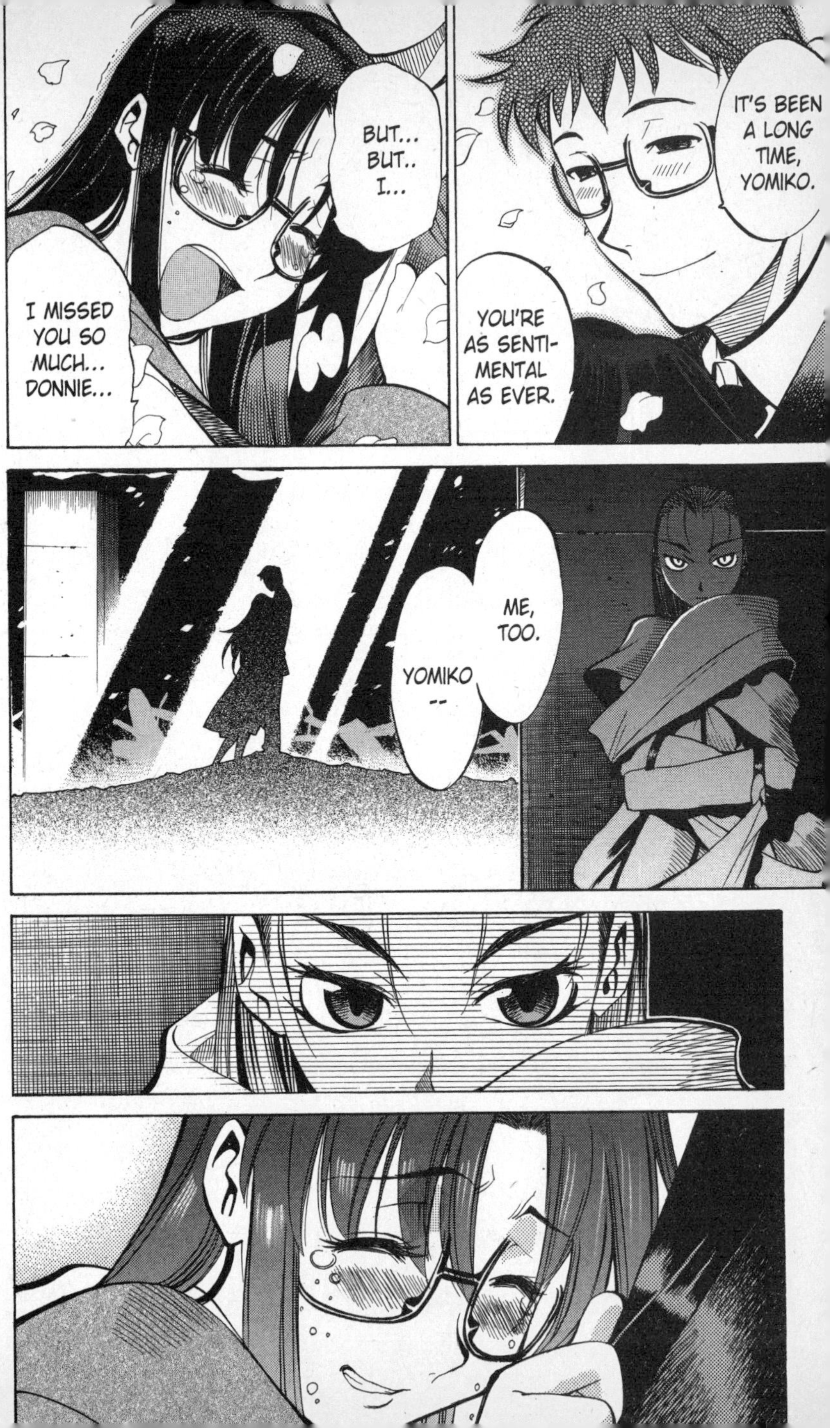
IT'S BEEN A LONG TIME, YOMIKO.
YOU'RE AS SENTI-MENTAL AS EVER.
BUT... BUT.. I...
I MISSED YOU SO MUCH... DONNIE...
ME, TOO.
YOMIKO --

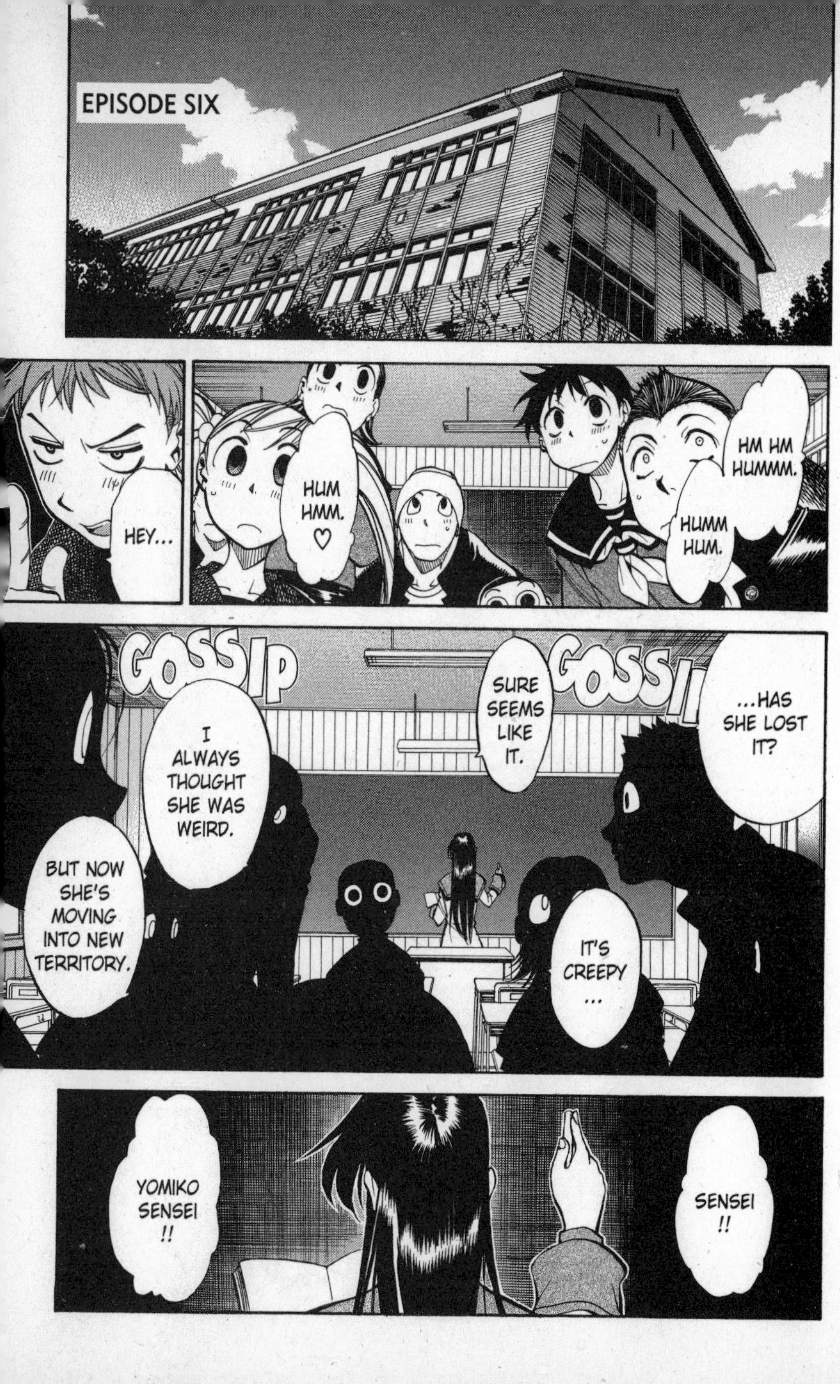
EPISODE SIX
HM HM HUMMM.
HUMM HUM.
HUM HMM. ♡
HEY...
...HAS SHE LOST IT?
GOSSIP GOSSIP
SURE SEEMS LIKE IT.
GOSSIP
I ALWAYS THOUGHT SHE WAS WEIRD.
IT'S CREEPY...
BUT NOW SHE'S MOVING INTO NEW TERRITORY.
SENSEI!!
YOMIKO SENSEI!!

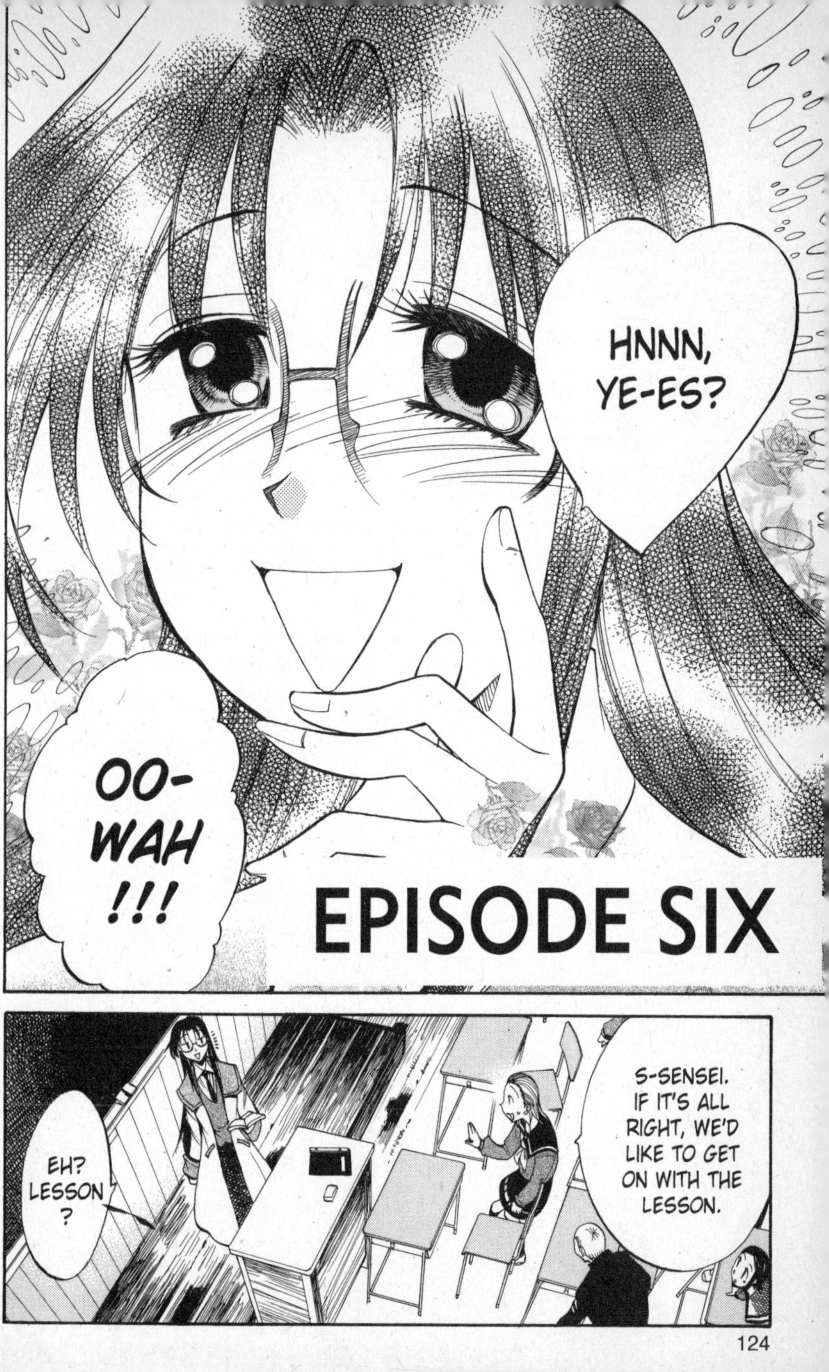
HNNN, YE-ES?
OO-WAH!!!
EPISODE SIX
S-SENSEI. IF IT'S ALL RIGHT, WE'D LIKE TO GET ON WITH THE LESSON.
EH? LESSON?

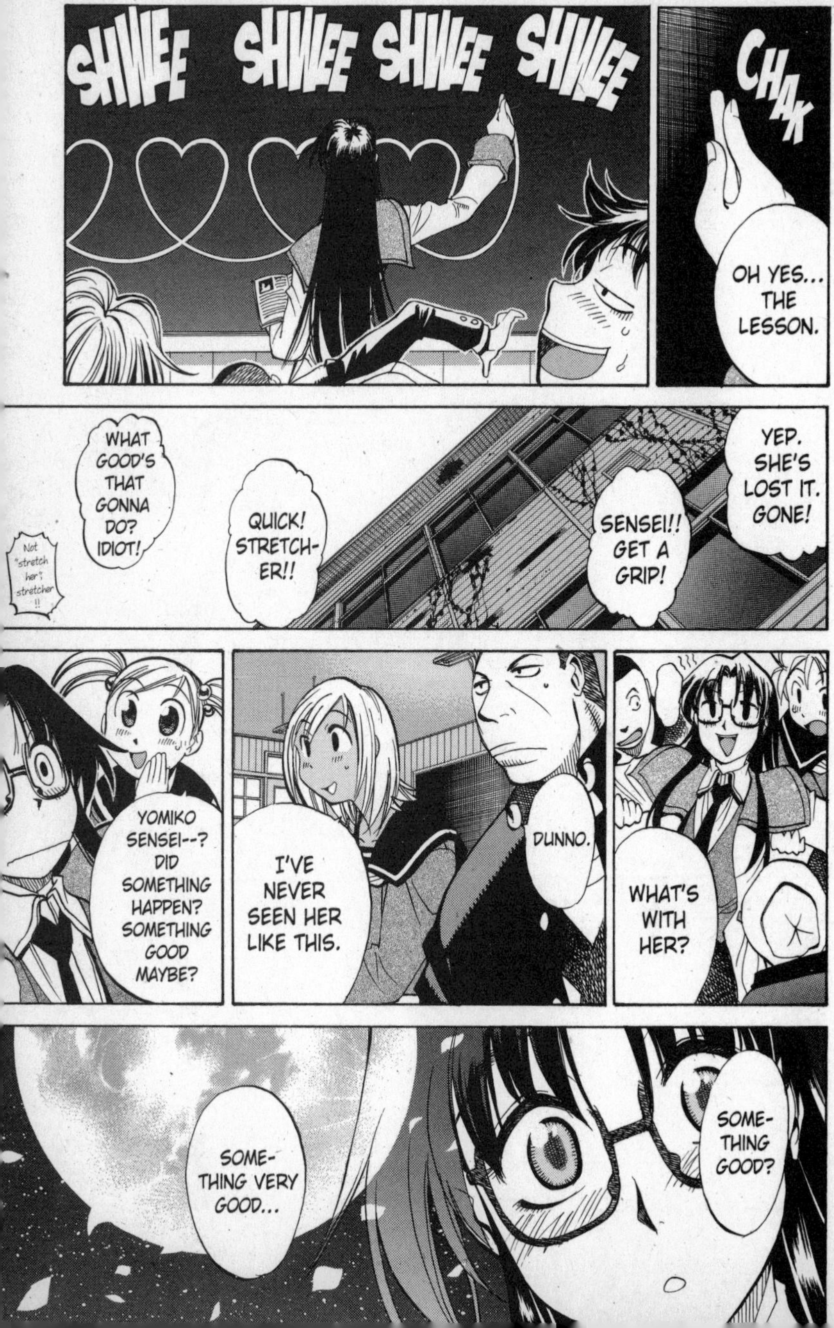
CHAK
OH YES... THE LESSON.
SHWEE SHWEE SHWEE SHWEE
YEP. SHE'S LOST IT. GONE!
SENSEI!! GET A GRIP!
QUICK! STRETCH-ER!!
WHAT GOOD'S THAT GONNA DO? IDIOT!
Not "stretch her," stretcher!!
WHAT'S WITH HER?
DUNNO.
I'VE NEVER SEEN HER LIKE THIS.
YOMIKO SENSEI--? DID SOMETHING HAPPEN? SOMETHING GOOD MAYBE?
SOME-THING GOOD?
SOME-THING VERY GOOD...

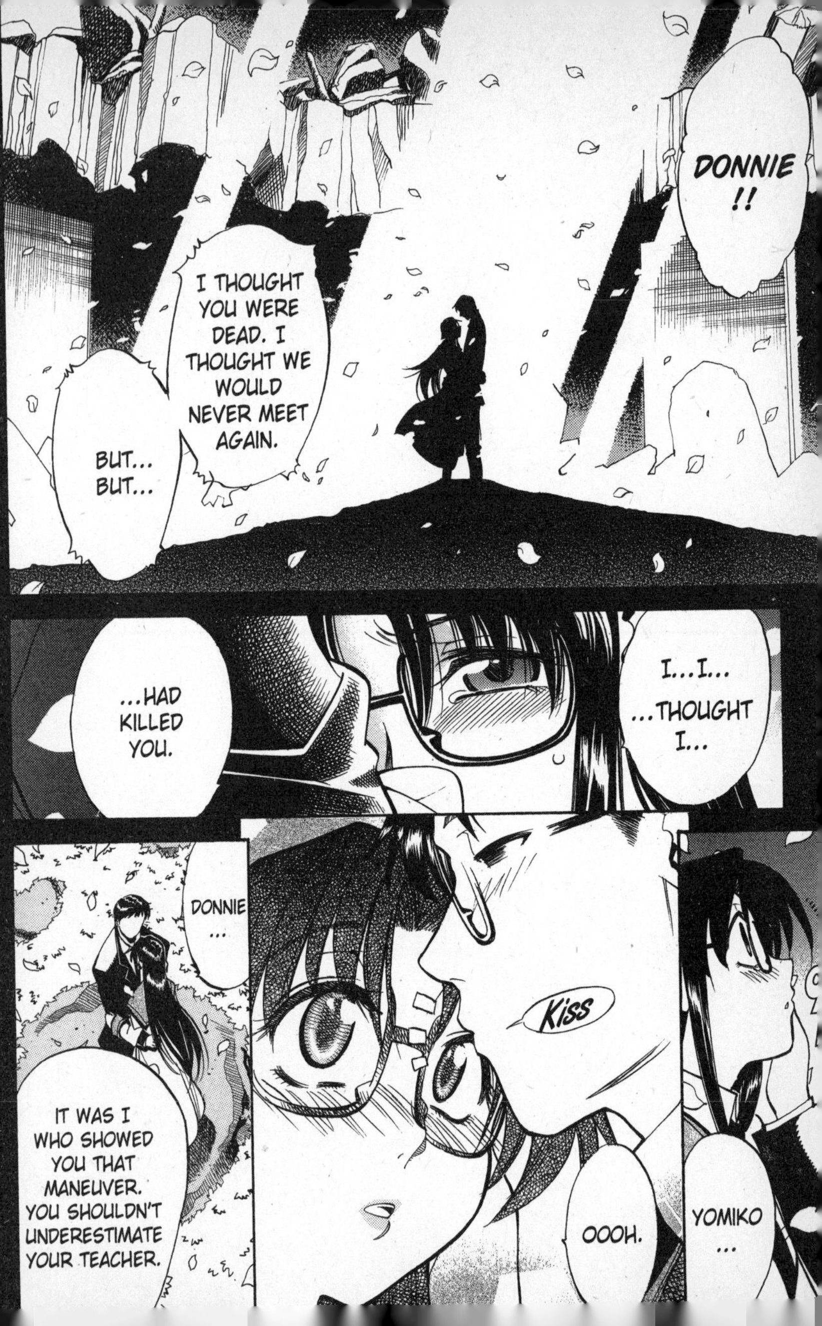
DONNIE !!
I THOUGHT YOU WERE DEAD. I THOUGHT WE WOULD NEVER MEET AGAIN.
BUT... BUT...
I...I... ...THOUGHT I...
...HAD KILLED YOU.
YOMIKO ...
Kiss
OOOH.
DONNIE ...
IT WAS I WHO SHOWED YOU THAT MANEUVER. YOU SHOULDN'T UNDERESTIMATE YOUR TEACHER.

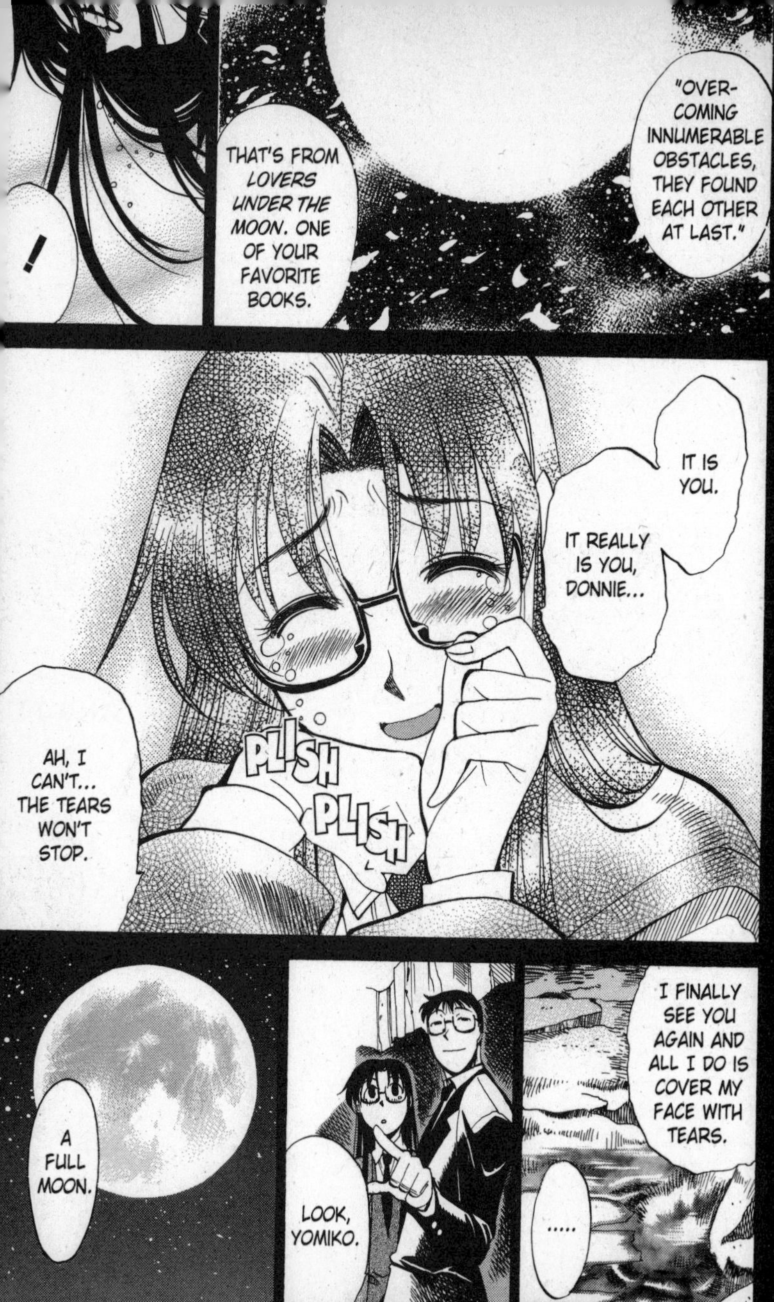
"OVER-COMING INNUMERABLE OBSTACLES, THEY FOUND EACH OTHER AT LAST."
THAT'S FROM *LOVERS UNDER THE MOON*. ONE OF YOUR FAVORITE BOOKS.
!
IT IS YOU.
IT REALLY IS YOU, DONNIE...
PLISH
PLISH
AH, I CAN'T... THE TEARS WON'T STOP.
I FINALLY SEE YOU AGAIN AND ALL I DO IS COVER MY FACE WITH TEARS.
.....
LOOK, YOMIKO.
A FULL MOON.

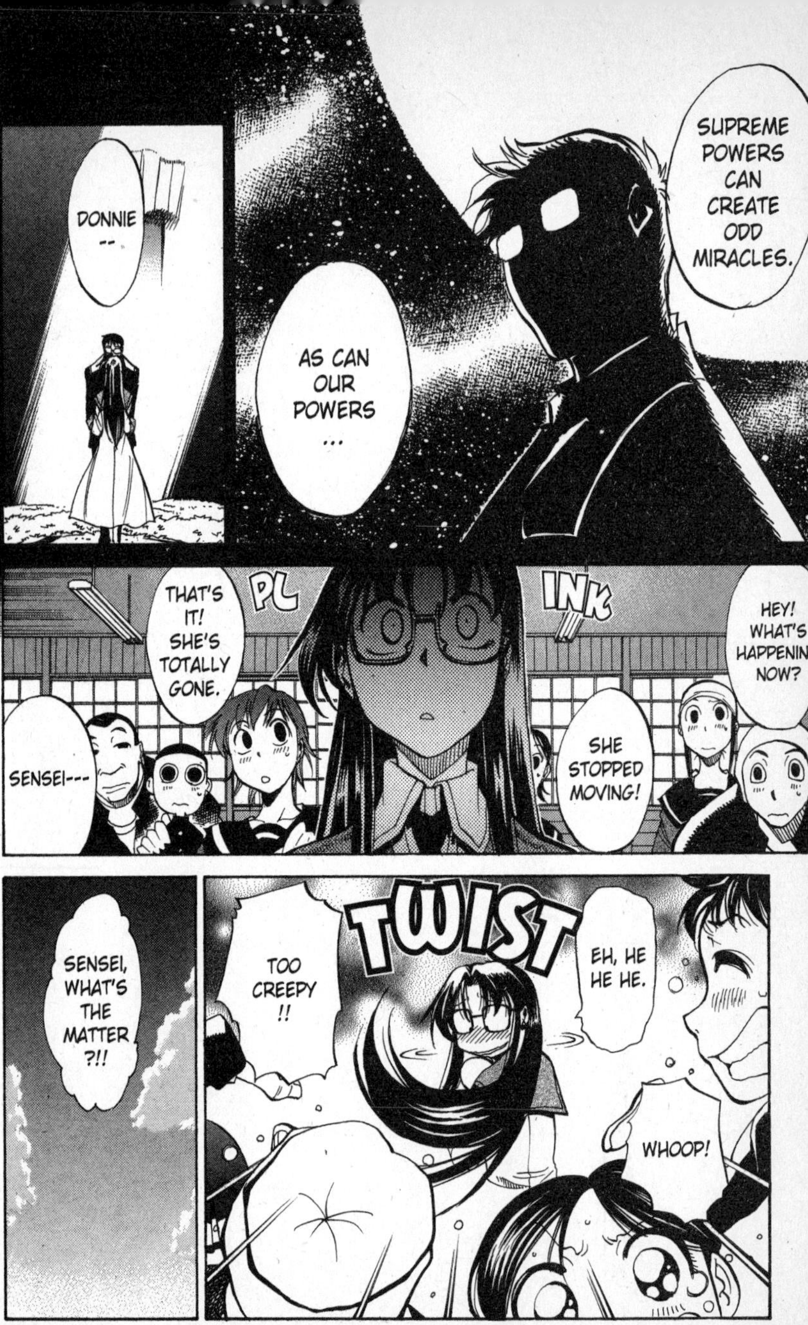
SUPREME POWERS CAN CREATE ODD MIRACLES.
AS CAN OUR POWERS ...
DONNIE --
PLINK
HEY! WHAT'S HAPPENING NOW?
SHE STOPPED MOVING!
THAT'S IT! SHE'S TOTALLY GONE.
SENSEI---
EH, HE HE HE.
TWIST
TOO CREEPY !!
WHOOP!
SENSEI, WHAT'S THE MATTER ?!!

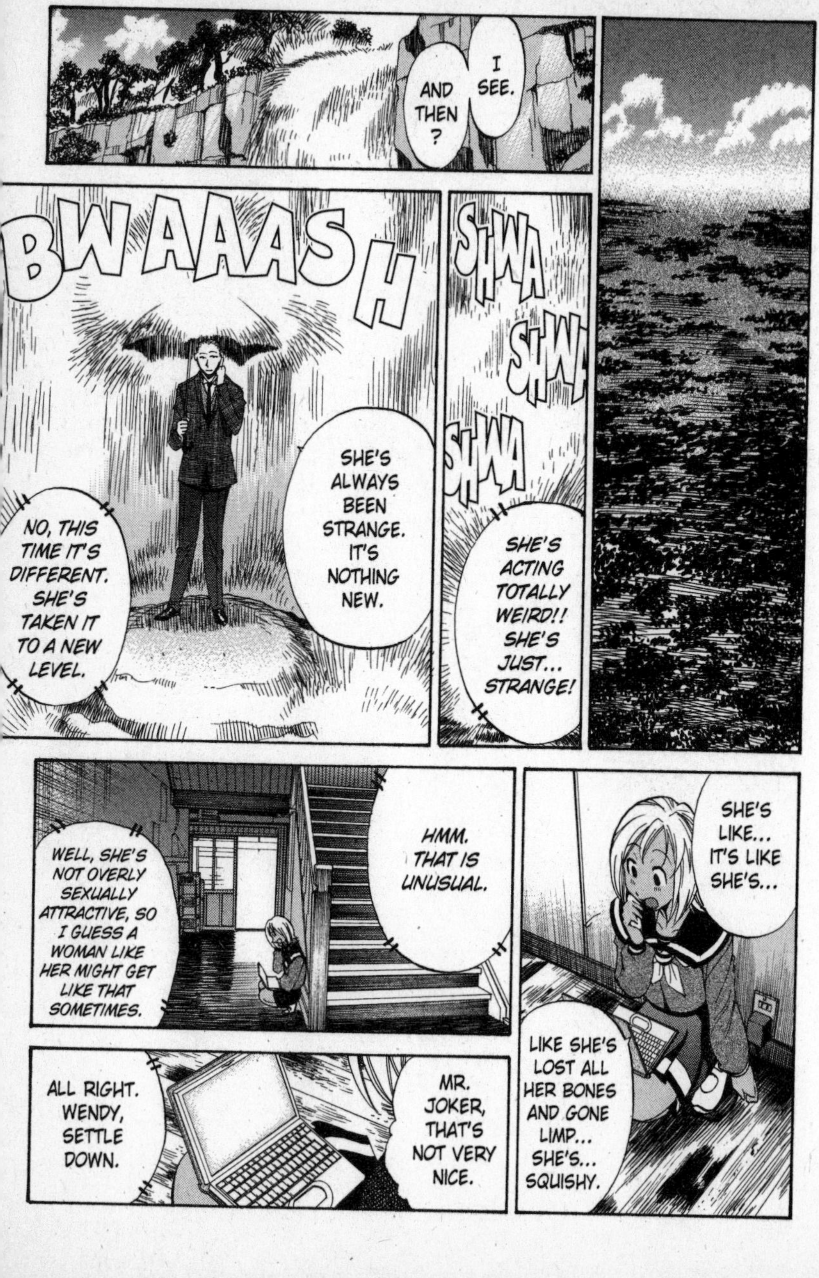
I SEE.
AND THEN?
SHWA
SHWA
SHWA
SHE'S ACTING TOTALLY WEIRD!! SHE'S JUST... STRANGE!
BWAAASH
SHE'S ALWAYS BEEN STRANGE. IT'S NOTHING NEW.
NO, THIS TIME IT'S DIFFERENT. SHE'S TAKEN IT TO A NEW LEVEL.
SHE'S LIKE... IT'S LIKE SHE'S...
LIKE SHE'S LOST ALL HER BONES AND GONE LIMP... SHE'S... SQUISHY.
HMM. THAT IS UNUSUAL.
WELL, SHE'S NOT OVERLY SEXUALLY ATTRACTIVE, SO I GUESS A WOMAN LIKE HER MIGHT GET LIKE THAT SOMETIMES.
MR. JOKER, THAT'S NOT VERY NICE.
ALL RIGHT. WENDY, SETTLE DOWN.

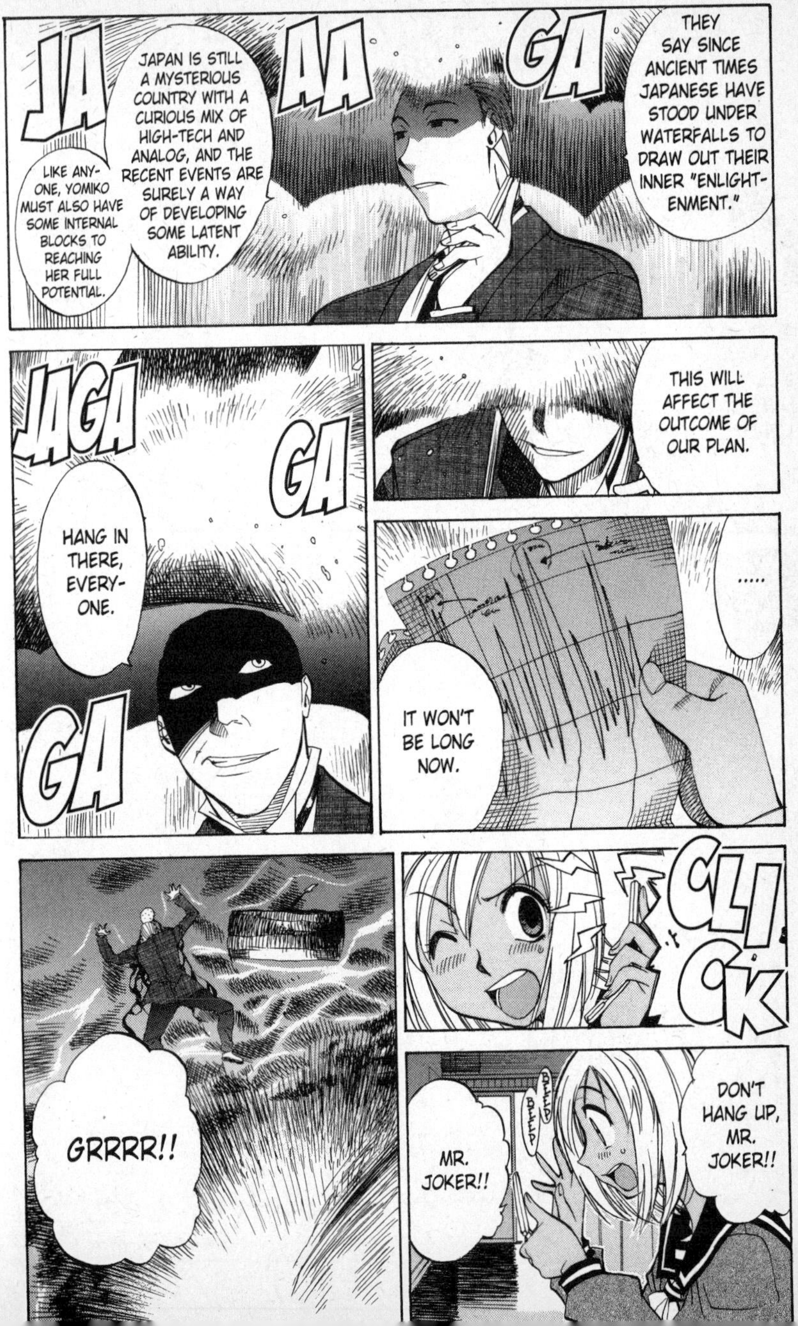

THEY SAY SINCE ANCIENT TIMES JAPANESE HAVE STOOD UNDER WATERFALLS TO DRAW OUT THEIR INNER "ENLIGHTENMENT."
GA
AA
JAPAN IS STILL A MYSTERIOUS COUNTRY WITH A CURIOUS MIX OF HIGH-TECH AND ANALOG, AND THE RECENT EVENTS ARE SURELY A WAY OF DEVELOPING SOME LATENT ABILITY.
JA
LIKE ANYONE, YOMIKO MUST ALSO HAVE SOME INTERNAL BLOCKS TO REACHING HER FULL POTENTIAL.
THIS WILL AFFECT THE OUTCOME OF OUR PLAN.
.....
IT WON'T BE LONG NOW.
GA
JAGA
HANG IN THERE, EVERYONE.
GA
CLICK
DON'T HANG UP, MR. JOKER!!
MR. JOKER!!
GRRRR!!

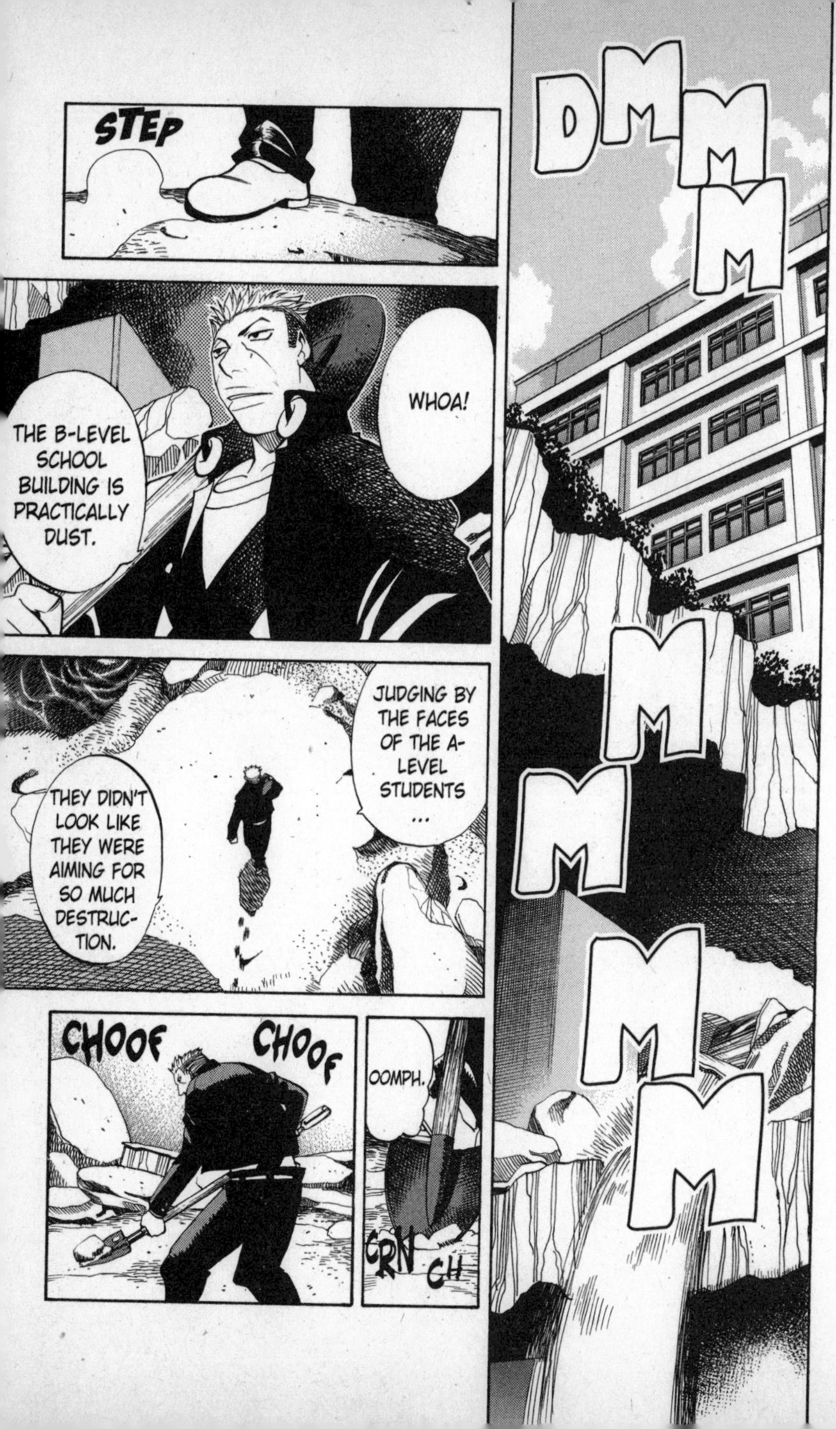
DMMMMMMMM
STEP
WHOA!
THE B-LEVEL SCHOOL BUILDING IS PRACTICALLY DUST.
JUDGING BY THE FACES OF THE A-LEVEL STUDENTS ...
THEY DIDN'T LOOK LIKE THEY WERE AIMING FOR SO MUCH DESTRUCTION.
OOMPH.
CRNCH
CHOOF
CHOOF

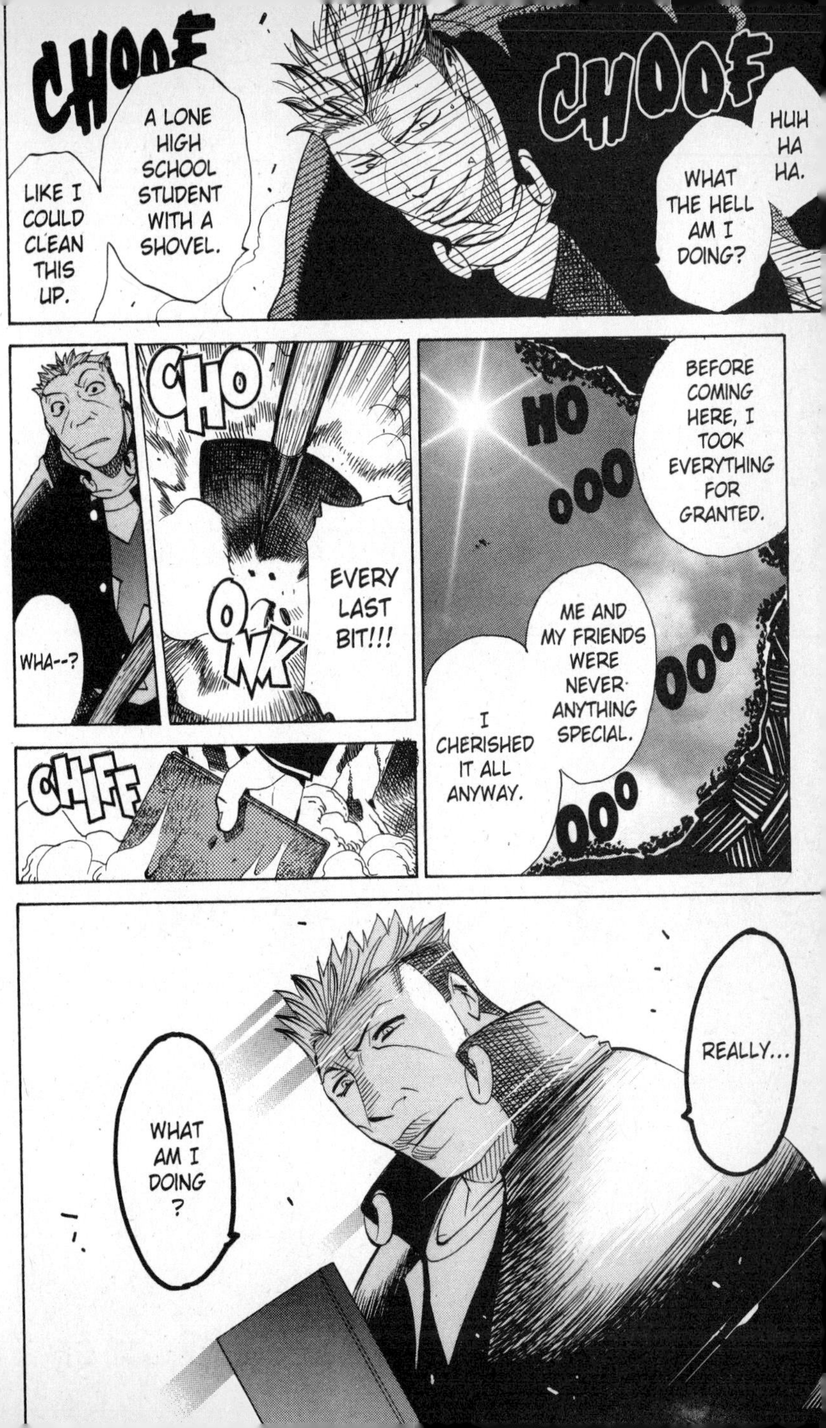
CHOOF
HUH HA HA.
WHAT THE HELL AM I DOING?
CHOOF
A LONE HIGH SCHOOL STUDENT WITH A SHOVEL.
LIKE I COULD CLEAN THIS UP.
BEFORE COMING HERE, I TOOK EVERYTHING FOR GRANTED.
HOOOOOOOOO
ME AND MY FRIENDS WERE NEVER ANYTHING SPECIAL.
I CHERISHED IT ALL ANYWAY.
CHO
EVERY LAST BIT!!!
ONK
WHA--?
CHIFF
REALLY...
WHAT AM I DOING?

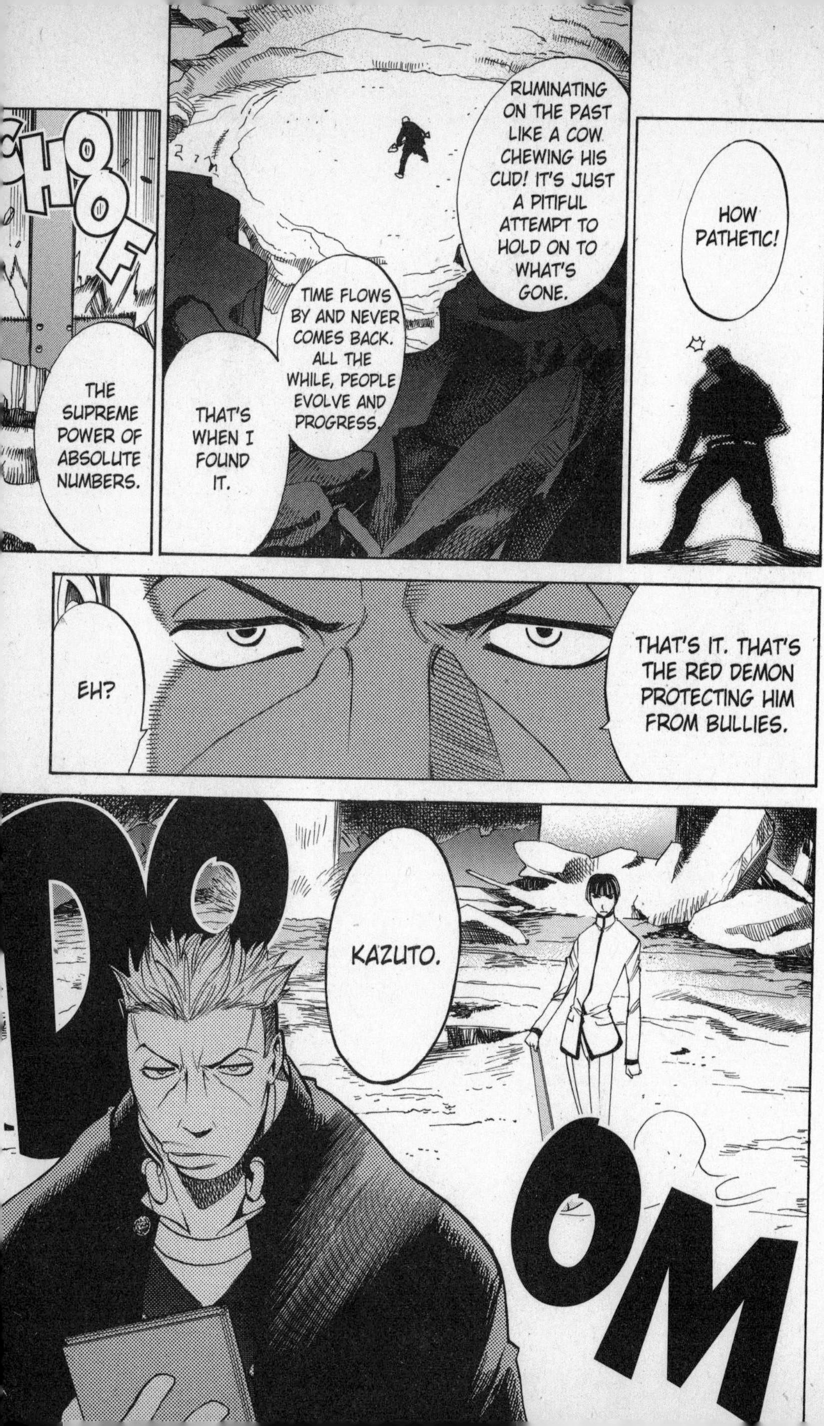
HOW PATHETIC!
RUMINATING ON THE PAST LIKE A COW CHEWING HIS CUD! IT'S JUST A PITIFUL ATTEMPT TO HOLD ON TO WHAT'S GONE.
TIME FLOWS BY AND NEVER COMES BACK. ALL THE WHILE, PEOPLE EVOLVE AND PROGRESS.
THAT'S WHEN I FOUND IT.
CHOOF
THE SUPREME POWER OF ABSOLUTE NUMBERS.
THAT'S IT. THAT'S THE RED DEMON PROTECTING HIM FROM BULLIES.
EH?
KAZUTO.
DOOM

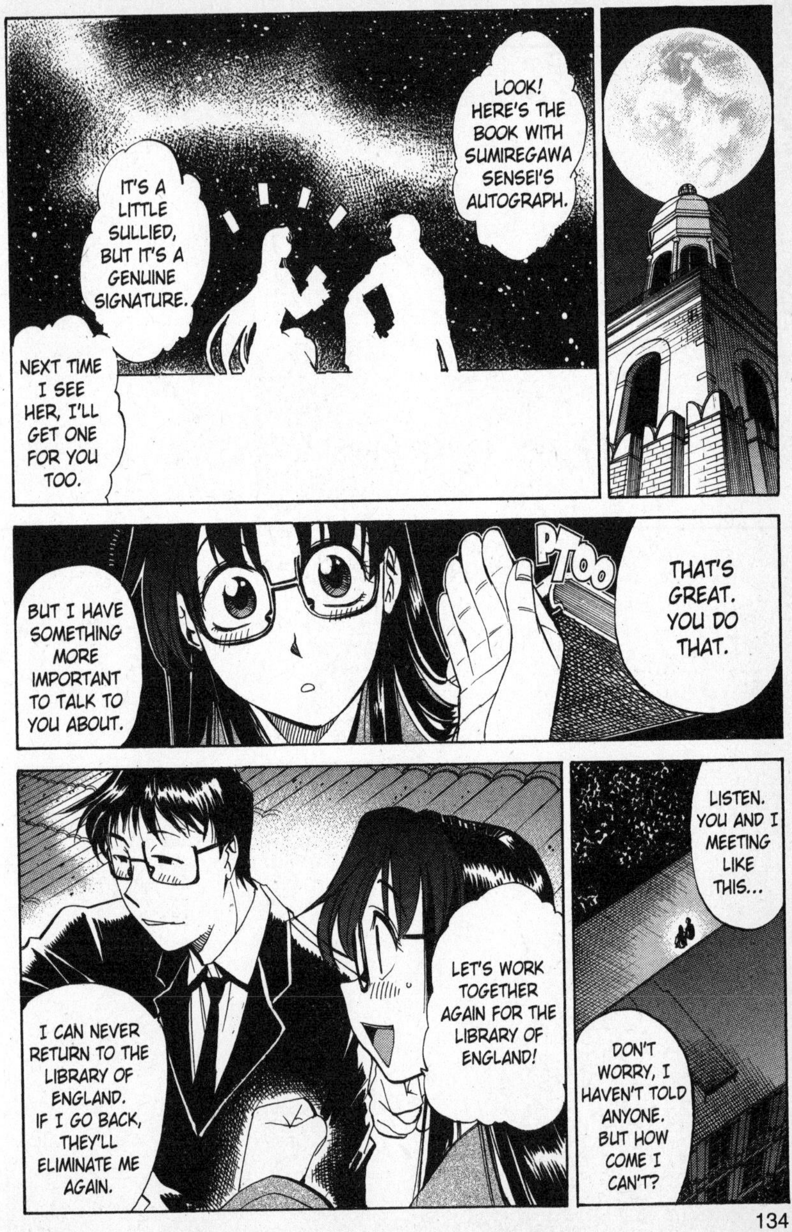
LOOK! HERE'S THE BOOK WITH SUMIREGAWA SENSEI'S AUTOGRAPH.
IT'S A LITTLE SULLIED, BUT IT'S A GENUINE SIGNATURE.
NEXT TIME I SEE HER, I'LL GET ONE FOR YOU TOO.
THAT'S GREAT. YOU DO THAT.
PTOO
BUT I HAVE SOMETHING MORE IMPORTANT TO TALK TO YOU ABOUT.
LISTEN. YOU AND I MEETING LIKE THIS...
DON'T WORRY, I HAVEN'T TOLD ANYONE. BUT HOW COME I CAN'T?
LET'S WORK TOGETHER AGAIN FOR THE LIBRARY OF ENGLAND!
I CAN NEVER RETURN TO THE LIBRARY OF ENGLAND. IF I GO BACK, THEY'LL ELIMINATE ME AGAIN.

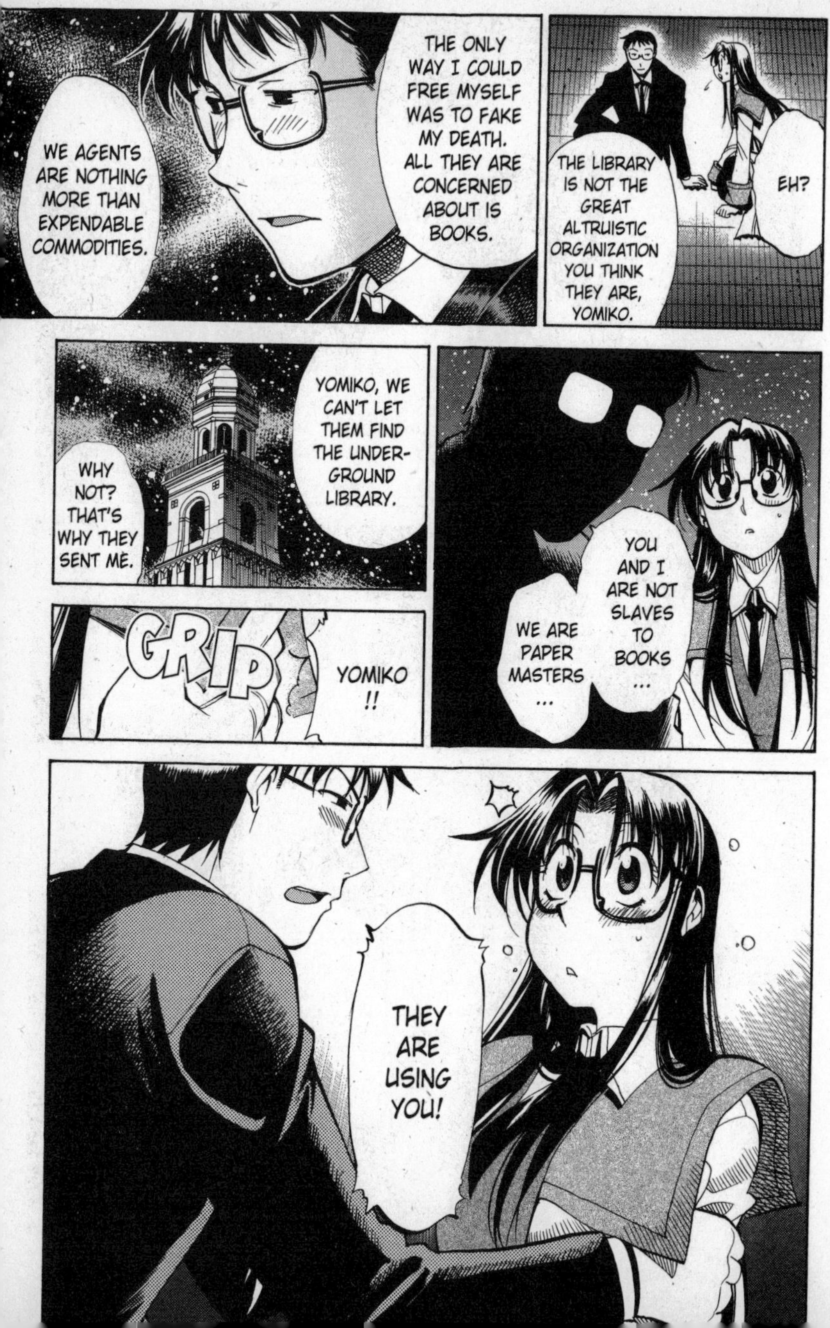
EH?
THE LIBRARY IS NOT THE GREAT ALTRUISTIC ORGANIZATION YOU THINK THEY ARE, YOMIKO.
THE ONLY WAY I COULD FREE MYSELF WAS TO FAKE MY DEATH. ALL THEY ARE CONCERNED ABOUT IS BOOKS.
WE AGENTS ARE NOTHING MORE THAN EXPENDABLE COMMODITIES.
YOU AND I ARE NOT SLAVES TO BOOKS ...
WE ARE PAPER MASTERS ...
YOMIKO, WE CAN'T LET THEM FIND THE UNDER-GROUND LIBRARY.
WHY NOT? THAT'S WHY THEY SENT ME.
YOMIKO !!
GRIP
THEY ARE USING YOU!

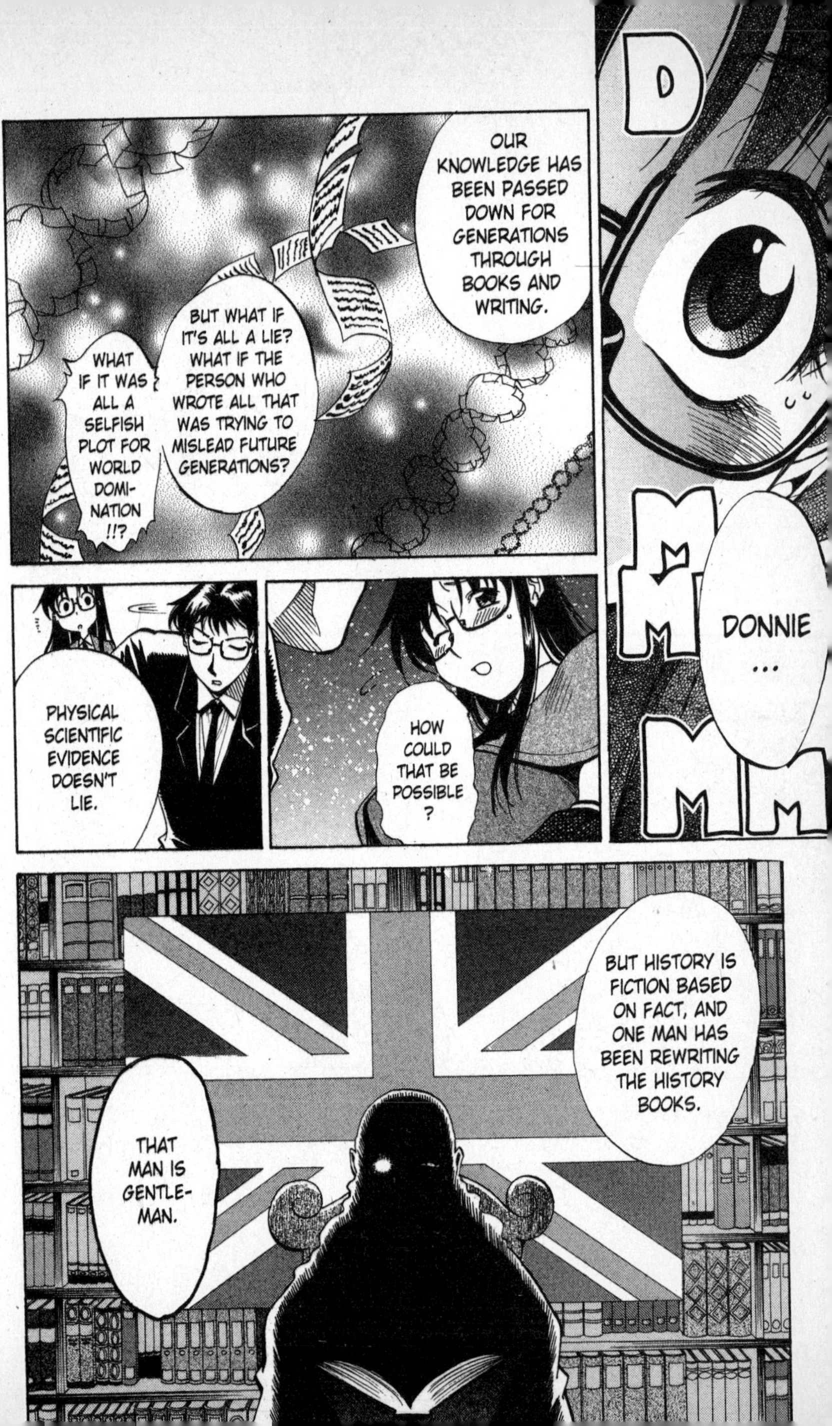

DOMMM
DONNIE ...
OUR KNOWLEDGE HAS BEEN PASSED DOWN FOR GENERATIONS THROUGH BOOKS AND WRITING.
BUT WHAT IF IT'S ALL A LIE? WHAT IF THE PERSON WHO WROTE ALL THAT WAS TRYING TO MISLEAD FUTURE GENERATIONS?
WHAT IF IT WAS ALL A SELFISH PLOT FOR WORLD DOMI-NATION !!?
HOW COULD THAT BE POSSIBLE ?
PHYSICAL SCIENTIFIC EVIDENCE DOESN'T LIE.
BUT HISTORY IS FICTION BASED ON FACT, AND ONE MAN HAS BEEN REWRITING THE HISTORY BOOKS.
THAT MAN IS GENTLE-MAN.

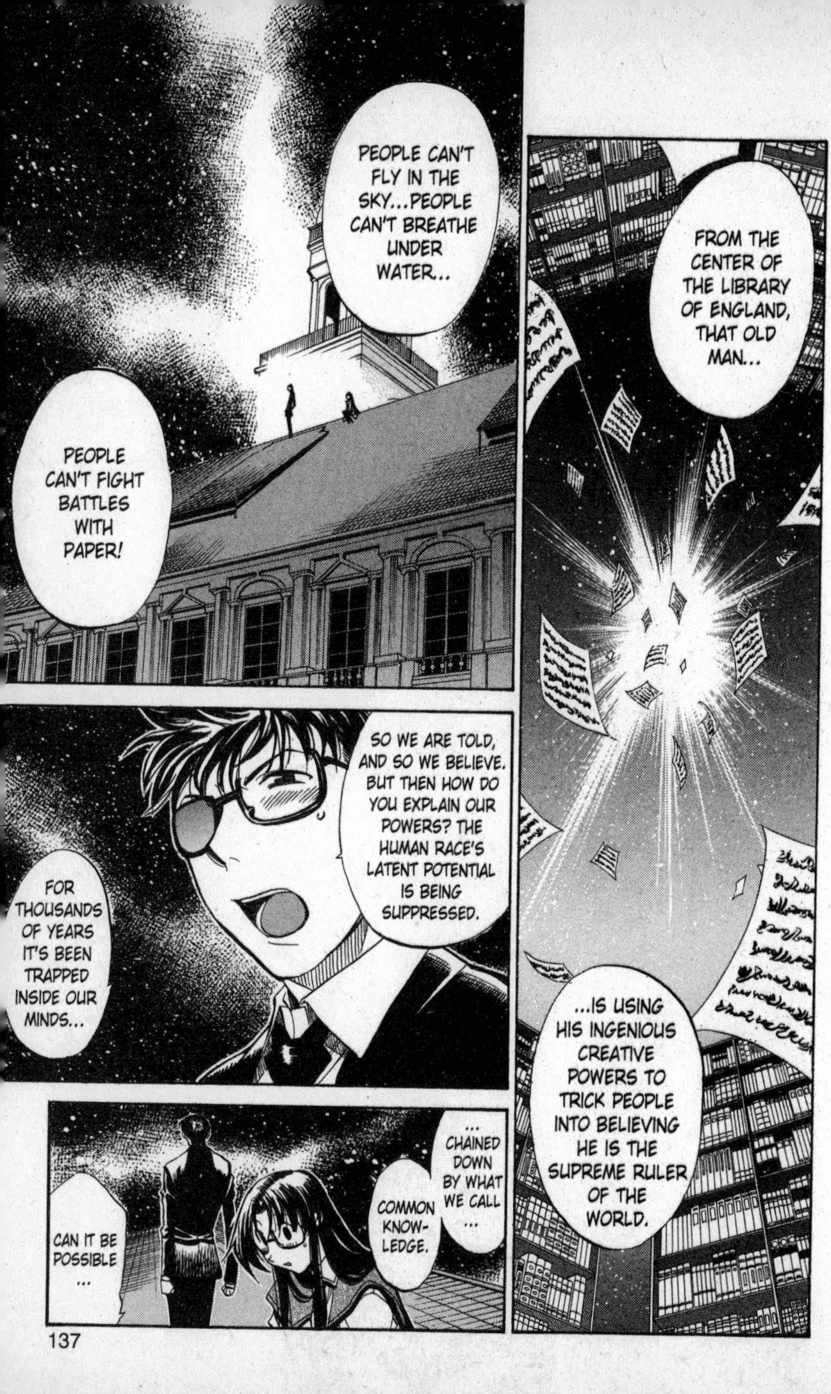
PEOPLE CAN'T FLY IN THE SKY...PEOPLE CAN'T BREATHE UNDER WATER...
PEOPLE CAN'T FIGHT BATTLES WITH PAPER!
SO WE ARE TOLD, AND SO WE BELIEVE. BUT THEN HOW DO YOU EXPLAIN OUR POWERS? THE HUMAN RACE'S LATENT POTENTIAL IS BEING SUPPRESSED.
FOR THOUSANDS OF YEARS IT'S BEEN TRAPPED INSIDE OUR MINDS...
...CHAINED DOWN BY WHAT WE CALL...
COMMON KNOW-LEDGE.
CAN IT BE POSSIBLE...
FROM THE CENTER OF THE LIBRARY OF ENGLAND, THAT OLD MAN...
...IS USING HIS INGENIOUS CREATIVE POWERS TO TRICK PEOPLE INTO BELIEVING HE IS THE SUPREME RULER OF THE WORLD.

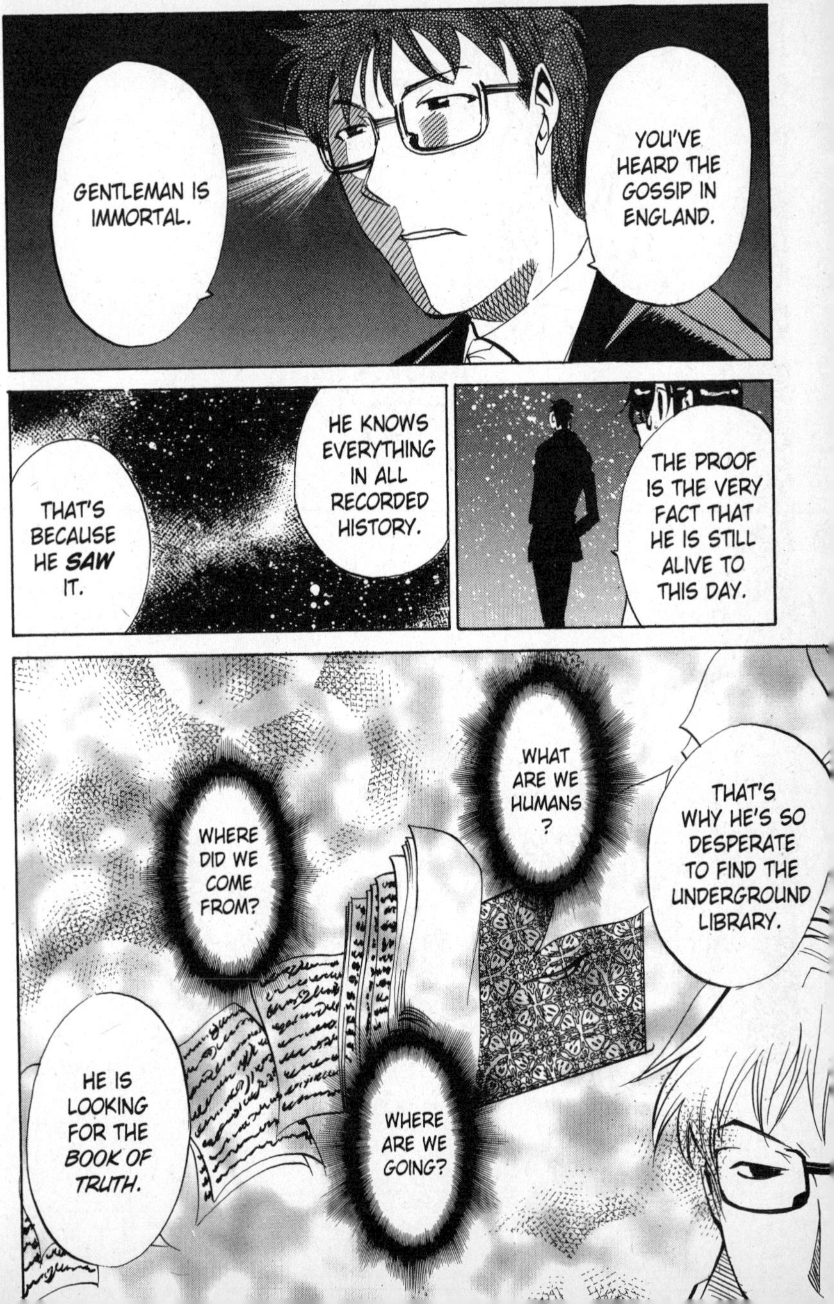
YOU'VE HEARD THE GOSSIP IN ENGLAND.
GENTLEMAN IS IMMORTAL.
THE PROOF IS THE VERY FACT THAT HE IS STILL ALIVE TO THIS DAY.
HE KNOWS EVERYTHING IN ALL RECORDED HISTORY.
THAT'S BECAUSE HE *SAW* IT.
THAT'S WHY HE'S SO DESPERATE TO FIND THE UNDERGROUND LIBRARY.
WHAT ARE WE HUMANS?
WHERE DID WE COME FROM?
WHERE ARE WE GOING?
HE IS LOOKING FOR THE *BOOK OF TRUTH*.

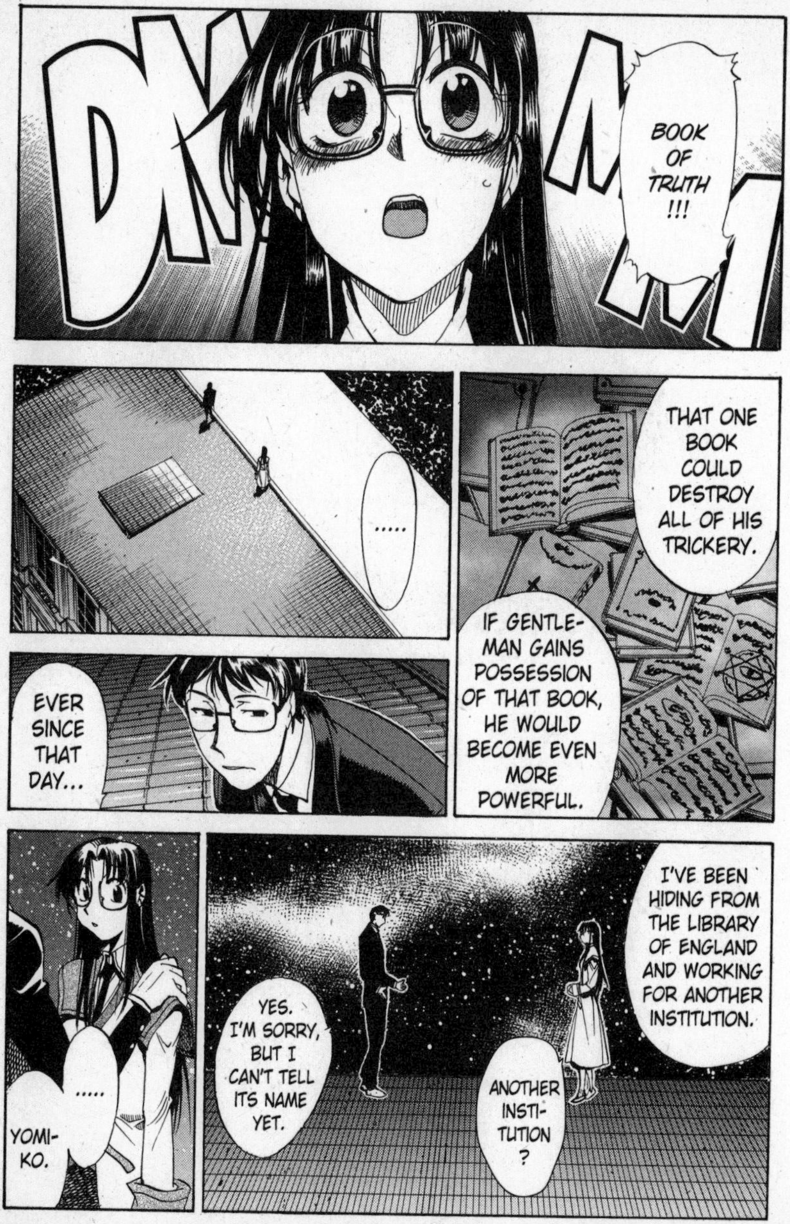
BOOK OF TRUTH !!!
THAT ONE BOOK COULD DESTROY ALL OF HIS TRICKERY.
IF GENTLE-MAN GAINS POSSESSION OF THAT BOOK, HE WOULD BECOME EVEN MORE POWERFUL.
.....
EVER SINCE THAT DAY...
I'VE BEEN HIDING FROM THE LIBRARY OF ENGLAND AND WORKING FOR ANOTHER INSTITUTION.
ANOTHER INSTI-TUTION ?
YES. I'M SORRY, BUT I CAN'T TELL ITS NAME YET.
.....
YOMI-KO.

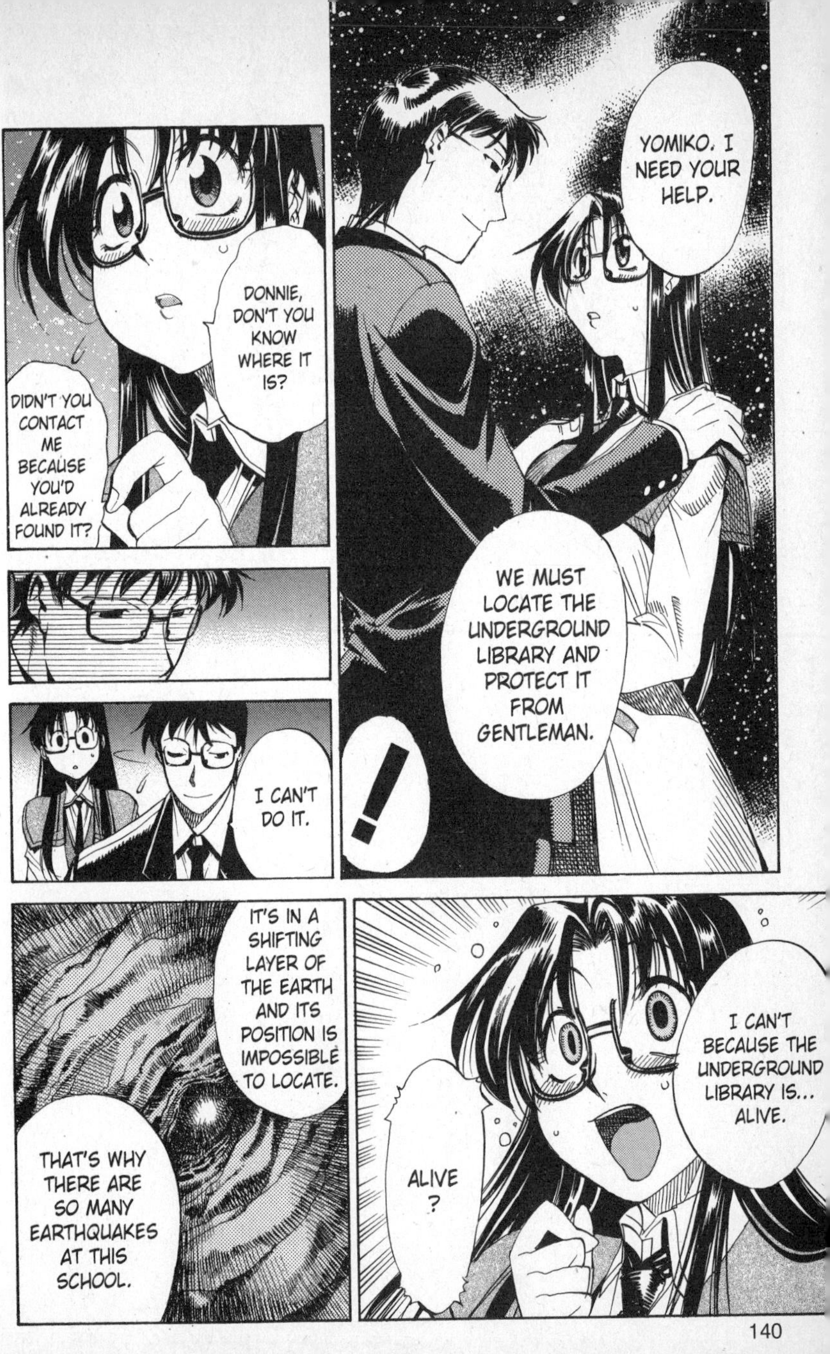
YOMIKO. I NEED YOUR HELP.
WE MUST LOCATE THE UNDERGROUND LIBRARY AND PROTECT IT FROM GENTLEMAN.
!
DONNIE, DON'T YOU KNOW WHERE IT IS?
DIDN'T YOU CONTACT ME BECAUSE YOU'D ALREADY FOUND IT?
I CAN'T DO IT.
I CAN'T BECAUSE THE UNDERGROUND LIBRARY IS... ALIVE.
ALIVE?
IT'S IN A SHIFTING LAYER OF THE EARTH AND ITS POSITION IS IMPOSSIBLE TO LOCATE.
THAT'S WHY THERE ARE SO MANY EARTHQUAKES AT THIS SCHOOL.

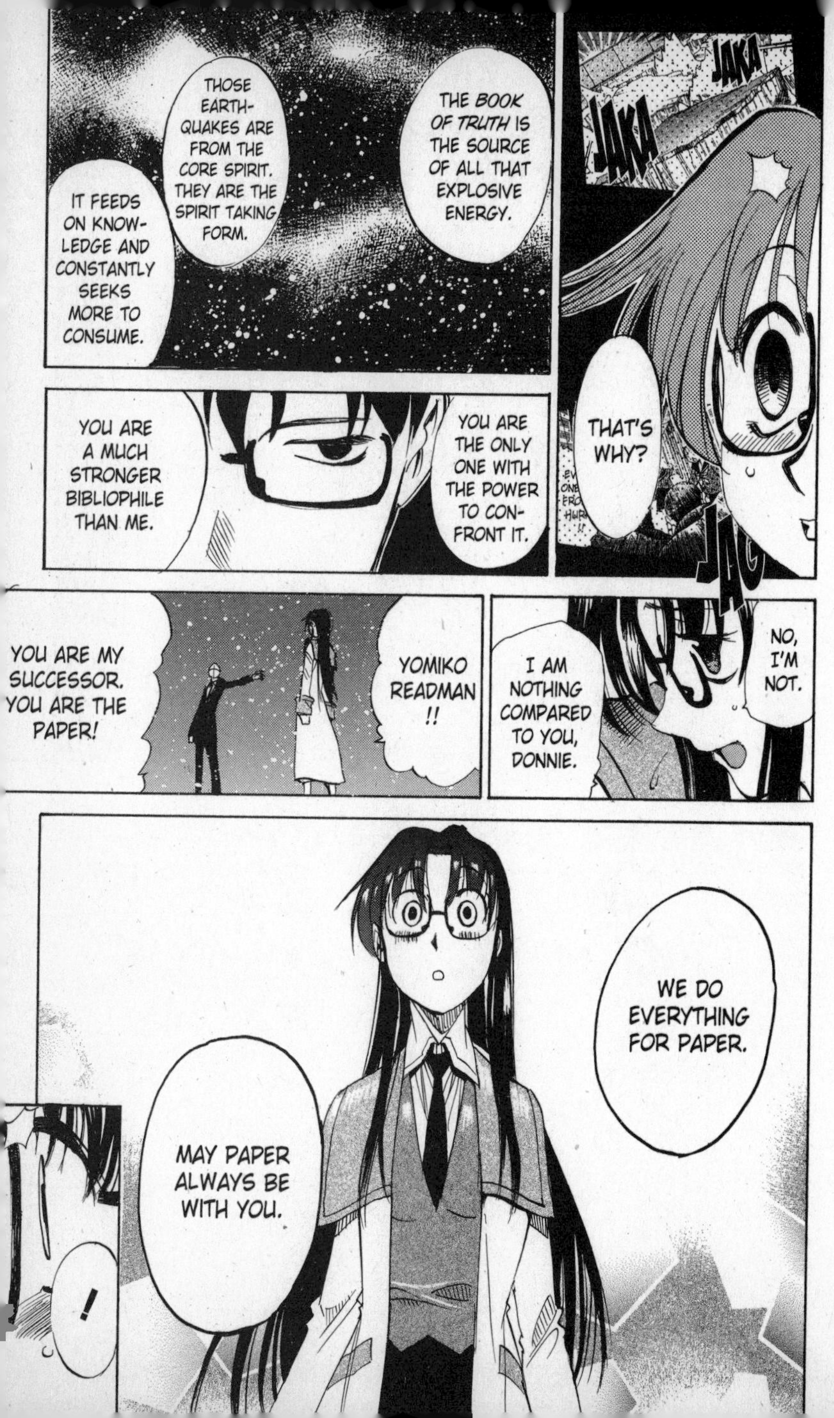
JAKA
JAKA
THAT'S WHY?
JAG
THE BOOK OF TRUTH IS THE SOURCE OF ALL THAT EXPLOSIVE ENERGY.
THOSE EARTHQUAKES ARE FROM THE CORE SPIRIT. THEY ARE THE SPIRIT TAKING FORM.
IT FEEDS ON KNOWLEDGE AND CONSTANTLY SEEKS MORE TO CONSUME.
YOU ARE THE ONLY ONE WITH THE POWER TO CONFRONT IT.
YOU ARE A MUCH STRONGER BIBLIOPHILE THAN ME.
NO, I'M NOT.
I AM NOTHING COMPARED TO YOU, DONNIE.
YOMIKO READMAN!!
YOU ARE MY SUCCESSOR. YOU ARE THE PAPER!
WE DO EVERYTHING FOR PAPER.
MAY PAPER ALWAYS BE WITH YOU.
!

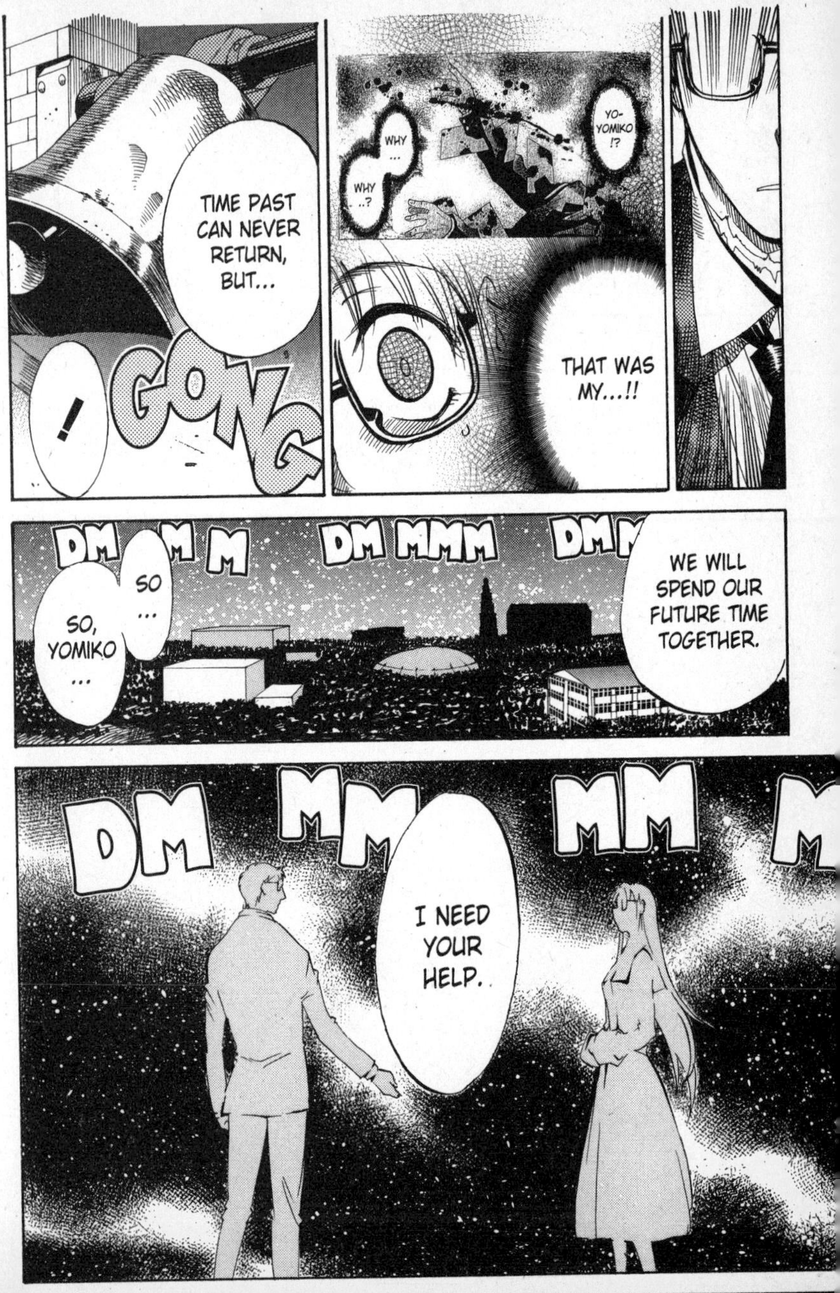
YO-YOMIKO !?
WHY ...
WHY ..?
THAT WAS MY...!!
TIME PAST CAN NEVER RETURN, BUT...
GONG
!
WE WILL SPEND OUR FUTURE TIME TOGETHER.
DM MMM
SO ...
SO, YOMIKO ...
DM MM MM
I NEED YOUR HELP.

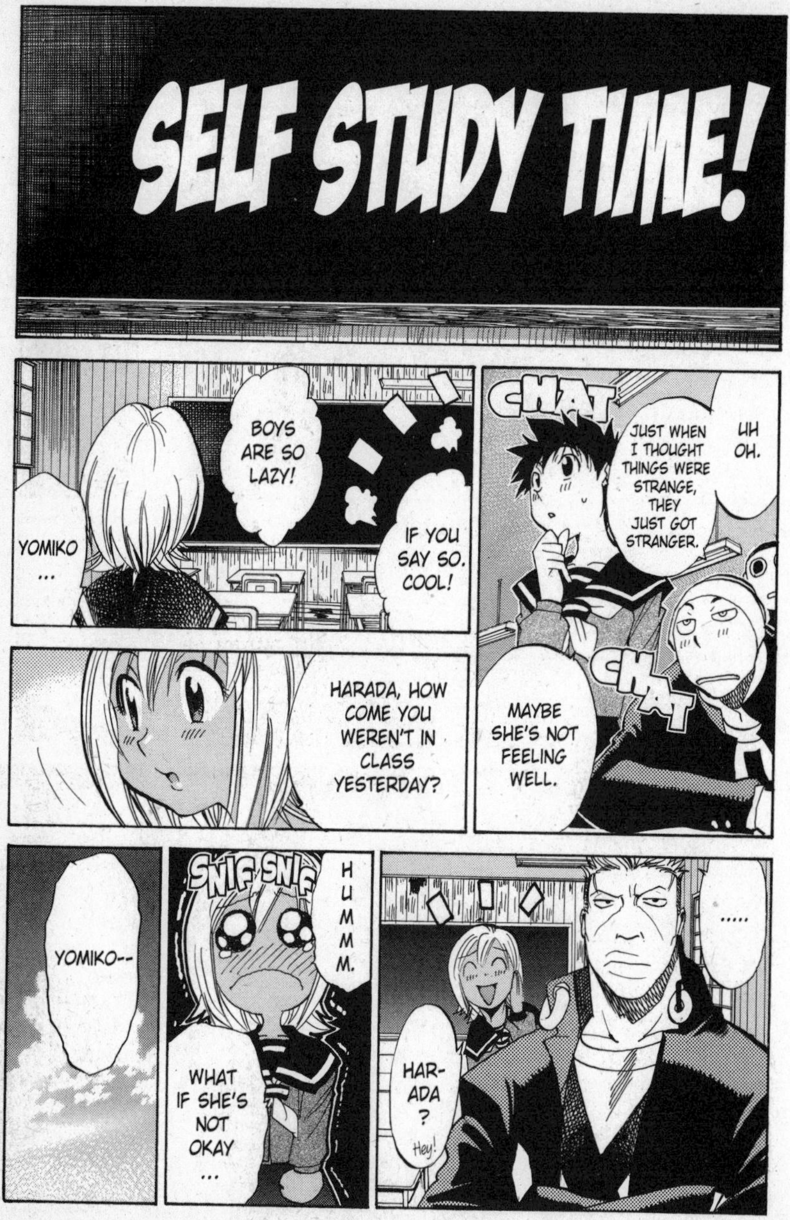
SELF STUDY TIME!
CHAT
UH OH.
JUST WHEN I THOUGHT THINGS WERE STRANGE, THEY JUST GOT STRANGER.
CHAT
MAYBE SHE'S NOT FEELING WELL.
BOYS ARE SO LAZY!
IF YOU SAY SO. COOL!
YOMIKO ...
HARADA, HOW COME YOU WEREN'T IN CLASS YESTERDAY?
.....
HAR-ADA?
Hey!
SNIF SNIF
HUMMM.
WHAT IF SHE'S NOT OKAY ...
YOMIKO--

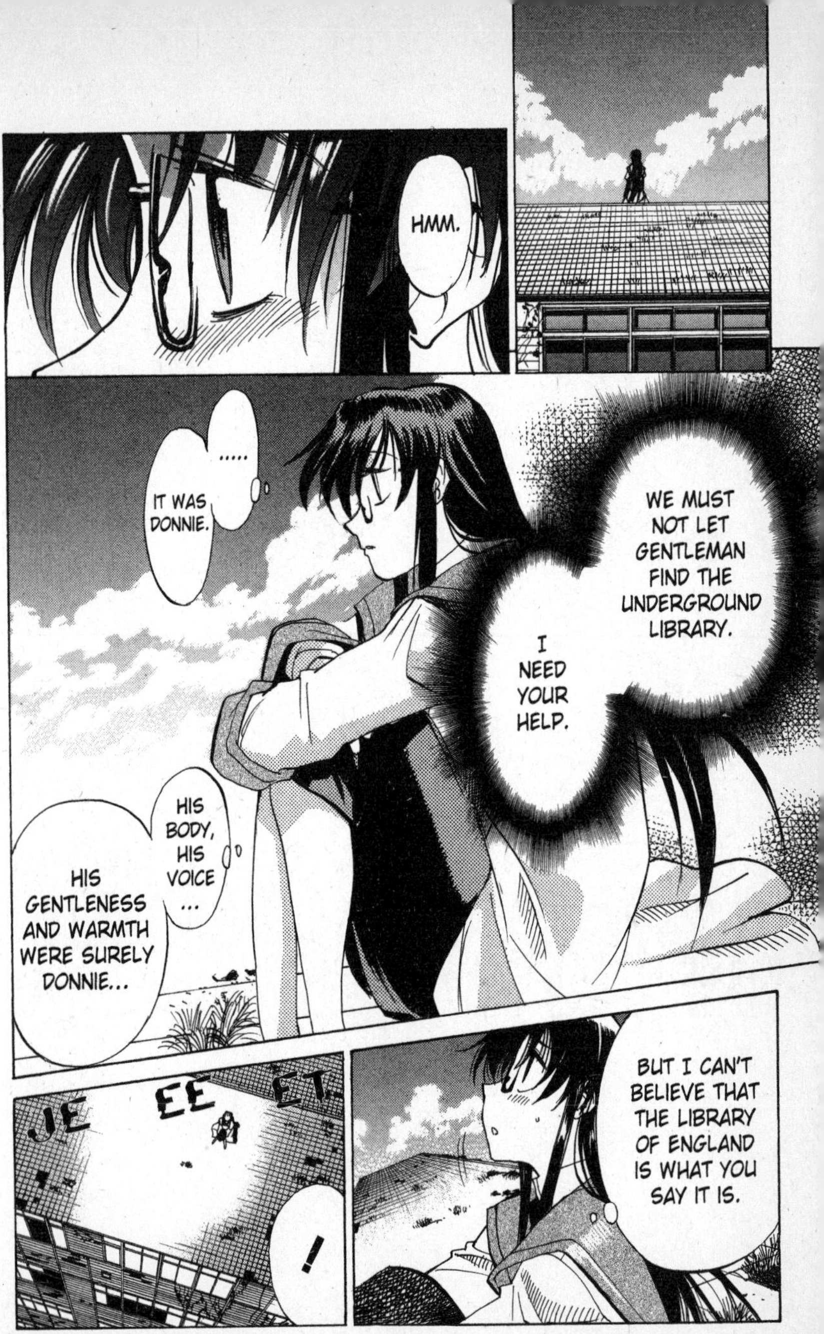
HMM.
WE MUST NOT LET GENTLEMAN FIND THE UNDERGROUND LIBRARY.
I NEED YOUR HELP.
......
IT WAS DONNIE.
HIS BODY, HIS VOICE ...
HIS GENTLENESS AND WARMTH WERE SURELY DONNIE...
BUT I CAN'T BELIEVE THAT THE LIBRARY OF ENGLAND IS WHAT YOU SAY IT IS.
JE EE ET
!

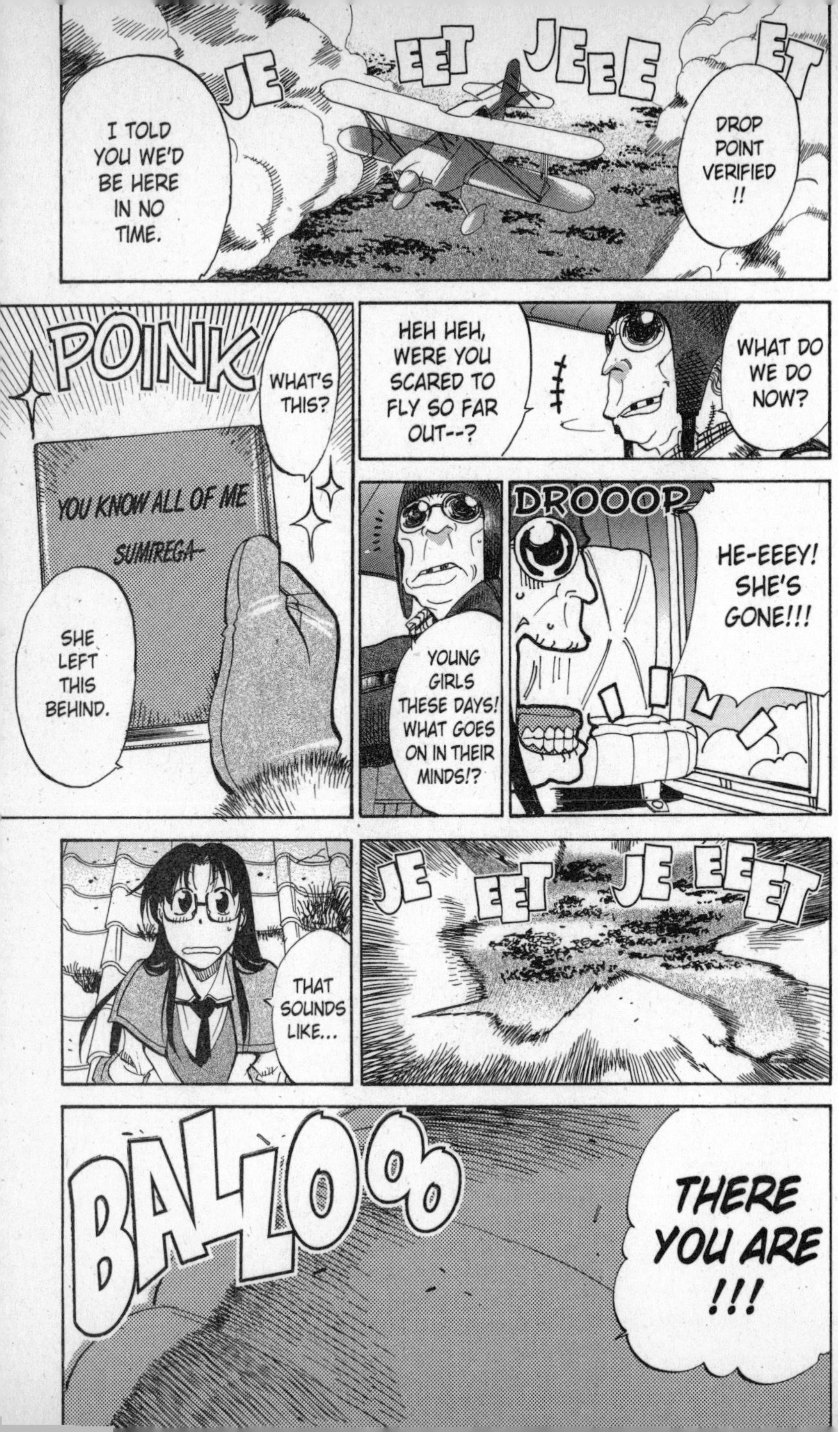
JE EET JEEE ET
DROP POINT VERIFIED !!
I TOLD YOU WE'D BE HERE IN NO TIME.
WHAT DO WE DO NOW?
HEH HEH, WERE YOU SCARED TO FLY SO FAR OUT--?
DROOOP
HE-EEEY! SHE'S GONE!!!
YOUNG GIRLS THESE DAYS! WHAT GOES ON IN THEIR MINDS!?
POINK
WHAT'S THIS?
YOU KNOW ALL OF ME
SUMIREGA
SHE LEFT THIS BEHIND.
JE EET JE EEET
THAT SOUNDS LIKE...
THERE YOU ARE !!!
BALOOO

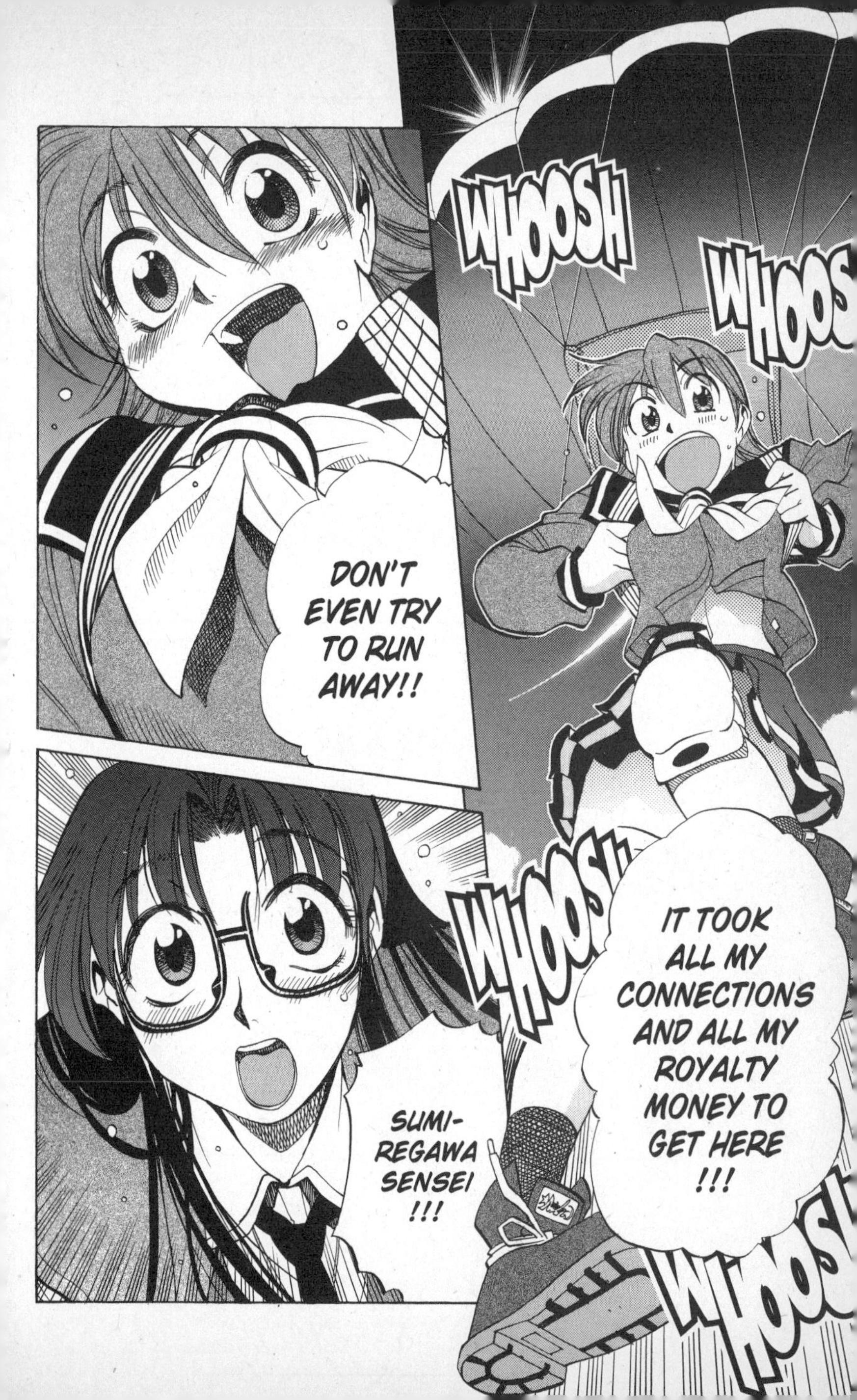
WHOOSH
WHOOS
DON'T EVEN TRY TO RUN AWAY!!
WHOOS
IT TOOK ALL MY CONNECTIONS AND ALL MY ROYALTY MONEY TO GET HERE !!!
WHOOS
SUMI-REGAWA SENSEI !!!

EPISODE SEVEN

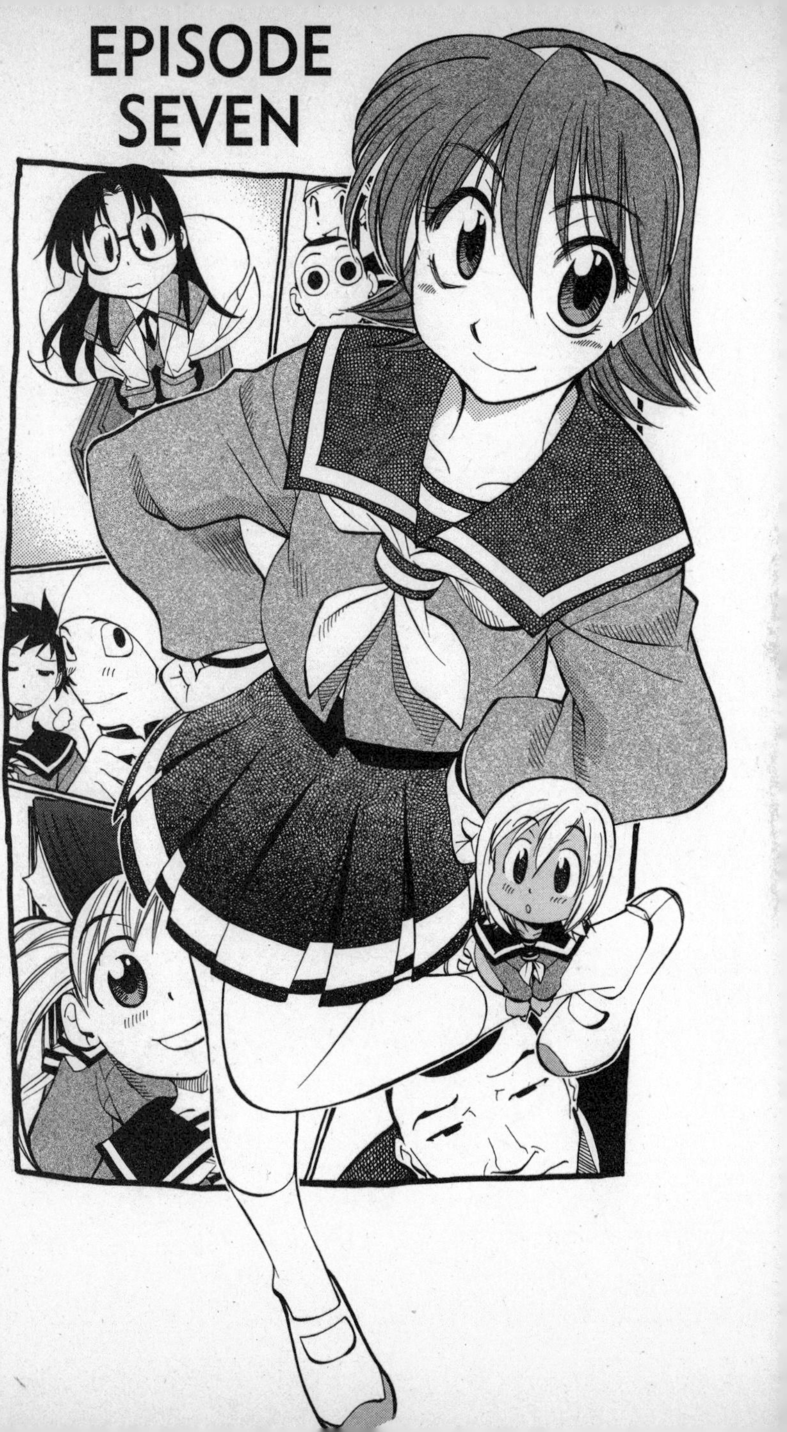

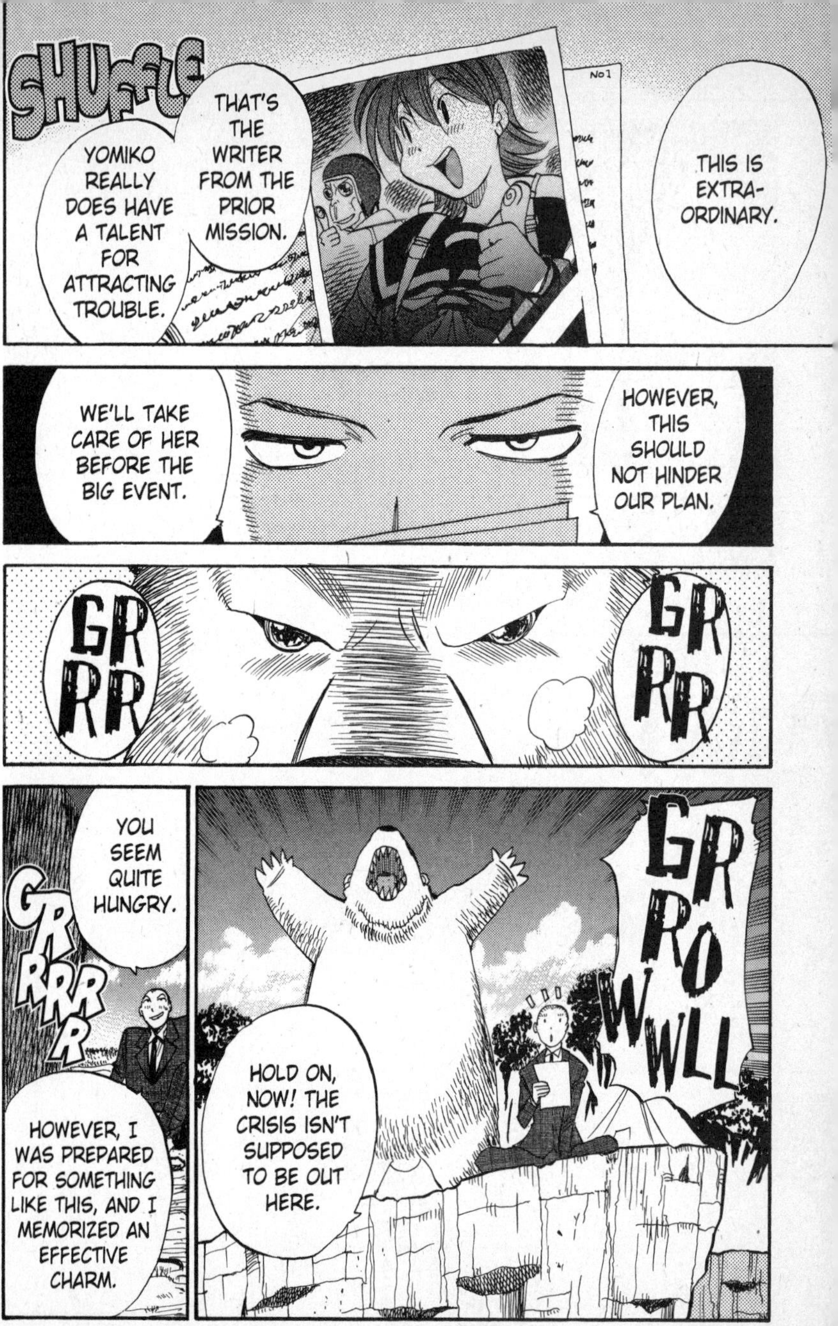
SHUFFLE
THIS IS EXTRA-ORDINARY.
THAT'S THE WRITER FROM THE PRIOR MISSION.
YOMIKO REALLY DOES HAVE A TALENT FOR ATTRACTING TROUBLE.
HOWEVER, THIS SHOULD NOT HINDER OUR PLAN.
WE'LL TAKE CARE OF HER BEFORE THE BIG EVENT.
GRRR
GRRR
GRROWWLL
HOLD ON, NOW! THE CRISIS ISN'T SUPPOSED TO BE OUT HERE.
YOU SEEM QUITE HUNGRY.
GRRRRR
HOWEVER, I WAS PREPARED FOR SOMETHING LIKE THIS, AND I MEMORIZED AN EFFECTIVE CHARM.

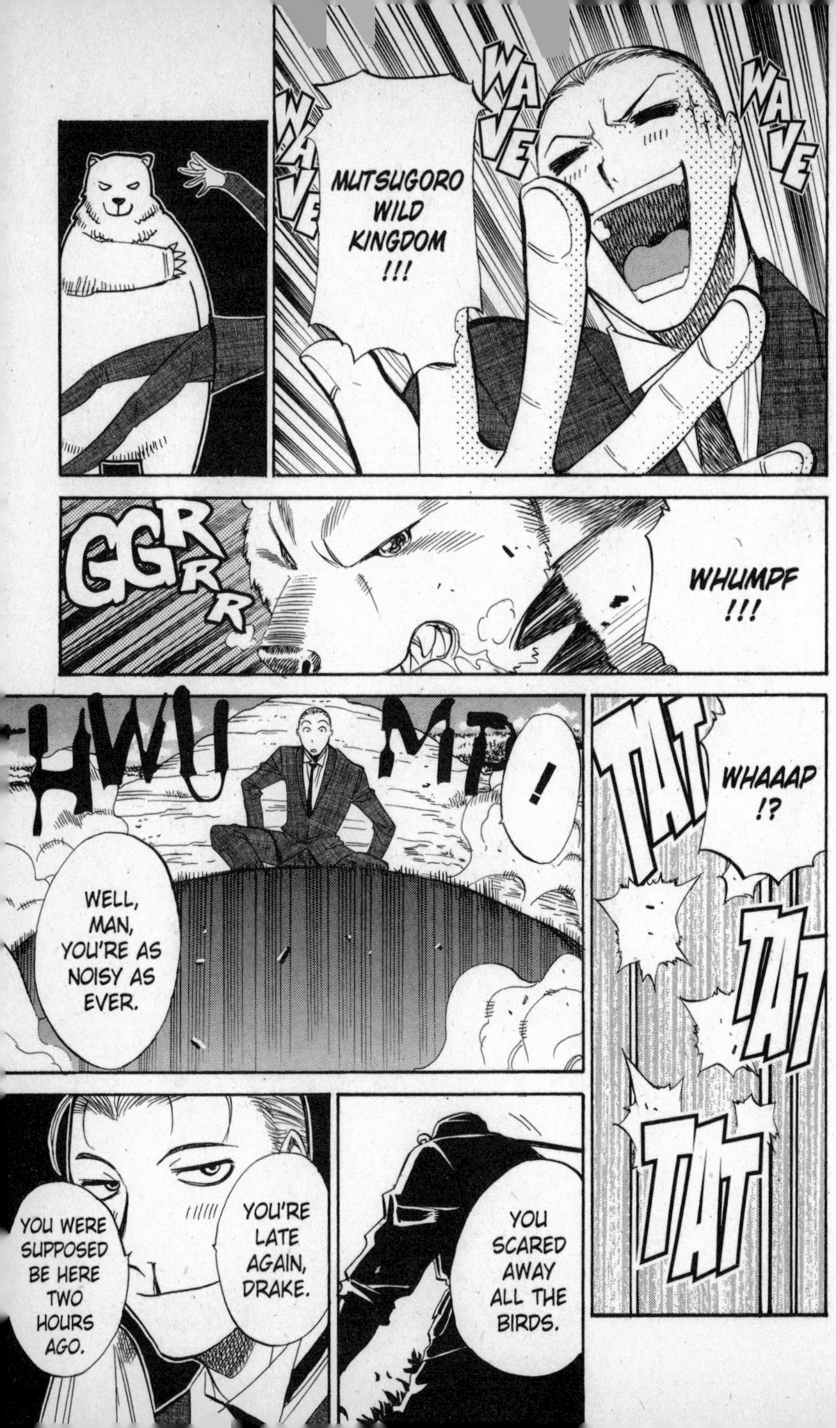
WAVE
WAVE
MUTSUGORO WILD KINGDOM !!!
WAVE
WHUMPF !!!
GGRRR
WHAAAP !?
TAT
TAT
TAT
HWUMP
!
WELL, MAN, YOU'RE AS NOISY AS EVER.
YOU SCARED AWAY ALL THE BIRDS.
YOU'RE LATE AGAIN, DRAKE.
YOU WERE SUPPOSED BE HERE TWO HOURS AGO.

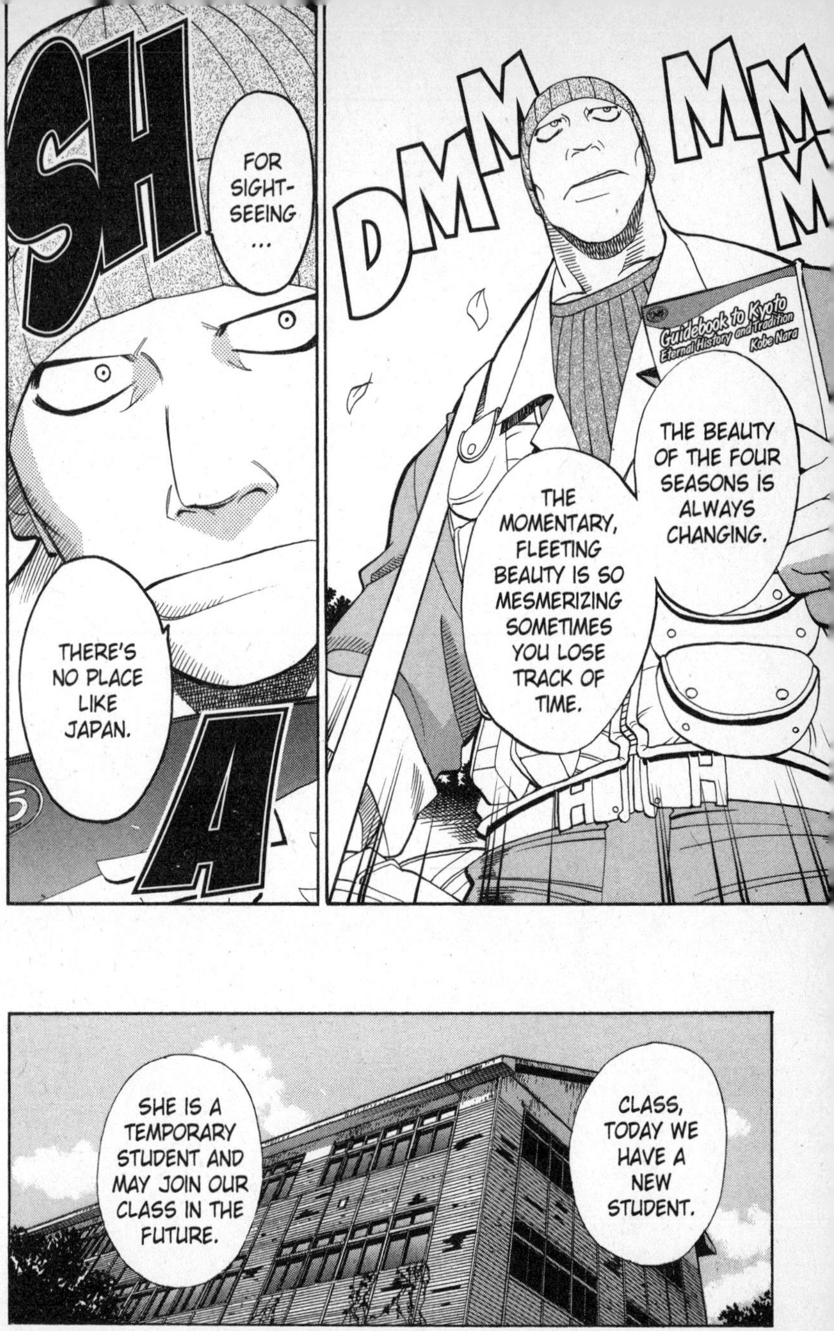
DMMMMMMM
Guidebook to Kyoto
Eternal History and Tradition
Kobe Nara
THE BEAUTY OF THE FOUR SEASONS IS ALWAYS CHANGING.
THE MOMENTARY, FLEETING BEAUTY IS SO MESMERIZING SOMETIMES YOU LOSE TRACK OF TIME.
SH
FOR SIGHT-SEEING...
THERE'S NO PLACE LIKE JAPAN.
A
CLASS, TODAY WE HAVE A NEW STUDENT.
SHE IS A TEMPORARY STUDENT AND MAY JOIN OUR CLASS IN THE FUTURE.

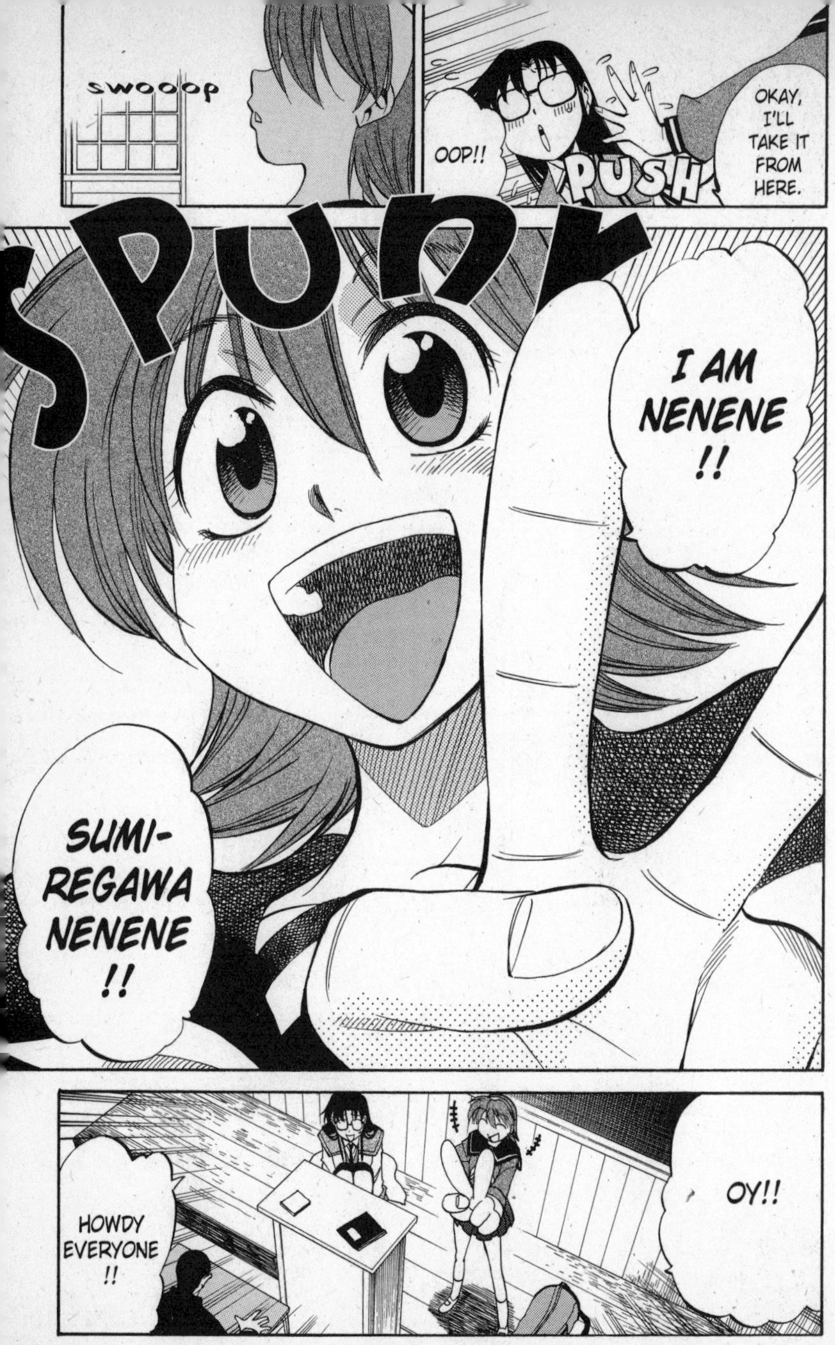
OKAY, I'LL TAKE IT FROM HERE.
PUSH
OOP!!
SWOOOP
I AM NENENE!!
SUMI-REGAWA NENENE!!
OY!!
HOWDY EVERYONE!!

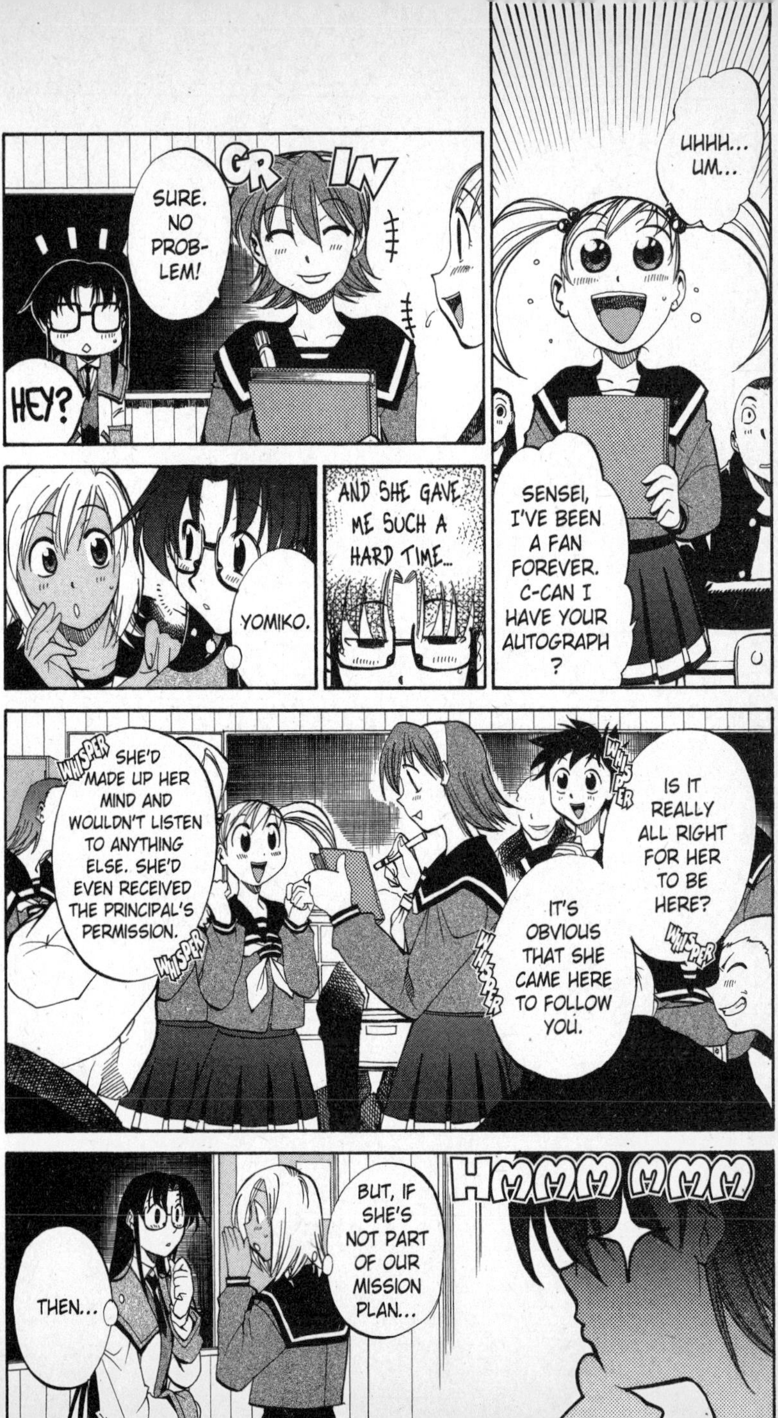
UHHH... UM...
SENSEI, I'VE BEEN A FAN FOREVER. C-CAN I HAVE YOUR AUTOGRAPH?
GRIN
SURE. NO PROB-LEM!
HEY?
AND SHE GAVE ME SUCH A HARD TIME...
YOMIKO.
WHISPER
IS IT REALLY ALL RIGHT FOR HER TO BE HERE?
WHISPER
IT'S OBVIOUS THAT SHE CAME HERE TO FOLLOW YOU.
WHISPER
WHISPER
SHE'D MADE UP HER MIND AND WOULDN'T LISTEN TO ANYTHING ELSE. SHE'D EVEN RECEIVED THE PRINCIPAL'S PERMISSION.
HMMM MMM
BUT, IF SHE'S NOT PART OF OUR MISSION PLAN...
THEN...

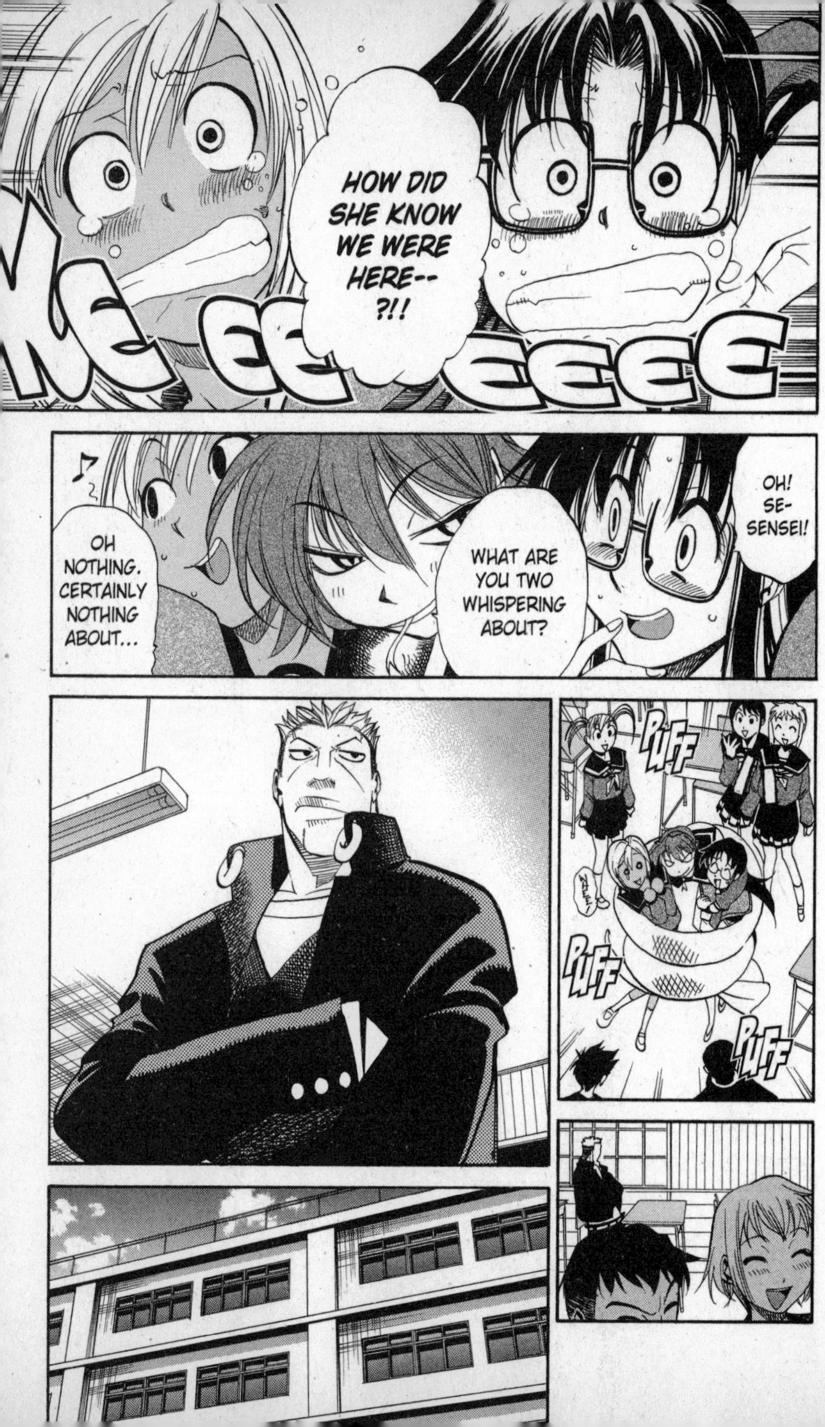
HOW DID SHE KNOW WE WERE HERE--?!!
OH! SE-SENSEI!
WHAT ARE YOU TWO WHISPERING ABOUT?
OH NOTHING. CERTAINLY NOTHING ABOUT...
PUFF
WHEE!
PUFF
PUFF

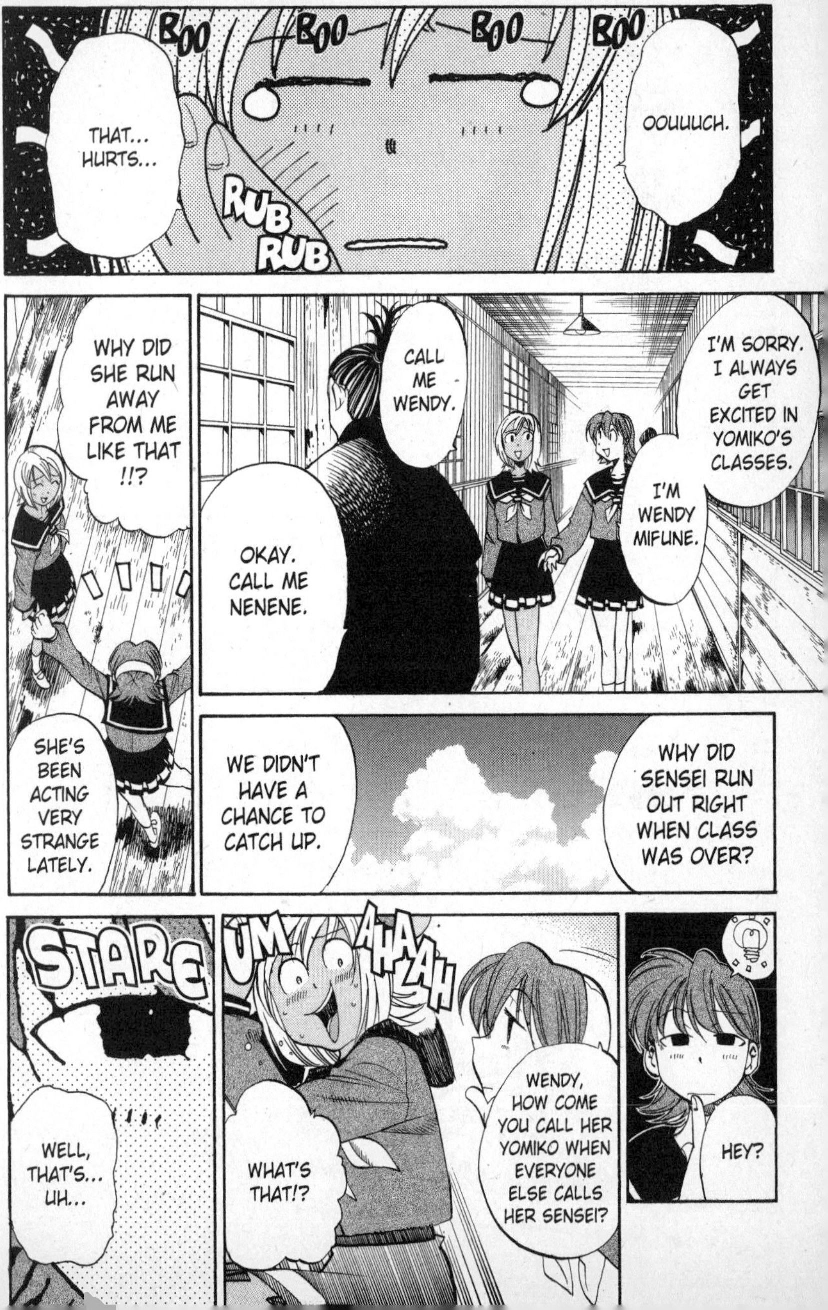
BOO
BOO
BOO
BOO
OOUUUCH.
THAT... HURTS...
RUB RUB
I'M SORRY. I ALWAYS GET EXCITED IN YOMIKO'S CLASSES.
I'M WENDY MIFUNE.
CALL ME WENDY.
OKAY. CALL ME NENENE.
WHY DID SENSEI RUN OUT RIGHT WHEN CLASS WAS OVER?
WE DIDN'T HAVE A CHANCE TO CATCH UP.
WHY DID SHE RUN AWAY FROM ME LIKE THAT !!?
SHE'S BEEN ACTING VERY STRANGE LATELY.
HEY?
WENDY, HOW COME YOU CALL HER YOMIKO WHEN EVERYONE ELSE CALLS HER SENSEI?
AHAAAH
UM
WHAT'S THAT!?
STARE
...
WELL, THAT'S... UH...

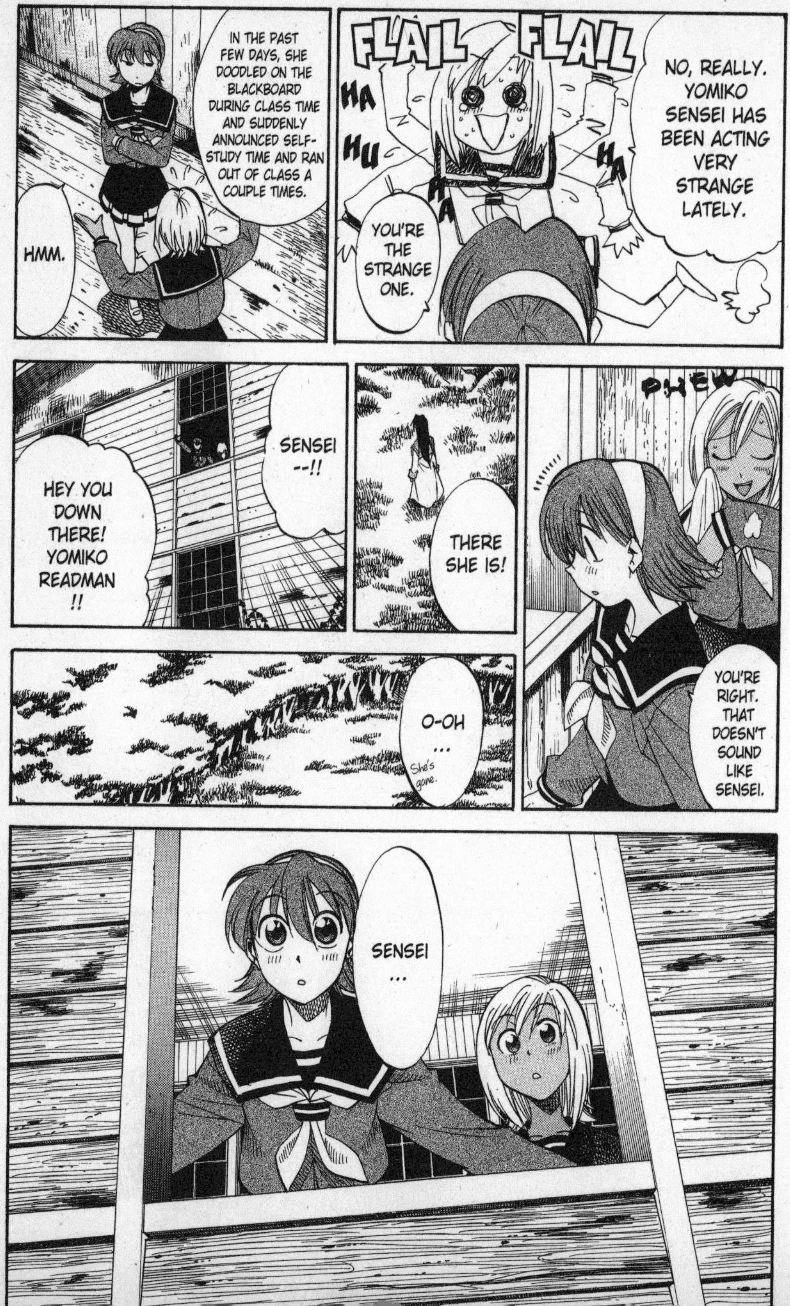
FLAIL FLAIL
NO, REALLY. YOMIKO SENSEI HAS BEEN ACTING VERY STRANGE LATELY.
HA HA HU HA HA
YOU'RE THE STRANGE ONE.
IN THE PAST FEW DAYS, SHE DOODLED ON THE BLACKBOARD DURING CLASS TIME AND SUDDENLY ANNOUNCED SELF-STUDY TIME AND RAN OUT OF CLASS A COUPLE TIMES.
HMM.
PHEW
YOU'RE RIGHT. THAT DOESN'T SOUND LIKE SENSEI.
THERE SHE IS!
SENSEI --!!
HEY YOU DOWN THERE! YOMIKO READMAN !!
O-OH ...
She's gone.
SENSEI ...

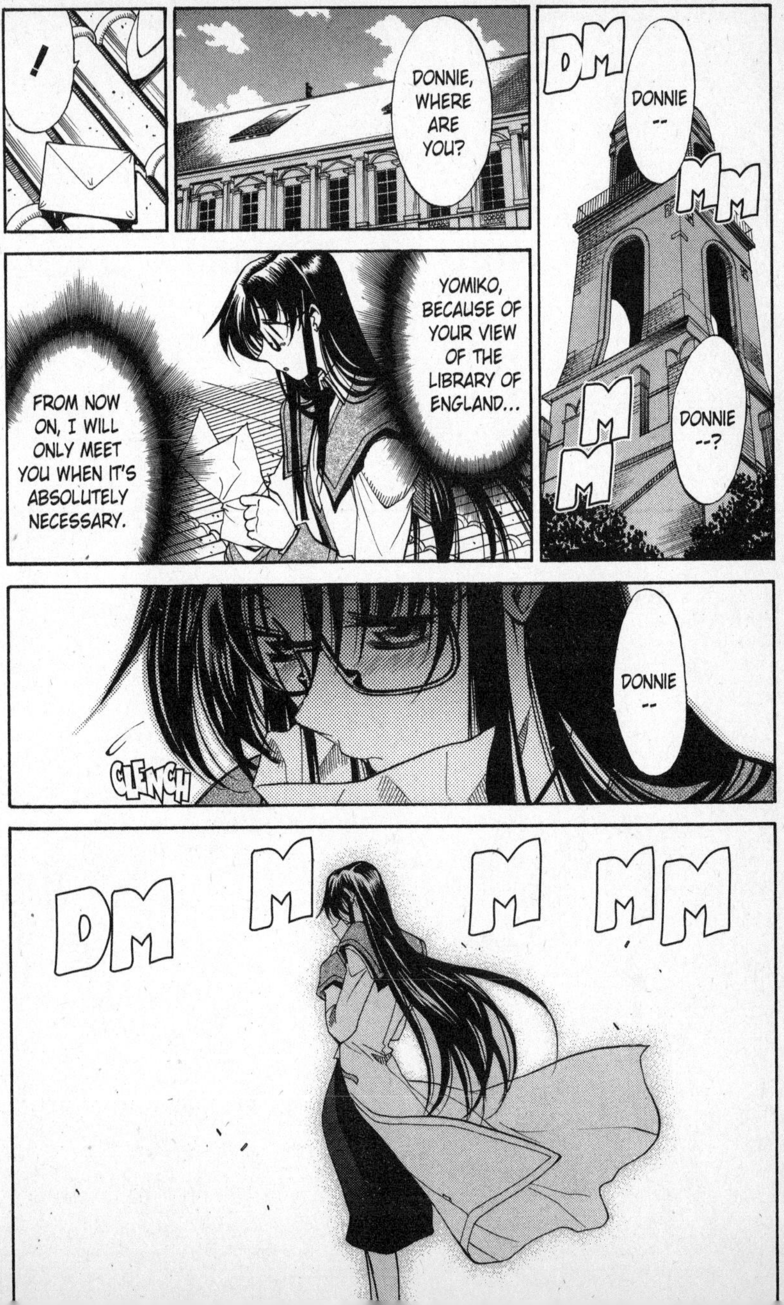
DM
DONNIE --
MM
DONNIE --?
M M M
DONNIE, WHERE ARE YOU?
!
YOMIKO, BECAUSE OF YOUR VIEW OF THE LIBRARY OF ENGLAND...
FROM NOW ON, I WILL ONLY MEET YOU WHEN IT'S ABSOLUTELY NECESSARY.
DONNIE --
CLENCH
DM M M MM

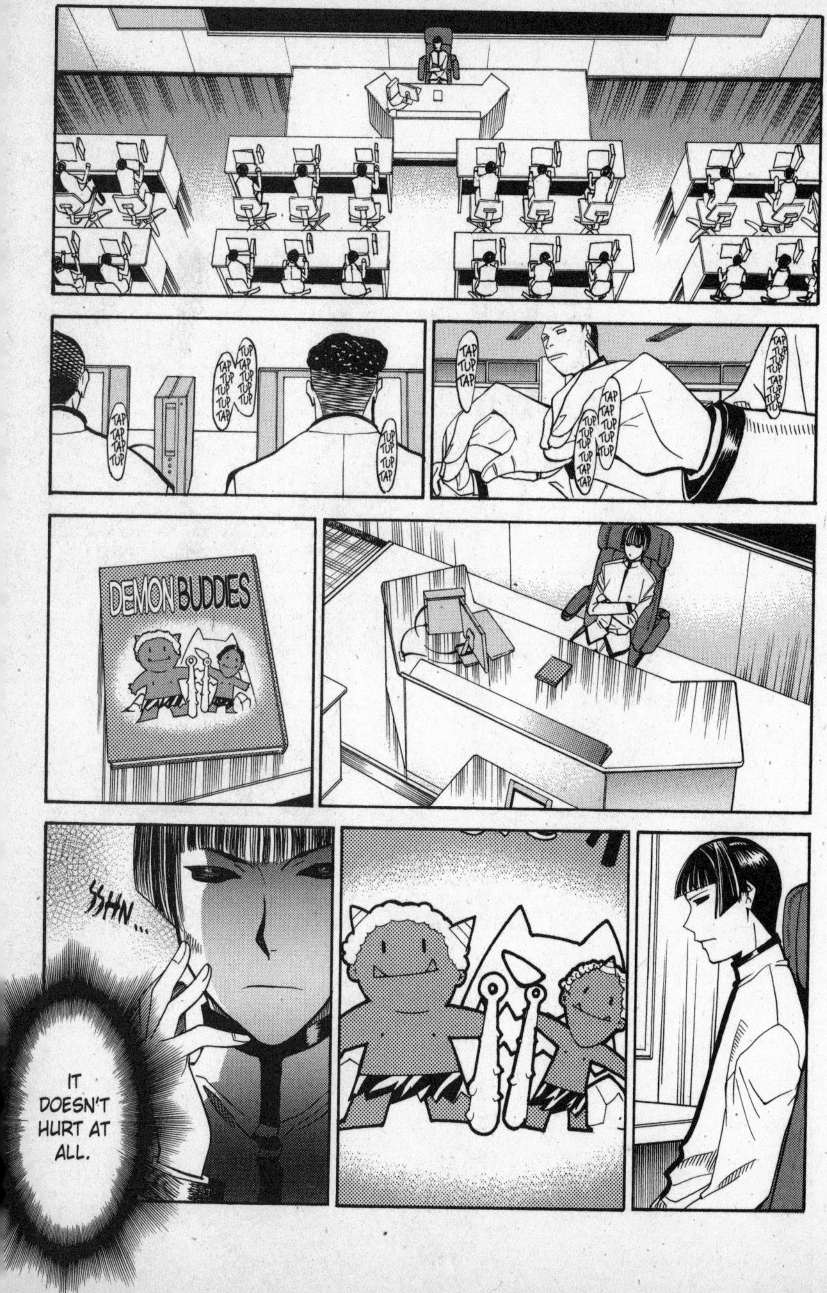
TAP TUP TUP TUP TAP TUP TUP TUP
TAP TAP TUP TUP TUP
TUP TUP TUP TUP TAP TAP
TAP TUP TAP
TUP TUP TUP TAP
TUP TAP TUP TUP TUP
TAP TUP TUP TUP TAP
TAP TAP TAP TUP
DEMON BUDDIES
SSHN...
IT DOESN'T HURT AT ALL.

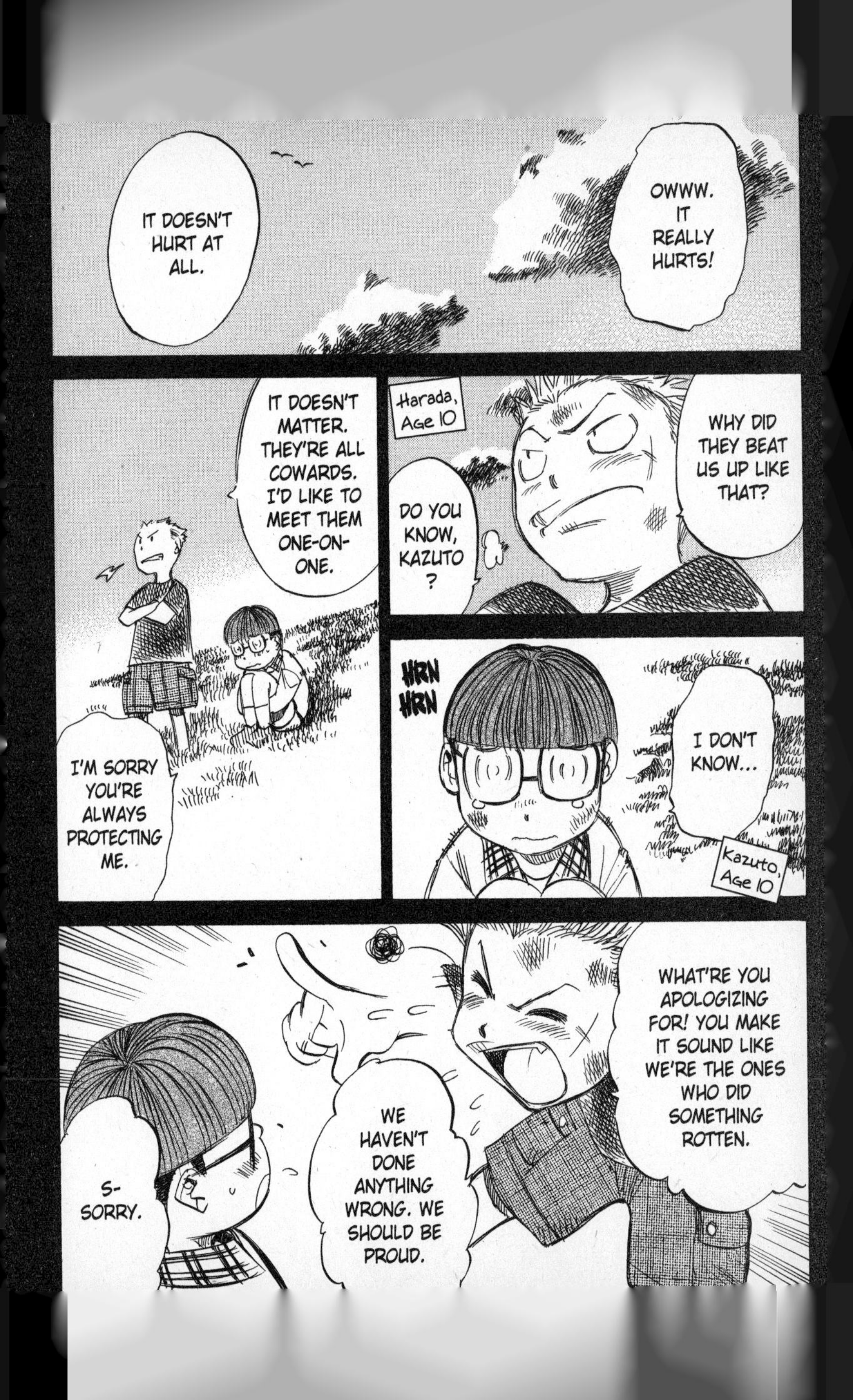
OWWW. IT REALLY HURTS!
IT DOESN'T HURT AT ALL.
WHY DID THEY BEAT US UP LIKE THAT?
Harada, Age 10
DO YOU KNOW, KAZUTO?
I DON'T KNOW...
HRN HRN
Kazuto, Age 10
IT DOESN'T MATTER. THEY'RE ALL COWARDS. I'D LIKE TO MEET THEM ONE-ON-ONE.
I'M SORRY YOU'RE ALWAYS PROTECTING ME.
WHAT'RE YOU APOLOGIZING FOR! YOU MAKE IT SOUND LIKE WE'RE THE ONES WHO DID SOMETHING ROTTEN.
WE HAVEN'T DONE ANYTHING WRONG. WE SHOULD BE PROUD.
S-SORRY.

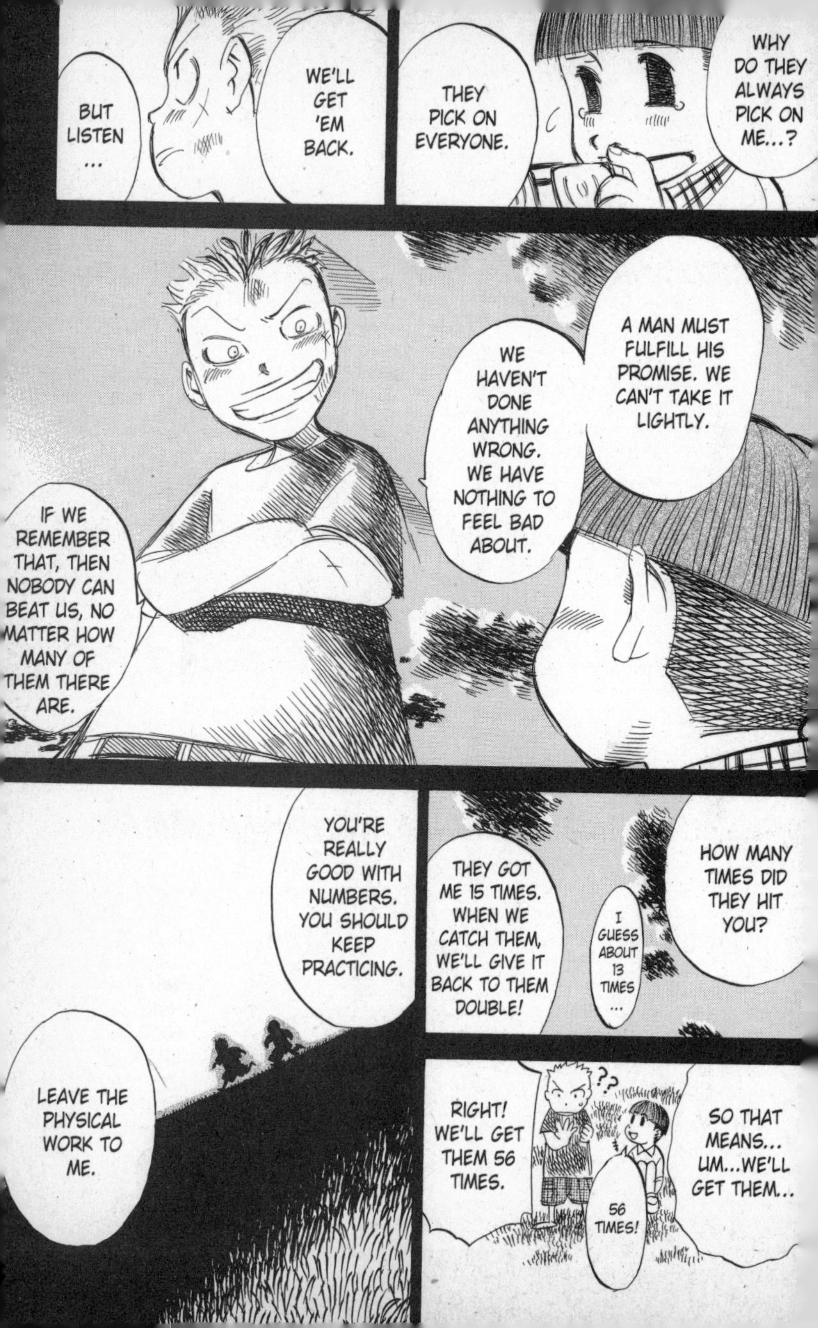
WHY DO THEY ALWAYS PICK ON ME...?
THEY PICK ON EVERYONE.
WE'LL GET 'EM BACK.
BUT LISTEN ...
A MAN MUST FULFILL HIS PROMISE. WE CAN'T TAKE IT LIGHTLY.
WE HAVEN'T DONE ANYTHING WRONG. WE HAVE NOTHING TO FEEL BAD ABOUT.
IF WE REMEMBER THAT, THEN NOBODY CAN BEAT US, NO MATTER HOW MANY OF THEM THERE ARE.
HOW MANY TIMES DID THEY HIT YOU?
I GUESS ABOUT 13 TIMES ...
THEY GOT ME 15 TIMES. WHEN WE CATCH THEM, WE'LL GIVE IT BACK TO THEM DOUBLE!
SO THAT MEANS... UM...WE'LL GET THEM...
56 TIMES!
RIGHT! WE'LL GET THEM 56 TIMES.
??
YOU'RE REALLY GOOD WITH NUMBERS. YOU SHOULD KEEP PRACTICING.
LEAVE THE PHYSICAL WORK TO ME.

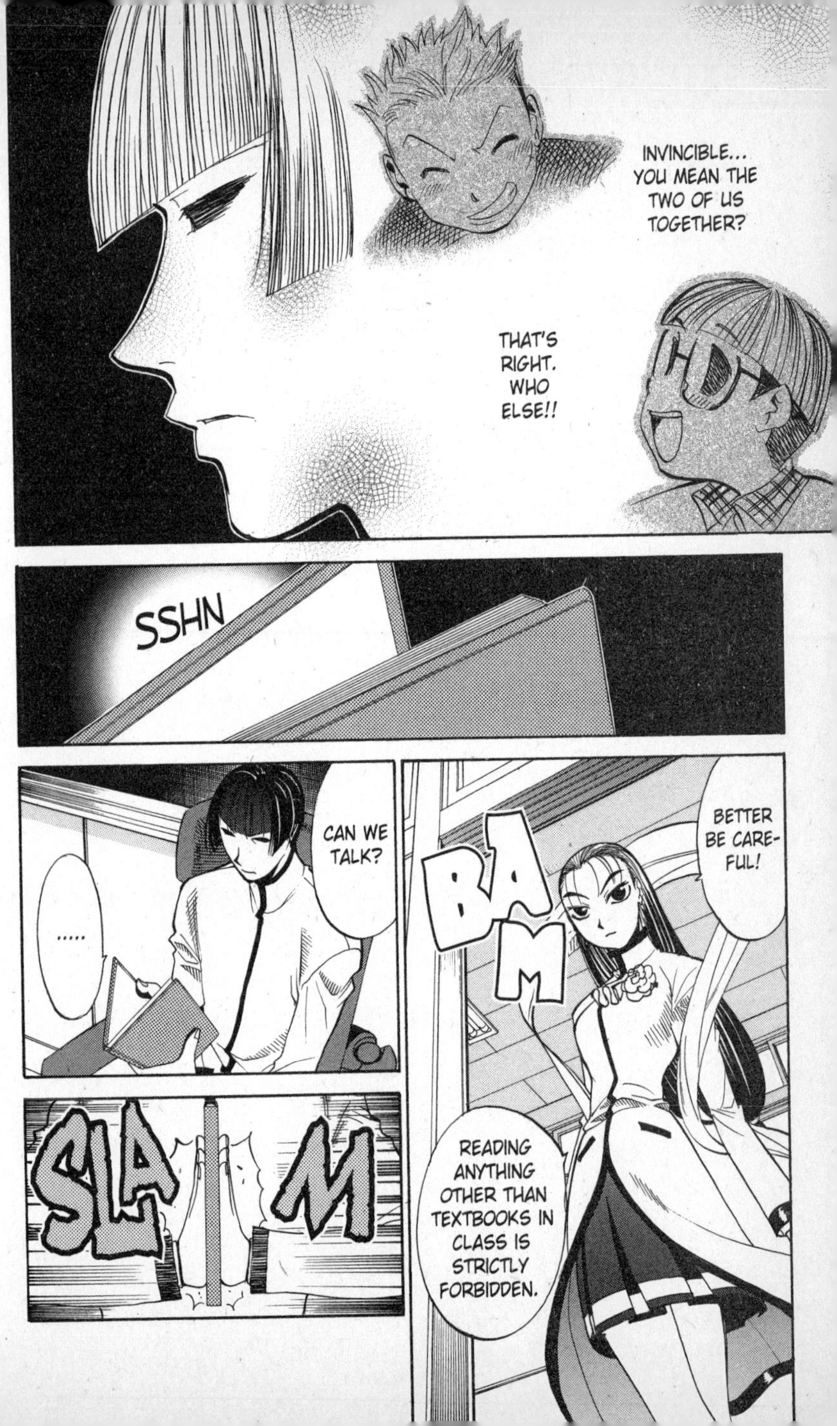
INVINCIBLE... YOU MEAN THE TWO OF US TOGETHER?
THAT'S RIGHT. WHO ELSE!!
SSHN
BAM
BETTER BE CARE-FUL!
READING ANYTHING OTHER THAN TEXTBOOKS IN CLASS IS STRICTLY FORBIDDEN.
CAN WE TALK?
.....
SLAM

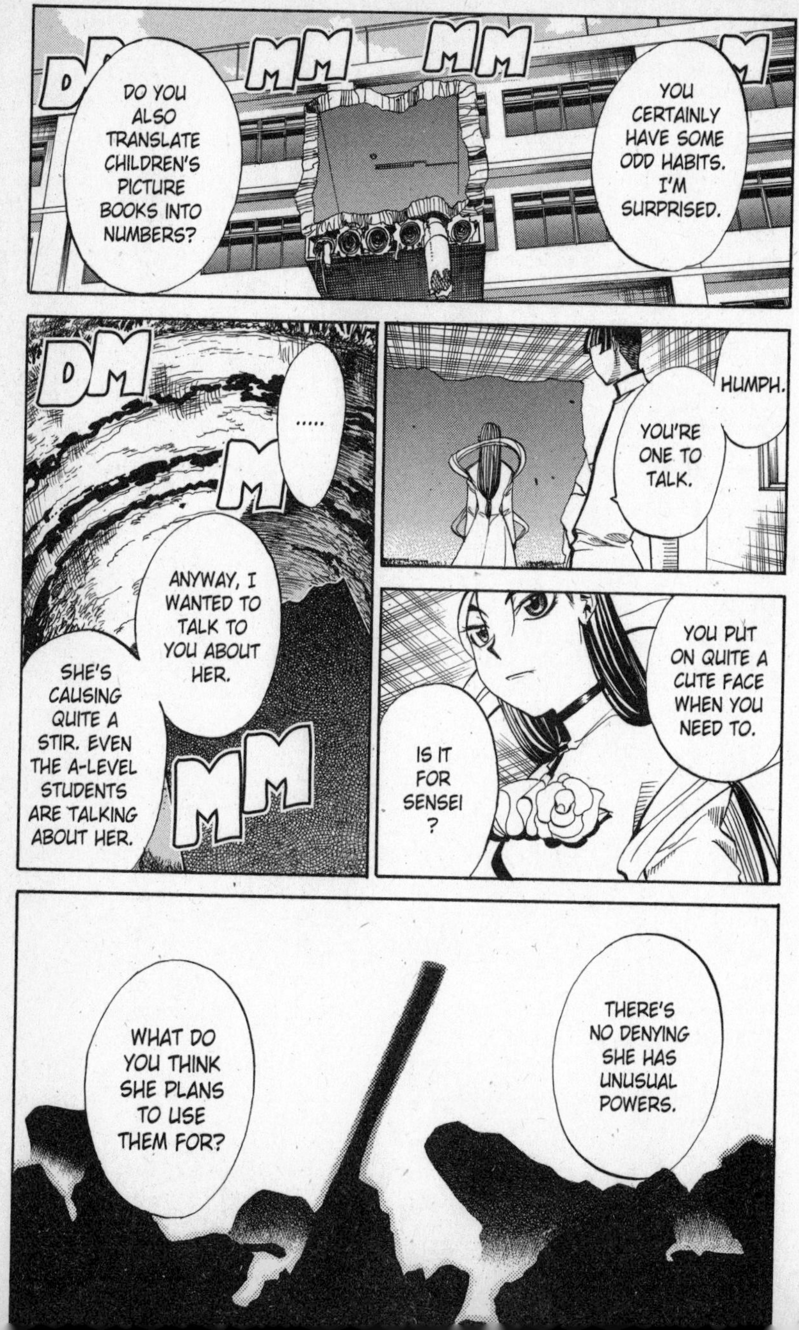
MM MM
YOU CERTAINLY HAVE SOME ODD HABITS. I'M SURPRISED.
DO YOU ALSO TRANSLATE CHILDREN'S PICTURE BOOKS INTO NUMBERS?
HUMPH.
YOU'RE ONE TO TALK.
YOU PUT ON QUITE A CUTE FACE WHEN YOU NEED TO.
IS IT FOR SENSEI?
DM
.....
M
ANYWAY, I WANTED TO TALK TO YOU ABOUT HER.
SHE'S CAUSING QUITE A STIR. EVEN THE A-LEVEL STUDENTS ARE TALKING ABOUT HER.
MM
THERE'S NO DENYING SHE HAS UNUSUAL POWERS.
WHAT DO YOU THINK SHE PLANS TO USE THEM FOR?

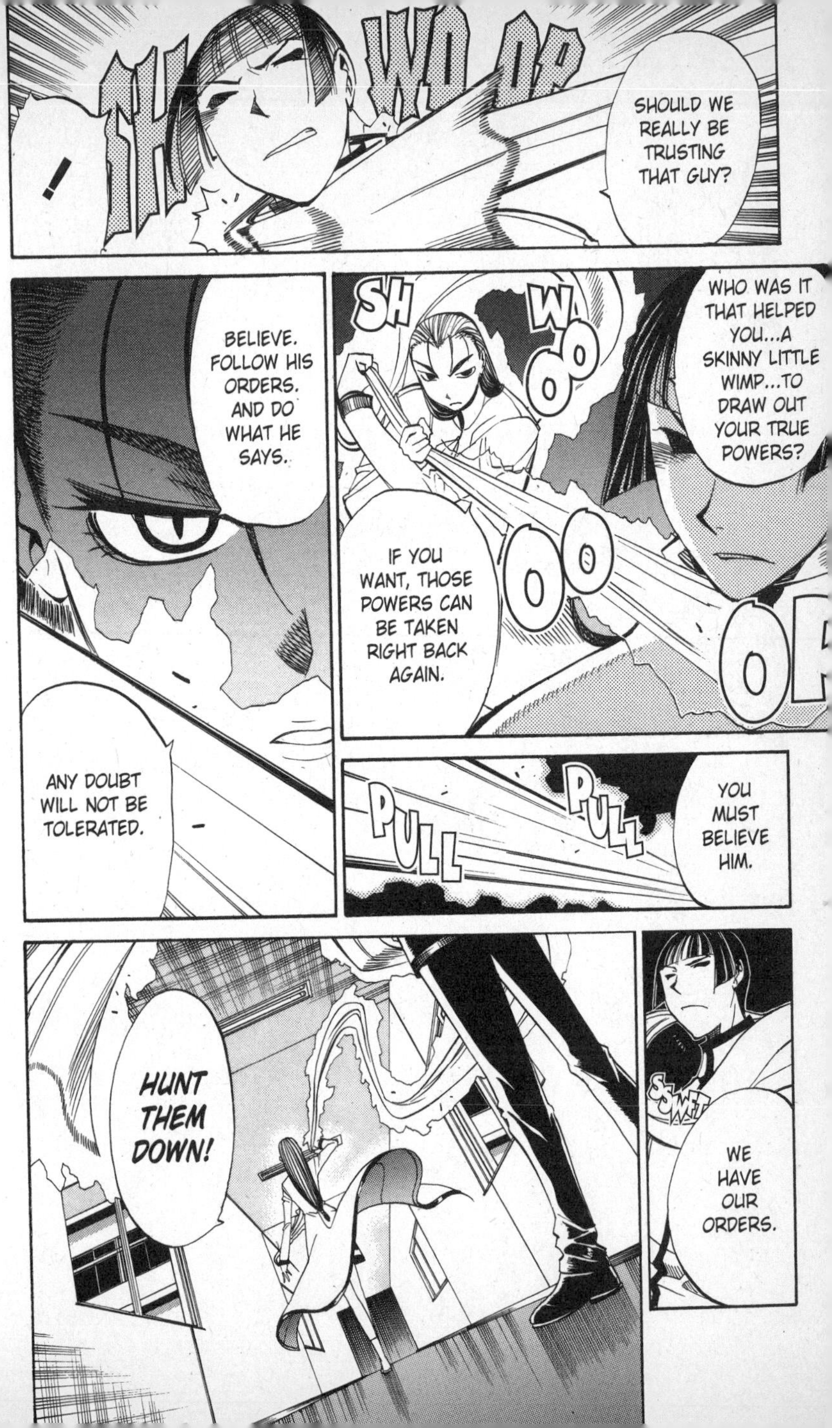
SHWO OP
SHOULD WE REALLY BE TRUSTING THAT GUY?
!
WHO WAS IT THAT HELPED YOU...A SKINNY LITTLE WIMP...TO DRAW OUT YOUR TRUE POWERS?
SHWOOOOOP
IF YOU WANT, THOSE POWERS CAN BE TAKEN RIGHT BACK AGAIN.
YOU MUST BELIEVE HIM.
PULL PULL
BELIEVE. FOLLOW HIS ORDERS. AND DO WHAT HE SAYS.
ANY DOUBT WILL NOT BE TOLERATED.
SWFT
WE HAVE OUR ORDERS.
HUNT THEM DOWN!

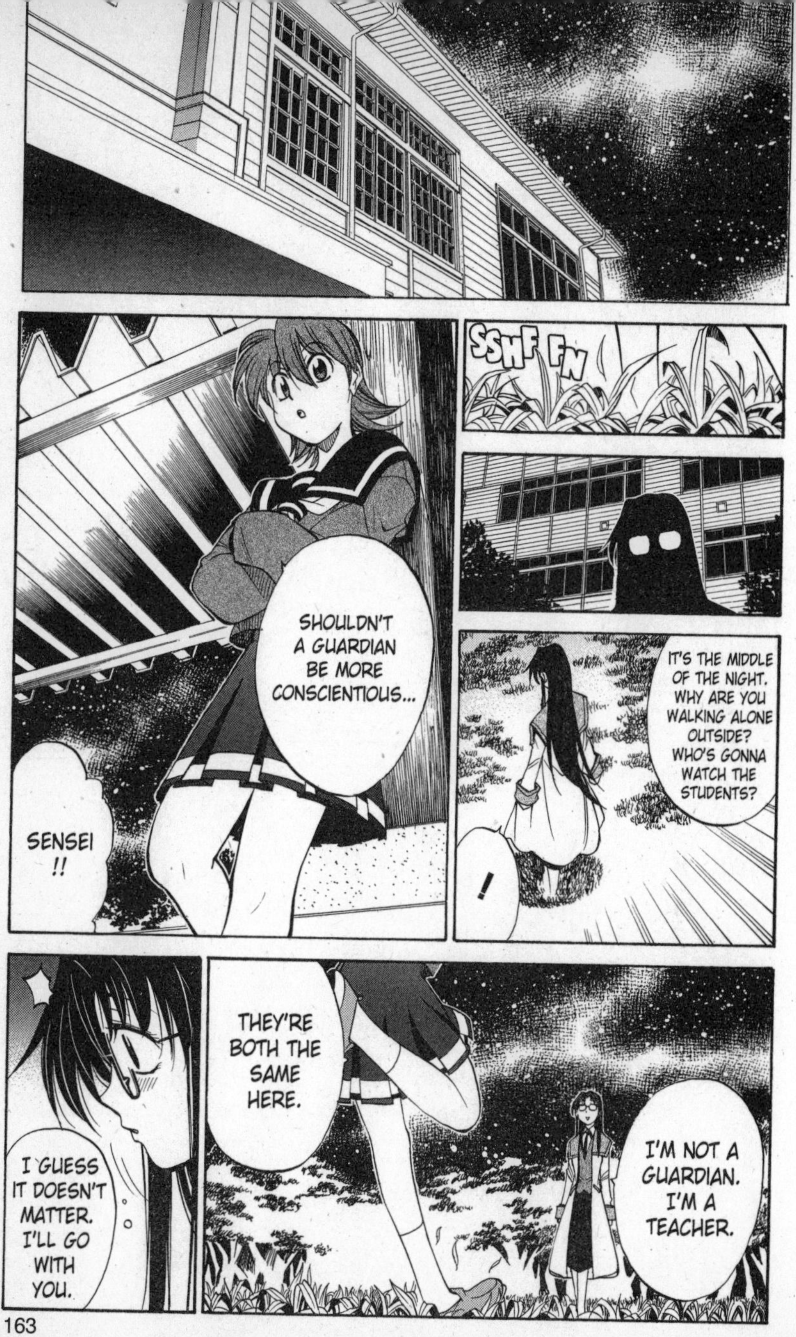
SSHF FN
IT'S THE MIDDLE OF THE NIGHT. WHY ARE YOU WALKING ALONE OUTSIDE? WHO'S GONNA WATCH THE STUDENTS?
!
SHOULDN'T A GUARDIAN BE MORE CONSCIENTIOUS...
SENSEI !!
I'M NOT A GUARDIAN. I'M A TEACHER.
THEY'RE BOTH THE SAME HERE.
I GUESS IT DOESN'T MATTER. I'LL GO WITH YOU.

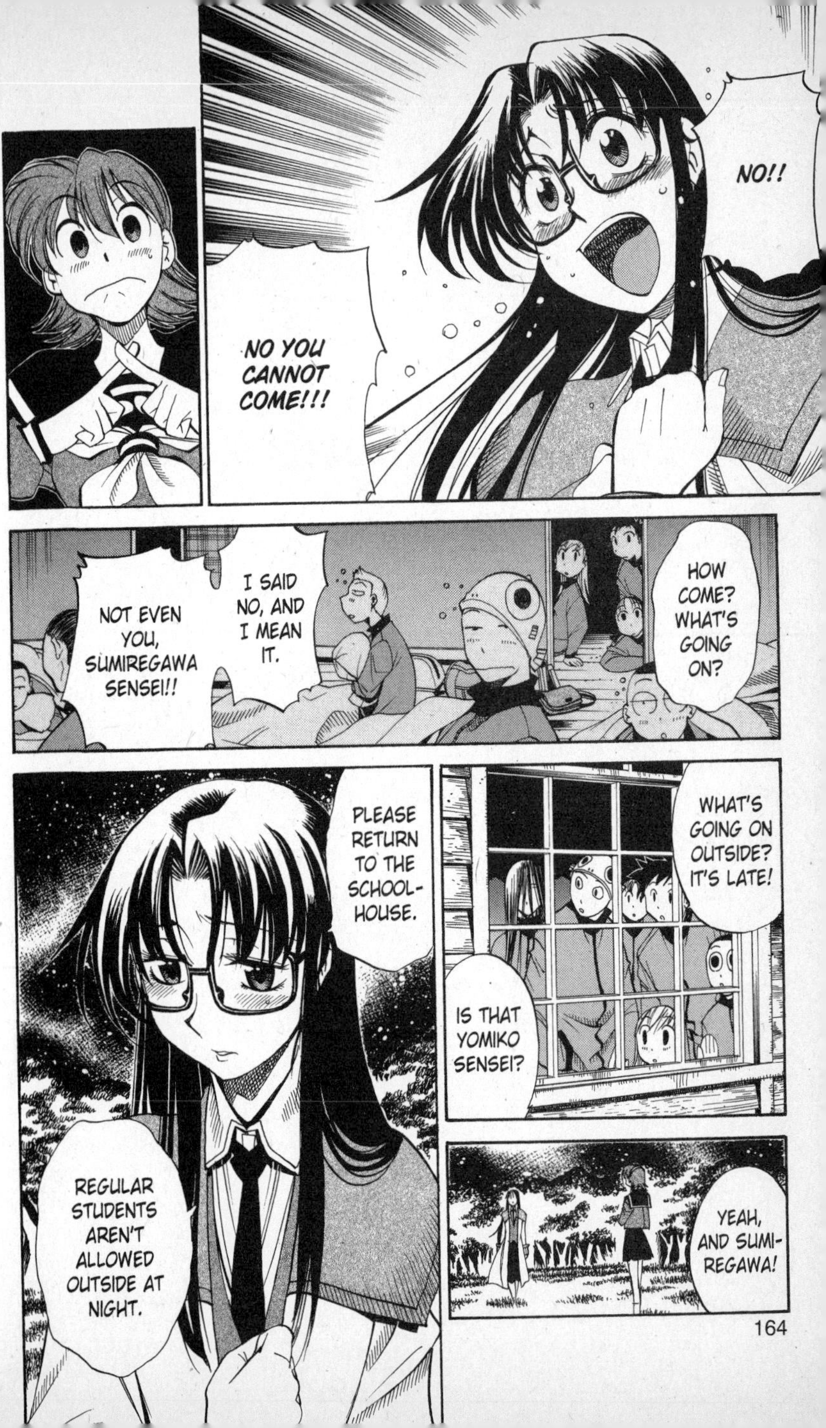
NO!!
NO YOU CANNOT COME!!!
HOW COME? WHAT'S GOING ON?
I SAID NO, AND I MEAN IT.
NOT EVEN YOU, SUMIREGAWA SENSEI!!
WHAT'S GOING ON OUTSIDE? IT'S LATE!
IS THAT YOMIKO SENSEI?
YEAH, AND SUMI-REGAWA!
PLEASE RETURN TO THE SCHOOL-HOUSE.
REGULAR STUDENTS AREN'T ALLOWED OUTSIDE AT NIGHT.

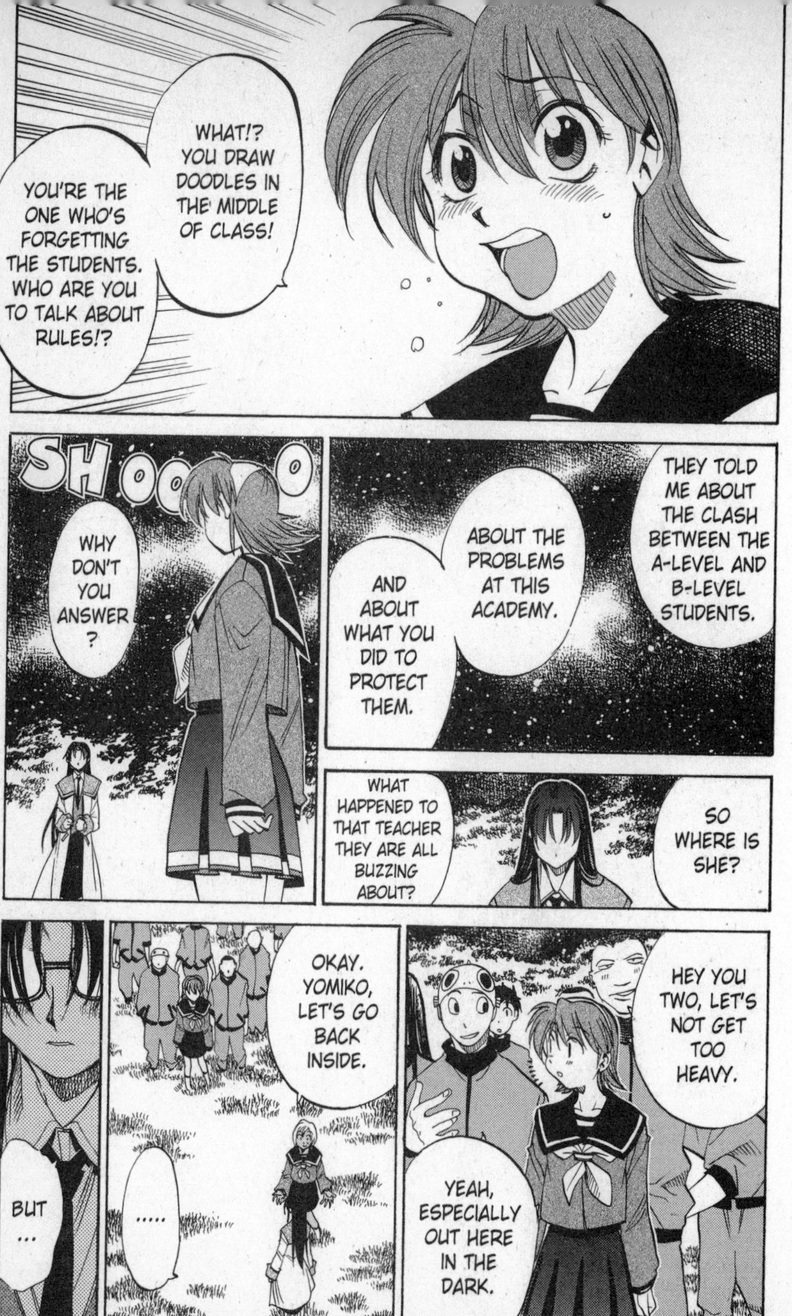
WHAT!? YOU DRAW DOODLES IN THE MIDDLE OF CLASS!
YOU'RE THE ONE WHO'S FORGETTING THE STUDENTS. WHO ARE YOU TO TALK ABOUT RULES!?
THEY TOLD ME ABOUT THE CLASH BETWEEN THE A-LEVEL AND B-LEVEL STUDENTS.
ABOUT THE PROBLEMS AT THIS ACADEMY.
AND ABOUT WHAT YOU DID TO PROTECT THEM.
SO WHERE IS SHE?
WHAT HAPPENED TO THAT TEACHER THEY ARE ALL BUZZING ABOUT?
SHOOOO
WHY DON'T YOU ANSWER?
HEY YOU TWO, LET'S NOT GET TOO HEAVY.
YEAH, ESPECIALLY OUT HERE IN THE DARK.
OKAY. YOMIKO, LET'S GO BACK INSIDE.
.....
BUT ...

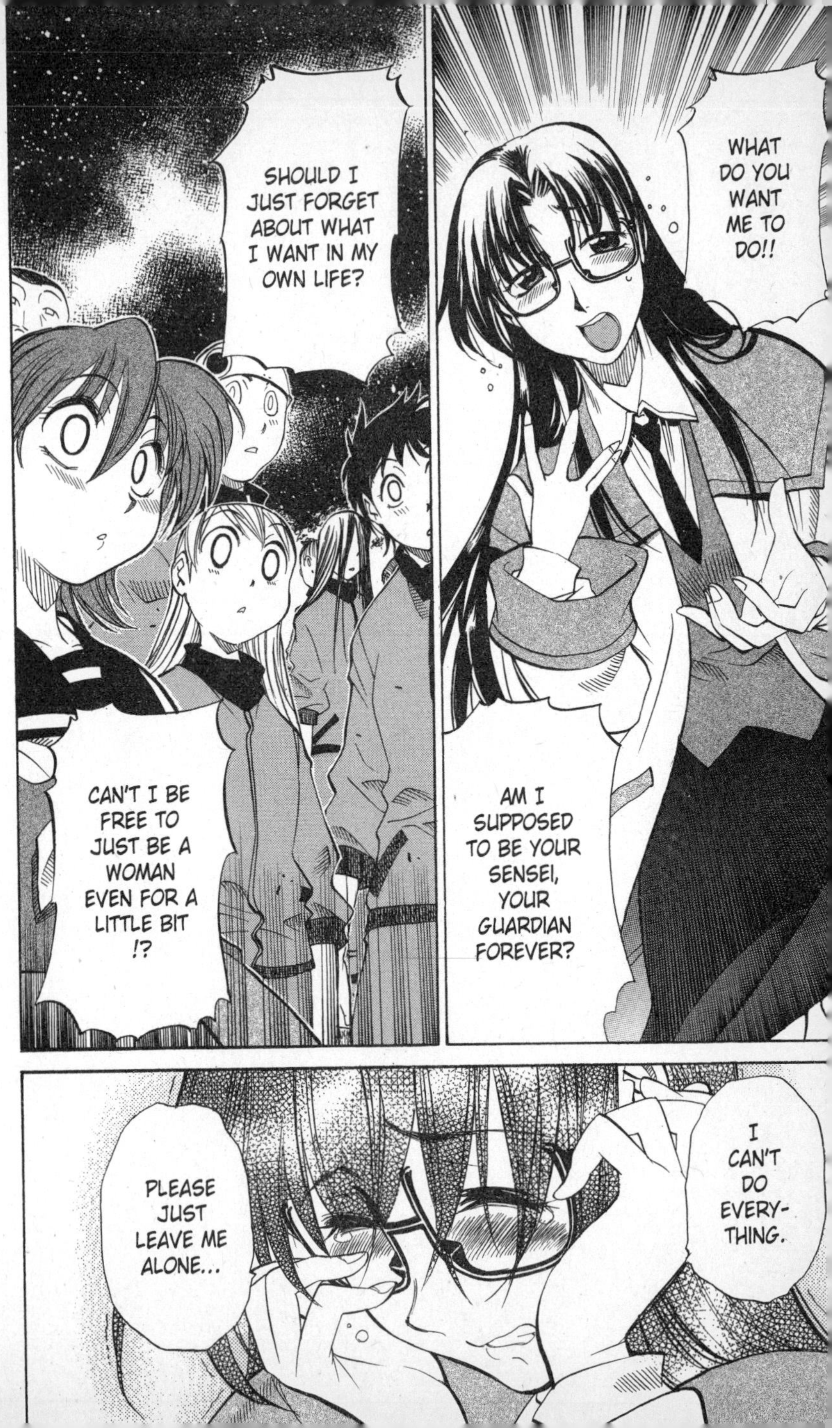
WHAT DO YOU WANT ME TO DO!!
AM I SUPPOSED TO BE YOUR SENSEI, YOUR GUARDIAN FOREVER?
SHOULD I JUST FORGET ABOUT WHAT I WANT IN MY OWN LIFE?
CAN'T I BE FREE TO JUST BE A WOMAN EVEN FOR A LITTLE BIT !?
I CAN'T DO EVERY-THING.
PLEASE JUST LEAVE ME ALONE...

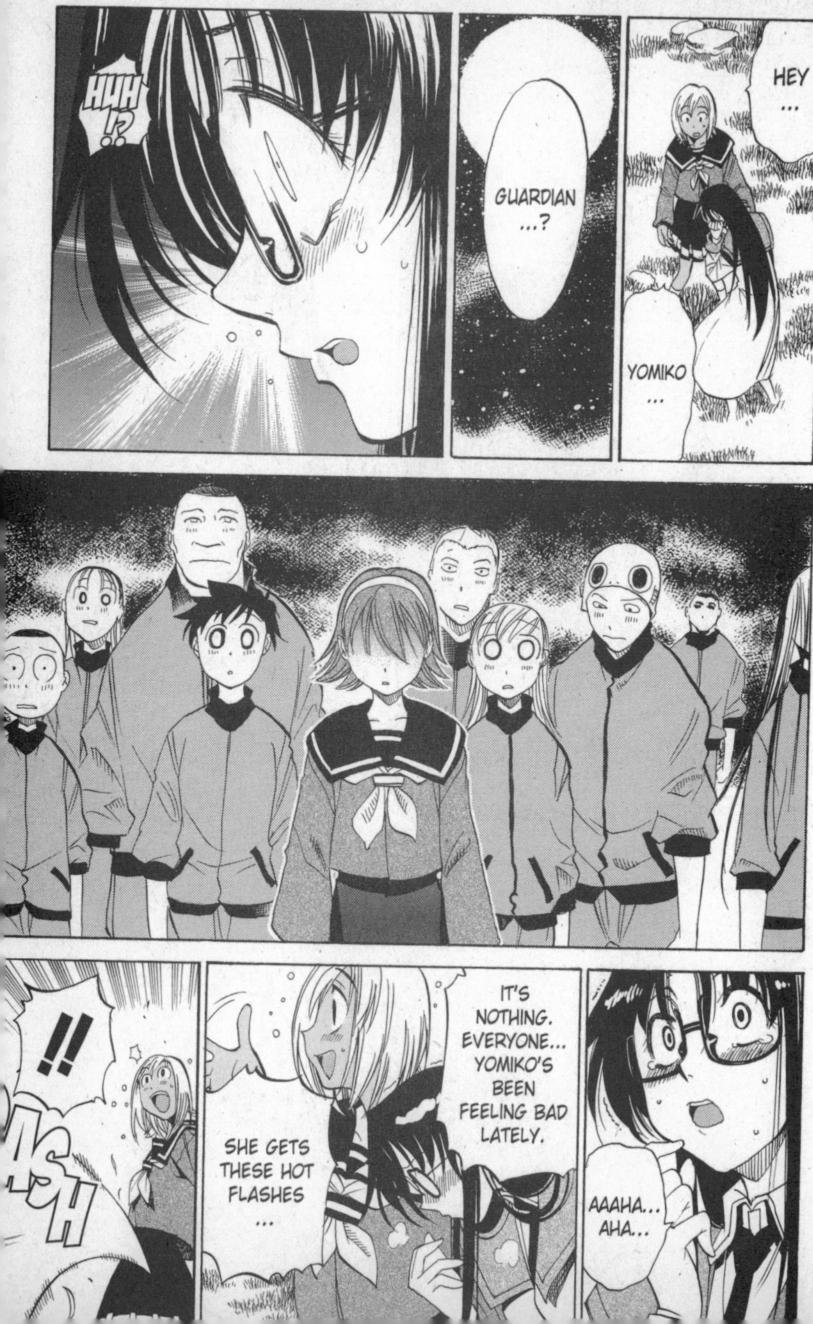
HEY ...
YOMIKO ...
GUARDIAN ...?
HUH !?
AAAHA... AHA...
IT'S NOTHING. EVERYONE... YOMIKO'S BEEN FEELING BAD LATELY.
SHE GETS THESE HOT FLASHES ...
!!

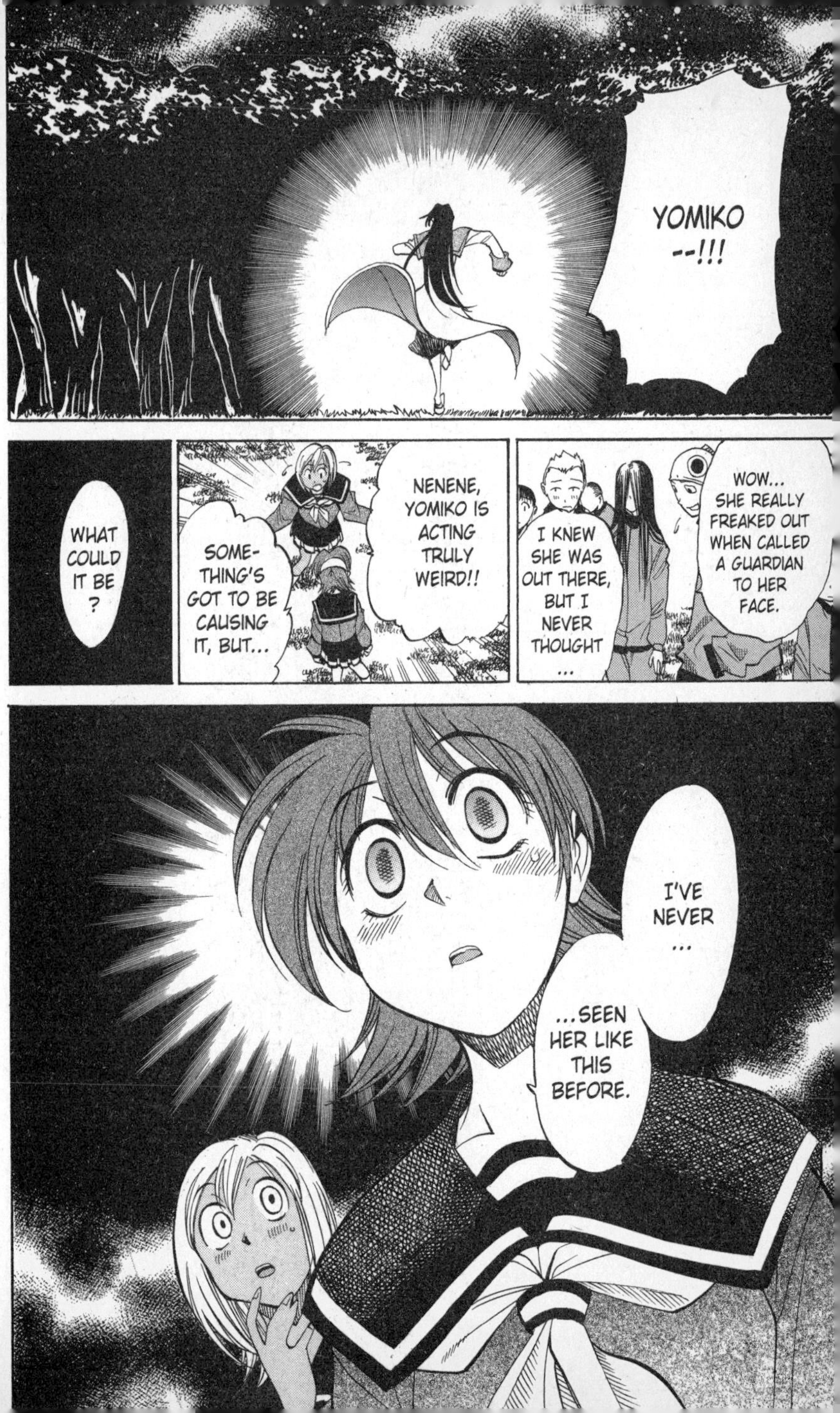
YOMIKO --!!!
WOW... SHE REALLY FREAKED OUT WHEN CALLED A GUARDIAN TO HER FACE.
I KNEW SHE WAS OUT THERE, BUT I NEVER THOUGHT ...
NENENE, YOMIKO IS ACTING TRULY WEIRD!!
SOME-THING'S GOT TO BE CAUSING IT, BUT...
WHAT COULD IT BE ?
I'VE NEVER ...
...SEEN HER LIKE THIS BEFORE.

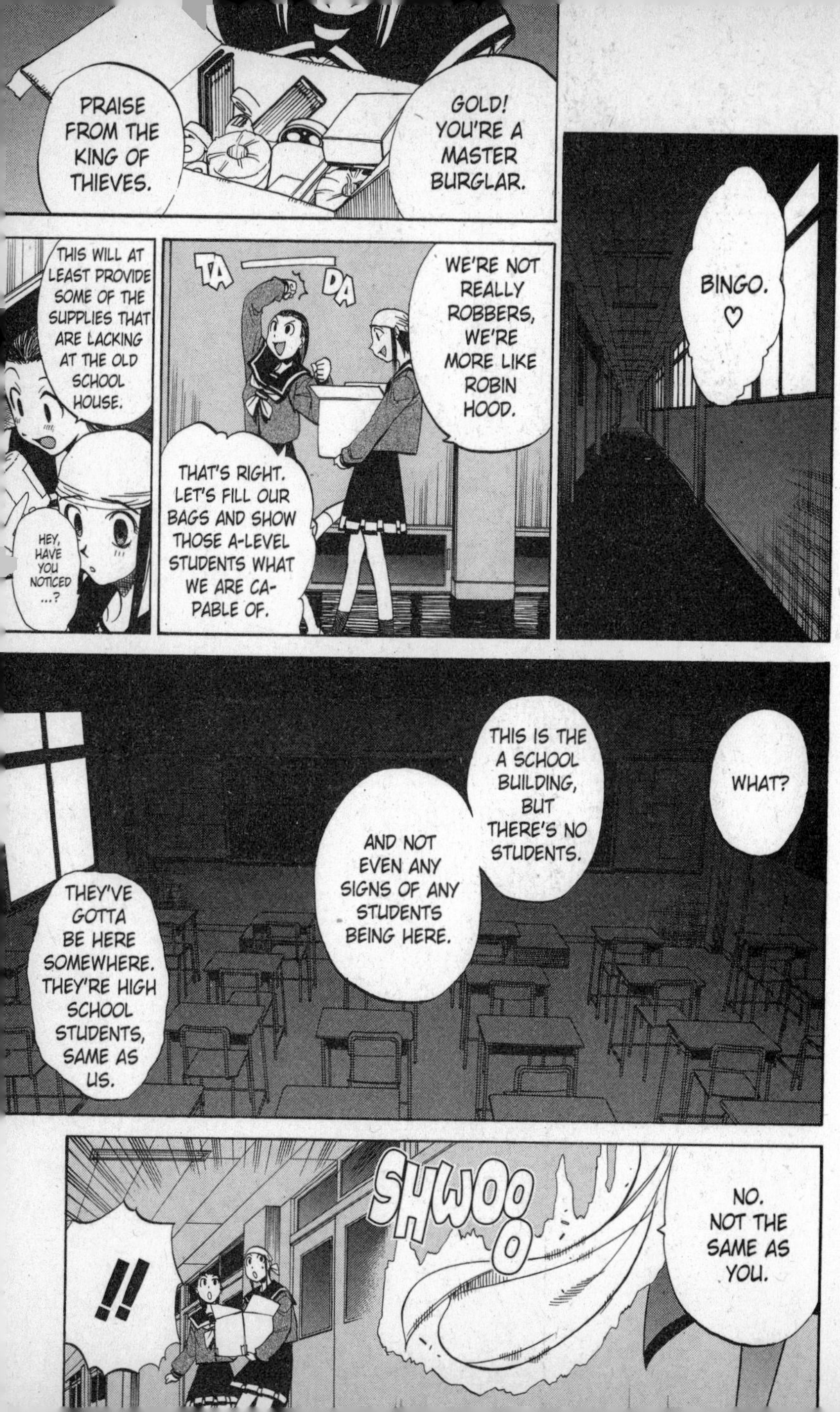
GOLD! YOU'RE A MASTER BURGLAR.
PRAISE FROM THE KING OF THIEVES.
BINGO. ♡
TA DA
WE'RE NOT REALLY ROBBERS, WE'RE MORE LIKE ROBIN HOOD.
THAT'S RIGHT. LET'S FILL OUR BAGS AND SHOW THOSE A-LEVEL STUDENTS WHAT WE ARE CA-PABLE OF.
THIS WILL AT LEAST PROVIDE SOME OF THE SUPPLIES THAT ARE LACKING AT THE OLD SCHOOL HOUSE.
HEY, HAVE YOU NOTICED ...?
WHAT?
THIS IS THE A SCHOOL BUILDING, BUT THERE'S NO STUDENTS.
AND NOT EVEN ANY SIGNS OF ANY STUDENTS BEING HERE.
THEY'VE GOTTA BE HERE SOMEWHERE. THEY'RE HIGH SCHOOL STUDENTS, SAME AS US.
NO. NOT THE SAME AS YOU.
SHWOOO
!!

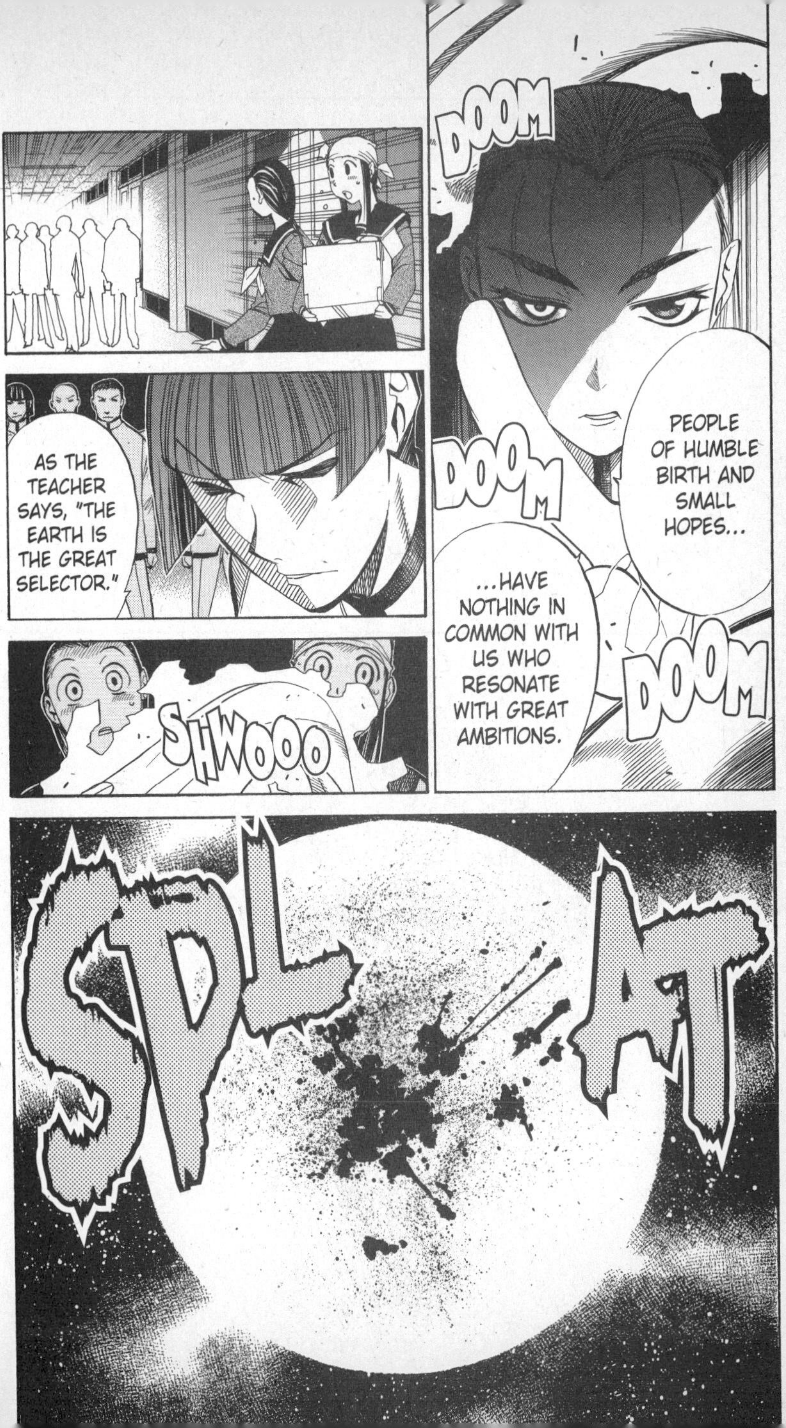
DOOM
PEOPLE OF HUMBLE BIRTH AND SMALL HOPES...
DOOM
...HAVE NOTHING IN COMMON WITH US WHO RESONATE WITH GREAT AMBITIONS.
DOOM
AS THE TEACHER SAYS, "THE EARTH IS THE GREAT SELECTOR."
SHWOOO
SPLAT

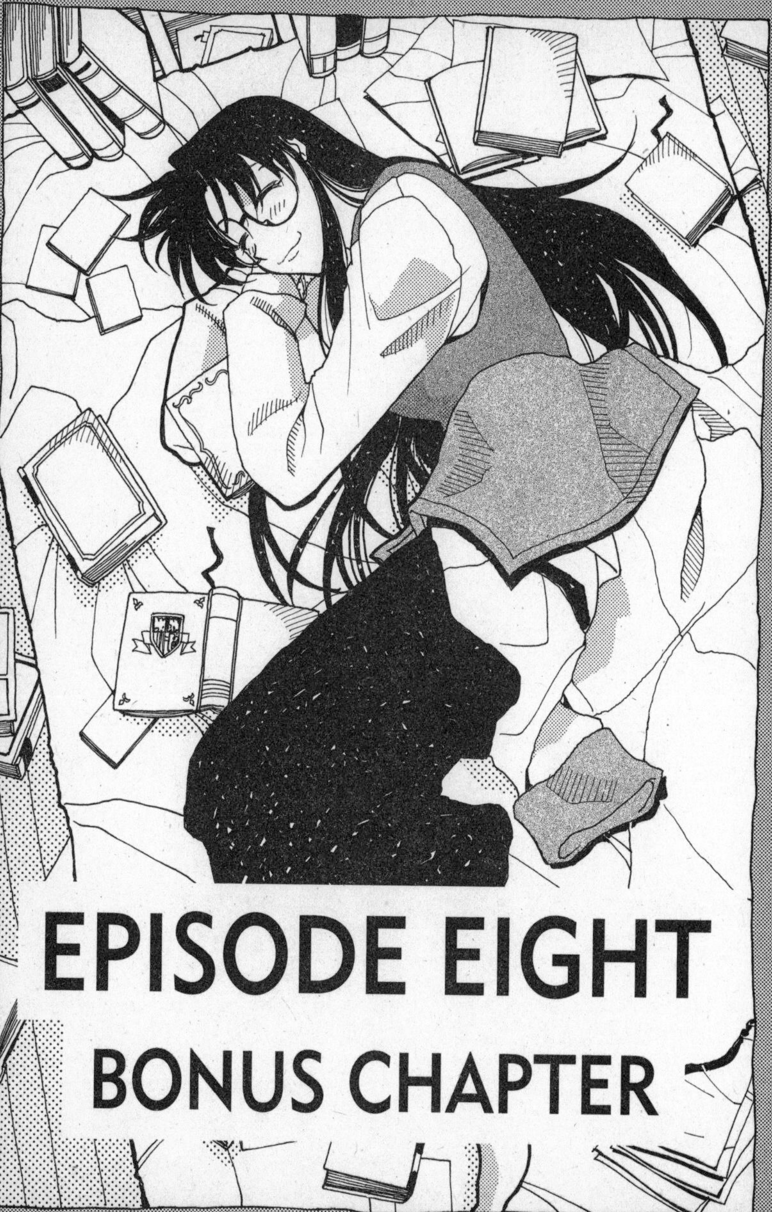
EPISODE EIGHT
BONUS CHAPTER

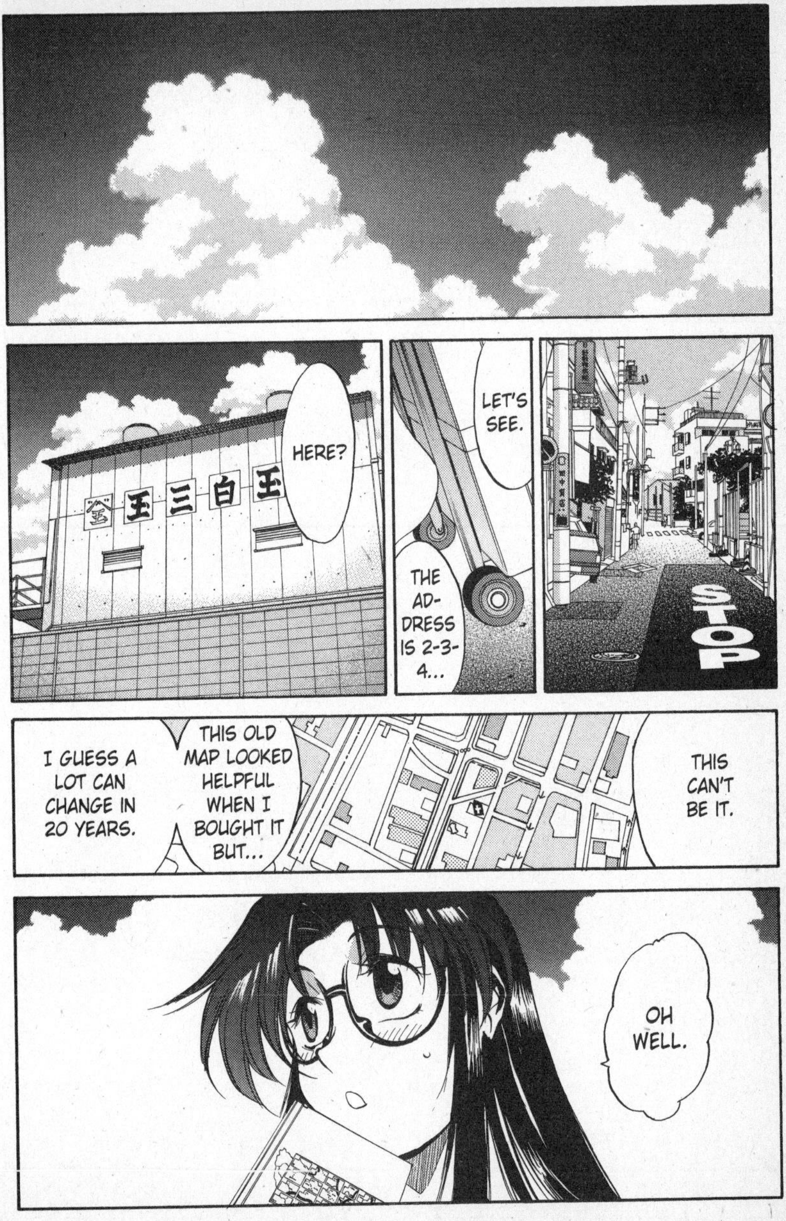
STOP
LET'S SEE.
THE ADDRESS IS 2-3-4...
HERE?
玉三白玉
THIS CAN'T BE IT.
THIS OLD MAP LOOKED HELPFUL WHEN I BOUGHT IT BUT...
I GUESS A LOT CAN CHANGE IN 20 YEARS.
OH WELL.

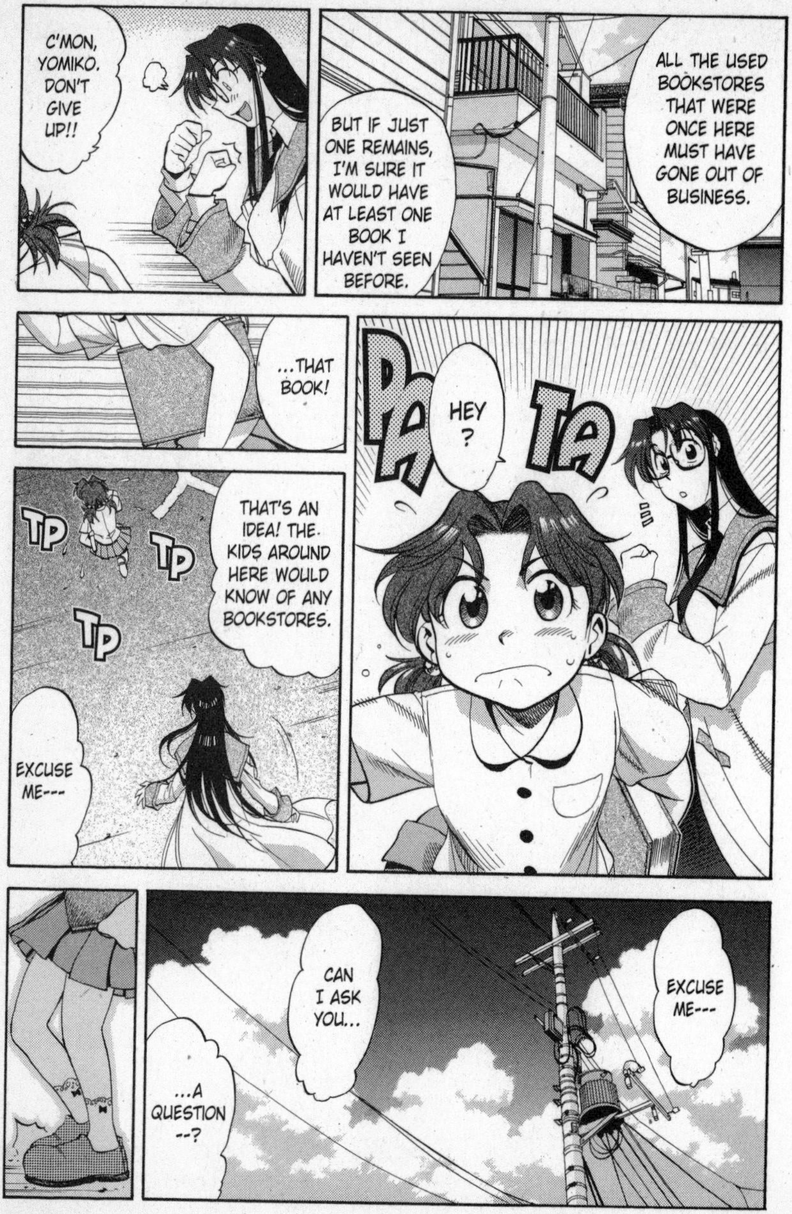
ALL THE USED BOOKSTORES THAT WERE ONCE HERE MUST HAVE GONE OUT OF BUSINESS.
BUT IF JUST ONE REMAINS, I'M SURE IT WOULD HAVE AT LEAST ONE BOOK I HAVEN'T SEEN BEFORE.
C'MON, YOMIKO. DON'T GIVE UP!!
PA
HEY?
TA
...THAT BOOK!
THAT'S AN IDEA! THE KIDS AROUND HERE WOULD KNOW OF ANY BOOKSTORES.
TP
TP
TP
EXCUSE ME---
EXCUSE ME---
CAN I ASK YOU...
...A QUESTION --?

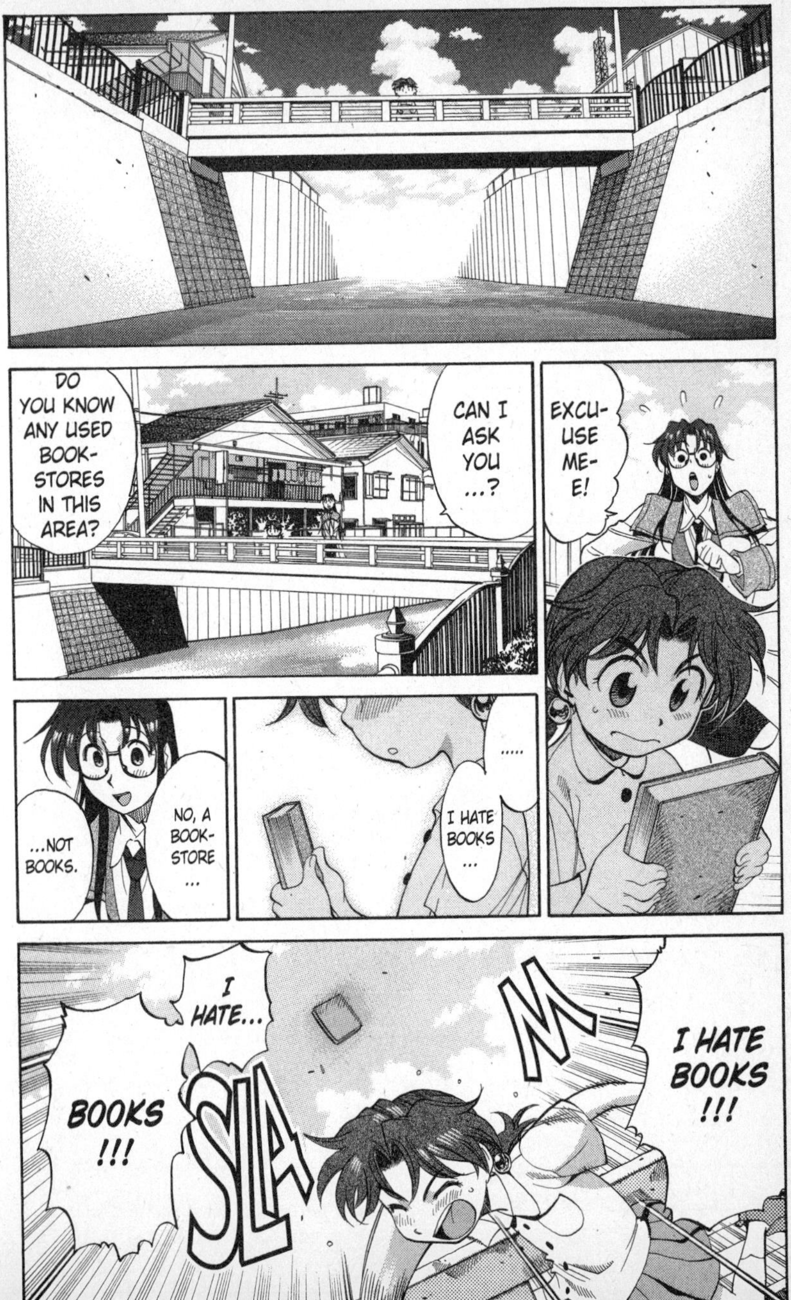
EXCU-USE ME-E!
CAN I ASK YOU ...?
DO YOU KNOW ANY USED BOOK-STORES IN THIS AREA?
.....
I HATE BOOKS ...
NO, A BOOK-STORE ...
...NOT BOOKS.
I HATE BOOKS !!!
SLAM
I HATE...
BOOKS !!!

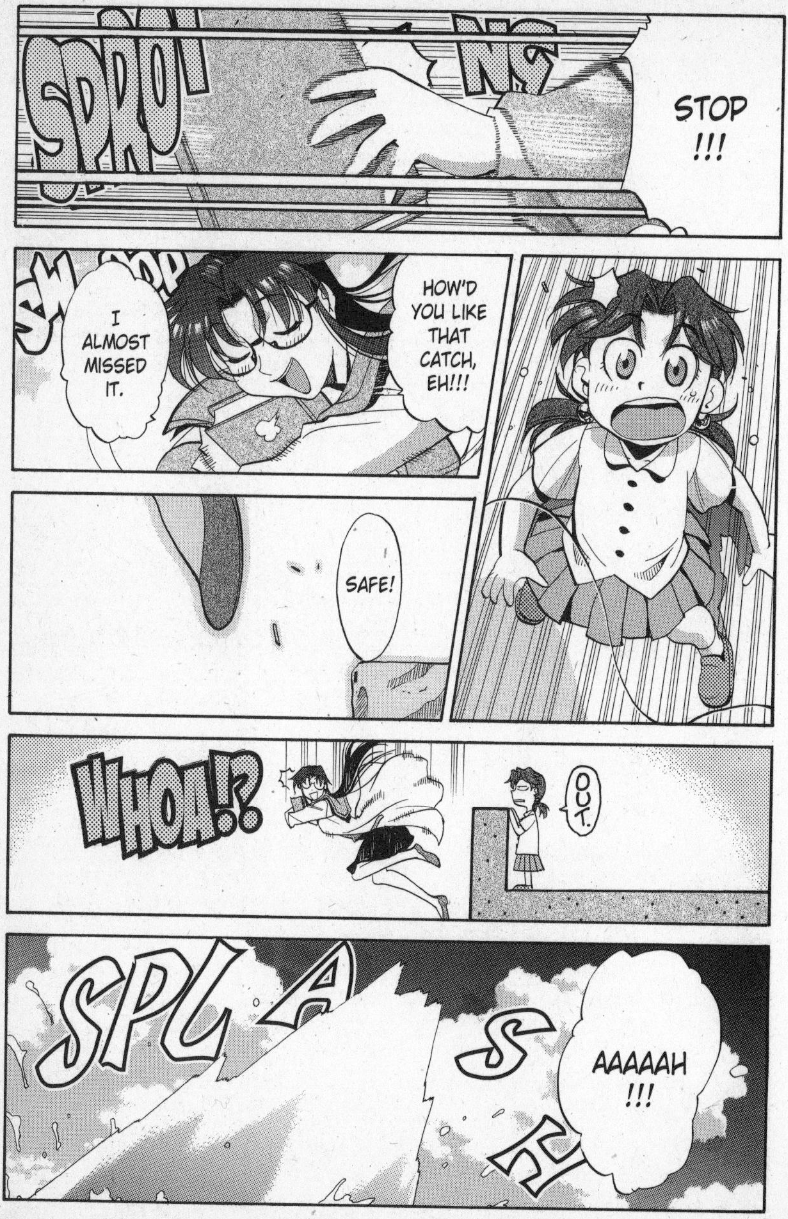
STOP !!!
SPROING
HOW'D YOU LIKE THAT CATCH, EH!!!
I ALMOST MISSED IT.
SAFE!
OUT.
WHOA!?
AAAAAH !!!
SPLASH

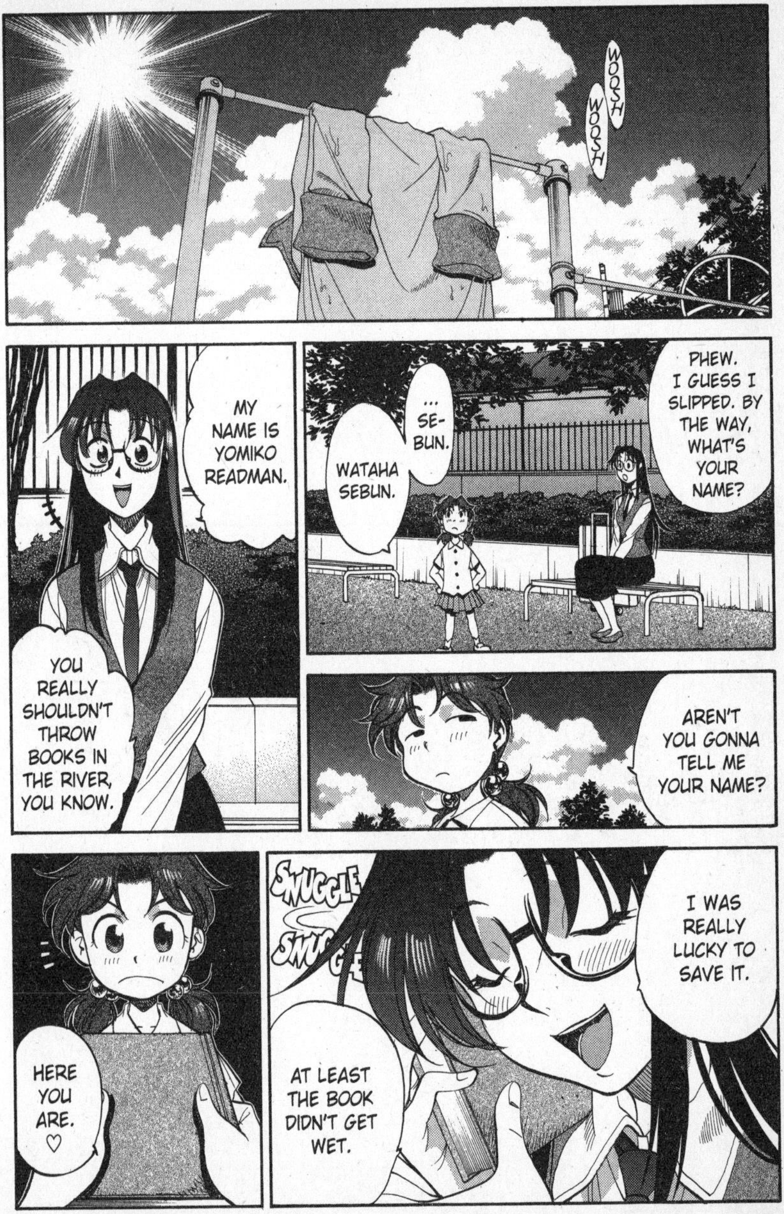
WOOSH
WOOSH
PHEW. I GUESS I SLIPPED. BY THE WAY, WHAT'S YOUR NAME?
... SE-BUN.
WATAHA SEBUN.
AREN'T YOU GONNA TELL ME YOUR NAME?
MY NAME IS YOMIKO READMAN.
YOU REALLY SHOULDN'T THROW BOOKS IN THE RIVER, YOU KNOW.
SNUGGLE
I WAS REALLY LUCKY TO SAVE IT.
AT LEAST THE BOOK DIDN'T GET WET.
HERE YOU ARE. ♡

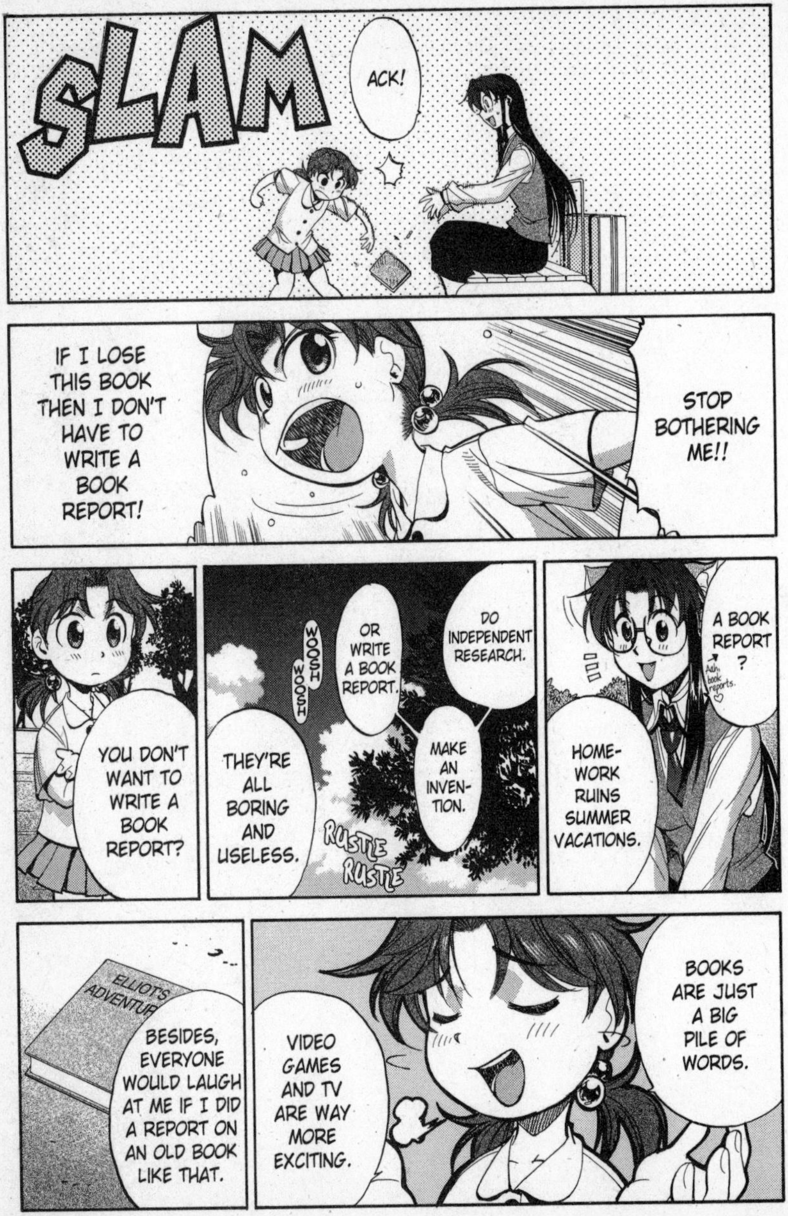
SLAM
ACK!
STOP BOTHERING ME!!
IF I LOSE THIS BOOK THEN I DON'T HAVE TO WRITE A BOOK REPORT!
A BOOK REPORT?
Aah, book reports. ♡
HOME-WORK RUINS SUMMER VACATIONS.
DO INDEPENDENT RESEARCH.
MAKE AN INVEN-TION.
OR WRITE A BOOK REPORT.
WOOSH WOOSH
THEY'RE ALL BORING AND USELESS.
RUSTLE RUSTLE
YOU DON'T WANT TO WRITE A BOOK REPORT?
BOOKS ARE JUST A BIG PILE OF WORDS.
VIDEO GAMES AND TV ARE WAY MORE EXCITING.
ELLIOTS ADVENTUR
BESIDES, EVERYONE WOULD LAUGH AT ME IF I DID A REPORT ON AN OLD BOOK LIKE THAT.

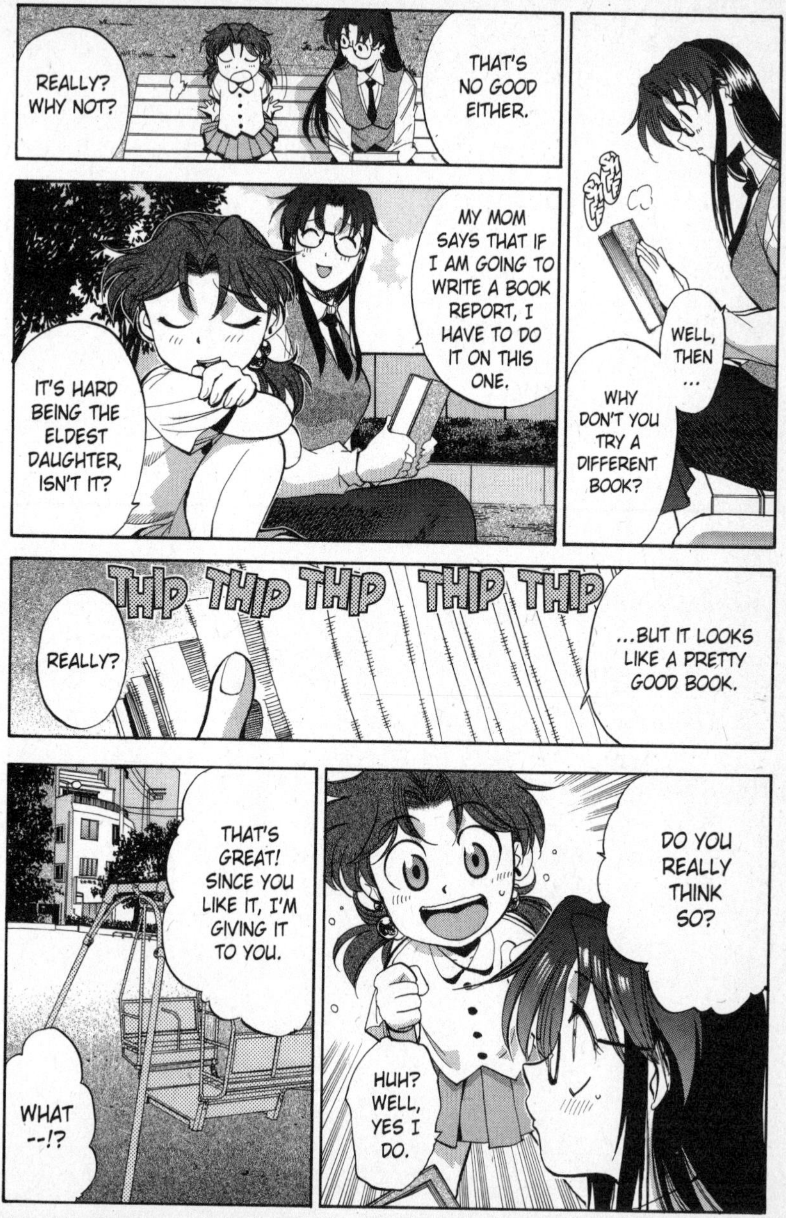
WELL, THEN ...
WHY DON'T YOU TRY A DIFFERENT BOOK?
THAT'S NO GOOD EITHER.
REALLY? WHY NOT?
MY MOM SAYS THAT IF I AM GOING TO WRITE A BOOK REPORT, I HAVE TO DO IT ON THIS ONE.
IT'S HARD BEING THE ELDEST DAUGHTER, ISN'T IT?
THIP THIP THIP THIP THIP
...BUT IT LOOKS LIKE A PRETTY GOOD BOOK.
REALLY?
DO YOU REALLY THINK SO?
HUH? WELL, YES I DO.
THAT'S GREAT! SINCE YOU LIKE IT, I'M GIVING IT TO YOU.
WHAT --!?

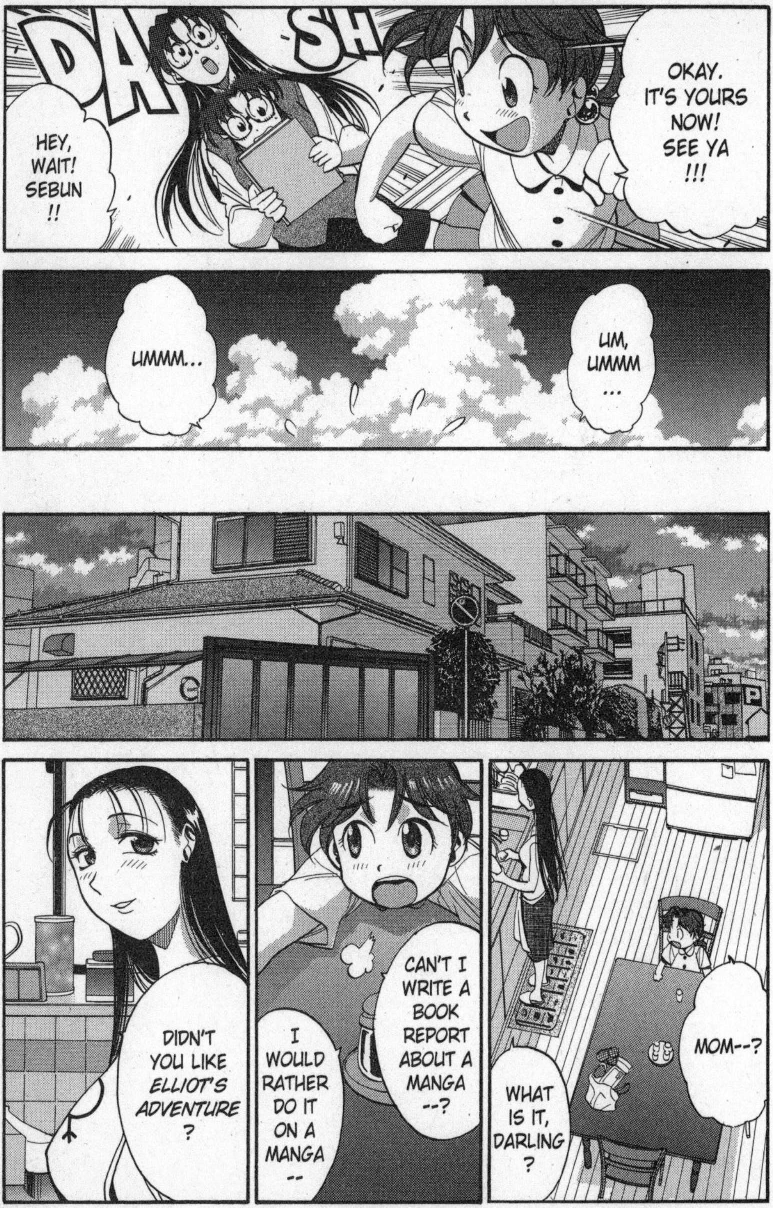
DA-SH
OKAY. IT'S YOURS NOW! SEE YA !!!
HEY, WAIT! SEBUN !!
UM, UMMM ...
UMMM...
MOM--?
WHAT IS IT, DARLING ?
CAN'T I WRITE A BOOK REPORT ABOUT A MANGA --?
I WOULD RATHER DO IT ON A MANGA --
DIDN'T YOU LIKE *ELLIOT'S ADVENTURE* ?

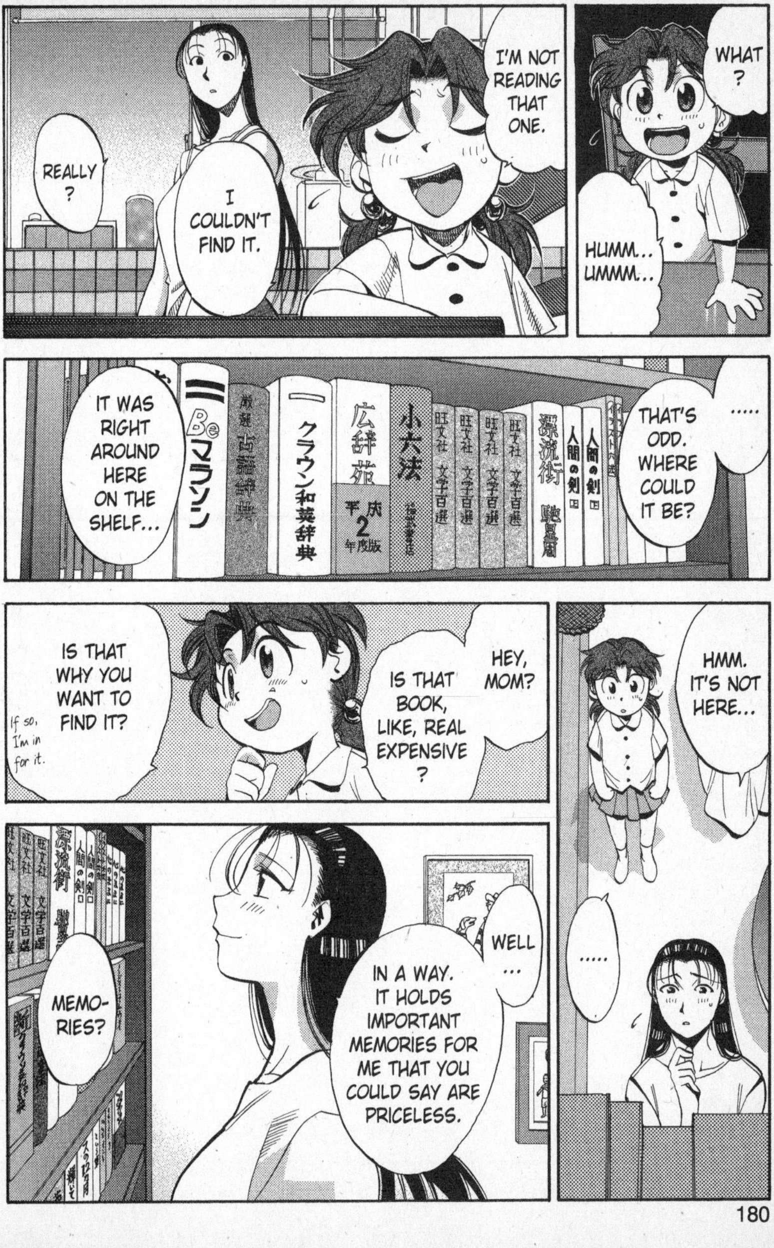
WHAT ?
HUMM... UMMM...
I'M NOT READING THAT ONE.
I COULDN'T FIND IT.
REALLY ?
.....
THAT'S ODD. WHERE COULD IT BE?
IT WAS RIGHT AROUND HERE ON THE SHELF...
小六法
広辞苑
クラウン和英辞典
HMM. IT'S NOT HERE...
.....
HEY, MOM?
IS THAT BOOK, LIKE, REAL EXPENSIVE ?
IS THAT WHY YOU WANT TO FIND IT?
If so, I'm in for it.
WELL ...
IN A WAY. IT HOLDS IMPORTANT MEMORIES FOR ME THAT YOU COULD SAY ARE PRICELESS.
MEMO-RIES?

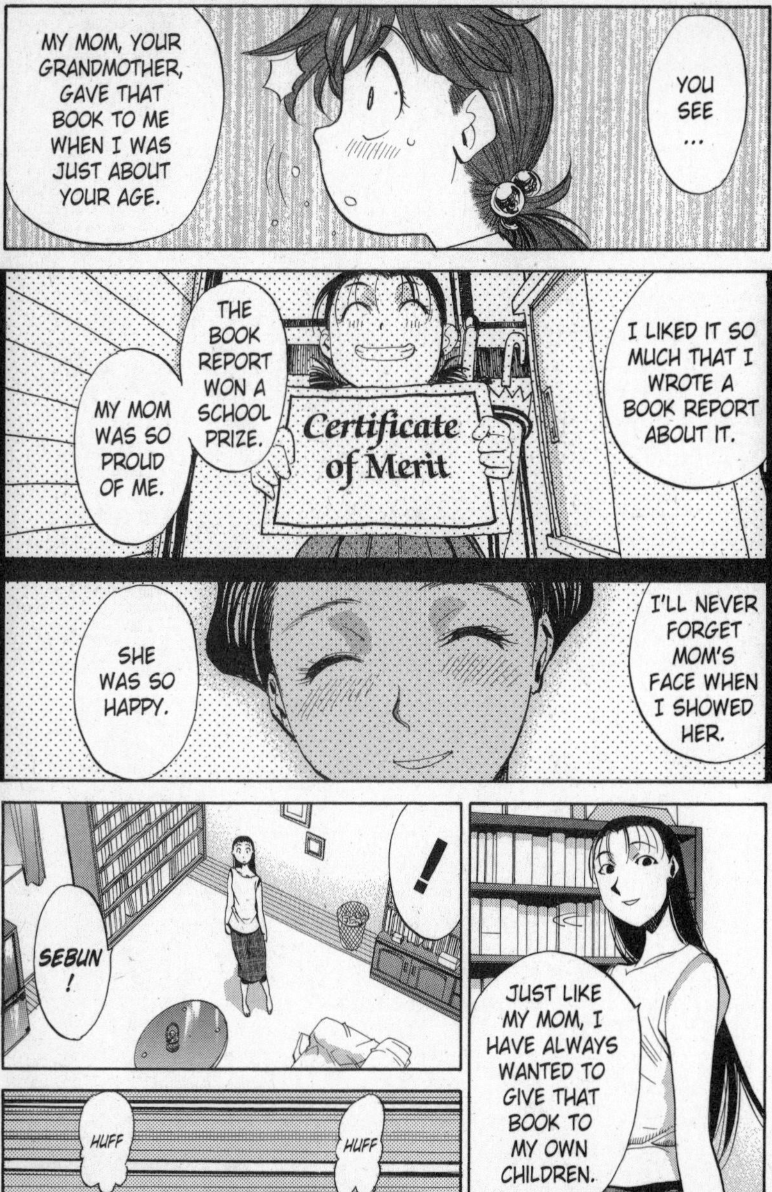
YOU SEE ...
MY MOM, YOUR GRANDMOTHER, GAVE THAT BOOK TO ME WHEN I WAS JUST ABOUT YOUR AGE.
I LIKED IT SO MUCH THAT I WROTE A BOOK REPORT ABOUT IT.
THE BOOK REPORT WON A SCHOOL PRIZE.
Certificate of Merit
MY MOM WAS SO PROUD OF ME.
I'LL NEVER FORGET MOM'S FACE WHEN I SHOWED HER.
SHE WAS SO HAPPY.
JUST LIKE MY MOM, I HAVE ALWAYS WANTED TO GIVE THAT BOOK TO MY OWN CHILDREN.
!
SEBUN !
HUFF
HUFF

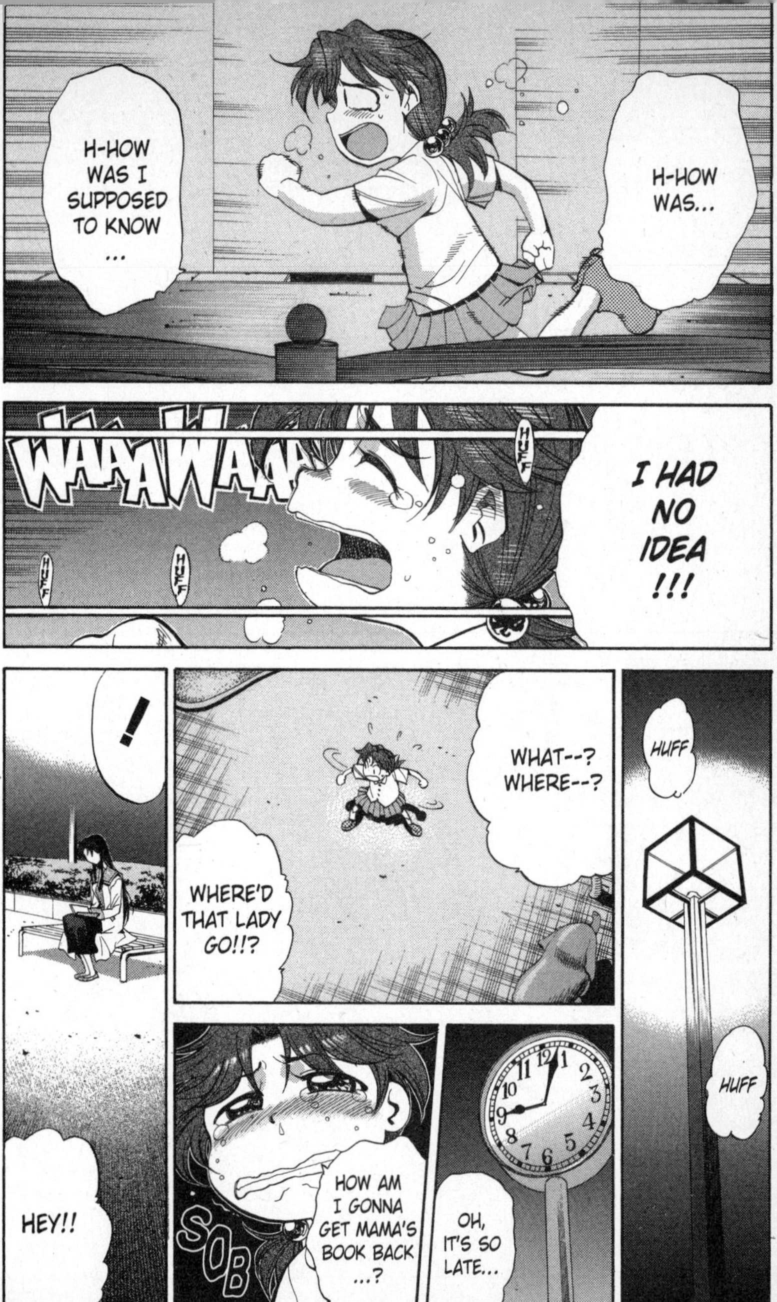
H-HOW WAS...
H-HOW WAS I SUPPOSED TO KNOW ...
I HAD NO IDEA !!!
HUFF
WAAAWAAA
HUFF
HUFF
HUFF
HUFF
WHAT--? WHERE--?
WHERE'D THAT LADY GO!!?
OH, IT'S SO LATE...
HOW AM I GONNA GET MAMA'S BOOK BACK ...?
SOB
!
HEY!!

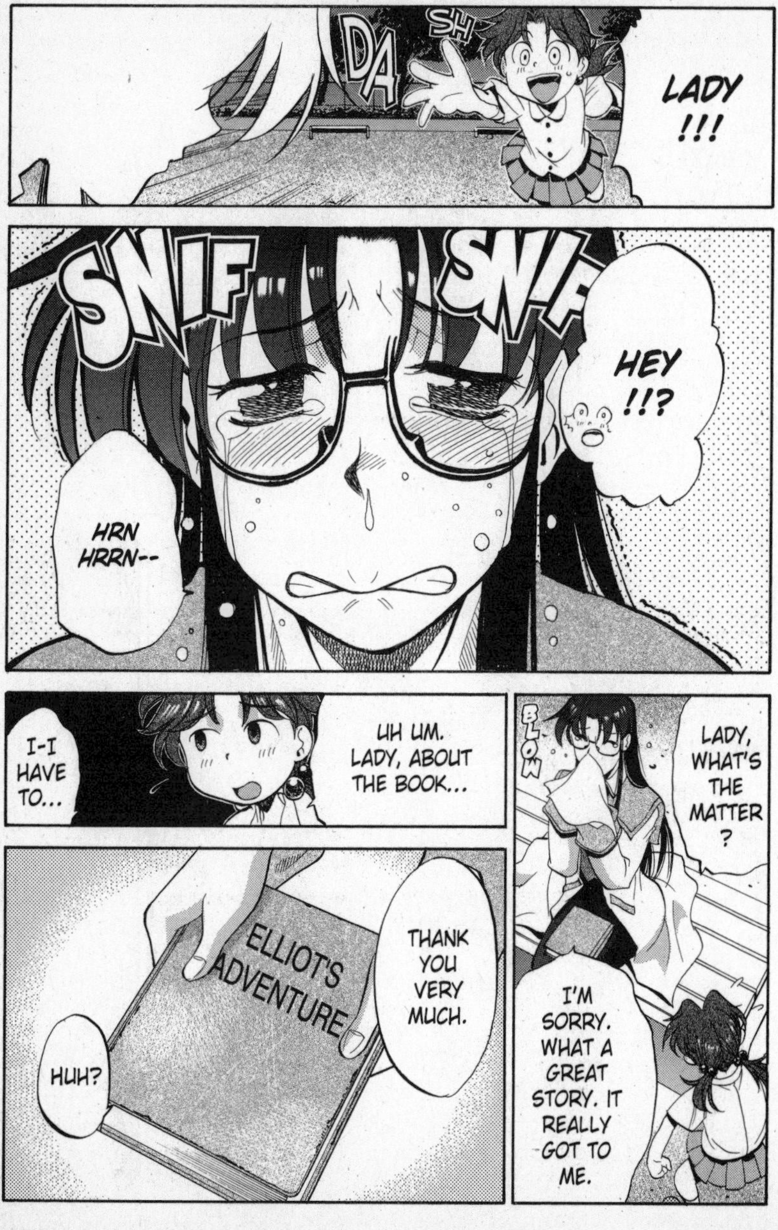
LADY !!!
DASH
SNIF
HEY !!?
SNIF
HRN HRRN--
LADY, WHAT'S THE MATTER ?
BLOW
I'M SORRY. WHAT A GREAT STORY. IT REALLY GOT TO ME.
UH UM. LADY, ABOUT THE BOOK...
I-I HAVE TO...
THANK YOU VERY MUCH.
ELLIOT'S ADVENTURE
HUH?

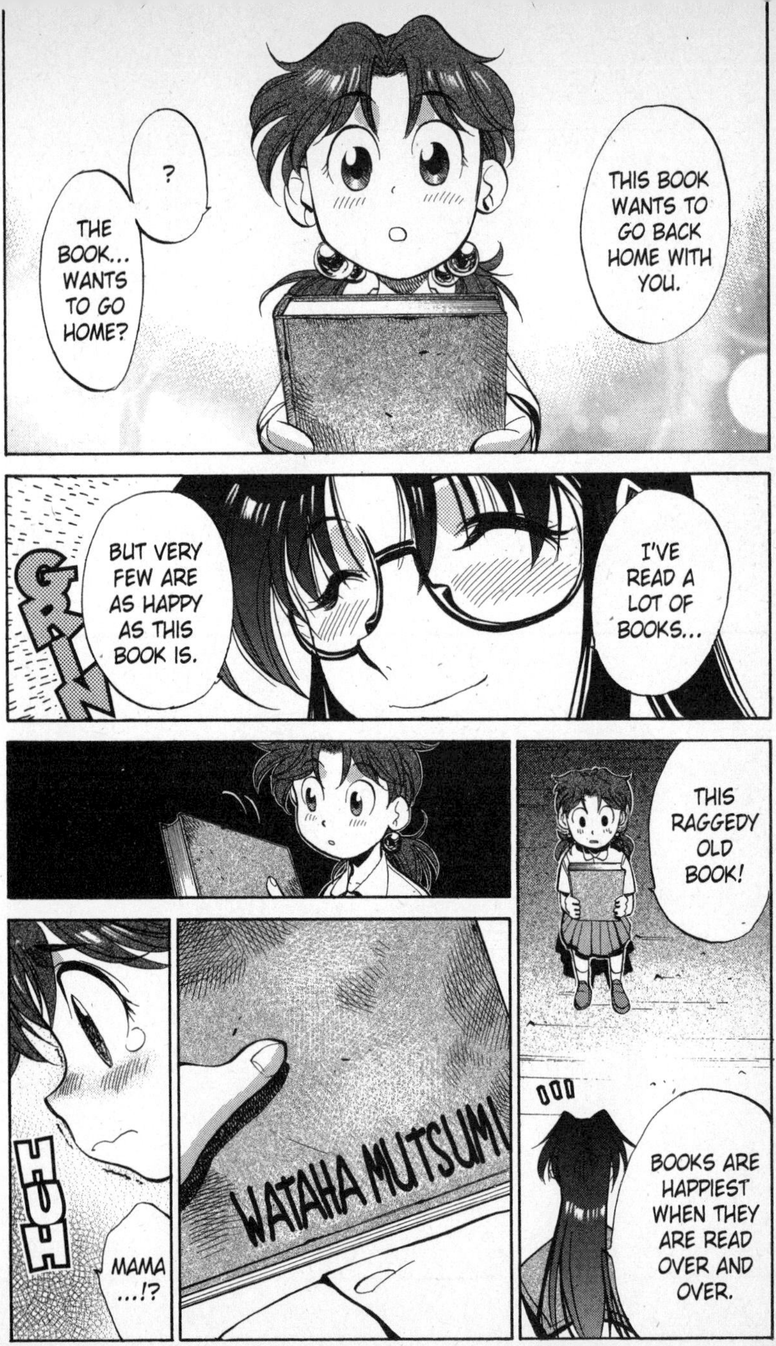
THIS BOOK WANTS TO GO BACK HOME WITH YOU.
?
THE BOOK... WANTS TO GO HOME?
I'VE READ A LOT OF BOOKS...
BUT VERY FEW ARE AS HAPPY AS THIS BOOK IS.
GRIN
THIS RAGGEDY OLD BOOK!
BOOKS ARE HAPPIEST WHEN THEY ARE READ OVER AND OVER.
WATAHA MUTSUMI
HUH
MAMA ...!?

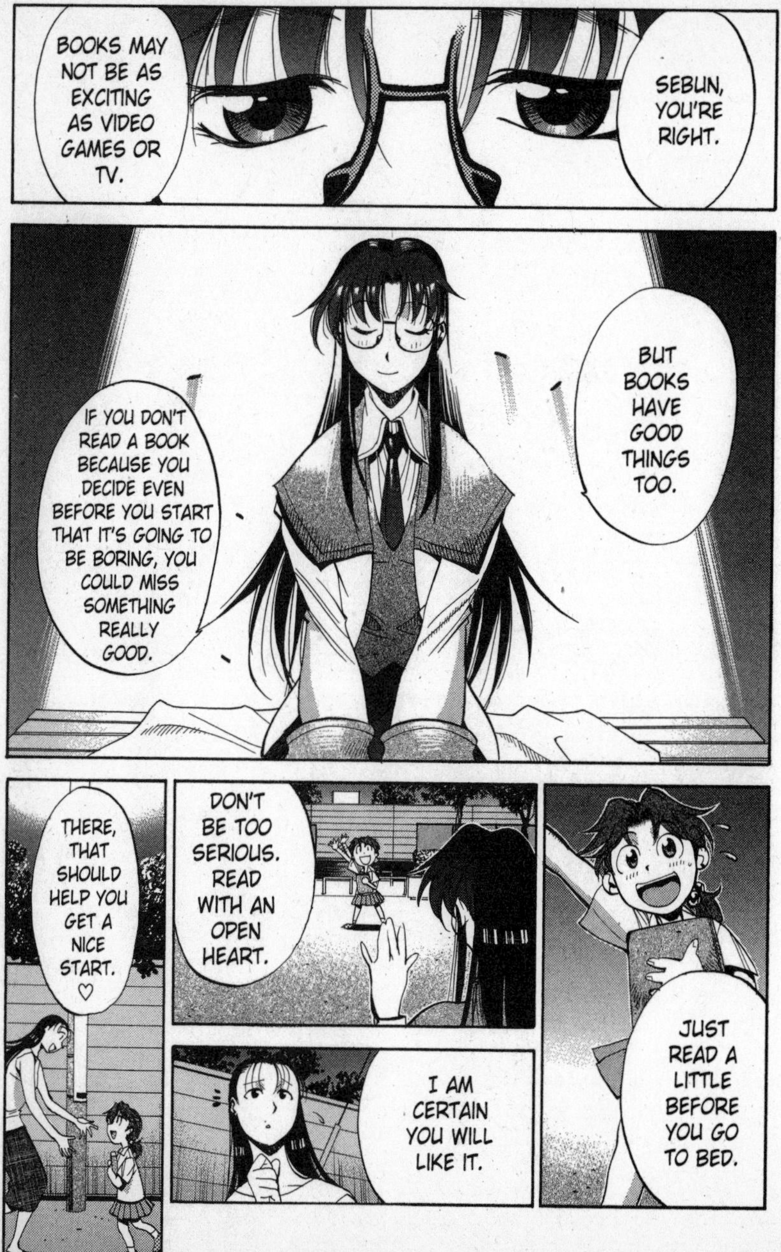
SEBUN, YOU'RE RIGHT.
BOOKS MAY NOT BE AS EXCITING AS VIDEO GAMES OR TV.
BUT BOOKS HAVE GOOD THINGS TOO.
IF YOU DON'T READ A BOOK BECAUSE YOU DECIDE EVEN BEFORE YOU START THAT IT'S GOING TO BE BORING, YOU COULD MISS SOMETHING REALLY GOOD.
JUST READ A LITTLE BEFORE YOU GO TO BED.
DON'T BE TOO SERIOUS. READ WITH AN OPEN HEART.
I AM CERTAIN YOU WILL LIKE IT.
THERE, THAT SHOULD HELP YOU GET A NICE START. ♡

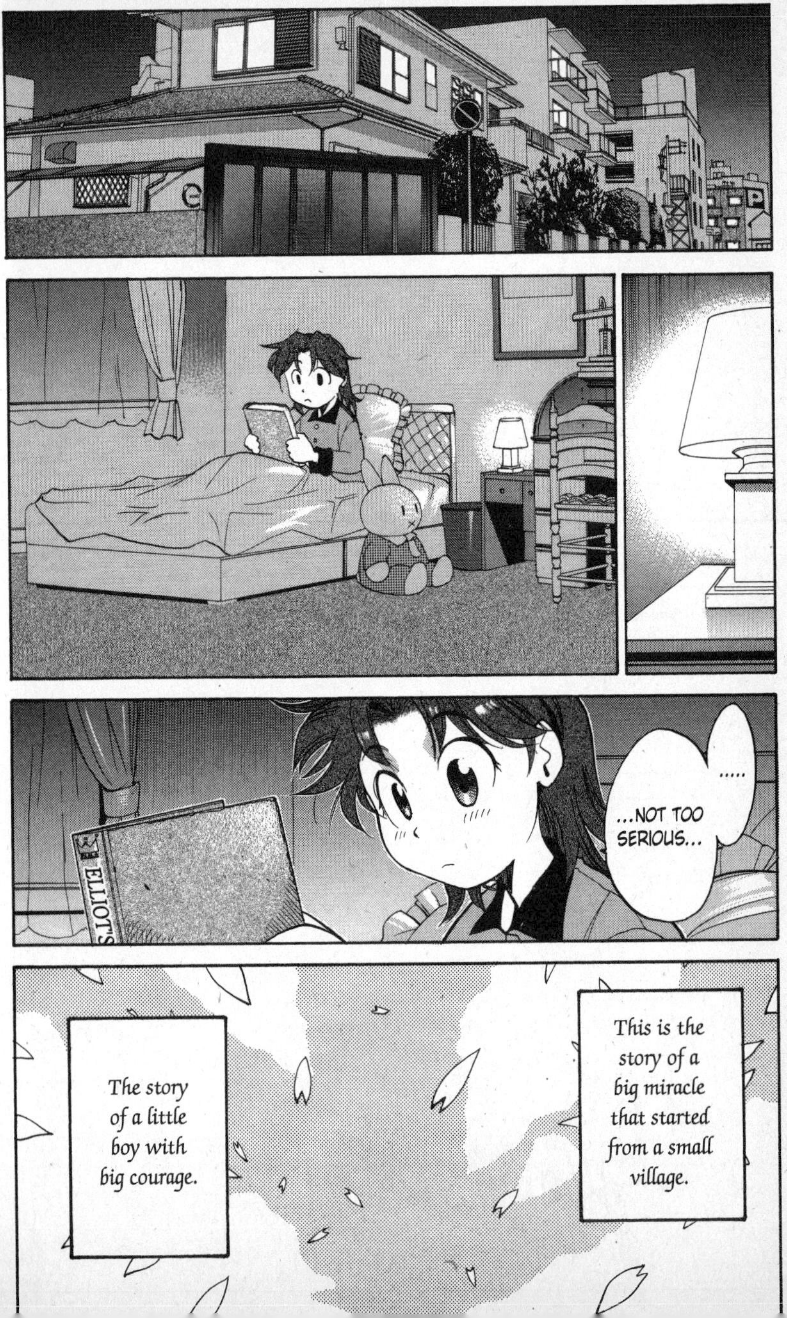
ELLIOT'S
.....
...NOT TOO SERIOUS...
This is the story of a big miracle that started from a small village.
The story of a little boy with big courage.

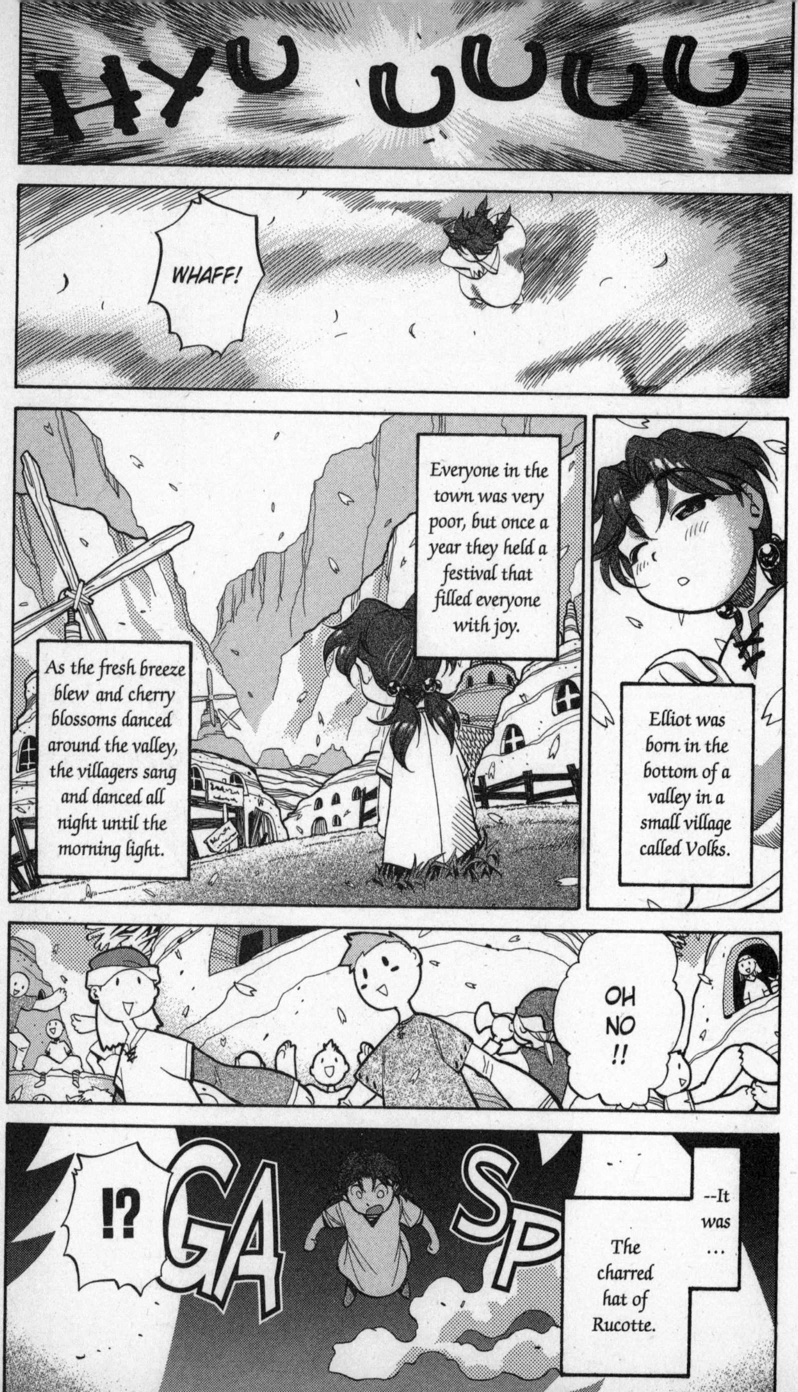
HYU UUUU
WHAFF!
Elliot was born in the bottom of a valley in a small village called Volks.
Everyone in the town was very poor, but once a year they held a festival that filled everyone with joy.
As the fresh breeze blew and cherry blossoms danced around the valley, the villagers sang and danced all night until the morning light.
OH NO !!
--It was ...
GASP
!?
The charred hat of Rucotte.

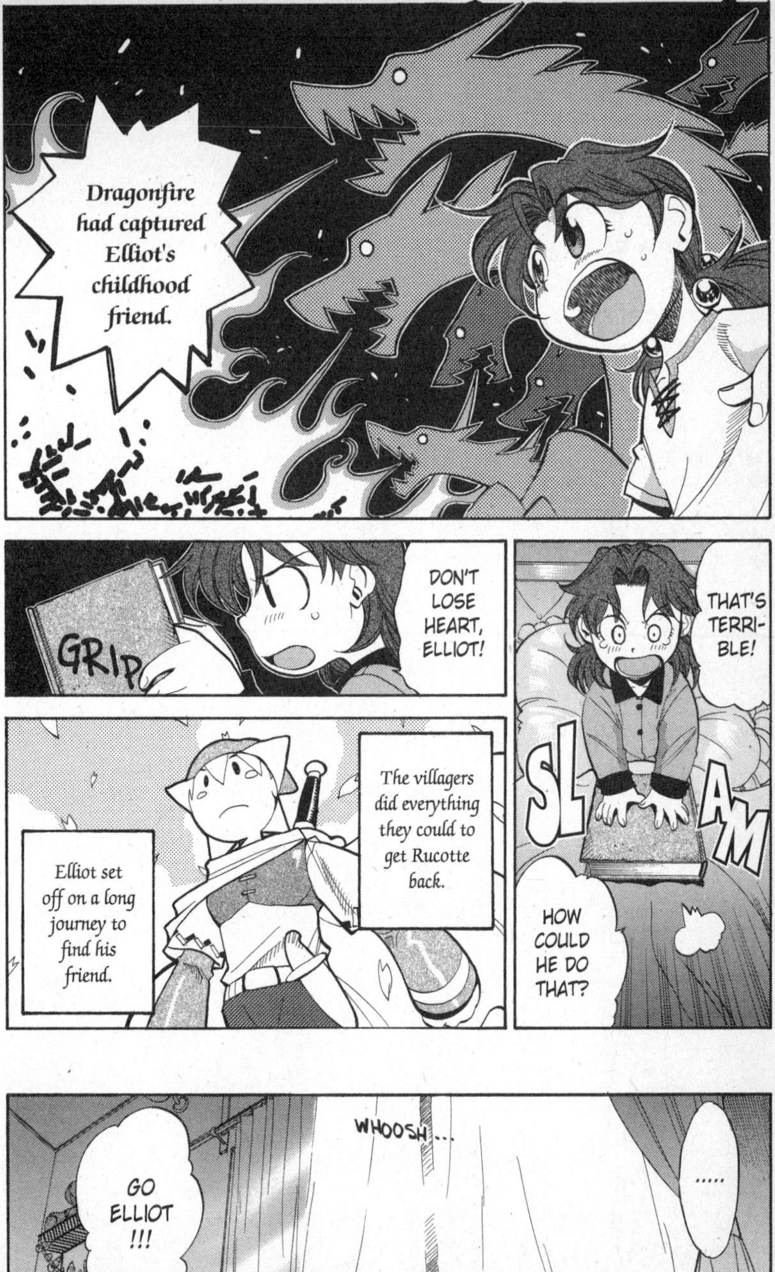
Dragonfire had captured Elliot's childhood friend.
THAT'S TERRI-BLE!
SL
AM
HOW COULD HE DO THAT?
DON'T LOSE HEART, ELLIOT!
GRIP
The villagers did everything they could to get Rucotte back.
Elliot set off on a long journey to find his friend.
.....
WHOOSH...
GO ELLIOT !!!

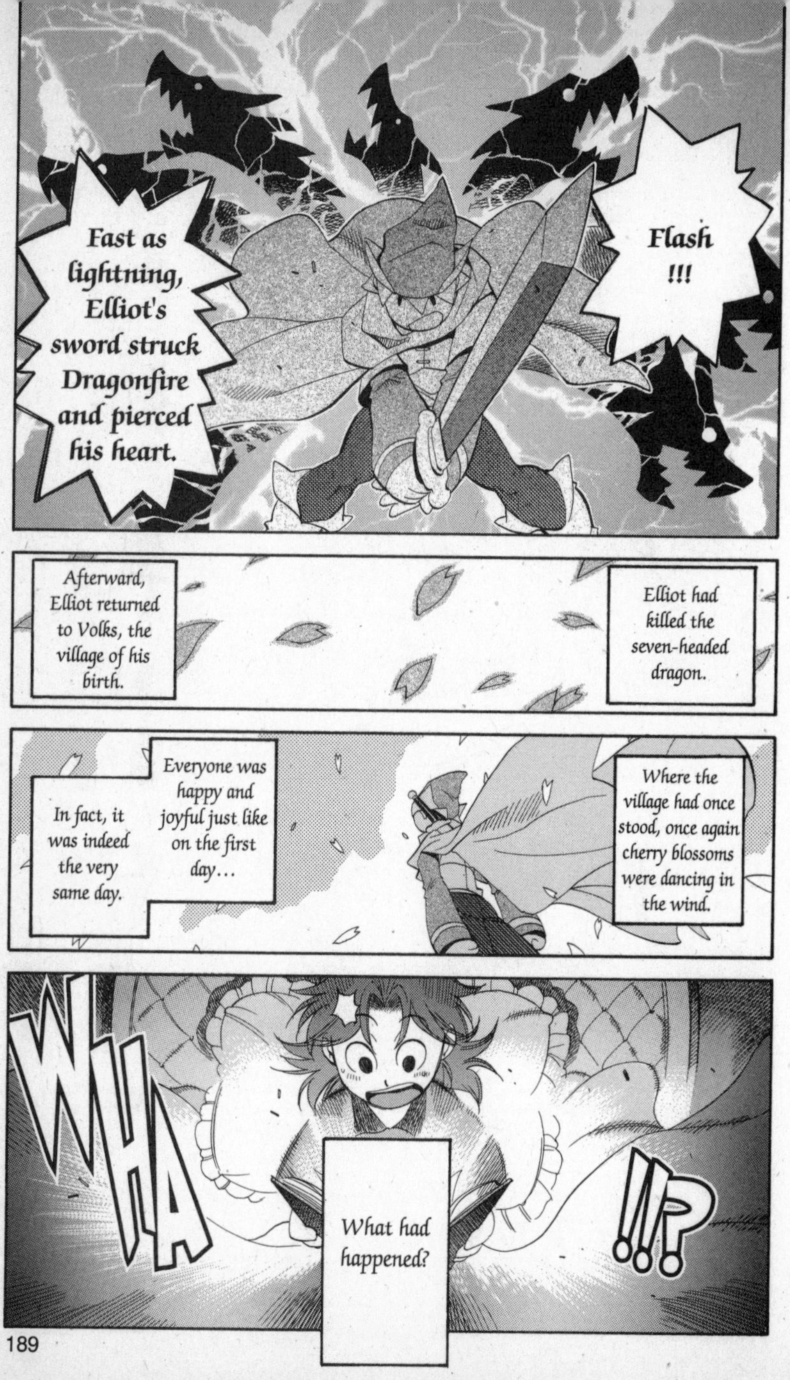

Flash!!!
Fast as lightning, Elliot's sword struck Dragonfire and pierced his heart.
Elliot had killed the seven-headed dragon.
Afterward, Elliot returned to Volks, the village of his birth.
Where the village had once stood, once again cherry blossoms were dancing in the wind.
Everyone was happy and joyful just like on the first day...
In fact, it was indeed the very same day.
WHA !!?
What had happened?

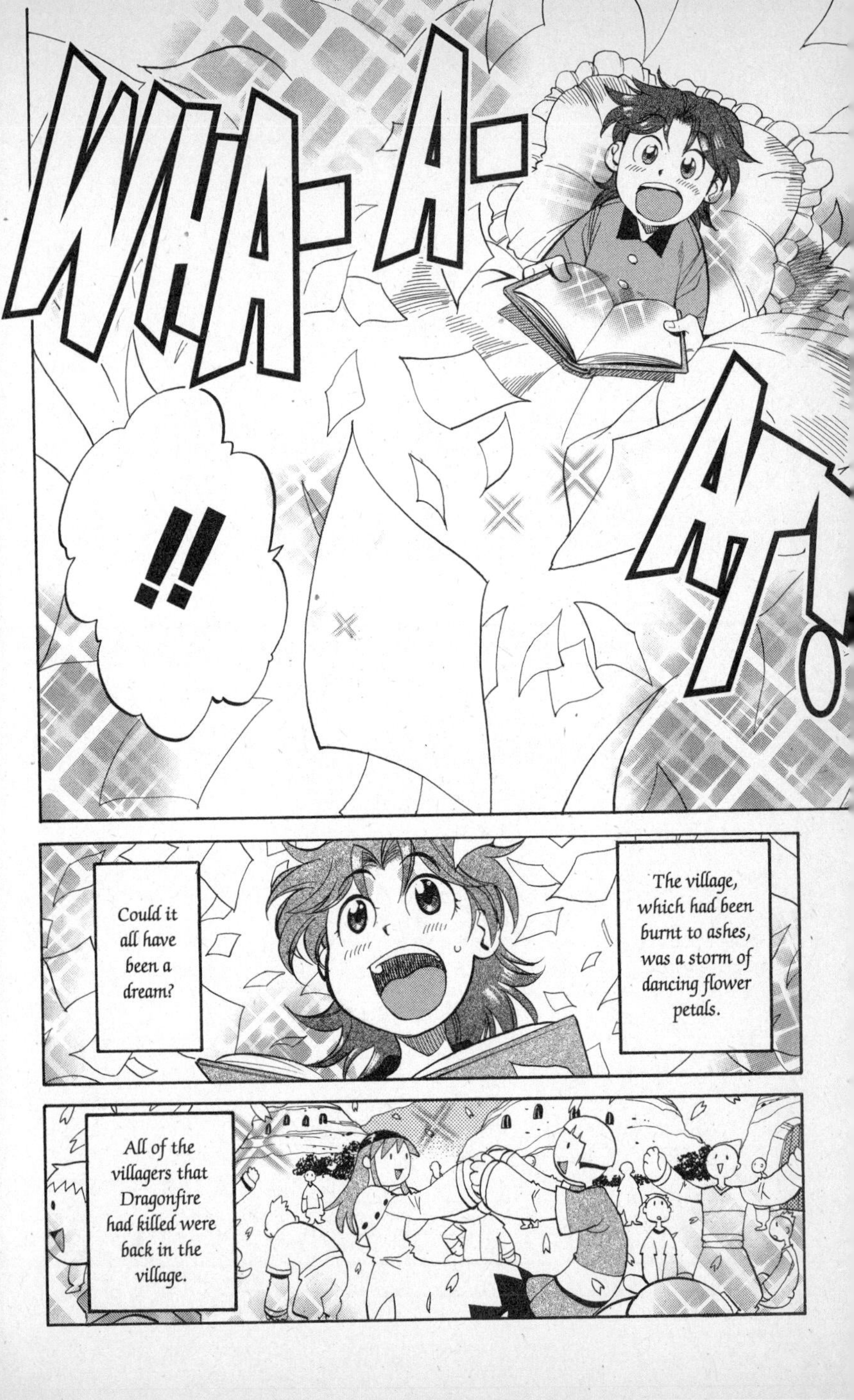
WHA-A-A-AT!?
!!
The village, which had been burnt to ashes, was a storm of dancing flower petals.
Could it all have been a dream?
All of the villagers that Dragonfire had killed were back in the village.

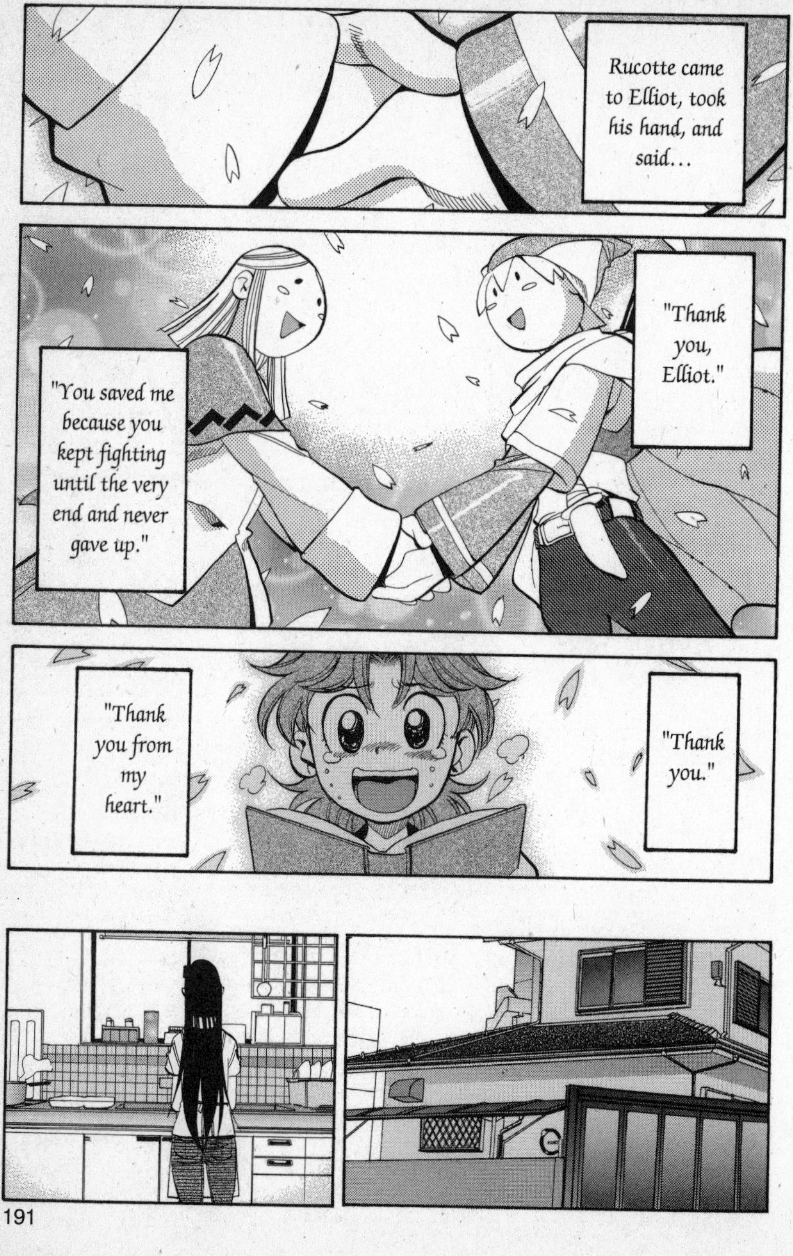
Rucotte came to Elliot, took his hand, and said…
"Thank you, Elliot."
"You saved me because you kept fighting until the very end and never gave up."
"Thank you."
"Thank you from my heart."

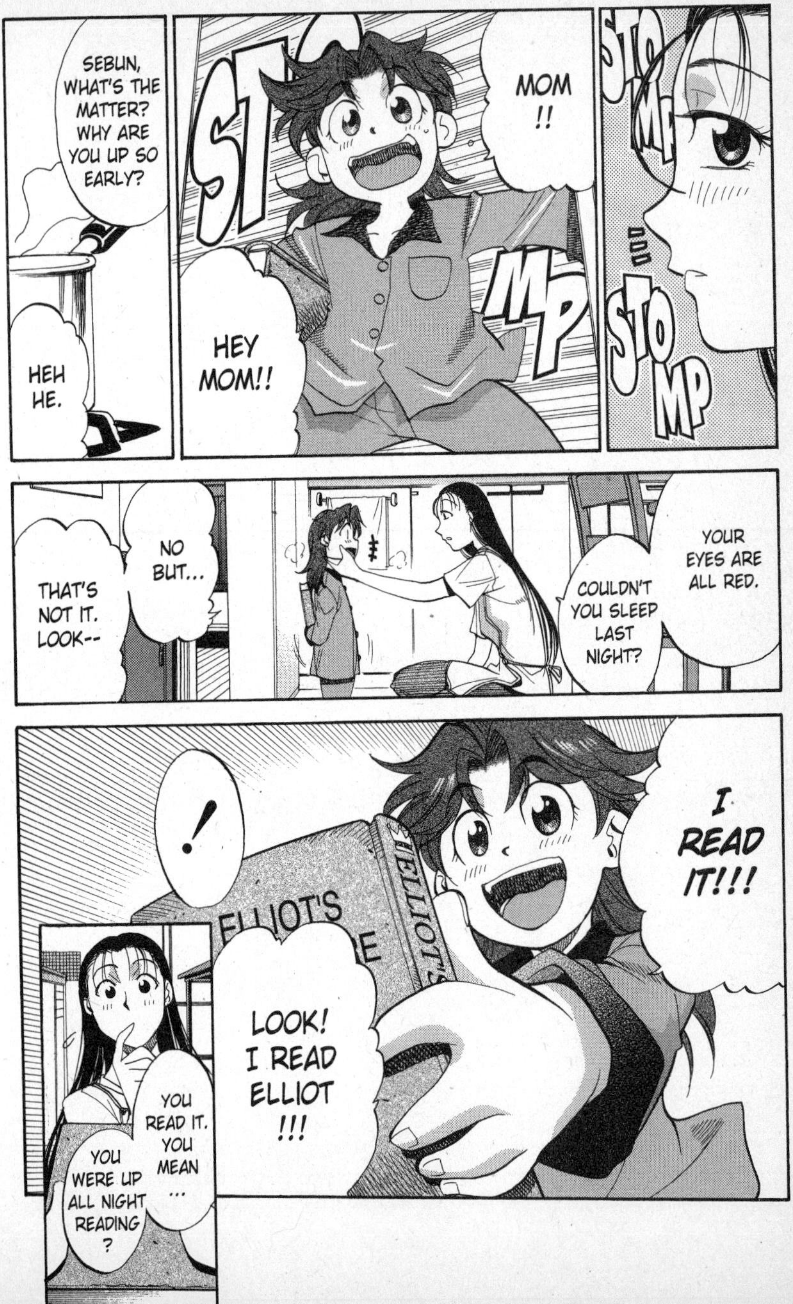
STOMP
MOM!!
STOMP
HEY MOM!!
SEBUN, WHAT'S THE MATTER? WHY ARE YOU UP SO EARLY?
HEH HE.
YOUR EYES ARE ALL RED.
COULDN'T YOU SLEEP LAST NIGHT?
NO BUT...
THAT'S NOT IT. LOOK--
I READ IT!!!
!
ELLIOT'S
LOOK! I READ ELLIOT!!!
YOU READ IT. YOU MEAN...
YOU WERE UP ALL NIGHT READING?

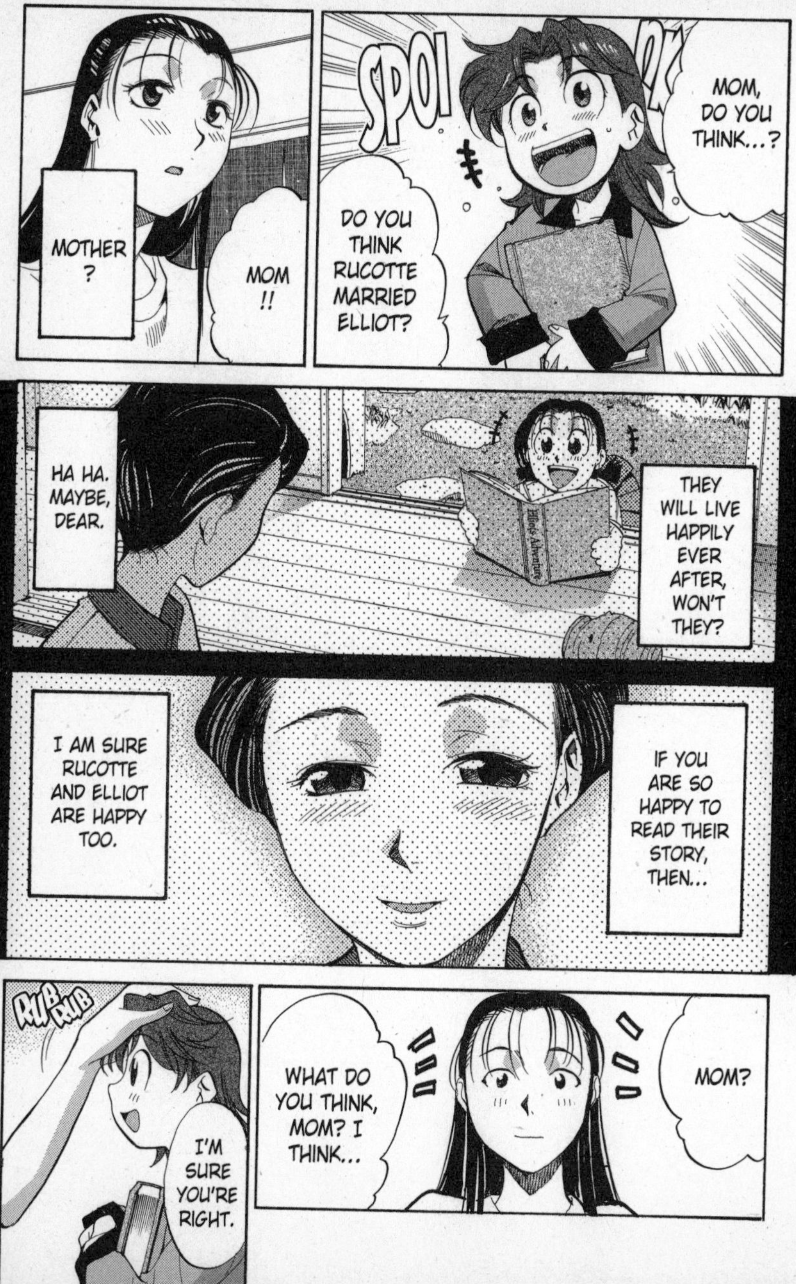
MOM, DO YOU THINK...?
SPOI
DO YOU THINK RUCOTTE MARRIED ELLIOT?
MOM !!
MOTHER ?
THEY WILL LIVE HAPPILY EVER AFTER, WON'T THEY?
Elliot's Adventure
HA HA. MAYBE, DEAR.
IF YOU ARE SO HAPPY TO READ THEIR STORY, THEN...
I AM SURE RUCOTTE AND ELLIOT ARE HAPPY TOO.
MOM?
WHAT DO YOU THINK, MOM? I THINK...
RUB RUB
I'M SURE YOU'RE RIGHT.

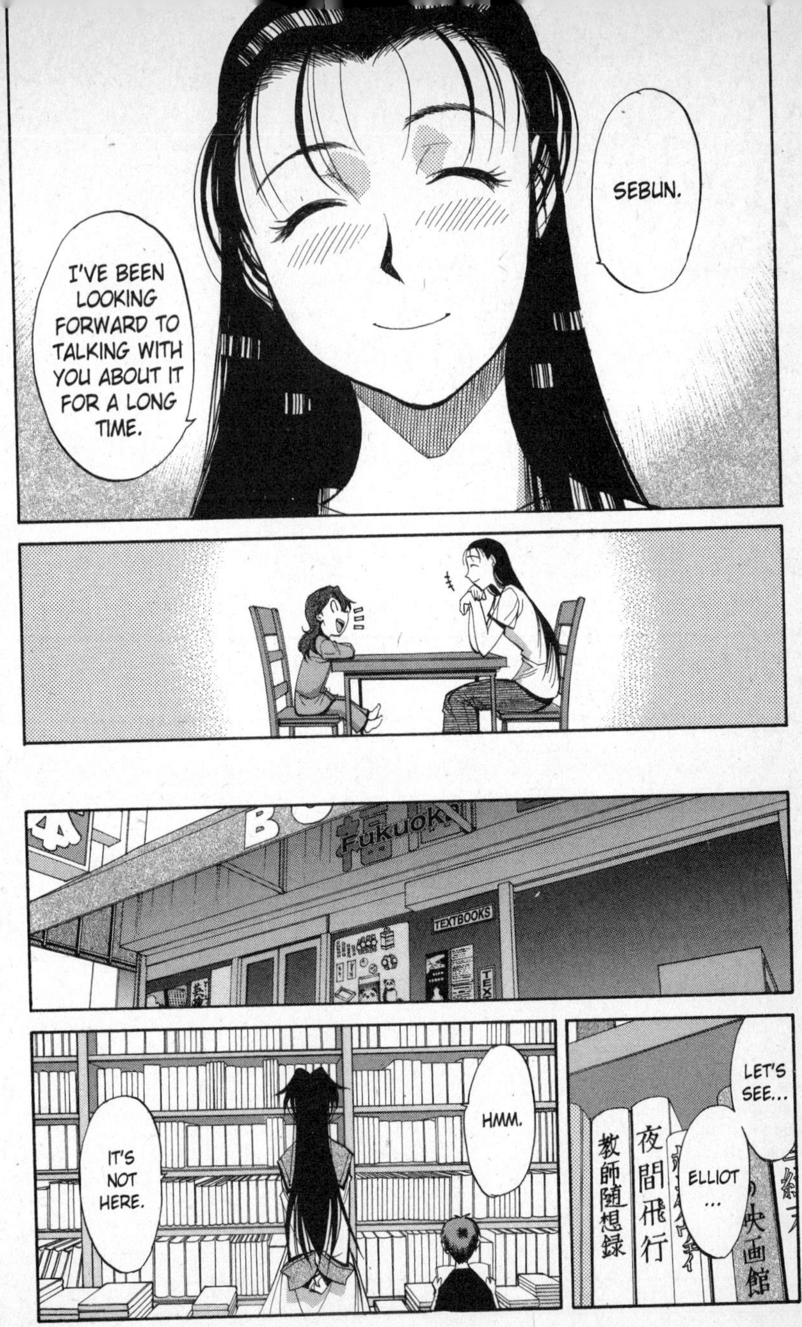
SEBUN.
I'VE BEEN LOOKING FORWARD TO TALKING WITH YOU ABOUT IT FOR A LONG TIME.
Fukuok
TEXTBOOKS
LET'S SEE...
ELLIOT ...
夜間飛行
教師随想録
HMM.
IT'S NOT HERE.

ULTRA READER KING YOMIOH

YOMIO SPECIAL NO. 2 A ROUNDTABLE MEETING OF THE CREATORS OF THE OVA VERSION OF *R.O.D*

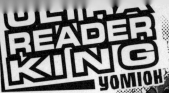

Kurata Hideyuki
(Original Creator, Script)
Ishihama Masashi
(Animation Character Design and Art Director)
Suganuma Eiji
(Mecha Design)
Tachibana Hideki
(Art Director Assistant)

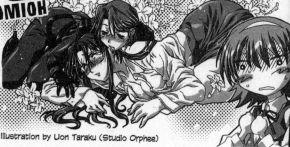

Illustration by Uon Taraku (Studio Orphee)

Kurata: Let's start by introducing ourselves and describing the work we are doing for R.O.D.
Ishihama: I am Ishihama. I am overseeing the animation character design and art direction.
Suganuma: I am Suganuma. I am doing the mechanical design for the telop [television opaque projector = text overlays, such as subtitles.]. I do other stuff too, but it's hard to say just what.
Kurata: Aren't you also the action director?
Suganuma: Well, that's what they told me at first (laughs). I'd never heard of mechanical design before.
Kurata: (laughs) Well, we've already stumbled onto our first surprise.
Tachibana: I am Tachibana. In the first film, I oversaw the art direction and lots of other things. I kinda did everything except the telop. I basically did odds-and-ends work and was the gofer.
Ishihama: The telop said you were Art Director Assistant.
Kurata: How could you remember cleaning up and not Art Director Assistant?
Tachibana: Doesn't Art Director Assistant fall under odds and ends?
Ishihama: Watch it now, let's not get provocative. (all laugh)
Kurata: Here we have gathered some of the main staff that produced the high quality anime. I would like to discuss with you all about *R.O.D* and what it was like working with Director Masunari Koji. I'd like to start with each of you describing how Masunari approached you to work on the series and about your work on the project.
Ishihama: I think I was probably the last one approached to work on *Read*. Masunari casually sent some work to me when I was still working for my previous company. It turned out to be the character design for the *Read* anime.
Kurata: You didn't know! (laughs) Didn't you ask what it was? (laughs)
Ishihama: No. We set a meeting at a family restaurant, and he showed up with his producer and director. He just said, "Will you do something for me?" I said, "Sure, I'll help," then he said, "It's a character design." (all laugh)
Kurata: So you started out as sort of just helping out with the project? What was your first impression of it?
Ishihama: That's right. (laughs). But my other work suddenly ended, so I was very fortunate to have this to work on. I had a feeling that Masunari wanted me for the project. When I went to see him about it, it turned out I was right.
Kurata: You lucked out.
Ishihama: When he said character design, he meant a complete design for the whole book. I thought it was a great opportunity and told him I'd do it.
Kurata: So can we say you came away with a good impression from your first contact with Masunari.
Ishihama: Certainly. He gave me the character design right from the very start. (laughs)
Kurata: Had he seen your previous work?
Ishihama: No. He must not have. (laughs)
Kurata: Why so modest? (laughs)
Ishihama: As I recall, he himself said so. (laughs)
Kurata: Wow! (laughs)
Ishihama: When he was doing NeoRanga, people who knew me were apparently dropping hints to him that I was available.
Kurata: I see. They brainwashed him. (laughs)
Ishihama: (laughs) Yes, something like that.

Suganuma: That's true. That did happen. (all laugh)

Ishihama: When Suganuma was brought in, I don't think the design production had even been finalized yet. When they called me, all the other staff was already in place. All I had to do was the work itself.

Suganuma: That's right. I always forget things like that. (all laugh)

Suganuma: That was a couple years ago, wasn't it?

Kurata: Yes. I seem to remember Uon asking me to create a character design proposal two years ago. So it must be about two and a half years since the very first drawings. This project has sure taken a long time. (all laugh)

Kurata: The world has changed quite a bit in that time. (all laugh) Hadn't it been a long time since you last worked so closely with Masunari?

Suganuma: Yes. It had been 10 years. The last time was when our studio did *Lamune & 40*, and I was an actor and illustrator.

Ishihama: I have always wanted to know, since you hadn't worked together for so long, what was Masunari's reaction when he heard you would be the action director?

Suganuma: Well, I'll tell you. It's easier when you're working behind the scenes, don't you think? (laughs)

Kurata: Easy!? Can you really call that project easy? (laughs)

Suganuma: Ishihama is a better lightning rod. He's the one you want to duke it out over the Internet. (all laugh)

Ishihama: I'm looking forward to the fight. I'd like lots of people to see the anime, enough so that it feels like a battle.

Suganuma: That's the part I like least. (all laugh)

Kurata: Tachibana, how did you get involved?

Tachibana: Me? I was first approached when I was working on NeoRanga. Then the project started up just when I had left my former company and had not decided on my next job. (laughs) I said, sure I'll work on it with you.

Kurata: It was that simple! (laughs)

Tachibana: Sorry guys. (laughs) At the time, Masunari was the only person who would still talk to me about work. (all laugh)

Kurata: What was your first impression of Masunari? Had you heard daunting stories about working with him? Did you have an image like that?

Kurata: Suganuma, I believe you might know Masunari longer than any of us.

Suganuma: Probably. I first met him about 15 years ago.

Kurata: Wow, 15 years! I was still in high school. (all laugh)

Suganuma: On top of that, since we have known each other for such a long time, he knows my work pace very well, so recently he hasn't been sending me anything that requires a lot of detail. He's sent me the opening packages for MAICO and Photon, but he no longer sends me work for, for example, specific frames in specific cuts. (laughs) Maybe he's trying to tell me something. (laughs)

Kurata: He probably doesn't want to bother you.

Suganuma: Could be. I would do it if he sent it to me, but it would probably just cause more problems for both of us. (laughs)

Kurata: (laughs) So, small jobs like that are a bother.

Suganuma: It's just nicer to work on a complete project. There was a period when I thought that people were purposely not sending me work. (all laugh)

Kurata: Did it feel like a mild case of blacklisting or something like that?

Suganuma: No, I never felt like I was being blacklisted.

Kurata: Was everyone just giving you space?

Suganuma: That's probably a better way to describe it.

Kurata: I didn't mean to pry. Sorry about that. (laughs)

Suganuma: Truth is, that may be all too true. (all laugh)

Suganuma: Three or four years ago I had problems with an anime project at JC that left me a bit dazed afterward. In fact, I think that may have been a reason he contacted me.

Kurata: You mean, a reason he called you at a relatively early stage of the project.

Suganuma: Could be. It was a bit suspect.

Kurata: How's that?

Suganuma: I mean, to be contacted about a project that is only half-developed. Ishihama may have felt the same.

Ishihama: The project was pretty much complete when he contacted me. The only thing it didn't have was the character design.

Suganuma: The concept must have progressed quite a bit by then.

Ishihama: The other people were already selected for the project.

Kurata: It did take quite a while to get the project ready to roll. This was the first time my company worked with SME and Visual Works, and it was difficult to get feedback from them. That could be why Suganuma was made to wait. (laughs)

Kurata: When you work, is there always a sense of fear involved?

Suganuma: You could say that. He and I belong to the same generation, so even though everyone knows that he is very strict with his projects, I don't really feel it. I can't say what it's like to be young and working for him.

Kurata: That's true.

Suganuma: To me he shows determination, effort and a desire to rise to a higher level. Anger at work quality or because a certain section is having problems can all be attributed to perfectionism. There may well be a good reason for him to get upset to a certain degree. He's just aiming high, so there is really nothing to be afraid about. That doesn't mean working on his projects is not a pain in the neck (laughs). That's a big factor. (laughs)

Kurata: Was *R.O.D* a pain in the neck?

Suganuma: Well, yeah it was. On the other hand, this project was divided up into sections very early on which greatly alleviated the pain.

Kurata: Is that so.

Suganuma: We each had a good idea of how much work he was going to give us, and he stayed within that range.

Kurata: It's interesting to hear such modesty when the final product is such high quality. Of course, I was amazed that the contraption made from the sketches of Lilienthal's glider actually flew. (laughs) Not to mention that the wings even flapped. (laughs)

[Note: Otto Lilienthal designed gliders in the late 1800s, making him one of the first humans to fly.]

Suganuma: That's because the original artwork was so good. I almost feel like I should apologize for the receiving credit for the first project because the original artwork made my job so easy.

shihama: Suganuma's standards are different from normal humans.

uganuma: No, it's true. I really didn't do that much on the first one.

hihama: The people at Studio Ebisu have gher standards than usual. They can take ally difficult jobs and whip them out like its utine work. Some of the work is really killer. (laugh)

rata: Will books two and three be the ne?

ganuma: Book two is going to be much ier for me. (laughs)

ata: How come? (laughs)

anuma: There's no Lilienthal glider in it. augh)

Tachibana: Before I spoke with him about the project specifics, people were telling me that he is really hard to work with. That was the only image they created of him inside me.

Kurata: So you thought it was daunting even before you met him?

Tachibana: Yep. (laughs)

Kurata: Didn't that make you apprehensive?

Tachibana: Incredibly.

Kurata: When you started working with him, was he as daunting as you had heard? Were you expecting him to demand constant revisions or grab you by the collar?

Tachibana: No. I'd heard he did that when he was young but not anymore. (laughs)

Kurata: (laughs) Did he do that when he was young? (all laugh)

Suganuma: I never actually saw him grab anyone by the collar. (laughs)

Tachibana: I heard he did one time during an argument.

Kurata: Do you think he is aware of his past reputation?

Suganuma: Well, I can say he had a fiery temper when he was younger.

Kurata: Past tense?

Suganuma: Compared to then, he is much more subdued now.

Kurata: That's a bit hard to imagine.

Suganuma: In terms of outward appearance, I'm way more scary than he is. (all laugh)

Kurata: That may be true. My impression of you is totally different after today. (laughs)

Suganuma: There is that element too. People tend to gather around Masunari Koji.

Kurata: You mean, his looks attract people to him? (laughs)

Suganuma: Yes! (laughs) When you actually work with him you understand. He's changed quite a lot, but in the past he did blow his top every once in a while. Maybe he did have a short temper, but he never just blew up for no reason. When people say he was scary, they don't mean it that way.

Kurata: You mean he had high expectations and was very particular about his work.

Suganuma: Yes, that's it. In fact, he never gets upset outside of work. I'm just the opposite, I usually get upset outside of work. (all laugh)

Kurata: Why outside of work? (laughs)

Suganuma: Studio Ebisu where we worked on *R.O.D* was always sparkling clean. I was always being told to straighten up or clean up. I couldn't believe it. (laughs)

Kurata: He has a very rare virtue. He has an image of being very strict, yet no one says they don't want to work with him.

Ishihama: I do know some people who think it's a pain in the neck and don't like to work with him.

Kurata: But that aspect didn't deter Suganuma and Tachibana.

Suganuma: The reward is the gratification from seeing your own work in the final versions of the film. Work is a pain in the neck because it's not simple, it's like a conundrum you create yourself and then have to figure out. After you finish, you realize that it was the complications that made it enjoyable. If you believe in your skills, then the work can be fun. I hope this doesn't sound too harsh. (laughs)

Kurata: It's the sense of accomplishment.

Suganuma: Exactly. When you are accountable for the success or failure of your work, you naturally feel responsibility for the work.

Kurata: That makes it worthwhile.

Suganuma: Yes.

Kurata: Tachibana, what do you think?

Tachibana: I think you're all amazing. (all laugh)

Kurata: Anything to add?

Tachibana: Well, I never had the luxury to think of it that way. The whole project was a mad rush for me for a whole year, and I still haven't finished. (laughs)

Kurata: Masunari told me the atmosphere in the *R.O.D* workroom changed when you joined the team,.

Tachibana: Did it?

Kurata: He said everything tightened up.

Ishihama: I know what you're talking about. Tachibana is very serious about his work.

Kurata: How about the others? (laughs) (all laugh)

Suganuma: Uh oh.

Ishihama: They got us.

Tachibana: Nice one. You've put your foot in your mouth this time. (laughs)

Kurata: Ishihama, this time you worked on character design and art direction. These must have been very challenging. What is your impression after your first project with Masunari?

Ishihama: Well, to be completely honest, I was allowed quite a bit of freedom and was able to do pretty much whatever I wanted. Overall, it was a lot of fun.

Kurata: Ho ho!

Ishihama: He was always open to my idea proposals and incorporated them into the final production.

Kurata: True, he does welcome idea suggestions.

Ishihama: Yes. And it's especially fun when someone accepts them all.

Suganuma: But doesn't that also make you a little nervous?

Ishihama: Well, there are always elements that will need tightening up. It's just a matter of learning how flexible or inflexible you can be with certain elements.

Suganuma: Funny, I've never had that experience. (all laugh)

Ishihama: I find Masunari very easy to understand. He may think I've got him all wrong, but my impression is that he is fun to work with.

Kurata: So you don't think he is strict at all?

Ishihama: Well, from the outside, the demands on an illustrator would certainly appear strict. But for me and my work, I never felt that he was being strict. He seems to be very aware that the more fun a work place is the better the work becomes.

Suganuma: In other words, he's receptive to ideas.

Ishihama: Yes, and I really respect him for that. A friend once told me, when you work with Masunari, he always takes care of you so you can work in an atmosphere of security. He said, you've got to do it, and when I did, I found it very enjoyable.

Suganuma: I think if you ask people for whom *R.O.D* is their first Masunari film to describe what makes a Masunari film different, they wouldn't be able to tell you. One film is not enough. You'd have to go back to *Lamune* and even further to his earlier films, then a vague image of what kind of director he is might take shape. Even then, though, you'd still probably have a hard time. (laughs)

Kurata: There are not many directors like that.

Suganuma: The current hot and popular directors all have their own unique features. That uniqueness is directly linked to a film becoming a big hit. However, these types of films also run the risk that people will quickly lose interest when the fad ends. Then they can easily disappear into obscurity. I wouldn't be surprised if Masunari is aware of this.

Kurata: That would make sense.

Suganuma: I am sure he would be just as glad to do a project where he was given center stage, like the cover picture of a magazine, but I don't think he would necessarily seek out that type of project on his own initiative.

Kurata: Tachibana, what do you think?

Tachibana: Me?

Kurata: Does the final *R.O.D* look to you like a Masunari film?

Tachibana: The first film is certainly a complete film and without a doubt a Masunari film, but...

Kurata: Does something seem different to you?

Tachibana: Somehow it seems different from his past films. It's really hard to describe what exactly.

Suganuma: That may be related to what Ishihama said earlier about the amount of freedom we had while making the film. It could have diminished the sense of Masunari's presence in the film.

Kurata: In the total balance, this works in the film's favor. I consider Masunari as very similar to Stanley Kubrick. There is really nothing out of the ordinary in Kubrick's films. He is so scrupulous and puts so much time and effort into each scene that the films are very difficult to make. Then the final product is absolutely superb. But you can't really say the films have a specific Kubrick color to them. It's very different from, say, the smokiness in a Ridley Scott film.

Suganuma: Yet after you see a few Kubrick films, they are unmistakably Kubrick.

Kurata: Yes! It gradually becomes visible. There are very few directors like this in anime.

Suganuma: It is like if Masunari Koji were a symphony conductor, the symphony members would change with each performance.

Suganuma: As this project took more and more time, I think things had become kind of stiff. Tachi loosened everything up in a good way.

Ishihama: Tachi's work ethic lit a fire under everyone's ass.

Kurata: That's a formidable achievement. When you saw the final film, did you feel the same sense of gratification that Suganuma talked about?

Tachibana: I've seen Masunari's films several times, and from the very beginning I had no doubt the final product would be a hit.

Ishihama: I wasn't so sure about it being a hit. (big laugh from all)

Tachibana: I meant a hit for me.

Kurata: When you say "hit," what do you mean? Do you mean in terms of numbers or personally, such as psychologically?

Tachibana: I mean from an animator's perspective. I was certain that as an illustrator, the final product would be a hit.

Kurata: That's something that can be said for this project. All the people I have met who worked on the product are confident about their contributions. The sound person and the music person, for example, both said they thought they did good work. In a way, that could be a problem because this is only the first film. (laughs) There are still two more to make. (laughs)

Tachibana: Don't make me think about it...

Ishihama: It's all useless unless we do a good job with all of three of them. (laughs)

Kurata: They say that for a TV series most of the hard work is put into the first season and that makes the production quality much higher at the beginning.

Ishihama: That's generally true. But I don't want this project to be like that.

Kurata: You sound very serious about it.

Ishihama: I am. I really want to make the next two films to be even higher quality than the first film.

Kurata: Overall, it sounds like you all have a positive image of Masunari, but I'm interested to hear what you think of his films. What do you find interesting about his films?

Tachibana: I am sure everybody has different reasons.

Kurata: That may be because the coloring of his films are not distinctively Masanari. Yet, even without this, the coloring of the final product does have a certain uniqueness. But if you ask me how, I really couldn't describe it.

Suganuma: One point that makes it easy to work with him is that he makes it very clear exactly what he wants you to do and what you should do. He also lets you know what he doesn't like. In fact, he doesn't even have to tell you that. You can tell by the look on his face. (all laugh)

Kurata: You can see it on his face.

Suganuma: Easily.

Ishihama: "Oh, I see you don't like it!" (laughs)

Kurata: You've known him for a long time.

Suganuma: That's obvious? (laughs)

Kurata: To round out our conversation, how about if each of you ends with a message about *R.O.D* that you'd like to send to Masunari. (laughs) Ishihama, would you like to start.

Ishihama: I'm always telling him what I think. That's how I gain his favor. I will just say, good luck on your next film. (all big laugh)

Ishihama: Regarding *Read*, we have more discussions about the next film scheduled tomorrow. Other than that, it is pointless to talk about it without Masunari present. Especially after all the events at the start of this film.

Suganuma: Tell us more!

Kurata: Yes, it sounds interesting.

Ishihama: Well, no, there was nothing really. (laughs) But I really don't want *Read* to fall apart. I want the next film to be made with the same tightness as the first. I'm already struggling with several points.

Kurata: So you seem to be saying, let's keep working hard. How about you, Suganuma?

Suganuma: We are already too deep into the next project to say anything now. (all laugh)

Ishihama: It's too late now.

Suganuma: It's not like we are saying or final farewells. (laughs)

Kurata: True. We're probably in for the long haul. Maybe until we die.

Suganuma: Could be.

Kurata: Stuck together for better or worse.

Suganuma: That too. There's no saying how long it will take. I have no idea. Sometimes I even wonder if I am working on *Read* even now. (laughs)

Ishihama: That's one point we'd all like you to become clear about!

Kurata: That's right. His team disbands after each project and very few people, if any at all, work under him again. In that way, too, he is like a symphony conductor. He assembles a team for a specific project and draws the very best out of that team.

Suganuma: That's another interesting point. After working with Masunari, you aren't left with a feeling that you want to continue working with him or want to work with him again. (laughs) (all laugh)

Kurata: You don't?

Suganuma: When you finish a Masunari project, you celebrate (laughs), say "see you later" and it's over. You really aren't looking ahead to another project.

Kurata: But it is good that you say "see you later" rather than that you'll never do it again.

Suganuma: That's right. It's more like saying, "Give me a call when you have another project." At the same time, you don't have the sense that you will be working together on the very next project.

Kurata: What do you think, Ishihama? You look like you want to say something.

Ishihama: I think you've got it right. With *Read*, we really had to give it our all or we wouldn't be able to do the job. It is easier to work when you don't have the next project already lined up.

Kurata: You sound a little emotional about it.

Ishihama: I am. Now that you mention it.

Suganuma: Thinking that you have another project afterward is like having a safety net.

Ishihama: You have to resolve yourself to the mindset of going all out until you get to the very end. Then you can say "see ya" or "banzai" and be done with it.

Kurata: For a professional to work like that is very cool. (all laugh)

Kurata: Working like that would also raise the tension in the film, which the viewers can look forward to. In terms of work style, I think it is easier to work on the very beginning stages rather than the later stages of a project. I've worked with numerous directors, but Masunari is the only one that I have thought I want to work with again. I guess I work differently than Suganuma, because I think it is easy to work with him. (laughs) Although, I have to say the first round of presentations was very difficult.

Ishihama: Nevertheless, I think that is a perfect example of Tachibana Hideki's character. He's saying he's going to do a great job on the next one right after doing a great job on the current one.

Kurata: It shows the determination to improve.

Tachibana: I heard that in the past from someone, maybe it was even Masunari, and it seems like that is what I am learning from him now. It's a sense that doing my very best now will somehow raise me to a new level. That's how I perceive my work now.

Suganuma: That's quite admirable.

Tachibana: If I don't give it all my energy now, then I am liable to burn out.

Kurata: That self-awareness is really good. How old are you?

Tachibana: Twenty-six.

All: So young! (laughs)

Tachibana: Is it such a big surprise? (all big laugh)

Kurata: You seem to already have a roadmap for your career. Where were we? (laughs) Ah yes. Add the "also." You will do your best on the next film also. Thank you all for coming.

All: Thank you.

Recorded at Studio Deen in April 2001

Suganuma: I just mean it is becoming hard to say how much I am putting into *Read* or to measure just how important my role is or how much I am actually contributing to the project as a whole. Without being clear on that, it is hard to say "good luck" because maybe I should actually be saying "I'm sorry". So for now, I'll just say, "Take care of yourself." (all laugh)

Kurata: I hear many nuances in "take care of yourself." (laughs)

Suganuma: It's true though. He doesn't have a really strong constitution, and I really do worry about him, particularly his tendency to overwork. He's the type whose condition is easy to see. It's very obvious when he is not feeling well. When making a movie, you can't just ignore it, it's impossible. That's why I hope he will take good care of himself.

Kurata: It had a deeper meaning than I thought. It comes from knowing him for 15 years. (laughs). How about you, Tachibana?

Tachibana: I will do my best on the next film.

Kurata: (laughs) That sounds like it too is filled with nuance. You aren't suggesting that you didn't try your best on this film, are you? Do you mean to add "also" in there?

Tachibana: Yes. Add "also" in there. Of course. (laughs)

Kurata: Pumping your fist won't appear in the transcript. (laughs)

Ishihama: I see your brain is already possessed by the next film.

Tachibana: No, not yet. I'm just following the line of thought you started.

DEPICTIONS OF MASUNARI KOJI

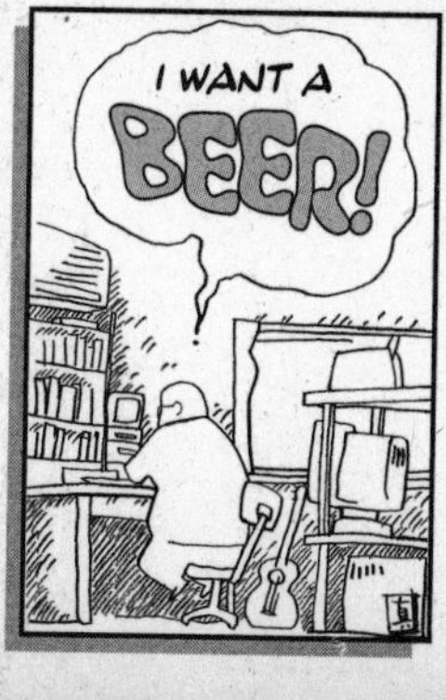
I WANT A
BEER!
◀ Ishihama Masashi

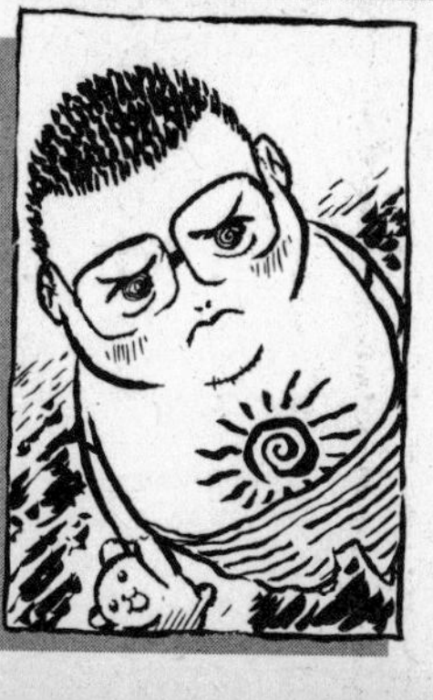
◀ Suganuma Eiji

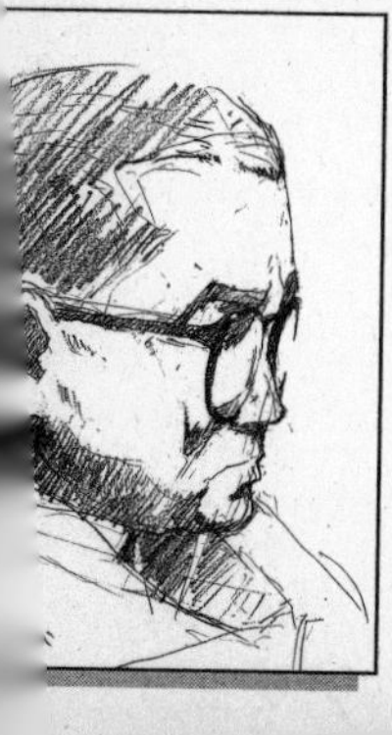
◀ Tachibana Hideki

Read or Die
Vol. 2

STORY BY **HIDEYUKI KURATA**
ART BY **SHUTARO YAMADA**

English Translation and Adaptation/Steve Ballati
Touch-up Art & Lettering/Mark McMurray
Cover & Graphic Design/Janet Piercy
Editor/Urian Brown

Managing Editor/Annette Roman
Director of Production/Noboru Watanabe
VP of Publishing/Alvin Lu
Sr. Director of Acquisitions/Rika Inouye
VP of Sales & Marketing/Liza Coppola
Publisher/Hyoe Narita

Printed in the U.S.A.

Published by VIZ Media, LLC
P.O. Box 77010
San Francisco, CA 94107

10 9 8 7 6 5 4 3 2 1
First printing, May 2006

www.viz.com

PARENTAL ADVISORY
READ OR DIE is rated T+ for Older Teen
and is recommended for ages 16 and up.
This book contains violence.

store.viz.com

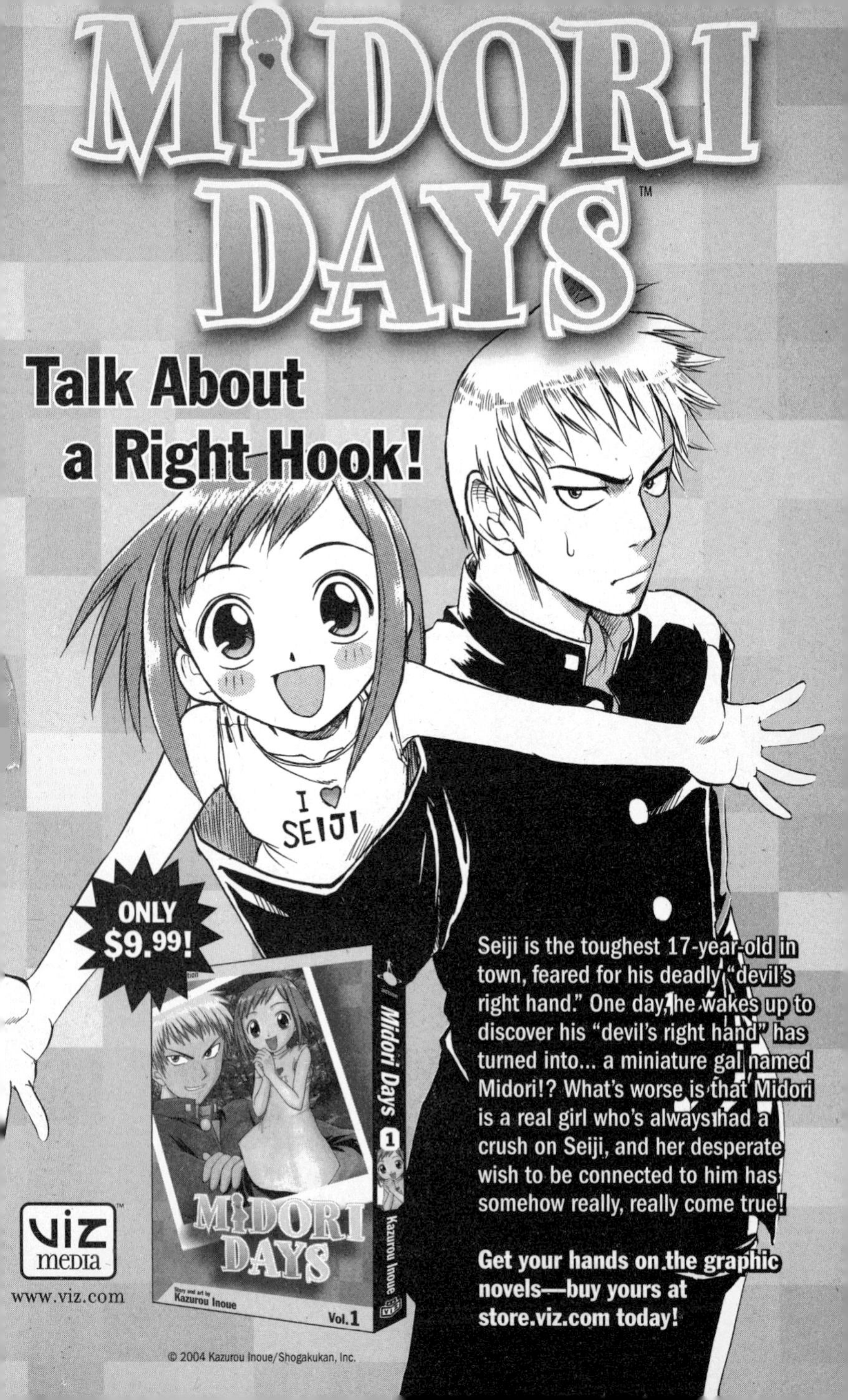
MIDORI DAYS™
Talk About a Right Hook!
I ♥ SEIJI
ONLY $9.99!
Midori Days 1
Kazurou Inoue
MIDORI DAYS
Story and art by Kazurou Inoue
Vol.1
Seiji is the toughest 17-year-old in town, feared for his deadly "devil's right hand." One day, he wakes up to discover his "devil's right hand" has turned into... a miniature gal named Midori!? What's worse is that Midori is a real girl who's always had a crush on Seiji, and her desperate wish to be connected to him has somehow really, really come true!
Get your hands on the graphic novels—buy yours at store.viz.com today!
viz media
www.viz.com
© 2004 Kazurou Inoue/Shogakukan, Inc.